RISK MANAGEMENT IN VOLATILE FINANCIAL MARKETS

FINANCIAL AND MONETARY POLICY STUDIES

Volume 32

Published on behalf of the
Société Universitaire Européenne de Recherches Financières (SUERF),
consisting of the lectures given
at the 19th Colloquium, held in Thun, Switzerland, October 1995

RISK MANAGEMENT IN VOLATILE FINANCIAL MARKETS

Edited by

FRANCO BRUNI

Bocconi University, Milan, Italy

DONALD E. FAIR

(formerly) Royal Bank of Scotland, London, United Kingdom

and

RICHARD O'BRIEN

Global Business Network, London, United Kingdom

Published on behalf of the Société Universitaire Européenne de Recherches Financières (SUERF)

with contributions from

Bill Allen	Colm Kearney
Julian Alworth	Mervyn Lewis
Sudipto Bhattacharya	Markus Lusser
Claudio Borio	Robert McCauley
Bruno Caillet	Phillip Morton
Andrew Crockett	Lionel Price
Philip Davis	Robert Raymond
Georges Gallais-Hamonno	Arjen Ronner
Charles Goodhart	Ad Stokman
Robert Gumerlock	Dirk Trappeniers
Martin Hellwig	Peter Vlaar
Glenn Hoggarth	Axel Weber
Svend Jakobsen	

KLUWER ACADEMIC PUBLISHERS
DORDRECHT / BOSTON / LONDON

A C.I.P. Catalogue record for this book is available from the Library of Congress

ISBN 0-7923-4053-1

Published by Kluwer Academic Publishers,
P.O. Box 17, 3300 AA Dordrecht, The Netherlands.

Kluwer Academic Publishers incorporates
the publishing programmes of
D. Reidel, Martinus Nijhoff, Dr W. Junk and MTP Press.

Sold and distributed in the U.S.A. and Canada
by Kluwer Academic Publishers,
101 Philip Drive, Norwell, MA 02061, U.S.A.

In all other countries, sold and distributed
by Kluwer Academic Publishers Group,
P.O. Box 322, 3300 AH Dordrecht, The Netherlands.

Printed on acid-free paper

Printed in the Netherlands

Table of Contents

Part E
THE MARJOLIN LECTURE

Editors' Introduction*

A spate of financial market shocks, including market crashes and institutional failures, have focused minds on the question of *risk* in the innovative, globalising marketplace of the 1990s. This volume examines the topic of risk management in volatile financial markets from three different perspectives: from a first perspective of market participants managing risk; from a second perspective of regulators and central bankers endeavouring to ensure stability and growth; and from a third perspective of academics seeking to understand and clarify the underlying trends and implications. The seventeen papers, a mix of technical and more 'accessible' work, juxtaposing case studies with broader appraisals, are presented in five main parts.

CENTRAL BANK PERSPECTIVES

In Part A two papers provide a central banking perspective, emphasising the greater weight being placed upon the market to deal with risk, with market participants needing to enhance their risk-management capabilities. Dr Markus Lusser, head of Switzerland's central bank, stressing that 'volatility is here to stay', calls for market forces rather than regulation to be the basic control mechanism for risk-taking activities. Andrew Crockett of the Bank for International Settlements (BIS), the 'central bankers central bank', observes that some institutions have lacked the necessary information and skills to assess risk exposure and that in some dramatic cases, the incentive structure for individuals and institutions has encouraged greater risk-taking than desirable.

VOLATILITY AND RISK

The five papers in Part B examine market developments in volatility and risk. Martin Hellwig of the University of Basle and Harvard University sees the problem coming not from an increase in risks *per se* but from the pressures of

---

* This volume has been edited by SUERF vice-president Professor Franco Bruni of Bocconi University, Milan, by Donald E. Fair, former Economic Adviser of the Royal Bank of Scotland, and by SUERF council member Richard O'Brien, principal, Global Business Network and Former Chief Economist of American Express Bank.

intense competition on banks and other financial institutions, as a period of oligopoly ends: more rather than less innovation is needed to help share undiversifiable risks, with more attention to correlations between different risks. Charles Goodhart of the London School of Economics (LSE), while questioning the idea that volatility has increased, concludes that structural changes have made regulation more problematic and calls for improved information availability on derivatives transactions.

In a thirteen country case study of the bond market turbulence of 1994, Borio and McCauley of the BIS pin the primary causes of the market decline on the market's own dynamics rather than on variations in market participants' apprehensions about economic fundamentals. Colm Kearney of the University of Western Sydney, after a six country study of volatility in economic and financial variables, concludes that more international collaboration in managing financial volatility (other than in foreign exchange markets) is needed in Europe. Finally, Stokman and Vlaar of the Dutch central bank investigate the empirical evidence for the interaction between volatility and international transactions in real and financial assets for the Netherlands, concluding that such influence depends on the chosen volatility measure. The authors suggest that there are no strong arguments for international restrictions to reduce volatility.

INSTITUTIONAL ISSUES AND PRACTICES

The six papers in Part C focus on what market participants are doing to manage risk. The opening paper by Philip Davis of the European Monetary Institute (EMI) highlights the effect of the behaviour of institutional traders on recent periods of market instability, warning that with the institutionalisation of portfolios still in its infancy the impact of institutional trading will grow, necessitating more research into institutional behaviour and the behaviour of global capital flows.

In the first of two papers contributed by the marketplace Robert Gumerlock of Swiss Bank Corporation demonstrates how the risk implications of fluctuations in market rates can be measured and an internal control system designed to protect a bank. In the following paper, from the corporate sector, Ronner and Trappeniers discuss the currency exposure management techniques pursued at Philips.

Academia then provides three specific studies. Svend Jakobsen of the Aarhus School of Business focuses on measuring value-at-risk for mortgage backed securities using data from the Danish market. Caillet and Gallais-

Hamonno of the University of Orleans suggest that the market for warrants on the Paris stock exchange reveals evidence of possible systemic risk. Finally, Lewis and Morton of the University of Nottingham examine risk management within the context of the retail banking experience.

POLICY IMPLICATIONS

The three papers in Part D broaden the focus to the policy implications, including the monetary policy perspective. Axel Weber's prize winning paper (*see The Prix Marjolin, below*) concludes that central bank intervention to try to stabilise exchange rates has had little lasting effect, either in the European context of the EMS or in the 'G3' context of the dollar-Deutschemark-yen rates. Alworth and Bhattacharya (of Mediolanum Consulenza and the LSE respectively) provide a wide-ranging examination of the regulatory framework and the effectiveness of recent measures such as capital adequacy rules. Finally in this section, a comparative study of monetary policy and market liberalisation in Poland, Russia and the UK, by Allen, Hoggarth and Price of the Bank of England, concludes that in Poland and Russia it would be better to identify monitoring ranges for monetary aggregates, rather than adhering to strict monetary targets.

THE MARJOLIN LECTURE

The concluding paper is the 1995 Marjolin Lecture by the Director General of the European Monetary Institute, Robert Raymond. The paper underlines the significant shift in recent years with respect to the roles and responsibilities of the 'authorities' and the market place, in order to cope with the trade off between price volatility and policy making, with central bankers now having to become media experts in dealing with the new relationship with markets, in stark contrast to their previous incarnation as 'silent gods'. In particular, policy makers now have to pay greater attention to 'the intrusion of time and space in monetary policy'.

SELECTION AND ACKNOWLEDGEMENTS

The papers in this volume were selected by the Council of the Société Universitaire Européenne de Recherches Financières (SUERF) from the contributions to the 19th SUERF Colloquium, held in Thun, Switzerland, in October 1995 under the chairmanship of SUERF President Jean-Paul Abraham. SUERF, founded in 1963, brings together more than twenty central banks, ninety private sector institutions and nearly three hundred individual members (particularly from academia). The Colloquia, held every eighteen months, focus on a key financial market topic in a plenary and workshop format.

The Council would like to extend its thanks to all the contributors and participants of the 19th Colloquium and especially to the SUERF council members in Switzerland, Aloys Schwietert of Swiss Bank Corporation and Joseph Bisignano of the Bank for International Settlements, to SUERF Council members Christian de Boissieu, Morten Balling, Martin Fase, Jürgen Pfister, Robert Raymond, Hans-Eckart Scharrer, and Jacques Sijben and Lianne Kieboom of the SUERF Secretariat, for their work in organising the meetings. SUERF also wishes to acknowledge the major financial support of the European Commission, the Bank for International Settlements and the Swiss National Bank and Swiss Bank Corporation who hosted the Colloquium at the SBC Training Centre in Thun. Additional support from Credit Suisse and Les Fils Dreyfus & Cie. was also gratefully received.

THE PRIX MARJOLIN

At the Colloquium SUERF was pleased to honour the memory of Robert Marjolin. A leading architect of post-war Europe, Robert Marjolin was the first head of the OECD, when set up as the OEEC to run the Marshall Plan, was the leading French negotiator of the Treaty of Rome, and then became Vice President of the European Commission, with responsibility for economic and financial affairs, for the first ten years of the Community. The Council of SUERF awarded the Prix Marjolin of ECU 2000 to Axel Weber of the University of Bonn and of the Centre for Economic Policy Research, for the best contribution to the Colloquium by an author of less than forty years of age. The award was presented by Robert Raymond who, as noted above, delivered the 1995 Marjolin Lecture at the Colloquium.

19 February 1996   FRANCO BRUNI
                                                         DONALD FAIR
                                                         RICHARD O'BRIEN

Part A
Central Bank Perspectives

G10

Volatility is Here to Stay — Some Thoughts on Its Implications

Summary

In a complex and changing world, stability in the sense of no overall volatility in the economy is not achievable. Neither international economic cooperation nor a transactions tax can eliminate volatility on financial markets. Because volatility is here to stay, central bankers, legislators and market participants have to make further efforts to deal with its implications. Although central banks have managed to reduce inflation significantly in recent years, they must keep up, or even increase, their efforts to fight inflation. Integral to fulfilling the core function of central banks "promoting price stability" is the need to understand the causes and implications of market volatility and to build up or to maintain credibility. Because it is a pure act of faith to believe that the consequences of volatility, unpleasant as they may be at times, could efficiently be prevented by regulation, any new calls for regulation should at least be treated with a good dose of scepticism. What is really needed in regard to regulation is the strengthening of market discipline and personal responsibility to the greatest extent possible. If market forces rather than regulation are to provide the basic control mechanism for risk-taking activities, the market must be able to assess the risks incurred by firms. Legislators and regulators should therefore increase their efforts to improve accounting standards, while market participants are encouraged to disclose more information about their risk exposures.

Markus Lusser studied law in Paris and at the University of Berne, where he was awarded a law doctorate in 1957. After undergoing practical training in an attorney's office and at various courts he set up practice as an attorney and notary public in 1958.

In 1959 Markus Lusser entered the Office of the Swiss Bankers' Association in Basle. He advanced to the position of managing director in 1979. He was also in charge of the secretariat of the Association of Swiss Holding and Finance Companies from 1959 to 1979. He contributed to the realisation of various joint undertakings of the Swiss banks. In particular, he was chairman of the Board of Directors of Eurocard Switzerland SA from 1978 to 1980.

In 1980 Markus Lusser was appointed to the Governing Board of the Swiss National Bank. He became vice-chairman in 1985 and was nominated chairman in 1988. In 1992, the Federal Council appointed him Swiss Governor of the International Monetary Fund (IMF) in Washington.

I. Volatility is Here to Stay — Some Thoughts on Its Implications

MARKUS LUSSER

The American satirist Ambrose Bierce once defined responsibility as a detachable burden easily shifted to the shoulders of God, fate, fortune, luck or one's neighbor. He added that in the days of astrology it was customary to unload it upon a star. As you know, unloading responsibility upon a star is not so easy any more — especially if you are a central banker. Let me therefore first confess that my feeling at the beginning of this colloquium is one of responsibility. Responsibility not for the stimulating program of this conference — for which the Société Universitaire Européenne de Recherche Financière (SUERF) deserves an enormous amount of credit — but, at least in part, for its cause: volatility in financial markets.

Don't get me wrong: Volatility was not invented by central banks nor was it a market reaction to the creation of the species called central banker. As the story of the seven years of plenty followed by seven years of famine in the Old Testament shows, volatile earning streams were an issue long before today's money was known, let alone central banks. Still, it cannot be denied that monetary policy has strong implications for volatility in the markets.

To be more specific, let me give you two examples. Since most central bankers nowadays think of themselves as bringing stability and not volatility to the economy, I hope you don't mind if these examples are taken from the past.

- First, let me remind you of the monetary policies which by market participants were characterized as "stop-and-go". Needless to say that these policies were in no way able to provide markets with an element of stability. On the contrary: the markets' task of pricing financial assets by forming expectations was made even more difficult. Hence, we have every reason to believe that these erratic policies increased overall volatility in the economy.
- Second, think of the consequences of the collapse of the Bretton Woods system. Under the old regime exchange and to a lesser degree interest rates were stable over long periods. But that came at a price: inflation

3

and the inability to pursue an independent monetary policy. As several countries were no longer willing to pay that price, the collapse of the system was only a question of time. Whether one thinks the benefits of floating exchange rates exceed the costs or not, one thing is clear: the monetary policy changes that took place after the collapse of the Bretton Woods system led to a dramatic and far-reaching shift of volatilities.

1. Volatility is Here to Stay or the Limits of International Economic Cooperation

Having said that monetary policy may have strong implications for markets' volatilities, let me emphasize that creating volatility is not what central banks are after. Quite the opposite is true: central banks have a keen interest in a smooth functioning of their economies. Yet we have to be realistic: in a complex and changing world, stability in the sense of no overall volatility in the economy is simply not achievable.

Take, for instance, exchange rates. Given the substantial differences in the structures of the various national economies and in the interests of governments, it should come as no surprise that there is no such thing as a single lead currency today. The existence of three major currency blocks — US Dollar, Deutsche Mark and Japanese Yen — is, among other things, a result of the fact that the exchange rate as an adjustment tool is still needed.

This is neither to say that stable exchange rates are not desirable nor that international coordination of economic policy is useless. Rather, economic policies are not necessarily compatible with stable exchange rates. Indeed, I regard international coordination as extremely useful. It serves at least two functions.

- First, it enables policy makers to exchange valuable information. Hence, inconsistencies between policies may be revealed and eliminated.
- Second, policies that are in a country's long-term interest but bear certain costs in the short-term may only be successful if they are supported by an international backing.

However, international economic coordination has its limit: it can only work if it serves the various countries' own interest. Remember: government officials and central bankers are paid for serving *their* people.

In a world characterized by risk-aversion, volatility comes at a cost. From time to time, a transactions tax — the so-called Tobin tax — is therefore advocated. Proponents argue that such a tax may reduce volatility by discouraging speculative and noise trading. In particular, it is hoped that the volatility not attributable to fundamentals — excess volatility — is reduced. Certainly, the costs attributable to volatility have to be taken seriously. As a central banker of a small and open economy, I'm especially concerned about the volatility of real exchange rates. Nonetheless, "throwing sand in the gears of financial markets" doesn't appeal to me. Whatever form a transactions tax may take, the costs imposed would almost certainly be much greater than the benefits. Hence, the arguments for such a tax seem to me at least as speculative as the speculation the tax seeks to eliminate.

2. IMPLICATIONS FOR CENTRAL BANKS

For these and other reasons, volatility in foreign exchange rates and on financial markets in general is here to stay. It is therefore legitimate to ask whether economic institutions are in shape to live with volatility and its perils. Although not among the endangered species in the economic system, central banks may be good candidates to look at first. As seen over and over again, the absence of real competition may cause serious problems with respect to fitness. Given the dramatically different ways central banks carry out their functions, I would like to consider three functions most — if not all — central banks have in common: promoting price stability, participating in the supervision of the financial system and being part of the payments system.

First and foremost, central banking is about promoting price stability while not hindering real growth. Integral to fulfilling this core function is the need for central banks — first — to understand the causes and implications of market volatility and — second — to build up or to maintain credibility.

– Understanding the causes and implications of market volatility helps in the conduct of monetary policy because it enables central banks to formulate a policy concept that is in line with their ultimate goal. Topics such as the choice of the intermediate variable of monetary policy or rules versus discretion clearly belong in this category. Because the debate on these issues has dragged on for many years, I do not intend to repeat the arguments in any detail today. Let me instead call your attention to the Swiss experience. Since the shift to a floating exchange rate in 1973, monetary policy in Switzerland is based on monetary targeting. The Swiss National Bank's experience with monetary targeting has been positive: in the last twenty years, no other central bank had a better inflation record than the Swiss National Bank. Only our German colleagues managed to get close to our average inflation rate of 3.1 per cent. Of course, this is not to say that other central banks did a bad job. It's just to say that monetary policy can make a

difference and being tough on inflation pays off in the end. However, since
we failed to achieve our ultimate objective — price stability — there's
still room for improvement. I therefore cannot help but conclude that the
Swiss National Bank — as well as other central banks — must keep up,
or even increase, the effort to fight inflation.
- The second attribute of a successful monetary policy is credibility. The
  higher the credibility of a central bank, the stronger its influence on markets' expectations and the lower the cost of disinflation. In monetary policy
  as in other fields, establishing and maintaining credibility is of course no
  easy task. But central banks nevertheless must pursue a policy that inspires
  confidence. Credibility and continuous communication are indispensable
  for the long-term success of monetary policy.

Another major responsibility of central banks is to promote a sound and
efficient financial system. Whether a central bank is directly engaged in the
supervision of financial institutions or not: as a lender of last resort the health
of the financial system surely is a matter of concern. Given the widespread
use of new and sometimes complex instruments, the challenges for central
banks certainly haven't become smaller in the last years. To assess the risks
of individual banks or in the banking system as a whole, for instance, requires
much more expertise than in the past. Still, the fundamental problem remains
the same: how can we encourage and maintain a financial system that is
sound without impairing its efficiency? Although one can't say the problem
has been solved, it is only fair to say it has been addressed by central banks
with at least some success. However, further work is needed. Because of this
and not because I want to promote Switzerland's ailing tourist industry, Basle
should stay high on central bankers' agendas.

Overseeing the payments mechanism is the third major function of central
banks. Here, volatility and its implications — among them an explosion of
financial activity — require extreme care on the part of central banks. Given
the amounts involved, the risks in the payment mechanism simply cannot
be taken lightly. Again, central banks are aware of the problems. In various
countries steps have been taken or will be taken to reduce or even eliminate
the credit risks in their large-value funds transfer system. However, various
problems are far from being resolved. The most important one concerns
transactions across borders and time zones. It must be a matter of great
concern for all interested in the safety and stability of the financial system
that there is no overlap in the hours in which transfers can be effected in
central banks funds for the US Dollar, Deutsche Mark and Japanese Yen.
Since the flows are likely to increase in the coming years, I consider devoting
resources to this issue a very promising investment.

3. OF REGULATION AND PERSONAL RESPONSIBILITY

As you see, there will be no lack of work for central bankers. Nor will there be for other institutions. If the past is a guide to the future, those involved in the design of regulations will be very busy. Why is that so? Why is regulation — despite the popularity of the expressions "deregulation" and "regulatory reform" — a growth business?

There are at least two explanations:

- First, society is getting more complex. This, in turn, is a result of technological progress and all that goes with it: a growing population density, an intensified specialization, a trend towards individualization, and a higher mobility. The more complex a society, the greater the potential for conflicts between its members. Whether justified or not, regulation often seems an appealing solution for these conflicts of interest.
- Second, regulation is a powerful vehicle for the realization of special interests. From government budgets to tax laws, the traces of rent-seeking behavior can be seen almost everywhere in the dense jungle of regulation.

It should therefore come as no surprise that financial market's volatility and its implications on market participants have been the subject of regulatory concern. True, there are legitimate concerns. In most countries the current accounting rules, for example, are inadequate and inconsistent, reducing rather than increasing the information about a firm's risk exposure. However, to think that regulation can easily resolve the problems of market volatility is just wrong.

In my view — and it's one I feel very strongly about — a tighter regulation of market participants would be the wrong answer to the challenges of market volatility. Piling up new regulations doesn't appeal to me because I have great doubts about their benefits. But they certainly have costs:

- First, there are the direct costs of regulation. They may crop up both at regulatory agencies and at regulated firms or their customers. The direct costs of regulation cannot be neglected. Take the costs of regulating the financial system in the United States. Financing regulators' activities amounts to about 800 millions US Dollars a year. But that's almost nothing compared with the costs to firms of complying with regulations. Estimates for these costs range from about 8 to 18 billion US Dollars a year. True, financial regulation in the US can hardly be characterized as a system of "few rules–low costs". However, it is only fair to say that the direct costs of financial regulation are probably substantial everywhere in the developed world and new regulations would in all probability increase them.

– Second, regulation gives rise to indirect costs. Does anybody believe that all the laws, decrees and rules in place do not create distortions in the allocation of economic resources? These indirect effects don't come cheap, either. What worries me most in that respect is that something essential often gets lost in the regulatory process; namely the personal responsibility of market participants. This is not just true in cases where it's clear that the buck is passed to the taxpayer. To some degree it is true for every kind of regulation. This is because regulation in general fosters the faith that somebody else is to blame in case of an unfavorable outcome. To see what may happen to personal responsibility you don't have to look at the aberrations of American product liability laws. The shift of responsibility can as well be seen in other areas. Is it a mere coincidence that banks' capital to asset ratios are much smaller today than they were about thirty years ago? To me, this trend reflects to a large degree the dramatically increased scale of government intervention in banking. One problematic aspect of this development is the increased tendency of depositors to believe that paying attention to the solvency of banks is no longer necessary. Whether this belief is justified or not, it certainly makes it easier for banks to maintain capital to asset ratios near the minimum level determined by regulation. Needless to say that the weakening of market discipline in general has far-reaching and expensive consequences. That these indirect costs of regulation hardly can be estimated doesn't make them any smaller. In fact, I suspect that they are even higher than the direct costs in most cases.

Given the substantial direct and indirect costs of regulation the calls for new regulation should at least be treated with a good dose of scepticism. The mere existence of asymmetric information doesn't justify new regulations. It is a pure act of faith to believe that the consequences of volatility, unpleasant as they may be at times, could be efficiently prevented by new regulation. This is especially true when it comes to corporations, pension funds or other sophisticated market participants. Trying to protect these institutions from the consequences of market volatility seems grotesque to me. What is really needed is a strengthening of market discipline and personal responsibility. Since Plato we know that "any unneeded law is a bad law". Taking this idea at face value and putting it into action is probably advice worth considering.

4. CORPORATE RISK MANAGEMENT: AN OUTSIDER'S VIEW

When the organizers of this conference invited me to give this speech, I wondered whether I would be the right person for the assigned topic, risk management in volatile financial markets. This is not because risk is a stranger to me or the Swiss National Bank. Although we haven't yet calculated any value-at-risk figures for the Swiss National Bank's portfolio, we run a substantial amount of risk in our books. It is not so much the topic as such that made me feel a little bit uneasy. It's rather the fact that I didn't quite manage to keep up with all the innovations in the field of risk management in the last few years. To put it mildly: I don't claim to be an expert in "shout options"[1] "roller coaster swaps",[2] "fairway bonds"[3] and many other clever new instruments. Nevertheless, I would like to contribute some comments on the topic of corporate risk management in volatile financial markets.

It seems natural to start with the question: "What is the rationale for managing financial risk?". I think important elements of an answer have emerged in the last four decades. Forty years ago — prior to the works of Modigliani, Miller, Sharpe and Lintner — the answer would have been straightforward: the owners of firms are risk averse, so the removal of risk must be beneficial. This argument didn't stand the test of time. Twenty years ago — after these great economists appeared on the stage — the message changed into the following: company owners can diversify, thus there is no advantage for a firm to hedge its financial exposures. The attitude toward managing financial risk was turned around completely. Yet firms remained risk-averse, and the new paradigm clearly needed refinement. Although no universally accepted paradigm has replaced the old one so far, recent academic research shows why risk may be expensive to firms and, hence, risk management may increase the value of firms. Risk may be costly to firms for various reasons: It enhances conflicts between a firm's stakeholders. It increases the costs of financial distress. It increases taxes when tax functions are non-linear. It may adversely affect the ability to make value-enhancing investments.

Of course, these theoretical findings don't necessarily solve all the specific problems firms are faced with. Problems like: How should exposures be identified and measured? Which exposures should be assumed? How to move from the current exposure to the desired one? Certainly, these questions will be the subject of subsequent papers by academics and market participants better qualified to explore them. Let me just give you my view on three specific aspects.

- First, I would like to point out that remarkable progress has been made in identifying and measuring the market risks in trading books. The value-at-risk approach — which has become almost a standard — enables firms to measure market risks in a way consistent with modern portfolio theory. It is more accurate than earlier methods. The value-at-risk approach is, therefore, undoubtedly, a very useful tool. However, it is only a tool. Even though the models are full of sophisticated statistics and maths, judgmental issues simply don't disappear. Since the results are heavily dependent on the assumptions made, the value-at-risk approach to measure market risks needs to be complemented by other techniques. This is not to say that these issues aren't appreciated by the institutions using these models. Rather, because the models will be used by an increasing number of institutions, the industry must ensure that awareness of the models' limits is kept high.

– Second, apart from price risks, other types of risk exist. Operating risk, for instance, is no small issue. Inadequate internal controls, inadequate procedures or even fraud can bring unexpected losses to a company. This type of risk certainly hasn't become smaller in the last twenty years. Today, derivatives markets allow institutions to make changes in their exposure almost instantaneously and to an extent that would have been hard to imagine twenty years ago. While this makes derivatives such a useful tool on the one hand, it should, on the other hand, also be clear that institutions operating in these markets must have effective risk control mechanisms in place. I therefore strongly welcome the attempts of market participants to establish best-practice standards for risk management. If derivative markets are supposed to develop without distortions, the imposition of burdensome regulation must be prevented. But on the other side, it is essential that market participants go on and improve these standards even further. After all, this is in their own best interest.

– Third, this is not to say that self-regulation should prevent risk taking by market participants. Given that volatility is here to stay, somebody has to take the risks. As long as the markets for risk management products work, losses — even big ones — are possible. Neither regulation nor self-regulation can rule them out. Rather, sensible self-regulation helps to assure the underlying integrity of the market. Furthermore, if market forces rather than regulation are to provide the basic control mechanism for risk-taking activities, the market must be able to assess the risks incurred by firms. This is the reason why disclosure is so important. Disclosure is the basis for well-informed investment decisions. I hope that the improvement of accounting standards and disclosure will lead to a system that allows investors to assess the exposure of financial and non-financial firms much better than today.

No doubt, a comprehensive exchange of views on these and other issues related to corporate risk management is needed. The strong presence of market participants from different countries in this room shows that they don't want to leave the field to academics, central bankers and regulators. In view of the importance of personal responsibility, this is clearly a good sign.

5. CONCLUDING REMARKS

Speaking of personal responsibility reminds me that my allotted time is running out. So let me leave you with the three main thoughts of my speech. First, because volatility is here to stay, central bankers, legislators and market participants will need to make further efforts to deal with its implications. Second, the decisions taken should be based on a proper understanding of the issues and the tradeoffs involved. This is why this conference is both timely and important. By bringing such a distinguished group of experts together, it promises to contribute significantly to the discussion. Third, let us find solutions which rely on market forces to the greatest extent possible. Solutions where responsibility is unloaded upon somebody else's shoulder or upon a star don't appeal to me. At the end of the day, this strategy does not pay off: as seen lately in the Baring's case, even a star may fall.

NOTES

1. "A path dependent option that allows the purchaser to lock in a minimum payout (the intrinsic value of the option at the time of the «shout») while retaining the right to benefit from further upside. So-called because when the option holder thinks the market has reached a high (call) or low (put), he «shouts» and locks in that level as a minimum" (Corporate Finance Risk Management & Derivatives Yearbook 1995, p. 43).

2. "A Swap in which one counterparty alternates between paying fixed and paying floating" (The Chase Guide to Risk Management Products, p. 29).

3. "Short-maturity FRN's that pay an enhanced coupon over Libor for every day that the Libor daily fixing remains within a predefined interest-rate range or that a specified foreign exchange rate remains within a predefined range" (Corporate Finance Risk Management & Derivatives Yearbook 1995, p. 39).

The Changing Structure of Financial Institutions and Markets: A Central Bank Perspective

Summary

Volatility in financial markets can be defined to include shifting pressures on financial institutions, as well as fluctuations in prices of financial assets. Many of the financial market disruptions which have occurred in recent years are related to changes that have been taking place in the structure of the financial industry, promoted by financial deregulation, technological advances and the internationalisation of finance. Existing institutions have sought to preserve market share against new intermediaries, and both have faced growing competition from markets in securitised assets.

The stability of financial markets and institutions is dependent on the availability and quality of financial information, and the market's incentive to use it to monitor the behaviour of financial transactors. The risk is that changes in the structure of the industry will not be accompanied by changes in the way the information needed to promote systemic stability is provided.

Although the creation of more types of financial asset and increased trading volumes should in theory improve welfare, Tobin and others have questioned whether this is so. However, there seems little justification for "sand in the gears". Admittedly, asset price bubbles have occurred from time to time, but it is hard to attribute these to new financial assets such as derivatives. These new assets have in fact improved the ability of economic agents to identify, price and manage risk. Properly used, they enhance systemic stability.

Still, much remains to be done to strengthen the financial system. Recent episodes have shown the importance of operational risk. Even if systems and controls are robust, liquid capital remains necessary to protect against risks consciously run, or unforeseen events. The classic distinction (due to Frank Knight) between risk and uncertainty, remains valid.

Andrew Crockett was appointed General Manager of the Bank for International Settlements in January 1994. Educated at Cambridge and Yale Universities, he previously held positions at the International Monetary Fund and the Bank of England. He is a former member of the Monetary Committee of the European Union and a former Chairman of Working Party Number 3 of the OECD. He has published two textbooks on monetary economics, as well as a number of articles and monographs.

II. The Changing Structure of Financial Institutions and Markets: A Central Bank Perspective

ANDREW D. CROCKETT

1. INTRODUCTION

It is hard not to contrast the physical location of this conference to the subject of the colloquium itself. "Risk, volatility, fragility and instability" seem far removed from the peaceful Lake of Thun. But perhaps this juxtaposition is quite appropriate. The topic, risk management in volatile financial markets, is probably best viewed from a perspective that is detached from the centres of financial turbulence, so that some sober reflection can take place without having to consult a Reuters, Telerate or Bloomberg screen.

I say this because while there is much to be concerned about in today's financial environment, there is also much with which to be satisfied. We certainly have observed a number of tumultuous events during the past ten years. But we have also seen the benefits of greater financial integration and efficiency, as financial institutions, markets and instruments expand and adapt to the changing needs of their customers.

In addressing the topic of risk management, let me begin with a story about Albert Einstein and the search for ideas. The story draws on an unusual event in literary and scientific history — the meeting between Einstein and the writer Ernest Hemingway. When Hemingway was a young man working as a reporter for the Toronto Star he was given the assignment of interviewing Einstein at Princeton University. During the interview Einstein asked Hemingway about the contents of a notebook Hemingway had with him, but never wrote in during the interview. Hemingway remarked that he had aspirations of one day becoming a novelist, and whenever he had a good idea he would jot it down. "Surely," he said to Einstein, "you too must have such a notebook" – "No, Mr. Hemingway," replied Einstein, "I don't have one. I don't have that many good ideas."

I too don't have that many good ideas, at least not new ones. You might say that I am here in search of some. Central bankers are looking for paradigms to help them understand the evolutionary changes in financial systems, the points

13

of potential structural stress, and the causes of the financial disturbances and volatility which form the subject of this colloquium. This understanding is just as likely to come from patient reflection on how to apply old insights as from innovative new discoveries. What I would like to do today is to share with you some of my concerns and discuss the ways in which official thinking is evolving on the general subject of stability in the financial system.

2. RISK MANAGEMENT IN A VOLATILE FINANCIAL INDUSTRY

SUERF is a rather unique institution. Every eighteen months it brings together academics, practitioners and public officials to discuss financial and monetary issues of interest to each of these groups. This is not an easy task. On occasions the three groups can be like ships passing in the night, acknowledging each others' presence at a distance. So it is something of a challenge to try to bridge their different perspectives on the topic of risk management in today's financial markets.

My first task is to define what the sponsors of this conference have called "volatile financial markets". As the papers reveal, most have interpreted this to mean markets in tradable financial instruments. My perspective is rather broader. I prefer to start by looking at risk management in a volatile financial *industry*, composed of institutions and markets. The extension of credit, whether in capital markets or through an institutional intermediary involves, in the language of academics, "imperfect information" and "agency problems"; or in plain language, the evaluation of credit and market risk and the monitoring and control of the borrowers' behaviour. The competition between markets and institutions in financing the private sector revolves around which of the two better solves these problems. Importantly, the difficulty that monetary and regulatory authorities confront in attempting to secure the stability of the financial system also depends on how problems of information and incentives are dealt with.

Many of the disruptions and transformations of financial systems which have occurred in recent years are related to changes that have been taking place in the structure of the financial industry, as existing institutions have sought to preserve market share against new intermediaries, and both have faced growing competition from markets in securitised assets. This brings the outside observer straight to the fundamental organisational question: namely, what is the structure of financial intermediaries and markets required to secure both efficiency and stability; and what should be the supporting role of the financial authorities in this pursuit?

In a very broad sense we are currently witnessing within financial systems evolutionary changes involving three forms of competition: competition between markets and intermediaries, between different types of intermediary (e.g. banks vs. nonbank) and between different types of markets and trading systems (e.g. cash vs. derivative markets, exchanges vs. OTC). The first type of competition is evident in most industrial economies and several emerging markets. It can be seen in the growth of securities markets, in the expansion in institutional investment and, unfortunately, in the weakness of some financial institutions. The second type of competition has resulted from deregulation and financial innovation, which have reduced the uniqueness of banks and subjected them to a much more hostile competitive environment. The weaknesses in some financial systems can be attributed to the aggressive behaviour of some non-bank financial intermediaries, a number of which were little regulated and poorly supervised. We also see considerable competition of the third type, with different financial centres competing aggressively for market share, and organised exchanges seeking to recover business from over-the-counter markets. A major consequence of greater competition has been an improvement in the welfare of users of financial services. But it has also led to greater variability in the fortunes of financial institutions.

Why does credit allocation proceed through different channels, and what causes the relative importance of these channels to change over time? The answer lies, in essence, in the comparative advantage of different forms of intermediation in gathering and analysing information on potential borrowers and in monitoring their behaviour. I want to emphasise the important role of *information* and *incentives* in the structure of financial systems and their role in ensuring or, if poorly structured, in undermining its stability. Let me explain specifically what I mean.

My point is a simple one: the stability of financial markets and institutions is dependent on the availability and quality of financial information, on the manner in which this information is provided to the market place and the market's incentive to monitor the behaviour of financial participants. Whether a financial system is weighted heavily towards intermediated finance or large capital markets, the stability of that system is greatly dependent on the information that lenders, whether they are banks, pension funds or individual depositors, have on potential borrowers and the incentives lenders have to monitor counterparties' behaviour.

The competition I referred to earlier between depository institutions and financial markets is a contest over the ability to determine the credit quality of potential borrowers, to monitor their performance and to efficiently manage risk exposure. It also involves the ability to analyse financial asset price behaviour in open markets — to understand the fundamental determinants of capital market behaviour. These issues are particularly important in an industry which previously has been heavily regulated, and where excess capacity is in evidence, as exists in some parts of the financial system. The risk is that changes in the structure of the industry will not necessarily be accompanied by changes in the way the information needed to promote systemic stability is provided. The opaqueness that has resulted from increasing off-balance-sheet items is a good example. A consequence is that the incentives that underpin stabilising activity may lose some of their force.

The problems of financial institutions in a more deregulated and competitive environment has caused the supervisory authorities to re-examine their role in ensuring the stability of the financial system. This has included not only a re-examination of the desired capital base of intermediaries, but also the need to improve the information and incentive structure in the financial industry. I will return to this topic towards the end of my remarks.

3. VOLATILITY AND RISK MANAGEMENT: THE ISSUES

Let me now narrow my focus and address specifically the issue of volatility in financial markets.

While advances in theoretical and applied finance have brought closer together the perspective of academics and financial practitioners, there still exists a healthy difference of opinion regarding how financial markets function and over the existence and potential causes of greater financial price volatility.

Consider the effects of having available more tradable financial assets. One view on the desired number of marketable financial assets is simply: the more the better. More choice in assets improves welfare because market participants are better able to create their preferred portfolio, and better able to protect themselves against risk. More trading is a logical corollary. This general argument stands behind much of the deregulation of financial markets since the early 1970s. At the same time, many outside the financial industry, including Nobel prize laureate James Tobin, have asked whether the proliferation of new instruments and advanced trading procedures have not led to greater financial asset "churning" and price volatility. There is a widespread impression in lay circles that asset price volatility has greatly increased and that new instruments and greater securities trading have been the root cause.

This latter argument can be questioned on its premise. It is not easy to detect in the data a substantial trend-like increase in asset price volatility in most of the major financial markets. To some extent, of course, the evidence depends on measurement techniques, period of observation and the particular market considered. However, research at the BIS suggests that in a number of markets recent asset price volatility is not much different from what we observed in the 1970s to mid-1980s. What may have changed, however, is what might be called "outlier volatility", i.e., the degree and frequency of sudden large price adjustments that go beyond what could be expected on the basis of conventionally calculated statistical distributions. The equity market crash in 1987, the European exchange market crisis of 1992, the long-term bond price slide in the spring of 1994 and the Mexican Peso crisis in December last year were all outlier events, difficult to anticipate given the price volatility just prior to these events. We should also recall that in a number of countries the major asset price bubbles have been in largely non-traded assets, in particular real estate, where few good hedging devices exist.

Academics and financial authorities are in search of the determinants of asset price bubbles and for the reasons that financial markets at times appear to overreact to new information. The changes in the structure of financial intermediation, resulting from deregulation, the rapid growth of institutional investment and cross-border portfolio diversification, have integrated financial markets in the direction of a seamless international financial web. Sizable movements in the price of traded assets now carry greater potential systemic implications, particularly if the financial infrastructure is not reinforced and the financial authorities unaware of possible stress points in the securities trading, clearing and settlement structure.

My general observation is that although average volatility may not have risen, the chances for large short-term but potentially disruptive price movements may indeed have increased. Put another way, the statistical techniques used to measure volatility may be inadequate to capture all the dimensions of the system's vulnerability to price movements. If the statistical distribution of price changes is "fat-tailed" rather than normal, it will convey a misleading sense of security to base systemic precautions on the premise that volatility has not increased.

This perspective is not inconsistent with several recent episodes of short-run swings in asset prices. Not infrequently the immediate trigger of a sudden increase in price volatility and of the disappearance of liquidity is difficult to identify. Neither analyses based on the fundamental determinants of asset prices nor explanations based on new instruments or trading procedures adequately explain the 1987 equity market crash or the 1994 bond market slide.

A number of people have argued that the periodic large asset price movements and bubbles seen in recent years are the direct result of the new instruments and trading techniques. Some have even gone so far as to suggest that certain financial instruments are inherently dangerous and that their use should be restricted.

My own view is that most sharp changes in asset prices result from a reappraisal by market participants of fundamentals. Even if the triggering event is small relative to the market reaction, it can set in motion a reconsideration of asset values that have gradually been allowed to get out of line. How does such a misalignment come about? Often, a trend which is initially justified by favourable fundamentals seems to continue when basic economic considerations no longer justify it. A selfsustaining process can take over — herd behaviour if you will — in which investors seek to take advantage of a rising price trend, each one individually hoping to exit the market before a correction comes.

It would be a mistake to blame the new instruments for this behaviour. The fundamental contribution of derivative instruments lies in their power to target risk; to break complex risks down into their constituent elements and to allow them to be separately priced and traded. This enables much more effective risk management. Intermediaries and end-users can more easily protect themselves against risks that they are unwilling to accept, by passing them on to others better placed or more willing to run them. In a world in which sudden large asset price changes have become more prominent, this capacity is an important protection. Under normal market circumstances, therefore, derivatives should be a force tending to add to stabilising properties and to strengthen market liquidity.

Of course, derivatives, like any tool, can be misused. Because derivatives are a sophisticated tool, their payoff characteristics are harder to calculate. And because they are a powerful tool, they can cause substantial damage in the wrong hands. An inexperienced road user can cause more harm in a Mercedes than on a bicycle. The answer is not to outlaw cars. It is to provide adequate driving instruction, introduce traffic regulation, and, possibly, to require third-party insurance.

Let me pursue the analogy by suggesting that two causes of road accidents are inadequate knowledge of a vehicle's controls, and driving too fast. Knowing how the vehicle works, in the case of derivatives, means not just knowing an instrument's intended payoff characteristics, but understanding the assumptions on which its value and volatility are based. There is now widespread agreement on the value-at-risk methodology in monitoring derivative exposure. But calculations of value at risk are based on four assumptions, none of which is likely to hold precisely. The first is that the model itself is correctly specified. The second is that the distribution of actual outcomes can be approximated by the normal distribution. The third is that the pattern of future outcomes will be the same as past outcomes. And the last is that liquidity is continuously available to permit trading without price jumps. The fact that these assumptions cannot be guaranteed to hold, and will undoubtedly be falsified in times of stress, argues for building additional safety margins into risk management practices.

Now for the second cause of road accidents. "Excessive speed" can be likened to the use of leverage. As I argued earlier, derivatives do not cause leverage; leverage can be achieved in many ways. But many of the new instruments significantly augment the ability to increase leverage for an initial capital position. Options, for example, clearly expand the borrowing and risk opportunity frontier. These greater leverage opportunities imply an increase in potential externalities from which unrelated market participants may not be able to protect themselves. The concentration in some derivative markets and the close linkages between cash and derivatives markets around the globe could, for example, potentially create serious liquidity problems during periods of market turbulence generated by expanded leverage opportunities. Here, and this is the end of my analogy, is where the need for third party insurance comes in to which I will return in a moment.

Excess leverage can also be an indirect cause of operational risk. The chance for a trader to recover from an earlier market loss by exploiting the leverage possibilities in derivative products clearly creates the need for improved internal risk management control systems. Operational risk has come to the fore in the wake of the recent experiences of Barings and Daiwa. Neither episode can be directly blamed on derivatives. But both highlight the willingness of management to suspend their critical faculties when confronted with traders undertaking operations which their superiors do not fully understand and which are, apparently, making money.

4. Ensuring against Instability: The Dilemma

Let me turn now to the issue of how to ensure greater stability in the financial system. In my opinion most of the major occurrences of financial disturbances and crises since the mid-1980s have been related to broad changes in the structure of financial intermediation and the difficulty of adjusting to these changes, rather than due to the development and proliferation of new trading and hedging instruments. And where problems have arisen with derivatives, they have typically been the result of human error and misjudgement. New derivative instruments have not yet been seen to be a primary source of systemic or contagion risk.

There may be a lesson in this observation. Allow me to draw three distinctions of use in understanding risk management in the new financial environment. The first is a distinction made by Professor Robert Merton between equity capital and hedging as alternative forms of risk management. Equity capital can be viewed as a financial "cushion", a general purpose form of risk management when the source of risk cannot be specifically identified. Hedging, on the other hand, can be thought of as a device used to control specific types of risk.

With this in mind, I want to recall a second important distinction made years ago by Professor Frank Knight, involving the difference between risk and uncertainty. Professor Knight defined risk as an uncertain event in which the distribution of possible outcomes is known, or can be approximated by the study of previous random outcomes. Uncertainty, on the other hand, is associated with events in which the distribution of outcomes is completely unknown.

Now let me combine these two distinctions to argue that hedging techniques and derivative instruments permit investors to confront Knightian risk. Knightian uncertainty, however, requires capital. Of course, the distinction in practice cannot be made as neatly as this. Hedging is subject to the practical problems of dealing with the estimation of the underlying structure (the "stochastic process") of random events. We see this in the need to estimate the variance of price behaviour in order to utilise Black-Scholes techniques for pricing options. So even Knightian "risk" requires capital, as well as hedging.

My third distinction draws on the notion of diversifiable and nondiversifiable risk. A diversified portfolio will have a lower volatility than the average of the volatilities of the individual assets. And in the limit, where the portfolio contains all the assets available in the market, the investor confronts only that risk which is undiversifiable. Once again, we are confronting a distinction between eventualities which can be insured against through portfolio management techniques, and those which can only be dealt with through an adequate capital cushion.

My reason for these distinctions is to emphasise that diversification and hedging opportunities have greatly increased in recent years, with improvements in financial technology, the growth of new instruments and financial markets. Both are useful in confronting diversifiable Knightian risk. But as we have seen, both are subject to practical limitations. At times some hedges may fail to work as anticipated and diversification opportunities may decline if prices in different markets begin to move similarly during stress periods. Moreover, all risk cannot be hedged or diversified away. Equity capital should be sufficient to absorb non-diversifiable risk — shocks to a financial institution which cannot be easily hedged or hedged at all.

From the experience of the last ten years I would argue that a number of institutions seriously overestimated their ability to hedge and diversify market and credit risk. We have also seen cases where institutions lacked the necessary information and the skills to properly assess risk exposure. In several dramatic cases, not only was information on risk exposure found wanting, but the incentive structure for individuals and institutions encouraged greater risk taking than was desirable, both from the point of view of the institution and the financial authorities. But the point I wish to emphasise is that in the vast majority of cases, the new financial instruments greatly improved the ability to manage risk. We should also remember that the events that attract the most attention have been those where new instruments have been misused and led to losses. There is little news value in a hedging operation that has successfully diversified risk.

I turn now to the need for protection against undiversifiable risk, or Knightian uncertainty. Clearly this requires a prudential capital cushion. The question is, how much? Since the uncertain event is, by hypothesis, unknowable, so too is the amount of capital required to protect against it. There is thus no scientific answer to the question. It is a matter of judgment. All that can be said is systemic protection requires both a strong capital cushion on the part of individual institutions and the availability of official support in the event of truly unforeseen shocks of major proportions. Because of the potential systemic implications of major failures in the financial industry, financial safety nets exist to limit the systemic damage that might arise from a sudden increase in non-diversifiable risk.

This presents a fundamental dilemma for financial authorities. An excessive or poorly structured safety net for the financial system may have the effect of insulating intermediaries from desired market discipline and create a perverse incentive structure by potentially encouraging greater risk taking. This can only be offset by increasing the market discipline of financial institutions. And market discipline can only result, as I emphasised earlier, from improvements in information and incentives. Greater transparency of the activities and risk exposures of financial intermediaries along with the incentives to monitor them, are a necessary ingredient to the fundamental health of the financial industry. This offers a promising field for practical research. We have recently become increasingly aware of the deficiencies of traditional forms of safety net, such as deposit protection and central bank rescues. How can the adverse effects of such arrangements on incentives be offset without compromising systemic stability?

5. CONCLUSION

Let me conclude by summarising the points I have been making in four simple propositions (in the spirit of Einstein's remark to Hemingway, these are not new ideas, but rather restatements of familiar insights).

Firstly, the process of change in financial structure is changing the relative ability of different institutions and markets to process efficiently the information that underpins the smooth-functioning of markets. This is the fundamental source of volatility and vulnerability in financial markets.

Secondly, since new instruments simply permit market participants to give effect to their portfolio preferences more readily, they cannot be seen as an independent source of financial volatility.

Thirdly, new instruments can be, and have been abused. Although they do not create new elemental risks, they facilitate both risk-taking and hedging and this can be a source of negative externalities.

Fourthly, hedging and new instruments can reduce risk, but they cannot do away with the need for adequate capital. There is no such thing as a perfect hedge and anyway some risks are inherently undiversifiable. The distribution of capital between the explicit capital provided by firms and the implicit capital provided by the authorities' safety net is one of the trickiest issues in financial market management.

I have no doubt that it will remain so, at least for so long as Einstein feels no need to take out his notebook!

Part B
Volatility and Risk

Financial Innovations and The Incidence of Risk in the Financial System

Summary

The paper argues that risk exposure of the financial system is mainly due to a lack of risk matching of assets and liabilities in traditional banking rather than the development of new financial markets and instruments. Increased competition between financial institutions has reduced the ability of banks to withstand undiversifiable risks from interest rate changes and macroeconomic developments. New instruments can help to improve the situation by taking these risks off the banks' accounts. However the correlation of explicit risks with counterparty risks in risk-shifting arrangements may make it difficult to assess the effectiveness of such arrangements. The problem is compounded by the fact that counterparty risk may depend on the entire network of inter-institution contracts which varies as time goes on. The paper suggests that, to a first approximation, a proper view of the risk exposure of the overall financial system can be obtained from a consolidated set of accounts which net out all inter-institution positions. As yet though, the fragmentation of regulatory and reporting systems precludes such a consolidation of accounts.

Martin Hellwig is a Professor of Economics at the University of Basle as well as Taussig Research Professor of Economics for 1995/96 at Harvard University. Born in Düsseldorf, he received his education at the Universities of Marburg and Heidelberg and the Massachusetts Institute of Technology. He has previously held academic positions at Princeton University and the University of Bonn. In 1992, he was President of the European Economic Association. His research interests include the foundations of macroeconomics and monetary theory, the economics of information, and financial economics, with special emphasis on banks and banking regulation.

III. Financial Innovations and The Incidence of Risk in the Financial System

1. INTRODUCTION

Risk in the financial system has become a central concern of practitioners and policy makers alike. Whereas in the 1950s and 1960s, bankruptcies and near-bankruptcies of banks and other financial institutions were the exception rather than the rule, in the 1980s and 1990s, they seem to have become commonplace, from Continental Illinois to Baring Brothers, from the American Savings and Loans Institutions to the Scandinavian and Japanese banks. In some instances, the risk exposure of financial institutions has even come to impose serious constraints on overall economic policy. American monetary policy from 1991 to 1993 was at least partly driven by a concern to re-establish the solvency of large American banks. More dramatically, the turnaround in Swedish fiscal and exchange rate policies in 1993 was triggered by the Swedish banking crisis and the ensuing constraints on the Swedish government.

In public discussion, the perceived increase in risk in the financial system is often linked to financial innovation and to the proliferation of new financial instruments over the past two decades. The outsider who looks at the development of the financial system is amazed by the spectacular growth of the markets for new financial instruments, by the remarkable contributions that these activities have been making to the earnings of financial institutions, and, to get to an item that even the outsider understands, by the private fortunes that trained professionals have made from activities in these markets. Given that the social usefulness of these activities is not obvious to somebody living on Main Street rather than Wall Street, the amazement is accompanied by

*I am grateful for the hospitality of Harvard University where this paper was written. I am also grateful for many stimulating discussions with Niklaus Blattner, Jürg Blum, Thomas Gehrig, Hans Gersbach, and Elu von Thadden. Finally, I am grateful for research support from the Schweizerischer Nationalfonds, the WWZ at the University of Basle, and the Taussig Chair at Harvard University.

unease, by a sense that these developments may be "unreal", like a house of cards that will eventually come tumbling down. Given the sense of unease, there is a ready market for doomsday warnings. Cases like Metallgesellschaft or Baring Brothers are major news stories. They play to the desire to be confirmed in one's unease, perhaps also to the desire to be entertained by the downfall of the great, especially if one doesn't understand what merits the "greatness" is based on.

However, the unease that comes from a lack of familiarity may not be a good guide to assessing the situation. Compare the media attention paid earlier this year to the cases of Baring Brothers and Crédit Lyonnais. Baring Brothers was by far the bigger media story — indeed the name of Baring Brothers even made its way into the Annual Report of the BIS. However, Crédit Lyonnais had by far the larger losses. To be sure, Crédit Lyonnais survived as an independent institution because it was bailed out by the French government. But losses borne by the taxpayer are still losses.[1]Nor are these losses any more palatable for involving "ordinary" credit operations rather than something as eerie as a Far Eastern index option.

The present paper tries to provide a more systematic discussion of risk in the financial system. I shall try to identify the factors that have led to an increase in risk since the 1970s. I shall also try to assess the role of the new financial instruments that have created so much excitement. To what extent do these instruments exacerbate existing risks or create new ones? To what extent do they actually improve the allocation of risks in the financial system? What is the role of risk management at the level of the individual institution and the level of the overall financial system?

2. RISK IN TRADITIONAL BANKING

In considering the financial system today, I am struck by the extent to which traditional depository institutions are exposed to risk. Given that deposit finance is a kind of debt finance, they are in the position of any debtor, namely, fluctuations in their asset returns do not affect their obligations to their financiers; such fluctuations affect the financiers *only* in the event of default. In addition, maturity transformation exposes them to refinancing risk, i.e., the risk that continued finance may not be available at all or may be available only at very high rates.

These considerations concern some of the most traditional banking operations. As the experience of the American Savings and Loans Industry shows even the transformation of savings deposits into home mortgages can be a very risky business indeed. Yet savings deposits and home mortgages account for a substantial portion of the financial sector's consolidated accounts.

Given the extent to which — by the letters of their contractual arrangements — depository institutions are exposed to risk, the surprising observation is *not* that the past decade has seen so many bank failures. The surprising observation is rather that preceding decades, say the 1950s or 1960s, had seen so few bank failures.

The stability of financial institutions in the 1950s and 1960s can largely be ascribed to the fact that effective risks were relatively small and interest margins relatively large:

– Fluctuations in market rates of interest were not very pronounced. Fluctuations in exchange rates were largely ruled out by the Bretton Woods system.
– Regulation, cartel practices, and consumer inertia served to restrict competition for deposits and to keep deposit rates low and stable.

With low levels of interest and exchange rate risks and assured refinancing at low deposit rates, depository institutions could use their oligopoly or cartel margins to smooth over most fluctuations in their asset returns. Moreover if in some years the margins did not suffice and an institution actually made losses, its oligopoly profits in subsequent years would provide a reliable source of funds for rebuilding equity without having to go to the market.

Depository Institutions today are in a rather different situation:

– Since the 1970s, fluctuations in nominal rates of interest have been more pronounced than ever before in this century. Moreover, since the abolition of the Bretton Woods system, fluctuations in exchange rates have also come to play a major role.
– At the same time, competition in banking and finance has intensified as (i) the removal of capital controls in the 1970s made room for international competition on a large scale, (ii) in some countries disintermediation or nonbank intermediation attacked the "cheap" deposit base of banks and savings institutions, and (iii) changes in computing and communication technologies reduced client inertia at the same time as they changed the balance of fixed and variable costs of financial institutions, making it more important to go for volume in order to cover overhead costs.[2]

In short, interest and exchange rate risk have become larger at the same time as intermediation margins have been eroded and the ability of financial institutions to rely on oligopoly rents to withstand shocks has been reduced. The erosion of oligopoly rents has also reduced the ability of financial institutions to rebuild equity after bad times without going to the market, thereby

enhancing their vulnerability to *successive* negative shocks. These developments have been more pronounced in some countries than in others, but the
direction of change seems to be everywhere the same.

These considerations suggest that the bank failures and banking crises of
the past decade are essentially the result of the lack of risk matching between
the assets and liabilities of traditional depository institutions. In the decades
before 1975, special circumstances prevented this lack of risk matching from
doing much harm. As these special circumstances have disappeared, the
underlying risk exposure of traditional depository institutions has come to
the fore, from the effective insolvency of a large fraction of American S&L's
as of 1980 to the more recent difficulties of banks all over the world with
real-estate finance and business loans in the recession.

To the extent that interest and exchange rate fluctuations are unlikely to
abate and the intensification of competition is likely to continue, we should
expect the lack of risk matching of assets and liabilities in traditional depository institutions to become even more of an issue in the future. To put it
more bluntly, unless risk matching of assets and liabilities is vastly improved,
we should expect to see more rather than fewer bank failures and banking
crises in the future. A major question for the future of the financial system
is whether the risk allocation in banking and finance can be improved before
banking crises become altogether unmanageable.

The full extent of the risk exposure of traditional financial institutions is
not always appreciated. Traditional concepts of risk in banking and finance
stand in the way of a proper perception of risk. Specifically, the traditional
classification of risk as either credit risk or market risk neglects the refinancing risks associated with maturity transformation as well as the *correlation*
between credit risk, market risk, and refinancing risk. A bank that uses savings deposits to finance fixed-rate loans or mortgages is not just subject to
the risk that debtors may default. It is also subject to the risk that at a time
of high market rates of interest the depositor may take his funds elsewhere
unless the deposit rate is adjusted to match market rates; given the effects of
high market rates of interest on securities and real-estate prices, this risk is
obviously correlated with (i) the risk that in the event of default the value of
the collateral does not cover the value of the loan and (ii) the risk that — in
the case of a fungible loan instrument – the market value of the instrument itself is depressed. Once the refinancing risks and their correlations with credit
and market risks are taken into account, it is clear that the risk exposure of
financial institutions can be much larger than the mere consideration of credit
and market risks would suggest.

As long as the competition for funds was restricted, the neglect of refinancing risks was not serious because these risks themselves were small. In certain countries where competition at the retail level is not yet so intense, e.g., in Germany, where money market funds were only recently admitted, one may still feel that refinancing risks are negligible. However, the experience of the United States shows that the situation can change very quickly. Moreover when the change comes, financial institutions that have previously neglected refinancing risks may find themselves trapped into long positions that hamper their ability to cope with the new situation. Considering that, e.g., in the German case, (i) political pressure from the European Union and the United States is likely to force an opening of the domestic financial system to international competition and (ii) further improvements in communication technologies are likely to reduce the role of branch networks and consumer inertia, the prospects of change in this case are clear, and a serious consideration of the refinancing risks associated with maturity transformation is called for.

3. INCREASED RISK IN BANKING AND FINANCE – A CONSEQUENCE OF
DEREGULATION AND INNOVATION?

An alternative assessment of the developments that have reduced safety in banking and finance would put more weight on the role of deregulation, innovation, and the recklessness of financial institutions. According to this view, the safety of banking and finance before the 1970s was due to the effectiveness of prudential regulation and supervision. Since then, financial innovation and deregulation have placed a wide range of activities outside of the domain of prudential supervision, permitting financial institutions to behave more recklessly than before. The consequences of such recklessness are to be seen in the fates of the American S&L's, the Swedish banks, and, more recently, Baring Brothers and the enterprising Mr. Leeson.

This alternative assessment seems to underlie much of the thinking of the regulatory community as evidenced, e.g., by the repeated warnings in the Annual Reports of the BIS.[3] It is also used to motivate the attempt of the Basle Committee of Banking Supervision to tighten regulation by extending capital adequacy requirements to "market risks" and to mobilize support for this attempt with the public.

I consider this assessment to be mistaken and harmful. It exaggerates the power of prudential regulation and supervision. It fails to recognize the fundamental unsoundness of traditional banking in a risky and increasingly competitive environment. Finally, it detracts from the potentially beneficial role of "new" financial instruments in actually reducing the overall risk exposure of financial institutions. These points are briefly substantiated in the following.

First, the deregulation of the late 1970s and early 1980s was not an autonomous policy measure, but was itself a response to the fact that traditional banking regulation was becoming untenable. In particular, deposit rate regulation was abolished because at a time when high market rates of interest created incentives for disintermediation, deposit rate regulation put depository institutions at a disadvantage in the competition for funds. Similarly, asset allocation rules in many European countries were abolished because they were seen to hamper competitiveness either immediately or in the coming Single European Market.[4] These observations suggest that the very viability of regulation in the earlier period was itself due to the fact that competitive pressures in the financial system were not very intense. They also suggest that any attempt to regulate without regard to viability in a competitive environment is likely to fail.[5]

Secondly, the incidence of bank failures and banking crises in the past decade does not warrant the assessment that new financial instruments involve more risk for financial institutions than old ones. Indeed given the size of derivatives markets today, the incidence of problems in this sector has been surprisingly low. The major problems have involved traditional banking operations, business lending and real-estate finance. Recklessness may have played a role, but it is not clear that this was due to deregulation. If one ascribes the Swedish banking crisis to recklessness induced by deregulation, how does one account for the crisis of large commercial banks in the United States in the late 1980s or of regional banks in Switzerland in the early 1990s? In all three episodes the institutions were hit by the bad performance of business loans in the recession and by the fall of real-estate prices that was induced by high interest rates and the recession — an instance of the lack of risk matching of assets and liabilities discussed earlier.[6] Even in the case of the American S&L's that deregulation left to "gamble for resurrection", one must take account of the fact that the worst offenders had in fact been technically insolvent at the time of deregulation, victims of the interest-induced refinancing risks that were associated with the maturity transformation from savings deposits to home mortgages.[7] To the extent that recklessness in banking has increased,[8] I would ascribe this to the overall worsening of profit outlooks due to increased competition rather than deregulation. There may be a tendency to replace lost oligopoly rents by premia on risk taking, especially, since the reduction in anticipated future oligopoly rents implies that the loss of future business is less of a penalty to bankruptcy due to current operations turning out badly.[9]

Thirdly, the development of new financial instruments has improved the scope for hedging risks to which one might otherwise be exposed. For instance, the packaged securitization of home mortgages in the United States has served to shift interest-induced refinancing risks of real-estate finance away from depository institutions to pension funds, which may be better able to bear them. The risk matching of assets and liabilities of depository institutions in the United States was thereby improved. From this perspective, the problem of the financial system today is *not* that there is too much financial innovation, but that there is too little. If we think of financial instruments as tools for trading risks, enabling financial institutions to improve the risk match of their assets and liabilities, then we would like to see more of these tools.

Unease about financial innovations is perhaps due to the fact that they have been an important tool of competition, from the invention of NOW accounts and money market funds in the 1970s to the latest derivative products. As such they have contributed to the erosion of the earlier restraints of competition as well as the erosion of earlier forms of regulation. Indeed they are still making life difficult for prudential regulation and supervision today.[10] However, the mere fact that innovations are initially unsettling should not detract from their potential benefits for the allocation of risk through the financial system.

4. THE PROBLEM OF RISK ALLOCATION AND THE FINANCIAL SYSTEM

At this point, it may be useful to take a step back and consider the overall role of the financial system in allocating risks. Whereas the regulatory community tends to look at this question primarily with a view to the safety and soundness of financial institutions, I shall be more concerned with *the efficiency of the allocation of risks.* An efficient risk allocation is not necessarily one where risks are avoided, but one where those risks are taken that are worth it and are shared in accordance with people's risk tolerances.

In this context, it is important to distinguish between diversifiable and undiversifiable risks. Loosely speaking, diversifiable risks are those risks that are relatively insignificant when many positions are combined and the law of large numbers comes into play. Undiversifiable risks are those risks that remain relatively significant even after all possibilities for exploiting the law of large numbers have been taken into account. In practice, any given position is likely to involve both, diversifiable and undiversifiable elements.

The risk that a saver withdraws his funds to finance an expensive medical treatment is likely to be diversifiable, the risk that he withdraws his funds because somebody else offers him better terms is likely to be undiversifiable. Whereas the incidence of medical needs would seem to be independent across savers, the competitor's better offer is likely to be addressed to all savers at the same time. The withdrawal risk associated with a savings account thus involves an undiversifiable as well as a diversifiable element. Similarly, the default risk on a loan is likely to involve an undiversifiable business-cycle component as well as a diversifiable borrower-specific component.

For practical purposes, it is useful to think about undiversifable risks in terms of a few driving factors, mainly price variables such as interest rates, exchange rates, or oil prices, and macroeconomic indicators. To be sure, these variables themselves are endogenous and reflect variations in preferences, technologies, and government policies. However for the purpose of this discussion, the exact source of risk is less important than the channel, e.g., the price variable, through which it affects the overall system and the allocation of resources in the system.[11]

An efficient allocation of risks in the overall economic system would require that:
- all diversifiable risks are in fact diversified,
- all undiversifiable risks are shared efficiently, i.e., in accordance with the participants' tolerances for these risks, finally that
- the overall exposure to undiversifiable risk reflects risk-return tradeoffs properly so that the costs and benefits of an increase in risk exposure just balance each other at the margin.

For concreteness, consider the economy's investments in residential housing yielding accommodation services in given location over a few decades. By making these investments, the economy incurs (i) the risk that the value of the accommodation services fluctuates, e.g., as the location in question becomes more or less attractive, and (ii) the risk that, as intertemporal prices (interest rates) may change, the discounted present value of the remaining accommodation services fluctuates. Both risks could be avoided if people were to live in tents rather than houses, but perhaps the gain in the quality of accommodation from living in houses rather than tents outweighs the costs of having to bear the associated risks. Given that the economy does use houses rather than tents for accommodation services, the associated risks have to be allocated. Efficient sharing of the — undiversifiable — interest rate risk requires that in the first place houses be owned by those who expect to hold them to maturity; they are not concerned about interim valuations anyway. If there are not enough people who expect to hold houses to maturity, the houses must be held, i.e., the interest rate risks must be shared by people with shorter horizons; in this case presumably, the returns from the high-quality accommodation services provide a suitable risk premium.[12] As for the uncertainty about the value of accommodation services in the given location, investors ought to diversify this away as much as possible by holding suitable portfolios of shares in houses in different locations.

In the absence of information problems, transactions costs, and the like, an efficient risk allocation would be achieved by a suitable system of direct markets without any recourse to financial institutions. Each homeowner would finance his investment by issuing a set of contingent claims that would provide for precisely the efficient amount of risks sharing. Investors would diversify by holding portfolios of such claims. To the extent that investors themselves are subject to uncertainty, e.g., about their investment horizons, this uncertainty also would be provided for efficiently in contingent-claims markets.[13]

From the perspective of the theory of "perfect" competitive markets, financial institutions serve mainly to overcome information problems, to reduce transactions costs, and to provide clients with readily available trading facilities. The bank that transforms savings deposits into home mortgages provides (i) the information service inherent in the assessment of creditworthiness and (ii) the insurance service inherent in allowing the depositor to withdraw his funds whenever he needs them. The actual risk allocation in this case depends on the details of the contractual arrangements. For instance, the allocation of the interest rate risk that is associated with the underlying real asset, i.e., the house, depends on whether the borrower has a fixed-rate or a variable-rate mortgage, whether the bank agrees to an interest rate swap with a third party, and whether the saver holds a standard savings deposit or, e.g., a fixed-interest bond.

Contractual arrangements will to some extent depend on information problems, transactions costs, etc., which affect the scope for risk sharing and risk diversification. How the financial system deals with these problems will affect the overall risk allocation, not only the extent of risk sharing and risk diversification, but also the availability of funds for investment and the costs of these funds. However it is important to keep in mind that once the pattern of real investments and their returns is fixed, the financial system can only allocate the risks inherent in this pattern; it does *not* annihilate given — undiversifiable — risks or create new ones.

5. FINANCIAL INNOVATIONS, RISK MANAGEMENT, AND THE PROBLEM OF RISK ASSESSMENT

The financial innovations of the past two decades have improved the scope for risk diversification as well as risk sharing. The development of mortgage-backed securities in the United States has improved the scope for geographical risk diversification as well as interest rate risk sharing. The development of variable-rate instruments, interest swaps and the like has expanded the scope for reallocating and sharing interest rate risks. Derivative instruments based on stock prices and indices, exchange rates, and raw materials prices have expanded the scope for reallocating and sharing the risks associated with these factors. The system seems to have come much closer to providing the scope for risk exchanges that would induce an efficient risk allocation. About the only major undiversifiable risk that cannot yet be traded is the business cycle risk of macroeconomic conditions affecting returns and financial needs.[14]

This being said, there are two reservations to be made. First, enthusiasm for securitization sometimes leads the participants to overlook incentive problems associated with contingent contracts. In the case of mortgage-backed securities, the ability to shift *all* return risks of the mortgages to the security holders must reduce incentives for care in initial credit-worthiness assessments of mortgage debtors. With a little more care in the design of the contracts, it should be possible to have instruments shifting location and interest rate risks without at the same time shifting borrower-specific default risks away from the mortgage-issuing institution. Without such additional fine-tuning of contract design, the holders of mortgage-backed securities may be in for unpleasant surprises.

Secondly and more importantly, the problem of counterparty credit risk in derivative contracts is bothersome. As I discussed above, the interest rate risks, exchange rate risks, etc. that one wants to hedge by derivative contracts are undiversifiable. *The derivative contracts do not annihilate these risks, they merely shift them to another party.* If the other party is not in fact able to bear those risks, it will default, and the protection provided by the derivative contract will break down.

In this context, it is important to see that *the counterparty credit risk of a derivative contract is correlated with the underlying risk to which the contract refers.* For instance, consider the situation of a bank that uses an interest swap to hedge the interest-induced valuation risk of a fungible fixed-rate security (or the interest-induced refinancing risk of a nonfungible fixed-rate security). If market rates of interest go up, the bank's claim on its partner in the interest swap goes up, and the partner's ability or willingness to fulfill the contract may be in doubt. Default is most likely in the very contingencies against which the bank most wants to hedge.

In the case of variable-rate mortgages, the problem of correlation of credit risk with the interest rate was shown quite dramatically at the time of high interest rates in the late 1980s and early 1990s. As the rates on outstanding variable-rate mortgages followed the market rates, many homeowners could not or would not pay the higher rates — the accommodation services of their houses not having followed suit;[15] when they defaulted, the creditors repossessing their properties found that the high interest rates had also depressed real-estate prices.

The assessment of counterparty credit risk poses major problems for the market participants and their supervisory authorities. In the case of the variable-rate mortgages mentioned above, the problem is perhaps not so difficult as it suffices to look at the position of the borrower and form a judgment taking into account the effects of the variable-rate clause.[16] In the case of contracts with other financial institutions, a mere look at the position of the counterparty is not enough. The counterparty in turn is involved in financial relations with third parties so its ability to pay in a crunch may depend on the counterparty credit risk in those further contracts. These in turn depend on the contractual engagements of the third parties with further, fourth, fifth, and sixth participants in the system.

The point of my argument is that a complex system of interbank dealings can obscure the actual risk exposure of the overall financial system and the institutions in it. For a simple example, consider a system with 479 institutions and suppose that the n-th institution takes in funds with a maturity of n months and lends out funds with a maturity of n+1 months. Any one institution will believe that it engages in almost perfect maturity matching. Yet the system as a whole transforms a one-month deposit into a forty-year mortgage. If all contracts are concluded on a fixed-rate basis, the system as a whole must be vulnerable to interest rate shocks. However no one institution is aware of this vulnerability nor is a supervisor who looks into any one institution's books. The vulnerability to interest rate shocks is completely hidden in the counterparty risks and their correlations with each other.

One might argue that each of the 479 institutions in the example must be contributing some equity protection so perhaps the additional risk obfuscation that any one of them contributes is compensated by the additional equity buffer. This may well be so, but it does not affect the basic point. I am not trying to say that a complex system of interbank dealings enhances systemic risk, only, that a complex system of interbank dealings makes it difficult, if not impossible to assess systemic risk exposure. The fact that we have no way to judge the tradeoff between additional obfuscation and additional equity merely confirms this point.

It has been suggested to me that the lack of transparency about the system's risk exposure can be overcome if participants look at market prices and use the information contained in them. This argument is not correct. Market prices reflect the behaviour of market participants. If market participants have a mistaken perception of risk, their behaviour — and hence, market prices — will reflect this mistaken perception of risk. Indeed market prices will then send the wrong signals for investment decisions. In the example of the 479 institutions, each of which engages in just a little bit of maturity transformation, the homeowner who takes out the forty-year mortgage will not be made to pay a risk premium for the interest-induced risks to which his real investment exposes the overall system.

To overcome the lack of transparency about the system's risk exposure, one needs information about the system as a whole. A preliminary approach would be to look at the consolidated position of the financial system *vis à vis* the rest of the world, nonfinancial firms and households. Such a consolidated position should provide information about, e.g., the overall amount of maturity transformation and the overall allocation of interest-induced risks.

Unfortunately, current reporting systems do not permit the construction of such consolidated accounts. The fragmentation of supervisory systems across countries and, in the case of the United States, across subsectors of the financial system seems to preclude the collection of data about the financial system as a whole.

6. CONCLUDING REMARKS

I conclude with a few remarks on the implications of the analysis for both, financial institutions and their supervisors. First, the intensification of competition in the financial sector has changed — and is likely to change even further — the scope for the handling of risks by financial institutions. As one looks forward, one needs to ask what system of risk management in the financial sector will be viable when reliance on oligopoly rents as a buffer has ended. The development of new financial instruments should therefore be encouraged, *not* because profits in derivatives may substitute for traditional rents,[17] but because the system needs more tools for sharing undiversifiable risks.

Secondly, practitioners and regulators need to stop thinking about risk in terms of credit risk and market risk with no correlation between the two.

They should add refinancing risks to the list. Even more importantly, they should take account of correlations between the different classes of risks. The "driving-factors approach" in the Basle Committee's recent espousal of bank models of market risks may provide a proper handle on these correlations. However, this approach needs to be extended to credit and refinancing risks as well as market risks.

As one proceeds in this direction, one may be tempted to put more weight on risks that are easily quantifiable, e.g., the explicit risks that are traded in an interest rate swap. After all, one is used to the idea that counterparty credit risks are small, and it seems hardly worthwhile to adjust a strategy that is based on Black-Scholes so as to take account of counterparty risks and the changes they undergo as everybody moves along. The development of strategies that are not subject to the professional's bias for quantifiability and yet are operational would seem to be a major task ahead.

To the extent that counterparty credit risks are difficult to assess, prudential supervision should begin to think in terms of the overall system rather than the individual institution. Bank supervisors have been used to look at each institution by itself, inferring stability of the system from the stability of the individual institutions. As shown in the preceding section, this approach may miss important elements of system risk exposure when the different institutions are involved in a complex tangle of contractual relations.

To assess system risk exposure, supervisors will have to make a substantial effort at coordinating reporting of interbank positions — with information about maturities and risk-shifting clauses — across financial subsectors and across countries. Achieving transparency through such coordination may actually be more important than some of the other efforts at regulatory coordination that are going on.

A final comment concerns the role of monetary policy. In this analysis I have treated interest and exchange rate fluctuations as if they were exogenous. In fact though, the large interest and exchange rate fluctuations that we have seen since the 1970s have been at least partly the results of national and international monetary policies. In terms of the safety of the financial system, much would seem to be gained if national and international monetary policies were to expose the system to fewer shocks. However, the use of monetary policy to subsidize financial institutions in order to reestablish solvency — as in the case of the United States from 1991 to 1993 — is *not* a solution to the problem; as the 1994 experience shows, permitting financial institutions to make substantial profits by playing the yield curve also enhances their vulnerability to the next interest rate shock.

NOTES

1. Indeed the systemic implications of the Crédit Lyonnais bail out may be rather more worrisome than those of the Baring Brothers failure.

2. For a more detailed account of these developments, see Hellwig (1994b).

3. See also OECD (1992).

4. See, e.g., Englund (1990), Mélitz (1990), Vives (1990).

5. In the case of the Basle Accord of 1988, the question of viability also arises because the Cooke ratios do not seem commensurate to the risks in question. 8 per cent may be a reasonable buffer for uncorrelated credit risks; it does not provide much protection against the threats to bank solvency that arise from refinancing risks and from correlated credit, market, and refinancing risks. The problem of correlated risks is further discussed below.

6. For evidence on the Swedish case see Berglof and Sjögren (1995), for evidence on the American case, Boyd and Gertler (1994).

7. For an account of prior insolvency and moral hazard in the S&L crisis, see, e.g., Benston, Carshill, and Olasov (1991), Dewatripont and Tirole (1994), or Kane (1989).

8. For a discussion of this issue in the American context, see Boyd and Gertler (1994).

9. For an elaboration of this argument, see Gehrig (1995).

10. Notice, e.g., the difficulties of the Basle Committee on Banking Supervision in coming to terms with the risk implications of derivatives, as evidenced by the dramatic change in approach from their 1993 proposals to their 1995 proposals.

11. For instance, the analysis of the allocation of interest rate risk does not depend on whether the interest rate risk is preference-induced or technology-induced, see Hellwig (1994a).

12. Interestingly, these efficiency conditions apply also in the case where investors are *ex ante* uncertain about their investment horizons. For details see Hellwig (1994a).

13. This is the essence of the Arrow-Debreu theory of risk allocation in competitive markets. For a more detailed account of the argument and its implications for the theory of financial institutions, see Hellwig (1994b).

14. One may wonder though to what extent certain stock indices would provide a handle for trading macroeconomic risks.

15. In the case of Switzerland, the indexing of rents to mortgage rates might seem to solve this problem, at least for rental housing; in fact though it merely serves to undermine the variable-rate clause of the mortgages as banks are subject to political pressure to keep mortgage rates low.

16. Note however the difficulties of assessing the role of counterparty credit risk on long-term contracts with final users in the Metallgesellschaft case; see, e.g., Culp and Miller (1995a,b), Mello and Parsons (1995).

17. Indeed, to the extent that derivatives operations rely on the exploitation of arbitrage opportunities, such profits are likely to be transitory.

REFERENCES

Basle Committee on Banking Supervision (1993), *The Prudential Supervision of Netting, Market Risks and Interest Rate Risk*, Bank for International Settlements, Basle.

Berglöf, E., and Sjögren (1995). *Combining Arm's-Length and Control-Oriented Finance – Evidence from Main Bank Relationships in Sweden*, ECARE Brussels, mimeo.

Boyd, J., and M. Gertler (1994). The Role of Large Banks in the Recent U.S. Banking Crisis, *Federal Reserve Bank of Minneapolis Quarterly Review* 18, 2–21.

Culp, C.L., and M.H. Miller (1995a). Metallgesellschaft and the Economics of Synthetic Storage, *Journal of Applied Corporate Finance* 7, 62–76.

Culp, C.L., and M.H. Miller (1995b). Hedging in the Theory of Corporate Finance: A Reply to Our Critics, *Journal of Applied Corporate Finance* 8, 121–127.

Dewatripont, M., and J. Tirole (1994). *The Prudential Regulation of Banks*, Cambridge: MIT Press.

Englund, P. (1990). Financial Deregulation in Sweden, *European Economic Review* 34, 385–393.

Gehrig, T. (1995). Capital Adequacy Rules: Implications for Banks' Risk Taking, to appear: *Swiss Journal of Economics and Statistics*.

Hellwig, M. (1994a). Liquidity Provision, Banking, and the Allocation of Interest Rate Risk, *European Economic Review* 38, 1363–1389.

Hellwig, M. (1994b). *Banking and Finance at the End of the Twentieth Century*, Discussion Paper No. 9426, WWZ Basle.

Kane, E. (1989). *The S&L Insurance Mess, How Did It Happen?* Washington: Urban Institute Press.

Mélitz, J. (1990). Financial Deregulation in France, *European Economic Review* 34, 394–402.

Mello, A.S., and J.E. Parsons (1995). Maturity Structure of a Hedge Matters: Lessons from the Metallgesellschaft Debacle, *Journal of Applied Corporate Finance* 8, 106–120.

Organization for Economic Co-Operation and Development (OECD) (1992). *Banks under Stress*, Paris 1992.

Vives, X. (1990). Deregulation and Competition in Spanish Banking, *European Economic Review* 34, 403–411.

Has Financial Risk Really Worsened?

Summary

Each generation believes that it faces greater difficulties, greater volatility in financial markets, than ever before. This is currently blamed on globalisation, derivatives and deregulation. But the evidence shows that, apart from Japan, volatility is not now (in 1995) historically high. Globalisation is no more advanced than it was before 1914, and should, anyhow, allow diversification and thereby reduce risk.

Similarly, there is no strong evidence that derivatives have destabilised spot markets, though OTC derivatives may have reduced transparency; and they have certainly further complicated financial regulation. Some even worry whether these structural processes might have weakened the authorities' grip on domestic monetary policy, a concern which is shown to be largely groundless. The additional leverage provided by derivatives, and certain aspects of dynamic hedging, may, however, have further complicated the authorities' ability to maintain a pegged exchange rate, but the basic difficulty of that exercise was known to be present beforehand.

In contrast, in the field of financial regulation, the speed, leverage, and complexity of international position-taking makes the possibility of regulation via externally imposed ratios, monitored via occasional balance sheet snapshots, of dubious viability. It will be necessary to rely more on internal managements' risk controls.

Charles A.E. Goodhart FBA is the Norman Sosnow Professor of Banking and Finance at the London School of Economics. Before joining the LSE in 1985, he worked at the Bank of England for seventeen years as a monetary adviser, becoming a Chief Adviser in 1980. Earlier he had taught at Cambridge and LSE. Besides numerous articles, he has written a couple of books on monetary history, and a graduate monetary textbook, *Money, Information and Uncertainty* (2nd Ed. 1989); and has published two collections of papers on monetary policy, *Monetary Theory and Practice* (1984) and *The Central Bank and The Financial System* (1995); and an institutional study of *The Evolution of Central Banks*, revised and republished (MIT Press) in 1988.

IV. Has Financial Risk Really Worsened?

C.A.E. GOODHART

1. INTRODUCTION

This Colloquium is entitled 'Risk Management in Volatile Financial Markets'. Perhaps we are being asked to infer that volatility has increased, both domestically and internationally, driven by the triumvirate of derivatives, globalisation and deregulation, which "have generated a new world characterised by high capital mobility". The initial prospectus, or outline, for this Colloquium went on to asseverate that "In the new financial environment, traditional anchors of expectations and policies such as monetary aggregates, exchange rates or interest rates are questioned." Indeed, with the level and rate of change of such financial variables being set increasingly at the international level, this may also "feed a possible 'decoupling' in individual countries between the financial sector and the real economy". In short, "Uncertainty prevails, requiring a better assessment and management of risks". Being a natural contrarian, I shall argue that this perception of worsening risk, though fashionable, has been much exaggerated. Volatility is *not* secularly increasing; the recent globalisation is not only desirable, but takes us back towards the condition that had already been obtained at the start of this century; the monetary authorities have *not* lost control over monetary policy; and the emergence of derivatives has *not* made the financial system riskier.

Indeed, the two eye-catching financial shocks this year, the collapse of Barings and the potential debt-deflation spiral in Japan, (plus the problems of Crédit Lyonnais), have been rather old-fashioned in format. In Barings an appalling lack of internal control allowed a rogue trader, who was supposed to be engaged in virtually riskless arbitrage, to take a punt and then to go on doubling up when that went wrong. In Japan credit risk assessments were too rosy during the boom; and the subsequent, and resulting, downturn was exacerbated by misguided macro monetary policies, whose deflationary rigour was signalled by excessively slow growth in the monetary aggregates, signals which the authorities ignored. Is not this familiar?

41

But the memory of the old is short and fallible, and the young see each event afresh. Indeed, there is a tendency for each new generation to believe that the extent and complexity of the problems that it faces are unprecedented, and that it has to overcome unique challenges to find new solutions. But, in reality, many of these difficulties are inherent in the system, and both they and the proposed answers, *mutatis mutandis*, often have a common form. So it is with problems of financial stability and control.

Many, including, I believe, our hosts in SUERF, worry whether financial markets have become more volatile. Yet, in the experience of my own country, the United Kingdom, the volatility of financial markets, (e.g. the equity market, the foreign exchange market, the property market or the bond market), has *not* been particularly marked in recent years; at least not by comparison with the severe disturbances of 1929–33, 1971–75 or 1979–82. Indeed the period, of slightly over a decade, from about 1971, when the Bretton Woods system collapsed, till after 1982, (when the industrialised countries restored their grip over inflation at the cost of high real interest rates and the associated LDC debt crisis), was one of almost continuous financial turmoil, after which a considerable degree of order and stability has been restored.

Nevertheless, the subsequent period has been punctuated by occasional extreme price movements in financial markets, notably the Stock Exchange crash on October 19th, 1987; the events in the foreign exchange market forcing ERM members off their narrow bands, in 1992 and 1993; the property bubble and bust in Japan and elsewhere 1989–1992; and, some might add, the rise and fall in bond markets in 1993/94, and even the recent disturbances in foreign exchange markets, particularly affecting the yen/dollar rate. Apart from the speculative attack on the ERM, it is difficult to relate these price movements convincingly (especially October 1987) to fundamentals. Consequently, there has been some inclination to ascribe the cause of such extreme price movements to destabilizing internal price dynamics, e.g. to portfolio insurance in 1987; to hedging of ERM positions in 1992 (I shall discuss this further later); and to a variety of stop-loss and hedging measures in 1989–92, and in the 1993/94 bond market collapse.

But stop-loss strategies have been known and used for decades, if not centuries. The levered, speculative positions perhaps adopted by hedge funds, (*perhaps*, since the extent of information on them is so limited), was earlier mirrored by speculators borrowing, often at call, to finance share holdings on a margined basis. There is little in the accusations and complaints about the way in which such levered speculators may destabilize markets that one cannot find matched in the annals of the 19th and early 20th centuries, see for example Sprague's (1910) *History of Crises under the National Banking*

System. Financial crises and manias, (as Kindleberger (1989) and others have documented), are hardly novel phenomena: nor is there any evidence that they are increasing in virulence. Rather the reverse. Of the five financial disturbances mentioned above, (October 1987, ERM, the property bubble, 1993/94 bond market, 1995 forex market), only the property bubble and bust left much of an adverse mark on real economies, though it is too early to document the real effects of recent exchange rate shifts.

One feature of these crises that has regularly surprised commentators, (even though that would be an oxymoron in a rational efficient world), has been the extent to which the financial disturbances have been internationally linked; this was even so to some extent with the ERM crises which, once started, reverberated from member country to member country despite their differing domestic conditions. While it is difficult enough to explain the October 1987 Stock Market crash, or the 1993/94 bond market gyrations, at their epicentre in the US, it is perhaps even harder to understand how and why such price movements were transmitted to other countries, and why such movements were dampened in some cases or aggravated in others; thus the percentage change in bond prices in the UK in recent periods has been even greater than in the US.

Financial markets are international, whereas the coverage of news media, and most people's first-hand knowledge, is local and national. Again, however, there is a tendency to believe that this globalisation of financial markets is new, a development of the modern age. In many respects, however, we are just managing to struggle back towards the global market that existed before 1914. By the Feldstein–Horioka criteria, (correlation of domestic investment and savings ratios) capital flows, and associated current account deficits/surpluses, were larger, as a percentage of GDP, for the major countries of the world prior to 1914, than since. The ease of migration of people, particularly from the Old to the New World, was far greater before 1914 than it has ever been subsequently. Whereas the international transfer of capital, unlike that of humans, has been somewhat restored, e.g. by the removal of exchange controls, to its pre-1914 condition, financial systems were then linked through the gold standard, in contrast to the present mode of largely floating exchange rates. As Morgenstern (1959) and others have documented, the gold standard resulted in national (short-term) interest rates being tied together even more closely than now. The major technical innovation tying international financial markets together was the (trans-oceanic) telegraph. Once this was in place, financial crises and disturbances occurring first in one country, e.g. 1890 Argentina, 1893 Australia, 1907 New York, would be transmitted rapidly, often via London, to the rest of the world. It is, at least, arguable that it was the separation and division of the world's economies between 1914 and, say, the 1960s by barriers to the movements of goods and capital (and people?) that was special and retrograde. If so, the returning globalisation of financial markets is part of an on-going, and desirable, trend.

One reason for the increased globalisation is the greater international diversification of asset holdings, e.g. by the large institutions, mutual funds, insurance companies and pension funds. But as we know diversification reduces risk (for a given mean expected return). The relatively low correlation between returns on the Tokyo and New York stock exchanges, e.g. in 1987 and again this year, has been a source of strength to asset holders everywhere.

One possible danger, however, is that the extent of positive covariance between movements in asset markets is itself time-varying, and can rise quite sharply during periods of market instability, as documented by King, Sentana and Wadhwani (1994). In so far as value-at-risk models are conditioned on historical data for asset market co-variances obtained over a normal calm period, these may seriously understate the extent of market covariance, and hence of portfolio riskiness, during occasional bouts of instability. In order to have some idea what stresses one needs to test, careful studies have to be made of how markets have operated under the rare cases of extreme pressure.

A further current trend can be seen in the continuing structural changes in markets and in financial institutions. The growth of the markets in derivative financial instruments, both in organized exchanges and over-the-counter, both absolutely and relatively to the underlying 'spot' markets is, perhaps, the most commonly remarked, and feared, feature of present developments.

It is not entirely clear, to me at least, why derivatives have been 'demonized' in this manner. They are, after all, redundant securities in the sense that equivalent positions can be constructed, with much effort and transactions costs, from the underlying spot positions. Indeed I have served on charitable trusts where the trustees have been unwilling to hedge a foreign asset position in the forward, or futures, market, because that is a derivative, but have been prepared to borrow foreign currency and use the proceeds to swap spot into domestic assets. Moreover, the great bulk of the studies of the effects of the introduction of derivatives, e.g. on the volatility of the underlying spot position, have reached a not guilty verdict, (see for example Board, Goodhart and Sutcliffe (1992) and the survey in Ayuso and Nuñez (1994) and Goodhart and O'Hara (1995).

Possibly as important a structural change, however, has been the effect of increased (international) competition in breaking down artificial barriers between markets and financial institutions both between, and within, countries. Such barriers were partly caused by, and undoubtedly much facilitated, financial regulation and supervision by national authorities within a domestic context. Such barriers, and distinctions, between markets and institutions have become eroded, and fuzzier. This has provided the authorities with a challenge, notably for regulatory control, which has been proving difficult to meet. We shall discuss this further later on.

Yet, this kind of problem is also not new. In the first half of the nineteenth century money predominantly took the form of coin, or of bank notes convertible into coin. The control of the monetary/financial system was for many, including many of the best economists of the day, e.g. Ricardo, synonymous with managing the issue of such bank notes, (the Currency School). No sooner was this done, e.g. by centralising note issue in the Central Bank, as was done in Peel's 1844 Bank Act, than the nature of both banks, with the growth of the branch-banking joint stock banks, and of money itself, transmuted. We are not *currently* facing quite as large a structural change to our concepts and to our institutional system, as occurred then. It is, however, quite possible that such changes may yet occur. For example, there is no inherent reason why the assets, which we can transfer in settlement of payments, i.e. money, need be restricted to bank liabilities, nor need they be in fixed-nominal-value form. In many ways mutual funds would represent a sounder basis for a monetary system than banks (Goodhart, 1993). It would not surprise me if, by the year 2010, we looked back at the decades of the 1980s and 1990s as being one of general stability and relatively little structural change.

It is as well to remind ourselves that many of the problems and disturbances that we face today are neither new, nor by most objective standards particularly virulent. I have highlighted three such concerns; first the extent of volatility in financial markets; second the increasing internationalization and the global links between such markets; and third the break-down of barriers, resulting in fuzzy boundaries, between markets and financial intermediaries within and between countries. I have also suggested that there is no particular reason for greater concern about these developments now than in earlier decades, perhaps less.

There is, however, one aspect of current developments that may, perhaps, be of increasing worry now, and which *is* linked to the growth of the new derivatives market. This is whether some of these innovations may have reduced the transparency of market positioning, and hence raised risks, for example by reducing the ability of both regulators and other market agents to interpret market signals, and to control risk adequately.

At the lowest level this syndrome is represented by a concern whether senior managers have sufficient understanding of the potential provided by the ability to deal in derivative markets to assess and to control the assumption of risk within their own institutions (e.g. Mr. Jett and Kidder Peabody and even more dramatically Mr. Leeson and Barings). Are internal control systems appropriate? At a slightly higher level, the existence of derivative markets allows financial intermediaries both to hedge risk and/or to take speculative positions not only extremely quickly, but also through quite complex mechanisms. Moreover, such financial engineering generates an increasing turnover in financial markets, which has so raised the size and scale of settlement and payments, for example in the foreign exchange market, that there is increasing concern about the dangers of potential failure in such (back-office) parts of the system. This is especially acute where there is no centralised market (e.g. in the OTC markets), and where netting procedures are not yet (legally) established. Under such circumstances the assessment of (credit) risk may become increasingly difficult. This inevitably raises questions about the adequacy of the traditional forms of (bank) regulation, based on certain, rather arbitrary, ratios for capital, and also perhaps liquid assets, applied against certain specified asset categories — with limited offsets — and checked against infrequent snapshots, (sometimes on preannounced, sometimes on random, occasions), of balance sheets.

Hayne Leland, one of the founding fathers of portfolio insurance, likes to distinguish between the effect that a few billion dollars of sales from portfolio insurance may have had on October 19th, 1987, and the virtually zero effect on markets of a *vastly* larger sale of shares a few months later. He then reveals that this latter was the new issue of NTT shares in Japan, which had been pre-announced and known well in advance, so that everyone could take their positions in response to it. Of course, major movements in prices have always triggered quasi-automatic reactions by stop-loss sales and margin calls, as already noted. But there *may* now be a qualitative change as the volume of quasi-automatic transactions, e.g. from option hedging, portfolio rebalancing, portfolio insurance, may be larger in relative amount or may, as we shall discuss in relation to exchange rate bands, be bunched together and triggered by a more particular event than in the past.

Markets, especially financial markets, work better when they have sufficient information. One of the questions raised by the growth of derivative markets is whether these have led to the generation of certain key bits of information, in particular sales/purchases that are quasi-automatically programmed to occur under certain specified market conditions, which should, perhaps, be more widely known to all market participants, but which data are *not* currently collected, collated and made publicly available. At least, following the Brockmeijer Report (BIS, 1995), Central Banks are now planning to collect a snapshot of commercial bank activity in derivatives markets, alongside their current BIS survey of foreign exchange activity.

2. CONTROL OVER THE INSTRUMENTS OF POLICY

Let me turn next to consider another worry expressed in the outline for this Colloquium which we have all received. This is that these structural processes, i.e. innovation, deregulation and globalisation, are somehow causing the authorities to lose their grip on domestic national monetary policy. This, too, is, I believe, exaggerated.

The main instrument of monetary policy consists of the Central Bank's ability to control the general level of short-term interest rates. It does so through having effective (monopsonistic) control over the outstanding volume of legal-tender, base money, (currency and deposits at the Central Bank), which it can manipulate on a short-term basis through open-market operations.

The main constraints on the proper operation of such monetary policy have been political. This has frequently taken the form of political pressures to keep interest rates lower than would be consistent with price stability. In unsettled circumstances such political imperatives have also adopted the guise of enforced emissions of monetary base to help finance public sector deficits, as is currently occurring, for example, in many of the Republics of the former USSR. There is, of course, nothing new about this. Indeed, the current fashion for the legislative adoption of Central Bank independence in many countries, as for example required for the member Central Banks of the European System of Central Banks under the Maastricht Treaty, indicates a desire to avoid such political interference in future.

There have been a few futuristic suggestions that the development of a cashless society ('smart' cards, etc.,) might so reduce, or somehow, alter the demand for cash that the Central Bank's control over short-term interest rates would be compromised. Such fears are unwarranted. Banks, and other financial intermediaries, will always want to settle in the unquestioned, 'good' funds of their Central Banks, rather than extend credit to counterparties. Moreover, alternatives to currency usually require electronic identification and hence lose anonymity, though that is not so, I understand, of the Mondex cards. Alas, much of the demand for cash in many countries is already related to illegal and black economy activities, but such activities *may* be as stably related to (calculated) nominal GDP as those activities becoming progressively cashless. It is, I believe, true that if the Central Bank did *not* have a monopoly on note issue, competition among commercial banks to issue their own notes would lead to a resolution of the problem of paying interest on such notes, (ending seigniorage and several arcane features of monetary economics at one swoop). Even then, I have argued (Goodhart, 1993) that the Central Bank could still control the general level of interest rates, by fixing the rate that it would pay on its own (note) liabilities.

Thus I start from the presumption that there is no current serious threat to the Central Bank's traditional ability to direct monetary policy via its command over short-term interest rates, whether from private financial dynamics or otherwise. Where, instead, such structural changes *have* caused problems for monetary control relates to questions of how to decide on which interest rate(s) to focus,[1] and how to monitor the effects of such interest rate changes, and through what transmission routes, on the economy.

The best known example of the resulting (control) problems caused by such structural changes has been the collapse of the stability of most demand-for-money functions, generally (though uncertainly) attributed to financial innovations, such as the payment of (market-related) interest rates on a widening category of (sight) deposits, the growth of money market mutual funds, etc., etc. The gyrations in M3 in Germany in 1993/94, and the Bundesbank's decision to lower nominal interest rates there in line with prospects for declining inflation, and nominal GDP, despite a surge in M3, provide a recent example. In earlier years, e.g. 1975–1982, it had been thought that intermediate monetary targets would, through a predictable link to subsequent movements in nominal incomes, provide a basis for informing Central Banks when to vary interest rates, so as to control monetary growth.[2] So far has fashion changed since then, owing in some large part to the apparent unpredictability of velocity, that the rates of growth of the monetary aggregates are not now given much weight by many Central Banks as information variables, among many other information variables (e.g. commodity prices, wages growth, etc.). For example, the rate of growth of bank lending and of broad money collapsed dramatically in several countries in 1990–92, including the UK and Japan, without producing any concerted campaign for a much greater counter-vailing reduction in interest rates, than was actually adopted. In the UK, of course, the conduct of policy was constrained first by ERM membership, and thereafter by a need for a strategic policy re-think.

Such structural changes have not only impaired the stability of demand for money functions, but they also have tended to alter the transmission mechanism whereby interest rates affect the economy. For example, constraints on the interest rates set by certain financial intermediaries, and associated limitations on the permitted activities of, and competition between, certain groups of intermediaries meant that policy-induced increases in interest rates would often lead to (somewhat) predictable shifts of funds, (e.g. away from housing finance specialists, such as UK building societies), and an associated rationing of loans to borrowers from those intermediaries. Thus persons, especially when borrowing on mortgage, and small companies could be rationed out of the market by tightening monetary policy: the authorities used the imperfections in financial markets to reinforce their grip.

That grip has been weakened by the undermining of such imperfections through the forces of competition and structural innovation. When the Central Bank now raises the *general* level of short term interest rates, it can no longer be confident of the effect on certain key interest rate *differentials*, (as it could in the past because of the imposed stickiness of competing bank/housing finance deposit rates). There is less, quasi-automatic rationing effect. In order to have the same overall impact on the economy the (relative) price effect of interest rate changes has to be greater.

The current situation, in those countries without exchange rate commitments, (either closed economies by benefit of size, e.g. US, or protected by exchange controls, and/or with floating rates), is to vary interest rates in a discretionary fashion, with the aim of achieving medium-term price stability, on the basis of a melange of information variables, including a variety of direct measures of inflation itself, capacity and unemployment variables, the exchange rate, monetary aggregates, etc. The weights attached to the various information variables are entirely subjective. It is not an intellectually tidy method of operating, but in a complex and structurally evolving world the resulting flexibility may be an operational advantage, particularly if the monetary authorities are rigidly precommitted to the goals to be achieved, e.g. a numerically specified inflation target, and given appropriate (pecuniary) incentives to meet their objective.

Even for a country with floating exchange rates, external influences are bound to have a major effect on the authorities' current decisions about the appropriate level of short-term rates, and the market's expectations of future probable domestic short-term rates. I shall shortly be discussing the authorities' ability to influence, control or peg exchange rates. So, longer-term interest rates, and the yield curve, in countries with floating rates are bound to be influenced by market assessments of (the domestic impact of) external forces. Beyond that normal effect of external factors on domestic interest rates, there has been some question in the course of recent years whether international capital flows had led to a worldwide adjustment in bond yields, that would seem in a number of countries to have driven some shorter-term (3 to 5 year) bond yields in a cycle, down, up and now down again which seems difficult to explain on the basis of plausible implicit domestic forward shorter-term interest rates. Once again the readjustment in bond yields appears to have been initiated in the US, with its effects radiating out from New York. The fluctuations in the price/yield changes have been somewhat difficult to explain even in the US, but considerably more so in Europe.

There is just a suspicion that we have seen some internationally co-ordinated over-reactions, perhaps driven in part by financial dynamics. Was the combined effect of the Basle capital adequacy risk ratios, and the bad debts on property loans in 1989-92, such as to make banks, and other financial intermediaries then overload their portfolios with government bonds? Was this driven-on further in 1993 by the actions of (inappropriately termed) hedge funds? Did an increasing proportion of these players put in place various forms of portfolio insurance policies to protect themselves against interest rate risk? How far does the insurance, risk-hedging, behaviour of the individual fund manager *worsen* aggregate risk, (especially where such individual strategies are not transparently revealed in advance to the market) by increasing the weight of trend-following, as compared with contrarian, market behaviour?[3]

While these concerns may, or may not, have some validity within a single country, they still do not address the question of the apparent *international co-ordination* of bond price/yield adjustment. But one of the features of derivative markets is that they can allow the differing kinds of risk inherent in a position to be separated, and either individually hedged or consciously assumed. A resident purchasing a foreign bond would, in the past, have simultaneously had to accept a currency, exchange rate, risk, as well as an interest rate risk. In so far as that currency risk can now be separately, and relatively cheaply, hedged, does it mean that foreign bonds have become much closer substitutes for domestic bonds? If so, will the course of bond yields around the world become much more sensitive to movements in the New York bond market? But, as I indicated earlier, there are no greater external constraints, assuming free floating exchange rates, on domestic Central Bank control of short-term money market rates than in former years. Does this, perhaps, mean that there will be a greater tension in future between international pressures and domestic factors, (e.g. the expected time path of future short rates), in the determination of bond yields in countries outside the US? If so, the ability of domestic Central Banks to control, or even to predict, the movement of *longer*-term bond yields, (despite their continuing control over shorter-term money market rates), may have become somewhat further impaired. Time will tell. But it would, perhaps, be as well not to become too excited about recent events in world bond markets. We do not fully understand what happened; it may prove to have been a once-off development that will not be closely repeated in future; it is doubtful whether the gyrations in these markets, unduly buoyant in late 1993, unduly depressed in the second quarter of 1994, actually had a seriously adverse effect on the world economy.

In short, so long as they do not commit themselves to trying to peg their exchange rate, Central Banks remain the masters of their own money markets. It is just that knowing how best to exert such mastery becomes even more difficult in a changing structural environment.

Let me turn next to the ability of the monetary authorities to control exchange rates. Of course, in the two main, canonical, regimes for exchange rates, free floating or completely fixed, there is no call for any conscious exchange rate policy.

Why, then, are Central Banks *not* content to adopt one, or other, of these canonical forms, which involve them in no exchange rate policies as such, but instead do they seek some half-way house requiring a conscious attempt at exchange rate management? A major problem with free-floating has been that real exchange rates have proven not only extremely volatile, but also subject to apparent serious medium-term misalignment: the worst case of this was the appreciation of the US Dollar in the mid-1980s, but recent developments in the yen, mark and dollar are also unsettling.

As this example from the 1980s suggests, there is no evidence, known to me, that recent market developments, e.g. the still increasing size of the foreign exchange (forex) market, the growth of derivative markets, etc., etc., have led to any *worsening* in the proclivity of the forex market to behave in a way difficult to explain in terms of fundamentals. Indeed, compared to the 1970s and 1980s, the forex market in the 1990s has, perhaps, been more responsive to fundamentals, [and that *includes* the recent debacle of the ERM in Europe].

With intervention providing relatively little control over free floating exchange rates, the monetary authorities may feel a need for some greater stability in exchange rates, vis-à-vis some neighbouring country, or set of countries, while not feeling prepared to abandon the option to undertake an independent monetary policy altogether: that is to move to a pegged, but adjustable, exchange rate.

A serious disadvantage for a local/regional economy within a currency board/currency union system is that asymmetric shocks may make the single interest rate, imposed at the centre, inappropriate for the region. But this disadvantage is, however, made considerably worse by the dynamics of a pegged, but adjustable, system, for reasons that have become known in the UK as the Walters' critique, after Sir Alan Walters, Mrs. Thatcher's adviser in the 1980s. When a country first enters such a system, or after a peg readjustment, the expectation is usually that the peg will be made to hold, if only for political credibility reasons, for, say, a year at least. Given that expectation, short-term interest rates will be driven down by capital inflows until they are only just above those in the centre country. But the country initially adopting, or readjusting the peg, is likely for a variety of reasons to have an inflation rate significantly above that of the centre country. Hence the first effect of pegging, somewhat paradoxically the more so the greater the credibility of that peg, is to introduce excessively low local real interest rates, a large capital inflow, and a further inflationary impulse.

One way to try to deal with the inflationary effect of too lax monetary policy in the early months/years of a pegged system is to counterbalance this with *extremely tight* fiscal policy. But this is usually politically not feasible. Instead, the norm unfortunately is for the inflationary gap between the peripheral and central country to remain, or worsen. This causes over time an appreciation of the *real* exchange rate, a worsening trade balance, and a weakening competitive position in the tradeable goods industry, as for example happened recently in Mexico. Eventually the continuation of the peg is perceived to be no longer credible. Once an expectation arises that the peg may be re-adjusted in the near future, the interest rate that becomes needed to prevent such speculation, and outward capital flows, becomes very high indeed. In such speculative crises in Europe, Sweden in 1992 resorted to overnight rates well in excess of 100 per cent p.a., as did Greece more recently (and for the time being successfully) in 1994.

There is, indeed, a further problem. If the country, whose pegged rate is suspect, also has high unemployment, a rise in interest rates may be perceived in the market as *politically* untenable, even if the Central Bank expresses its willingness to impose such high rates. So a rise in interest rates, under such circumstances, may, at any rate initially, reinforce rather than quell speculation. This syndrome was believed to have been a factor both in the attacks on £ in September 1992, and on the French Franc in Summer 1993.

Moreover, this possible perverse effect of raising interest rates, to defend the peg, has probably been exacerbated by internal financial dynamics, as analyzed in the paper on 'Dynamic Hedging and the Interest Rate Defence' by Garber and Spencer (1994), and emphasized by the discussant's comments by Paolo Kind, (Perugia Conference, NBER, July 1994). Essentially, portfolio managers will shift funds between national bond markets (as already noted in Section 2) to take advantage of local interest rate differentials. They will simultaneously hedge their currency risk by taking out a put option, with that option coming into the money once the local exchange rate falls below the weak band limit. A rise in interest rates, to protect the currency, will tend to force the forward rate, assuming that the spot rate is near the lower limit, below that level. This will cause those intermediaries who have written the put options to undertake hedging sales. If there has been a large volume of prior capital inflows, on a pure comparative interest-rate play, there could be a massive volume of puts, requiring hedging sales when, and if, an interest rate hike (to protect the currency) drives the forward rate below the lower band. So a Central Bank, which has raised its interest rate, in the expectation that this should strengthen the spot exchange rate, might instead be faced with an unexpected wave of hedging-driven sales. It was suggested by Paolo Kind at Perugia that this had, indeed, played a role in driving the Italian Lira out of the ERM in September 1992.

3. REGULATION

Where I would argue that the structural processes at work have necessitated a reconsideration of our ideas and approaches is in the field of financial regulation. This has been undertaken by *national* regulatory authorities, but within the commercial banking system on the basis of *internationally* co-ordinated capital adequacy requirements.

The Basle CARs concentrated initially on only one kind of risk, credit risk. There are, however, many other kinds of risk, e.g. interest rate risk, liquidity risk, exchange rate risk, etc., etc., not to speak of risk of fraud. The current tendency of the authorities appears to be to stick with the building block approach, i.e. to assess each kind of risk separately, to measure the extent of each risk inherent in certain blocs of assets and/or liabilities, and to allow only limited and usually ad hoc offsets within and between blocs. Moreover, the capital requirements for these differing kinds of risk are, it appears, to be treated as additive, despite the fact that such different risks are not necessarily positively correlated.

At the same time as the attempt to extend the Basle building-block approach to cover a wider range of risk is increasing the complexity of the system, and further weakening whatever intellectual underpinning it once may have had, the development of the derivatives markets has been allowing banks to adjust their overall positions, vis-à-vis certain of these risks, either to hedge or to speculate, very rapidly, often through a rebalancing of their off-balance sheet position. It has become much more difficult to assess a bank's overall riskiness from a snap-shot of its balance sheet; the interaction of on and off-balance sheet positions needs to be properly reviewed; and the latter, if not the former, can be swiftly changed once the snap-shot has been taken, so the adequacy of

the snap-shot itself as representative of a bank's 'normal' riskiness is subject
to greater doubt.

Against this background there is an increasing chorus of voices arguing for
a radical reconsideration and recasting of The Basle CAR approach. Thus the
lead article in the July/August 1994 Financial Regulation Report, (Financial
Times Business Information), has opined that:

"The debate over regulating derivatives activities has highlighted the complexity
of banks' risk-management techniques and the crudity of the existing (and proposed)
Basle capital adequacy guidelines.

There is now a real issue as to whether regulators can hope to capture the risk profile
of individual institutions through the application of simple, static capital rules and
whether it might be better to leave the task of risk measurement to banks themselves.

It is against this background that Charles Taylor, Executive Director of the Group
of Thirty, has proposed a radical overhaul of the way in which regulators approach
their task. He argues in "A New Approach to Capital Adequacy for Banks", Centre
for the Study of Financial Innovations, July 1994, that the present Basle régime is
fundamentally flawed because it measures risk by focusing on the classification of
instruments rather than risk types and by failing to take account of the sophisticated
risk-management models currently employed by major financial institutions. As a
result it discourages rather than promotes good risk management."

Many of the critical comments on the present regulatory system have suggested that, rather than attempt to impose a common, and inevitably simplistic,
(since it must be capable of application to the smallest, least sophisticated
banks), system of ratios, the supervisors should instead assess, and try to build
on, banks' own risk management schemes, possibly with a fall-back system
to be imposed on (small) banks with inadequate systems of their own. Thus,
in the same Financial Regulation Report, as above, Patrick Fell of Coopers
& Lybrand argued that:

"Historically most banks and brokers worldwide have had to comply with externally determined capital regimes which have little in common with the way in which
management monitors risk. The obvious example is the Basle agreement framework,
which looks only at credit risk, and even in this area applies a much more simple
régime than that which banks should normally put in place.

In the last couple of years supervisors have started to focus on the growing complexity of instruments (notably derivatives) whose risks are far less susceptible to
assessment through mechanistic techniques than, for example, simple lending business. Supervisors are beginning to realize that such risks can only be understood
when viewed through the microscope of the firm's *own* risk management system.
Use of any other less sophisticated approach merely gives a result which is incorrect

(rather than one which is necessarily prudent).

In conclusion he states that:

"The move towards the use of risk models for supervisory assessments and capital calculations is inevitable, and in general is highly to be recommended. Supervision and management control can then move along the same path, rather than along linked, but not necessarily parallel paths. Supervisors will have a greater incentive to encourage good management practice, while management will feel that supervisory compliance is not merely a bureaucratic overlay, but rather something which can assist the company in meeting its own control objectives."

Many of the senior officials involved in bank regulation, especially in the US, and reputedly including Alan Greenspan, are coming to the opinion that, rather than the Regulators trying to impose a common set of ratios on (all) banks *ex cathedra*, much more weight has to be placed on assessing, and seeking to build on and to improve, banks' own internal risk-control methods. While trying to build on the basis of banks' own internal risk-control models would seem preferable to attempting to impose a single, common and simplistic model from outside, nevertheless it is not sufficient. However good the (internal) control system may be, losses can still be made, and capital impaired.[4] In particular banks may fail to monitor and enforce their own internal risk management systems, however good these may be on paper. This appears to have been the problem in the case of Barings. The willingness of the Bank of England to see Barings fail, rather than bail it out, should help to reinforce in commercial bank managers' minds the importance of adequately maintaining their own internal control systems. Beyond that, it is difficult to see what lessons the Barings disaster may have for the *external* system of supervision and regulation (see Board, Goodhart, Power and Schoenmaker, March 1995, a paper prepared for the Select Committee on the Treasury and Civil Service of the House of Commons, on the regulation of derivatives in the light of the Barings collapse). The external supervisor cannot possibly oversee all internal operations; to make the internal audit a formal document for presentation to the external supervisors would probably so change its very nature that there would be no advantage gained.

So, however good a bank's own internal control system may be, serious losses can still be made. Once capital is impaired, the danger of loss, perhaps from the conscious assumption of riskier strategy by management, loss to depositors, deposit insurance or taxpayers, increases.

Thus, in addition to providing an outside overview, almost a form of consultancy, on banks' internal risk control models and methods, the supervisors will want to impose increasing constraints on bank activities pari-passu with a worsening decline in its capital, with a view to closure, or enforced takeover, before its capital is exhausted. For this purpose capital can be defined quite widely, including subordinated debt, and should be measured, as far as possible, in terms of market or current (present) values, rather than at historical accounting cost. Probably the best approach along these lines is the proposal developed by George Benston for Structured Early Intervention and Resolution (SEIR), (Benston, 1993, 1995).

4. CONCLUSION

Let me end on a slightly heretical note. It is commonly suggested that derivatives could be dangerous if they were to facilitate and to encourage speculation, but that their use to hedge risks and to insure positions is good and blameless. May I suggest that both claims need much qualification.

Since no one can see into the future, no one can really have a firm view on the present fundamental value of assets. Given the risks involved in taking a position, few are, therefore, willing to speculate on fundamental values. The concept that current asset values are 'anchored' by their expected future value is wishful thinking. There are too few speculators prepared to take and hold a view about future fundamentals to do so.

By contrast, the same uncertainties make us keen to hedge and to insure positions. Our realisation of the limitations of our own foresight makes us both unwilling to speculate on fundamentals, and too willing to follow the herd. But whenever markets turn sharply down, such portfolio insurance will lead in due course to stop loss sales, whether by those who have written put options, or by other mechanisms. The easier it is to hedge long asset positions, and the less we know about the resulting sales that may be forced in spot markets once the hedges are activated, the more likely it may be that a sharp downturn in asset values would be transmuted into a rout. In so far as derivatives make it both easier to follow hedging strategies, and at the same time difficult to observe what contingent transactions would be triggered by future asset price sales, they could exacerbate market volatility, especially under disturbed conditions.

Since it would obviously be nonsensical to seek to penalize hedging strategies, the best solution would seem to be to arrange for more data on such contingent transactions to be provided. Since such information is both a public good, and might harm the commercial interest of any single private sector institution making such data available in isolation, there is a clear case for the public sector authorities to collect, coordinate and publish such data.

NOTES

1. Many academics, e.g. McCallum in his paper for the Bank of Japan (1993a and b), would argue that the Central Bank should determine a growth rate for the monetary base rather than interest rate levels. This is a long-running argument, which I address in several papers elsewhere (e.g. *Economic Journal*, November 1994). For present purposes, my claim is that, in practice, Central Banks have, and will continue to, set policy on the basis of interest rate, not monetary base, control, so that the discussion should proceed on this realistic, practical basis.
2. This practice used to infuriate monetarist economists, who argued for the superiority of monetary base control as the operational technique. As already noted, in Note 1, Central Banks never accepted the arguments or precepts of monetarists in this respect.
3. When markets move extremely sharply, this is frequently attributed to speculation. In practice, hedging strategies are just as, or more likely, to exacerbate trends. Be that as it may, it takes detailed knowledge of an agent's portfolio position to be able to distinguish between a speculative, and a hedging, transaction.
4. Moreover, some (small) banks may not have developed (sufficiently good) internal risk control models of their own. In such cases the supervisors will probably feel the need for a (relatively simple) fall-back risk control system which could be imposed on those banks. An adaptation of the present Basle system might fill such a need.
   Alternatively there could be a (partial) private sector solution. Perhaps partly to prevent some less satisfactory and binding set of official control mechanisms, J.P. Morgans have made publicly and freely available their risk-metric system. It may be in the interests of large and successful private sector institutions to develop and to market proprietary risk control systems which smaller banks may be encouraged to adopt.

REFERENCES

Ayuso, J. and S. Nuñuz, (1994), 'Los Derivados solve Deuda y la Volatalidad del Mercado al Contado, El Caso Español', Paper presented at 7th Symposium of *Moneda y Credito*, Madrid, November.

Benston, G.J., (1993), 'Safety Nets and Moral Hazard in Banking', paper presented at the Bank of Japan Conference, Tokyo, Oct 28-29, on *Financial Stability in a Changing Environment*, now published, eds. K. Sawamoto, Z. Nakajima and H. Taguchi, London: Macmillan, 1995.

Board, J., C. Goodhart, M. Power and D. Schoenmaker, (1995), 'Derivatives Regulation', LSE Financial Markets Group, Special Paper No. 70, (March); also presented to House of Commons Select Committee of the Civil Service and the Treasury enquiry into the regulation of financial derivatives.

Board, J., C. Goodhart and C. Sutcliffe, (1992), *Inter-market Volatility Linkages: The London Stock Exchange and London International Financial Futures Exchange*, (Securities and Investments Board: London, June).

Brockmeijer Report, (1995), *Issues of Measurement Related to Market Size and Macroprudential Risks in Derivatives Markets*, prepared by the Euro-Currency Standing Committee of the G-10 Central Banks, (Bank for International Settlements: Basle, February).

Fell, P., (1994), 'Capital Adequacy' *Financial Regulation Report*, Financial Times Business Information, July/August: 2-7.

Financial Regulation Report, (1994) 'Re-casting financial regulation', *Financial Regulation Report*, Financial Times Business Information, July/August: 1-2.

Garber, P. and M. Spencer, (1994) 'Dynamic Hedging and the Interest Rate Defense', paper presented at the Perugia Conference, July 1-2, on 'Microstructure of Foreign Exchange Markets', organized by J. Frankel, G. Galli and A Giovannini, (proceedings forthcoming).

Goodhart, C.A.E., (1993) 'Can we improve the structure of financial systems?', *European Economic Review* 37 (2/3) (April): 269-91.

Goodhart, C.A.E., (1994) 'What should Central Banks do? What should be their macroeconomic objectives and operations?' *Economic Journal*, Vol. 104, No. 427, November, pp 1424-1436.

Goodhart, C.A.E. and M. O'Hara, (1995), 'High Frequency Data in Financial Markets: Issues and Applications', Introductory lecture at Conference on 'High Frequency Data in Finance', Olsen and Associates, Zurich, (March); forthcoming *Journal of Empirical Finance*.

Kindleberger, C.P., (1989) *Manias, Panics and Crashes*, 2nd Edition, London: Macmillan.

King, M., E. Sentana and S. Wadhwani, (1994), 'Volatility and links between national stock markets', *Econometrica*, 62, 4, (July), 901-933.

McCallum, B.T., (1993a), 'Specification and Analysis of a Monetary Policy Rule for Japan', *Bank of Japan Monetary and Economic Studies*, 11:1-45.

McCallum, B.T., (1993b) 'Monetary Policy Rules and Financial Stability', paper presented at Bank of Japan Conference, Tokyo, Oct 28/29, on *Financial Stability in a Changing Environment*, now published, eds. K. Sawamoto, Z. Nakajina and H. Taguchi London: Macmillan, 1995.

Morgenstern, O., (1959) *International Financial Transactions and Business Cycles*, National Bureau of Economic Research, Princeton, N.J.: Princeton University Press.

Sawamoto, K., Z. Nakajima, and H. Taguchi, eds., (1995), *Financial Stability in a Changing Environment*, Proceedings of a Bank of Japan Conference held in Tokyo, 1993, London: Macmillan.

Sprague, O.M.W., (1910), *History of Crises under the National Banking System*, National Monetary Commission (Sixty First Congress, Second Session, Senate Doc # 538; Washington, D.C; Government Printing Office).

The Anatomy of the Bond Market Turbulence of 1994

Summary

This paper examines the sharp rise in bond yield volatility across the major bond markets in 1994. The analysis covers thirteen industrialised countries and is largely based on OTC data for implied bond yield volatility. We conclude that the market's own dynamics seem to provide a stronger explanation than variations in market participants' apprehensions about economic fundamentals. We identify three market dynamics: downward markets increase volatility; volatility spills over from certain markets onto others; and it can rise in the wake of substantial withdrawals of foreign investments. We find more limited evidence that monetary or fiscal policies accounted for the rise in volatility, at least by our measures. Moreover, changing expectations about growth and inflation, while perhaps at work in particular countries, do not offer much of a general explanation.

Claudio E.V. Borio is Head of Section in the Monetary and Economic Department of the Bank for International Settlements with responsibilities primarily for the analysis of banking, finance and regulation and the corresponding chapter in the BIS Annual Report. He was previously an Economist in the Country Studies branch of the Economics and Statistics Department of the OECD, and has also worked as a Research Fellow and Lecturer in Economics at Brasenose College at the University of Oxford. He has written numerous publications in the fields of monetary economics, banking and finance, and holds a Doctorate in Economics from Oxford University.

Robert N. McCauley is an economist with the Bank for International Settlements. His previous fourteen years at the Federal Reserve Bank of New York featured assignments as economist to the Interagency Country Exposure Review Committee in Washington, and as secretary to the Bank's Financial Policy Committee and Board of Directors. On leaves, he worked for the Congressional Joint Economic Committee in 1988, and taught international finance and the multinational firm at the University of Chicago's business school in 1992. Mr. McCauley has published on international comparisons of the cost of capital, capital flows, banking and the Euromarkets, IMF programs, direct investment, and US corporate finance.

V. The Anatomy of the Bond Market Turbulence of 1994

CLAUDIO E.V. BORIO and ROBERT N. MCCAULEY*

INTRODUCTION

The bond market sell-off of 1994 has begun to show up on lists of market events against which risk management systems are judged. One such list includes the 1987 stock market crash, the 1990 Gulf war, the 1992 European exchange rate mechanism turbulence, the 1994 bond market decline and the 1995 Kobe earthquake (Market Risk Task Force, 1995).

In contrast to the 1987 stock market crash, however, our understanding of the 1994 bond market decline has not benefited from a series of official post-mortems and from subsequent published studies. This paper steps into this lacuna and asks why *volatility* rose across the major bond markets in 1994, with increases ranging from 5 percentage points in the US market to 10 or more elsewhere.[1] The analysis covers thirteen industrialised countries[2] and is largely, though not exclusively, based on OTC data for implied bond yield volatility (see Box for more details).

The market's own dynamics seem to provide a stronger answer than variations in market participants' apprehensions about economic fundamentals. We identify three market dynamics: downward markets increase volatility; volatility spills over from certain markets onto others; and it can rise in the wake of substantial withdrawals of foreign investments. We find more limited evidence that monetary or fiscal policies accounted for the rise in volatility in 1994, at least by our measures. Moreover, changing expectations about growth and inflation, while perhaps at work in particular countries, do not offer much of a general explanation.

*The views expressed are those of the authors and not necessarily those of the Bank for International Settlements. We would like to thank Henri Bernard, Angelika Donaubauer and Gert Schnabel for statistical assistance, Wilhelm Fritz for technical help and Stephan Arthur for preparing the graphs.

Graph 1

Bond yield volatility since 1993

In percentages

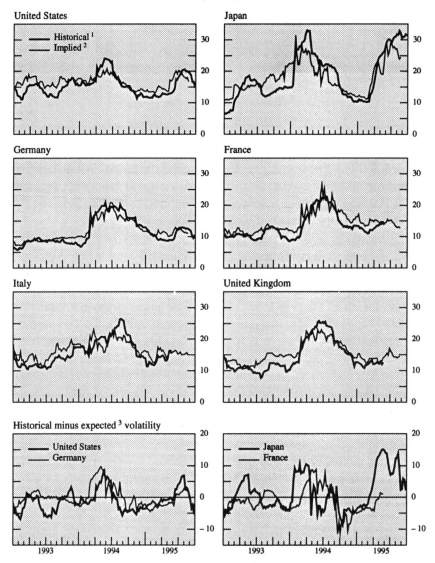

[1] Historical volatility is measured as the annualised standard deviation of daily percentage changes in bond yields calculated over the preceding ninety-one calendar days.   [2] Yield volatility implied in three-month over-the-counter, at-the-money option contracts on ten-year benchmark government bonds, plotted at the time the contract is struck.   [3] Expected volatility is implied volatility plotted at the time the contract expires so as to be aligned with historical volatility (e.g. the point in December is equal to the difference between historical volatility as plotted in December and implied volatility as plotted in September).

Sources: Datastream, J. P. Morgan and national data.

1. THE EVENTS

Volatility rose sharply in the world's major bond markets last year, accompanying the early stages of a bear bond market (Graph 1). Volatility generally began to increase in February, soon after the tightening of monetary policy in the United States. The main exception was Japan, where the rise started in January.

The scale and persistence of the increase were not uniform across countries. Measured by the standard deviation of daily percentage changes over a sliding three-month window, the rise was comparatively modest and short-lived in the United States and especially large and persistent in ERM countries. In Europe, volatility generally peaked in mid-year, about one month later than in the United States and a whole quarter behind Japan.

The overall picture is broadly similar when gauged by the movements of the implied volatility of three-month over-the-counter at-the-money option contracts on ten-year benchmark government bonds, the main focus of this paper (Graph 1, top six panels). The main difference is that the increase in volatility in the US market looks smaller.

If implied volatility measures market expectations about realised volatility during the life of the option's contract, the evidence indicates two surprises in 1994: participants initially failed to anticipate the turbulence and subsequently overestimated its persistence (Graph 1, bottom two panels). This pattern, uniform across countries, suggests that implied volatility is firmly anchored to the behaviour of historical volatility in the proximate past.

A look at the rise in volatility from a longer-term perspective highlights both the scale and the unusual international incidence of the increase (Graph 2). Last year's rise appears to be the third such global episode since the beginning of the 1980s. The first two took place, respectively, in the early 1980s and around the stock market crash of 1987. In 1994 volatility reached close to record highs and persistence in some of the countries with the lowest interest rates and better inflation records, such as Germany and the Netherlands. In Europe, it also typically exceeded the levels observed at the time of the ERM turbulence in 1992 and 1993.

BOX — THE DATA

Much of the present research draws on a database of weekly yield volatility for three-month at-the-money over-the-counter options on ten-year benchmark government bonds in thirteen major markets as quoted at the market close on Thursdays by a leading market-maker, J.P. Morgan (Watts, 1994 and 1995). Supply and demand in the market for options set the premium price; and this price, together with interest rates, can be used to back out an implied volatility through an option pricing formula. Admittedly, market-makers' methods for mapping premium prices into and out of implied volatilities vary somewhat across firms and over time. However, the difference between these pricing models are subtle enough for market-makers to find it convenient to quote their options in terms of the implied volatilities.

OTC market quotations have a number of advantages over volatilities embodied in the prices of exchange-traded options. They exist for government bonds that are not exchange-traded. And they are quoted for the same maturity at every observation. By contrast, exchange-traded contracts exist only at monthly or longer intervals. Successive quotations on the same contract thus differ if implied volatility varies across contracts with different maturities. While interpolating techniques have been developed to deal with this problem, the constant-maturity aspect of the over-the counter quotations avoids it altogether.

Relying on over-the-counter quotations for implied volatility from a single market-maker raises questions regarding the reliability (or what might be called the intersubjective truth) of the data. At the outset, recall that financial markets have confronted this problem in the past. The most famous example is the London Interbank Offered Rate (LIBOR) for bank deposits, which, just as an OTC option contract, can expose the buyer to the selling bank's credit risk. Big syndicated loan contracts with interest rates tied to LIBOR will typically specify the five leading banks whose quotations are to be averaged. The difference between an unquestioned acceptance of LIBOR and of our OTC quotations thus reduces from the principle of using over-the-counter prices to the practical question of whether one can rely on one dealer's prices.

Those in charge of monitoring the accuracy of a dealer's valuation of its book typically use quotations of competitors as a benchmark. It is therefore natural to do the same in our case. A comparison of the J.P. Morgan quotations with scattered ones from Hong Kong Banking Corporation's London affiliate (Midland Montague) was reassuring. Given differences in the timing of the quotations and the need to convert price into yield volatility through a standard approximation, the remaining small discrepancies indicated that the J.P. Morgan quotations were a satisfactory basis for the analysis. (See Borio and McCauley, 1995, for details).

A final issue is the choice between price and yield volatility. Price volatility is the most useful measure of the variability of holding period returns. It would therefore be the natural choice in the context, say, of "value-at-risk" models. But when it comes to making international comparisons of volatility levels, yield volatility appears to be more appropriate. The reason is that it controls for differences in the duration of the bonds linked to differences in nominal yield levels and cash-flow profiles. This is also useful in longer-term time series when the benchmark bonds change.

As an illustration, consider the comparison between the benchmark US Treasury bond and its Swedish counterpart in mid-September 1995. The US security had a coupon of 6.5 per cent, the Swedish instrument one of 6.0 per cent. Since krona yields exceeded dollar yields by a sizable margin, the Swedish bond sold at a heavy discount; the US security, by contrast, traded close to par. As a result of the deep discount, the Swedish bond approached the long duration of a zero coupon bond. Measured in terms of yield, the implied volatility of the US security was higher, 18.2 per cent against 16.5 per cent. In terms of price volatility, however, the Swedish bond appeared to be considerably more volatile, 10.3 per cent against 8.2 per cent.

Graph 2

Bond yield volatility: a longer-term perspective

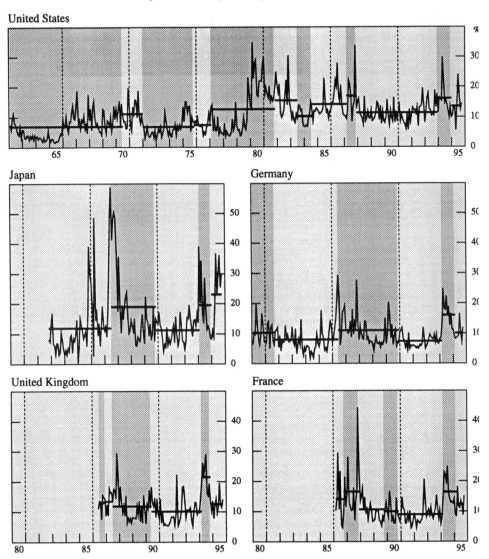

Note: Volatility is measured as the annualised standard deviation of daily percentage changes during calendar months in the yield on ten-year benchmark government bonds. The shaded (unshaded) areas represent bear (bull) markets and the horizonta lines the average volatility during these periods.

Sources: Datastream and national data.

TABLE 1
Persistence of implied bond yield volatility[a]

	Persistence parameter[b]	$\bar{R}^2$	Sample begins on[c]
United States	0.90***	0.81	31.08.92
Japan	0.93***	0.87	31.08.92
Germany	0.96***	0.93	31.08.92
France	0.90***	0.81	31.08.92
United Kingdom	0.96***	0.92	31.08.92
Italy	0.84***	0.73	31.08.92
Canada	0.95***	0.90	31.08.92
Belgium	0.94***	0.90	31.08.92
Netherlands	0.97***	0.94	31.08.92
Spain	0.77***	0.58	16.11.92
Denmark	0.92***	0.83	14.02.94
Sweden	0.94***	0.89	14.02.94
Australia	0.88***	0.77	21.03.94

Note: In this and subsequent tables and graphs, one, two and three asterisks denote statistical signifcance at the 10, 5 and 1% level, respectively.
[a] Yield volatility implied in three-month over-the-counter at-the-money option contracts on ten-year benchmark government bonds. [b] Autoregressive parameter of AR(1) process estimated by OLS on weekly data. [c] The sample ends on 22.05.95 for all countries.

2. THE POSSIBLE EXPLANATIONS: MARKET DYNAMICS

2.1. Persistence

The most powerful feature of the dynamics of volatility is its tendency to persist over time, that is, to revert to its mean only gradually. This feature obviously leaves open the question of the force or forces that drive volatility up in the first place and thus cannot *explain* the events of 1994. Nevertheless, since an econometric evaluation of any other factor must take persistence into account, we report in Table 1 the relationship between implied bond volatility in two successive weeks as captured by the autoregressive coefficient. The power of this dynamic factor is evident: it accounts for anything as much as 58 to 93 per cent of the variance of volatility.

Graph 3

**Stylised relationship between implied bond yield volatility and
changes in bond yields[1]**

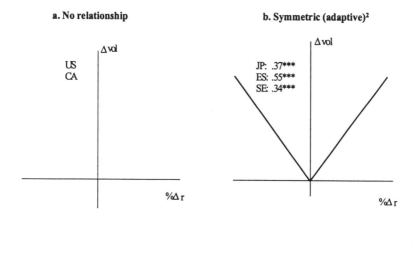

a. No relationship

US
CA

b. Symmetric (adaptive)[2]

JP: .37***
ES: .55***
SE: .34***

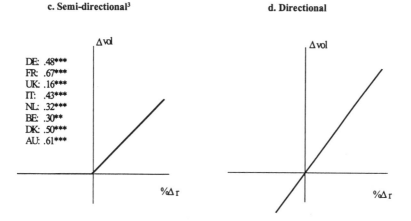

c. Semi-directional[3]

DE: .48***
FR: .67***
UK: .16***
IT: .43***
NL: .32***
BE: .30**
DK: .50***
AU: .61***

d. Directional

Note: AU: Australia; BE: Belgium; CA: Canada; DK: Denmark; FR: France; DE: Germany; IT: Italy;
   JP: Japan;   NL: Netherlands; ES: Spain; SE: Sweden; UK: United Kingdom; US: United States.

[1] Coefficient estimates of the suitably transformed weekly percentage change in the bond yield (first difference
in the logs; Friday to Thursday) in an AR(1) regression for implied bond yield volatility.   [2] Coefficients on the
absolute value of the change.   [3] Coefficients on positive changes only.

2.2. *Impact of Market Movements*

The twenty-year-old observation (Black, 1976; Hentschel, 1995) that price declines in the stock market are associated with higher volatility applied with particular force to the 1987 crash. For the 1994 bond market decline, we find strong but not ubiquitous evidence that a rise in bond yields over a week pushed implied bond volatility at the end of that week higher (Graph 3). For eight of the thirteen countries, volatility appears directional in our sample period: it rises in response to declines in bond prices but fails to respond significantly to equivalent increases. The data suggest that the United States and Canada are exceptions in that implied volatility does not react at all to proximate market movements. Also, in Japan, Sweden and Spain the response appears to be symmetrical: increases and decreases in yields have a similar effect. The fairly precisely estimated magnitude of the effect of a market move is substantial; its one-third to one-half range suggests that a rise in long rates from 6 to 7 per cent — a 16 per cent increase — might raise volatility by 5 to 8 percentage points.

For Japan we hypothesise that two deflationary developments, the appreciation of the yen in early 1994 and again in early 1995, destabilised the bond market (and the money market, see below). These exchange rate movements would work to change expectations of the price level and set in train market anticipations of changes in short-term interest rates and in fiscal policy.

Our short period analysis of implied volatility finds reinforcement in a longer view of the behaviour of realised volatility (Loeys, 1994). In Graph 2 the shaded bear market periods appear to experience higher volatility as a general rule. Thus, in the German market, for example, recent events echo those during two previous bear markets: at the onset of German reunification and at the wearing-off of the euphoria of the 1986 oil price collapse.

It is difficult to say what lies behind the apparent directionality of volatility. Several potential explanations can be put forward. These include asymmetries in inflation risks (Friedman, 1977), in the ability and willingness of risk-averse market-makers to provide liquidity and in investors' reactions to market movements, especially if they hold leveraged portfolios. Explanations can also relate to option trading strategies and opportunistic issuing patterns by borrowers (Borio and McCauley, 1995). No doubt this is an area that merits further research.

2.3. Foreign Disinvestment

Unlike in the 1987 stock market crash (Aderhold, Cumming and Harwood, 1988), international capital flows seem to have played a key role in the 1994 turbulence in the bond market. In particular, volatility rose significantly in continental Europe as foreign investors liquidated their holdings of government bonds.

The association between foreign selling and volatility is quite striking, as can be seen in Graph 4. For example, foreign investors liquidated over DM 13 billion of their holdings of German public debt securities in March 1994, a month in which implied bond volatility leapt by 4 percentage points. Regression analysis suggests that foreign liquidation of bonds of Fr.fr. 187 billion in France, DM 39 billion in Germany and Lit. 27 trillion in Italy in the first half of 1994[3] raised implied bond yield volatility in these markets by 14, 9 and 6 percentage points respectively. These estimated effects are not significantly tainted by any correlation between sales and market movements. Once directionality is allowed for, the estimated coefficients are very similar.[4]

In our view the relationship between foreign sales and volatility reflects the greater proclivity among foreign investors to leverage their holdings of bonds. As bond prices fell, leveraged investors had to sell, in the same way as shallow-pocketed equity investors receiving margin calls.

Table 2 indicates the large scale of leveraged bond investment leading up to 1994. It is presumed that bond investments by banks and securities firms can be taken as a sign of leverage owing to the predominantly short-term liabilities of these financial firms. The partial evidence suggests that banks' and securities firms' leveraged positions were building up at a rate of $50 billion per quarter in the course of 1993, only to shrink rapidly in the first two quarters of 1994. Note especially the activity of UK-based securities firms, likely buyers and sellers of European bonds.

2.4. Market Spillovers

In October 1987 price changes in one market mimicked price changes in others. Studies of the 1987 stock market crash have indeed documented substantial spillovers of volatility across markets (Bennett and Kelleher, 1988; Hamao, Masulis, and Ng, 1990; King and Wadhwani, 1990). Such spillovers seem less a feature of the *usual* interrelations of global bond markets than of global stock markets. Nevertheless, in 1994 spillovers multiplied to create an interesting hierarchy of influence.

Graph 4

Bond yield volatility and bond sales by non-residents in Germany, France and Italy

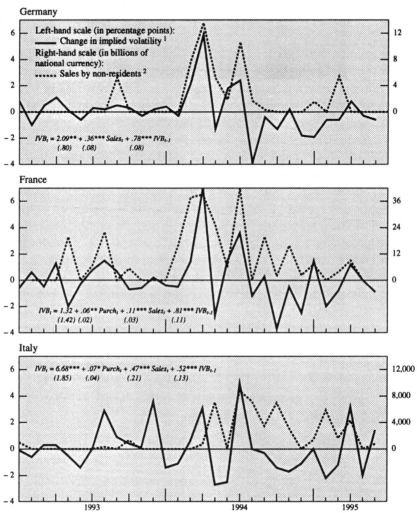

¹ As defined in Graph 1.   ² Net sales are truncated at zero. For Germany, public sector DM-denominated bonds; for France, OATs and BTNs; for Italy, BTPs.

Sources: J. P. Morgan and central banks.

TABLE 2
Selected indicators of leverage in international bond markets

	1991	1992	1993	1994			
				Q I	Q II	Q III	Q IV
			in billions of US Dollars				
United States	131	99	76	9	–26	–17	–22
Commercial banks[a]	111	105	73	17	–6	–20	–18
Securities dealers[a]	20	–6	3	–8	–20	3	–4
United Kingdom	19	53	136	–43	–18	0	..
Banks[b]: gilts	–2	6	16	2	0	–1	3
foreign bonds	15	24	52	–5	–1	7	19
GEMMs[c]: gilts	..	..	9	–9	0	–1	..
Securities dealers:							
foreign bonds	6	23	59	–31	–17	–5	3
Total	150	152	212	–34	–44	–17	..
Memorandum items:							
Interbank financed[d]	7	54	182	–54	–48	–1	17
Repo financed[e]: *Spain*	..	8	24	–8	–8	–4	–2
Sweden	..	..	13	–5	–3	–6	2

[a] Treasury and agency securities for banks and corporate and foreign bonds for securities dealers. [b] Including building societies. [c] Gilt-edged market-makers. [d] Cross-border interbank domestic currency lending by banks in Europe as an indicator of movements in non-residents' bond purchases hedged against exchange rate risk. [e] Indicators of Treasury bond purchases by non-residents financed through repos. Sources: National data and BIS.

In contrast to the two other forms of market dynamics just discussed, spillovers cannot explain the general rise in volatility. That is, the market's decline and foreign disinvestment can be considered as (perhaps unsatisfactory) prime movers. Spillovers represent no more than a force that spreads volatility around.

Simple correlations show that bond yield volatility is more closely related across countries when volatility is high (Singleton, 1994). While 1993 saw quite variable patterns of volatility within the G-3 and across Europe, in 1994's highly volatile markets volatility co-varied considerably across borders; Japan was the exception (Graph 5).

Graph 5

International correlations of implied bond yield volatility *

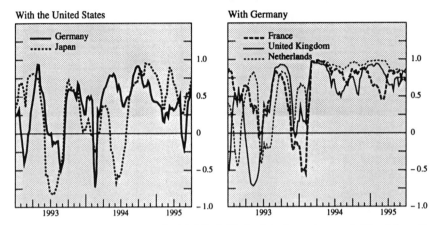

* The correlation coefficient between weekly implied yield volatilities is calculated over a sixteen-week sliding window and is plotted at the point corresponding to the last observation.

Sources: J. P. Morgan and BIS calculations.

Similarly, lagged volatility in a foreign market adds explanatory power to own lagged volatility when the effect of the latter falters (Graph 6). We find that such spillovers vary in size and direction over time.[5] They were sparse before the US tightening of monetary policy in February 1994, with Frankfurt and London each exerting some influence on other European markets (Graph 7). They became much more pervasive thereafter, when New York broadcast its volatility widely and London appeared to transmit its volatility to continental Europe (Graph 8).

3. THE POSSIBLE EXPLANATIONS: DOMESTIC ECONOMIC FACTORS

Domestic economic factors, including the inflation record and money market volatility, help to explain cross-sectional differences in bond volatility. They do not, however, offer much help in explaining the 1994 episode. In particular, changes in expected inflation and growth did not correspond to changes in volatility.

Graph 6

The explanatory power of persistence and spillovers: rolling regressions *

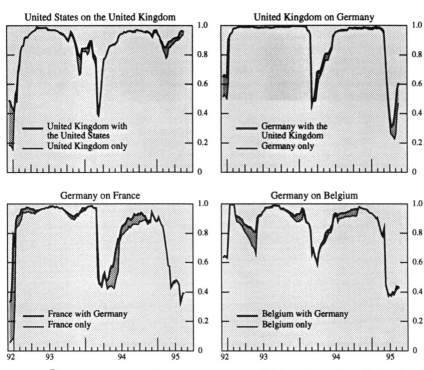

* Uncentred $\bar{R}^2$ from (de-meaned) AR(1) rolling regressions for market i to which the previous week's volatility in market j is added. The regressions are run over a sixteen-week window.

3.1. Inflation Performance and Expectations

Inflation performance and expectations set the background level of volatility. For evidence, consider the US time series and the cross-section of European countries.

In the 130 years following the Civil War, the most volatile period in US bond markets was the spell of record-high rates fifteen years ago (Wilson, Sylla and Jones, 1990). If inflationary expectations drive yields, then the highest inflation expectations in US history produced the highest yield volatility. A moving average of monthly yield volatility of the ten-year bond peaks in common with yields early in the 1980s (Graph 9).

Graph 7
Volatility spillovers
August 1992-January 1994

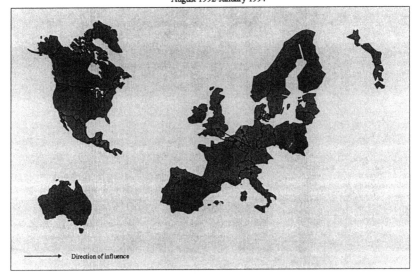

Graph 8
Volatility spillovers
February 1994-May 1995

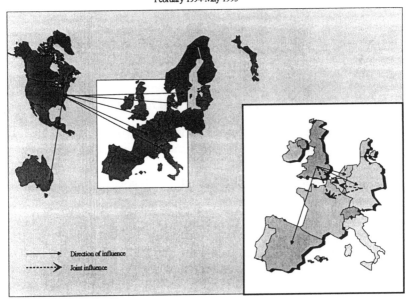

Graph 9

Volatility and the ten-year Treasury bond yield in the United States *

In percentages

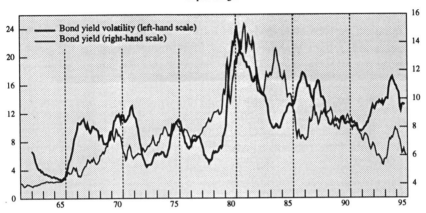

* Volatility is measured as the twelve-month moving average of the annualised standard deviation of daily percentage changes during calendar months.

Graph 10

Implied bond yield volatility and yields in European bond markets

Averages of weekly data, in percentages

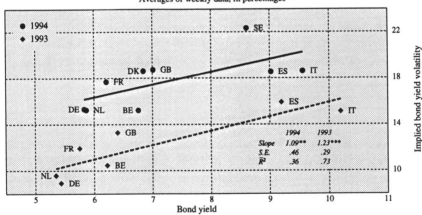

Sources: J. P. Morgan, Datastream and national data.

Within Europe, lower-inflation economies enjoy generally less volatile bond markets. In both 1993 and 1994, the excess of yield volatility of Italian government bonds over that of their German counterparts more or less matched the 4 to 5 percentage point excess of Italian government bond yields over German yields (Graph 10). If international differences in bond yields reflect inflation performance and expectations (as filtered through exchange rate expectations), then higher volatility joins higher yields as the price of inflation.

3.2. Revisions of Inflation and Growth Expectations

While volatility reflects long-term inflation performance, changes in volatility in 1994 bore little relation to market participants' revisions of inflation expectations. What is more, the same negative result holds in the case of changes in growth expectations (Table 3). True, some important instances did suggest a relationship; the striking revision of estimates of German growth in the first half of 1994 is one such example. But the relationship does not seem to possess any generality. More formal econometric evidence supports this conclusion (Borio and McCauley, 1995). We have not, however, abandoned this relationship altogether. We are in the process of investigating the explanatory power of changes in the cross-sectional dispersion of opinion (Consensus Economics, 1992–95).

Put differently, our evidence indicates that if expectations about inflation and output growth played a role in the rise of volatility then this role was only indirect i.e. it operated through their impact on the *level* of yields and hence through one of the identified market dynamics. Whether the sharp increase in bond yields last year was itself fully explicable in terms of fundamentals is a question not addressed here, but one about which some doubts remain (BIS (1995)).

3.3. Money Market Volatility

In the cross-section, money market volatility was associated with bond market volatility across a dozen markets in 1994 (Graph 11). We measure money market volatility as the standard deviation of the daily percentage change in three-month LIBOR three months forward in order to avoid the very close control of the central bank over the shortest rates.

On the basis of the time series, we find evidence of a relationship between *realised* money volatility and *implied* bond volatility in almost all of the markets considered. The relationship in Tokyo is clearly apparent, especially

TABLE 3
Volatility of market participants' growth and inflation forecasts

	Growth[a]			Inflation[a]		
	1993[b]	1994[b]	change	1993[b]	1994[b]	change
	in percentage points					
United States	0.11	0.10	-0.02	0.08	0.03	-0.05
Japan	0.25	0.07	-0.17	0.06	0.06	-0.01
Germany	0.17	0.17	0.00	0.04	0.05	0.01
France	0.16	0.06	-0.11	0.10	0.06	-0.04
Italy	0.09	0.14	0.05	0.10	0.06	-0.04
United Kingdom	0.06	0.05	-0.01	0.08	0.15	0.07
Canada	0.06	0.07	0.00	0.06	0.16	0.09
Australia	0.16	0.12	-0.04	0.09	0.10	0.01
Belgium	0.15	0.07	-0.08	0.07	0.06	-0.01
Netherlands	0.12	0.11	0.00	0.07	0.08	0.01
Spain	0.10	0.07	-0.03	0.12	0.08	-0.05
Sweden	0.10	0.10	0.00	0.08	0.13	0.05

[a] Standard deviation of the monthly changes in the forecast for average annual GDP growth and consumer price inflation respectively over two years. [b] Year in which forecasts are made. Source: © The Economist, London (various issues), and BIS calculations.

in January 1994, when the rise in bond yield volatility echoed instability in the money market (Graph 12).

For seven of the thirteen markets, money and bond market volatility co-vary significantly at the weekly frequency (Table 4). In the United States, Germany, the United Kingdom, the Netherlands, Spain, Denmark and Sweden, 1 or 2 per cent of (Friday through Thursday's) money market volatility shows up in the respective Thursday close bond volatilities.

More volatile money markets tend to show a significant influence on the respective bond markets only at the monthly frequency (same table). In Japan, France, Belgium and Australia, money market volatility shows a generally stronger effect on bond volatility.

The link between money market and bond market volatility seems to have strengthened in 1994. For instance, in the United States there was no significant transmission of volatility along the yield curve before February 1994, but thereafter 2 per cent of money market volatility appeared in bond volatility.

The tightening of the relationship between money and bond volatility becomes evident when US *implied*, rather than *realised*, money volatility is

Graph 11

Implied bond yield volatility: relationship with money market volatility

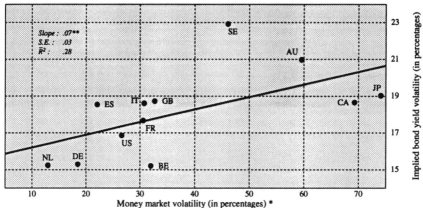

* Annualised standard deviation of the daily percentage change in the yield on three-month LIBOR three months forward; monthly average for 1994. The measure avoids the direct influence of the authorities on spot short-term rates and is therefore a better indicator of market expectations.

Sources: J. P. Morgan, national authorities and BIS.

Graph 12

Implied bond yield volatility and historical money market volatility in Japan

In percentages

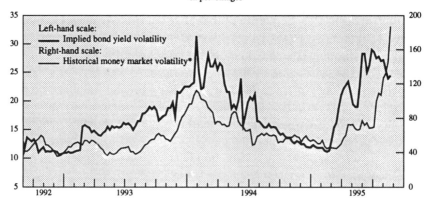

* Annualised weekly volatility, calculated over a one-week window, with an imposed zero mean; nine-week moving average.

Sources: J. P. Morgan and national authorities.

TABLE 4
Implied bond yield volatility and realised money market volatility: regression results[a]

	Weekly			Monthly[b]		
	Whole sample	Earlier period	Later period	Whole sample	Earlier period	Later period
United States	0.012** (0.005)	0.005 (0.006)	0.018** (0.007)	0.006 (0.024)	–0.027 (0.029)	0.036 (0.040)
Japan	0.004 (0.007)	0.018 (0.011)	–0.005 (0.008)	0.066*** (0.019)	0.041*** (0.014)	0.095* (0.053)
Germany	0.025** (0.010)	0.010 (0.008)	0.032** (0.015)	0.006 (0.059)	0.032 (0.062)	–0.046 (0.107)
France	0.005 (0.005)	0.004 (0.005)	0.010 (0.012)	0.044** (0.017)	0.030** (0.012)	0.118** (0.052)
Italy	0.011 (0.010)	0.011 (0.015)	0.017* (0.009)	0.008 (0.011)	0.005 (0.014)	0.030 (0.052)
United Kingdom	0.009* (0.005)	0.011* (0.005)	0.015 (0.017)	0.004 (0.016)	0.006 (0.017)	0.038 (0.110)
Canada	0.004 (0.003)	0.009* (0.005)	0.001 (0.002)	0.004 (0.010)	0.023 (0.014)	–0.008 (0.012)
Belgium	–0.003 (0.006)	0.004 (0.003)	–0.012 (0.010)	0.025c (0.015)	0.008 (0.006)	–0.062*** (0.014)
Netherlands	0.017*** (0.006)	0.001 (0.004)	0.054*** (0.017)	0.009 (0.021)	–0.004 (0.016)	0.053 (0.084)
Spain	0.006 (0.006)		0.003 (0.010)	0.018 (0.016)	0.037 (0.026)	0.017 (0.025)
Denmark[d]			0.020* (0.011)			0.063 (0.057)
Sweden[d]			0.023* (0.009)			0.070** (0.031)
Australia[d]			0.009 (0.008)			0.049 (0.029)
Japan (period split at end-1993)	0.004 (0.007)	0.004 (0.007)	0.003 (0.010)	0.066*** (0.019)	0.035** (0.015)	0.090*** (0.029)

[a] The table shows the coefficient of money market volatility in an AR(1) regression for implied bond yield volatility. The data are weekly. Money market volatility is measured as the standard deviation (around an imposed zero mean) of the implied three-month LIBOR three months forward calculated over non-overlapping one-week horizons (Friday to Thursday). Standard error are shown in brackets. Blanks indicate missing data. [b] Month-end data. [c] Marginal significance level equal to 10.06%. [d] Data are missing for earlier period. See Table 1.

Graph 13

**Implied bond yield and money market volatility
and monetary policy in the United States**

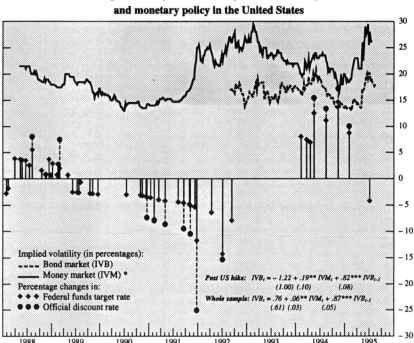

Implied volatility (in percentages):
- - - - Bond market (IVB)
——— Money market (IVM) *
Percentage changes in:
♦ ♦ ♦ Federal funds target rate
● ● ● Official discount rate

Post US hike: IVB$_t$ = $-1.22 + .19^{**}$ IVM$_t$ $+ .82^{***}$ IVB$_{t-1}$
                   (1.00) $(.10)$ $(.08)$

Whole sample: IVB$_t$ = $.76 + .06^{**}$ IVM$_t$ $+ .87^{***}$ IVB$_{t-1}$
                   $(.61)$ $(.03)$ $(.05)$

1988   1989   1990   1991   1992   1993   1994   1995

* Derived from three-year caps on three-month LIBOR.

Sources: Chase Manhattan, J. P. Morgan and the Federal Reserve Board.

juxtaposed to implied bond volatility (Graph 13). Moreover, with the benefit
of these data, the transmission of volatility gains strength, from 1–2 per cent
to some 5 per cent over the whole period and to 20 per cent after February
1994. This result suggests that our crude measure of realised weekly money
volatility may understate volatility transmission by a factor of 4 or 5 over the
whole sample.[6]

On balance, international differences in money market volatility of 40
percentage points or more suggest a fairly weighty role for this factor in the
cross-sectional analysis. But even our high estimates of volatility transmission
along the yield curve point to only a modest role for money market volatility
in making sense of the turbulence of bond markets in 1994.[7] In fact, in a
number of countries, money markets were actually more stable in 1994 than

in 1993. And for the countries where both money and bond market volatility rose in 1994, the increase in money volatility was too modest to explain much of the rise in bond volatility.

3.4. Fiscal Policy Uncertainty

We are able to measure the variation in market participants' views about fiscal policy at a high frequency only for one country. Italy's government debt is so large that movements in the spread between government and private fixed-rate borrowing costs largely reflect changing judgments about fiscal policy. In other markets, they mirror primarily movements in private sector default risk, and hence the business cycle, as well as other specific demand and supply factors. In fact, in Italy the configuration of private and public debt rates is unique in favouring private debtors. The best of these can raise long-term funds on better terms than those enjoyed by the Italian government (Giovannini and Piga, 1992; Banca d'Italia, 1995).

At times the rise in Italian government yields and the associated increase in volatility seem to have reflected the deterioration in the government's credit standing. Yields on Italian government bonds rose in relation to the cost of private debt in the summer of 1994, when investors' hopes for a businesslike budget process waned, and again in March 1995, when events in Mexico turned investors against financing unsustainable debts, whether domestic or external (Graph 14).

Regression analysis suggests that in Italy a 10 basis point widening of the spread between public and private debt costs pushes up implied bond yield volatility by a third of a percentage point. Accordingly, the widening of the swap spread in the late summer of 1994 would account for around 2 percentage points of the rise in volatility during that period.[8]

This widely appreciated but hitherto unquantified impulse to Italian bond yield volatility has no obvious parallel in other countries. Until some such evidence is found for the other dozen markets considered, we must provisionally judge the role of fiscal uncertainty in 1994's bond market turbulence to be specific to one market rather than a general factor.

CONCLUSIONS

The observation that the highest volatility ever recorded in US bond markets occurred fifteen years ago cautions against many popular conceptions. The highest volatility did not require developed markets for bond futures and

Graph 14

Government bond yield and swap rate in Italy
In percentages

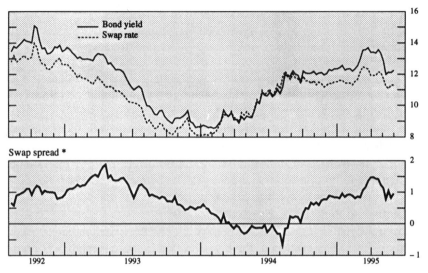

* Difference between the ten-year benchmark government bond yield and the ten-year swap rate.
Sources: Datastream and Reuter.

options, new forms of leveraged investment or even a substantial presence of foreign investors.

That said, in the bond market turbulence of 1994 we find more evidence of the bond market's own dynamics at work than of measurable uncertainty regarding fundamental macroeconomic and financial factors.

Let us step back and compare the 1994 bond market decline with the 1987 stock market crash. Obviously, the bond market decline was a more diffuse and less global event. The notion that at least some markets were overvalued is probably more widely accepted for the 1987 stock market crash than for the 1994 bond market decline (Hardouvelis, 1988; Bank for International Settlements, 1995).

In terms of the market dynamics which we have emphasised, both incidents reinforce the connection between bear markets and high volatility. An interesting question might be whether the stock market returned to normal volatility faster than did global bond markets in 1994. Both incidents saw an intensification of spillovers and a broadening of their geographical scope. But the importance of foreign disinvestment distinguishes the 1994 bond market decline from the 1987 crash, and this may make it more modern. Similarly, foreign investors' extensive use of leverage sets the 1994 episode apart from the crash of 1987, when leverage remained a domestic phenomenon.

The role of fundamentals in the two cases remains problematic. In 1987 observers vaguely pointed to the effect of interest rate volatility, including that associated with Japanese disinvestment in US bonds, to frictions between the US and German authorities and to other factors. For our part, we have had little success in linking revisions of growth and inflation expectations to the pattern of increases in bond yield volatility last year. And there is just a little weight to be given to the view that increased uncertainty regarding monetary policy drove up bond volatility.

NOTES

1. This report is a particular application of the findings presented in our longer paper, "The economics of recent bond yield volatility". The interested reader is referred to that paper for a more detailed treatment of the points distilled here.

2. The United States, Japan, Germany, France, the United Kingdom, Italy, Canada, Australia, Belgium, Denmark, the Netherlands, Spain and Sweden.

3. February to June for France and Germany; March to July for Italy.

4. In the case of France directionality actually drops out altogether. In those of Germany and Italy, at 7 and 5 percentage points respectively, the estimated influence of foreign rates is only slightly lower.

5. The tests were based on AR(1) regressions for market i to which the previous week's volatility on market j was added. The picture presented here is a simplified one. For a more comprehensive map, see Borio and McCauley (1995).

6. In Borio and McCauley (1995) an additional econometric procedure is used to quantify this bias. The estimates indicate that the adjustment typically varies between 2 and 5 across countries.

7. Moreover, the causal link may even have run from bond to money market volatility. As leveraged investors unwound their holdings of bonds, the reduction in their demand for short-term funds may have disturbed money markets.

8. The preferred equation included only positive changes in the swap spread (ΔSP^+) and positive percentage changes in the swap rate (ΔRW^+, approximated by the first difference in the logs) as controlling variable. Asymmetries are again at work:

$$IVB_t = 2.76^{***} + 2.92^* \Delta SP^+ + 0.44^{***} \Delta RW^+ + 0.80^{***} IVB_{t-1}$$
$$(0.65) \quad (1.54) \quad\quad (0.11) \quad\quad\quad (0.04)$$

REFERENCES

Aderhold, R., C. Cumming and A. Harwood (1988). "International linkages among equities markets and the October 1987 market break". Federal Reserve Bank of New York *Quarterly Review*, 13(2), pp. 34-46.

Banca d'Italia (1995). *Annual Report*, 1994.

Bank for International Settlements (1995). *65th Annual Report*, Basle.

Bennett, P. and J. Kelleher (1988). "The international transmission of stock price disruption in October 1987". Federal Reserve Bank of New York *Quarterly Review*, 13(2), pp. 17-33.

Black, F. (1976). "Studies of stock price volatility changes", in *Proceedings of the Business and Economic Statistics Section*. American Statistical Association, 177-81.

Borio, C.E.V. and R.N. McCauley (1995). *The Economics of Recent Bond Yield Volatility*, BIS mimeograph.

Consensus Economics (1992 and 1995, various issues). *Consensus Forecasts. A Digest of International Forecasts.*

Friedman, M. (1977). "Nobel lecture. inflation and unemployment". *Journal of Political Economy*, 85, pp. 451-72.

Giovannini, A. and G. Piga (1992). "Understanding the high interest rates on Italian government securities". Centre for Economic Policy Research, 720.

Hamao, Y., R.W. Masulis and V. Ng (1990). "Correlations in price changes and volatility across international stock markets". *The Review of Financial Studies*, 3(2), pp. 281-307.

Hardouvelis, G.A. (1988). "Evidence on stock market speculative bubbles. Japan, the United States, and Great Britain". Federal Reserve Bank of New York *Quarterly Review,* 13(2), pp. 4-16.

Hentschel, L. (1995). "All in the family. nesting symmetric and asymmetric GARCH models". *Journal of Financial Economics*, 39, pp. 71-104.

King, M.A. and S. Wadhwani (1990). "Transmission of volatility between stock markets". *The Review of Financial Studies*, 3(1), pp. 5-33.

Loeys, J. (1994). "Strategies in bear bond markets", in *Volatile Markets: Risks and Opportunities*, J.P. Morgan, pp. 1-15.

Market Risk Task Force, International Swaps and Derivatives Association, Inc. (1995). *Planned Supplement to the Capital Accord to Incorporate Market Risks. Comment*, 31st July.

Singleton, K.J. (1994). "Persistence in international interest rate correlations". Prepared for the Berkeley Program in Finance, September.

Watts, M. (1994 and 1995, various issues). "Global options analysis". J.P. Morgan Securities, Ltd., London.

Wilson, J.W., R.E. Sylla and C.P. Jones (1990). "Financial market panics and volatility in the long run, 1830-1988", in E.N. White (ed.), *Crashes and Panics. The Lessons From History*, Homewood, Il. Dow Jones-Irwin.

Volatility and Risk in Integrated Financial Systems: Measurement, Transmission and Policy Implications

Summary

The issue of financial market volatility has become increasingly important in recent times. Concern has been focused upon whether volatility has risen, whether deregulation and innovation alter the amount of systemic volatility or redistribute it, whether global financial integration leads to faster transmission of volatility across frontiers, how financial managers can most efficiently manage risk and what role regulators ought to play.

The analysis presented here first overviews developments in the measurement of volatility. In doing so, it employed a comprehensive dataset of economic and financial variables for 6 countries (Britain, France, Germany, Italy, Japan and the US) over the period January 1973–December 1994 to illustrate the traditional and recently developed measures of volatility. A by-product of this includes an assessment of the relative volatilities of the economic and financial systems of the countries included in the sample. The analysis then focuses on the international transmission of financial volatility by presenting the results of a vector autoregressive model which describes the international transmission of stock market volatility.

The analysis finally examines three current issues which are faced by regulators and policymakers who are concerned about financial volatility and its transmission. *First*, does portfolio insurance cause financial volatility, *second*, can circuit breakers, margin requirements and price halts lead to a sustainable reduction in volatility and *third*, should inter-market clearing and credit mechanisms be improved and should one regulator oversee the various markets? The prevailing view seems to be that the answer to the first two questions is negative and to the final question is positive. Overall, the conclusion is reached that more international collaboration in managing financial volatility in markets other than the foreign exchange market should be on the European agenda.

Colm Kearney is Professor of Economics at the University of Western Sydney where he heads the Department of Economics at the Macarthur campus. He holds degrees from University College Dublin, the University of Essex and the University of Western Ontario, and his Ph.D. degree is from the University of Warwick. He has held visiting appointments including the Central Bank of Ireland and the Federal Parliament in Canberra where he served as Economic Consultant to the Australian Finance Minister during the early 1990s. His research and publications are in the area of international finance and macroeconomics.

VI. Volatility and Risk in Integrated Financial Systems: Measurement, Transmission and Policy Implications

COLM KEARNEY

1. INTRODUCTION

The issue of volatility and risk has become increasingly important in recent times for financial practitioners, regulators and researchers. Amongst the main concerns which are currently expressed include (i) have the world's economic and financial systems become more volatile in recent times, (ii) has financial deregulation and innovation led to an increase in financial volatility or has it successfully permitted its redistribution away from risk averse operators towards more risk neutral market participants, (iii) is the current wave of financial innovation leading to a complete set of financial markets which will efficiently distribute risk, (iv) has global financial integration led to faster transmission of volatility and risk across political frontiers, (v) how can financial managers most efficiently manage risk under current circumstances, and (vii) what role ought regulators play in the process?

The issue of volatility and risk has been extensively examined within the economics, finance and econometrics disciplines. In economics, Poole's (1976) classic article demonstrates how disturbances to the financial or goods markets can be transmitted to either interest rates or real output depending upon the policy stance adopted by the authorities, while Dornbusch's (1976) equally classic analysis demonstrates how sticky goods market prices have the effect of shifting the burden of adjustment to disturbances which initially hit the goods markets onto financial asset prices such as interest rates and the exchange rate. The main issues which continue to be investigated include (i) does price volatility impede the growth and/or the stabilisation of real output (see *inter alia* Barone-Adesi and Yeung (1990)), (ii) does inflation volatility affect interest rates which in turn impede capital investment, (see *inter alia* Cooley 1993) and (iii) does exchange rate volatility impede international trade (see *inter alia* Bailey, Tavlas and Obstfeld (1988))?

Within the finance literature, the main issues which have recently been investigated include (i) does output volatility determine the volatility of common stock prices (see *inter alia* Chung (1989)), (ii) does the volatility of stock prices determine their underlying value (see Scott (1991) and Timmermann (1993)), (iii) do financial derivatives raise underlying asset price volatility, (iv) has the volatility of stock markets increased over time, (see Peel, Pope and Yadav (1993)) and (v) are the world's financial and capital markets transmitting volatility more quickly (see Agmon (1972), Koch and Koch (1991), Malliaris and Urrutia (1992) and Chan, Karolyi and Stulz (1992))?

Coincidentally with the growth of these literatures, econometric developments in time series modelling have made important contributions to the description, measurement and modelling of volatility and its persistence in economic and financial time series data. The main innovation in this regard has been the development of the ARCH (autoregressive conditional heteroscedasticity) model by Engle (1982), its generalisation to GARCH (generalised ARCH) by Bollerslev (1986) and many subsequent extensions and generalisations.

The purpose of this paper is threefold. It begins in the next section by presenting an overview of developments in the measurement of volatility. In doing so, it employs a comprehensive dataset of economic and financial variables for six countries (Britain, France, Germany, Italy, Japan and the United States) over the period January 1973–December 1994 to illustrate the traditional and recently developed measures of volatility. A by-product of this section includes a current assessment of the relative volatilities of the economic and financial systems of the countries included in the sample. Section 3 turns the focus of attention to the international transmission of financial volatility. More specifically, it presents the results of a vector autoregressive model which describes the international transmission of stock market volatility. Section 4 then turns to an examination of the current issues which are faced by regulators and policymakers who are concerned about financial volatility and its transmission. The final section of the paper summarises the main points and draws together the conclusions.

2. MEASURING FINANCIAL VOLATILITY AND RISK

The market clearing prices of financial assets are determined by the forces of supply and demand which impact on the market. If these forces remain largely stable over time, the corresponding financial asset prices will not change much. If, however, the factors determining the supplies and demands do change significantly, the relevant financial asset prices will exhibit correspondingly significant changes as they move to restore market equilibrium.

This is what is meant by financial asset price *volatility*, and it has three dimensions: frequency, size and speed. Frequent, large and fast price changes which amount to volatile financial asset prices are a reflection of well-functioning financial markets. They imply that the forces which cause shifts in the supplies and demands of financial assets are met by appropriate price shifts which act to restore equilibrium in the markets.

There is a general concern amongst many financial market participants, analysts and regulators that the degree of financial asset price volatility may have increased over recent decades. What are the important factors which cause financial volatility? There are many potential explanations, but amongst the most important are:

- Institutional change (such as the move away from the Bretton Woods system of fixed exchange rates),
- Deregulation of financial institutions and markets (such as the easing of balance sheet restrictions and the ending of interest rate controls);
- Financial innovations in products, services and markets (such as derivative products and program trading);
- Technological development (such as advances in computer hardware and software technology and in communications), and
- Globalisation of international financial markets.

There has been extensive analysis and debate about the relative importance of these and other determinants of recent trends in financial asset price volatility. The interested reader is referred to the work by the Federal Reserve Bank of Kansas City (1988), Finnerty (1988) and Marshall and Bansal (1992) for more complete treatments and discussion.

Of more importance in the current context is that because financial volatility reflects the efficient functioning of financial markets, it should not generally be of concern to regulators. Such volatility, however, is capable of exposing market participants (such as financial intermediaries, industrial corporations and governments) as well as non-participants (such as private individuals) to significant degrees of financial *risk*. It is this risk which causes concern for all risk-averse agents and which frequently propels regulators to attempt to mitigate the degree of price volatility.

What do we mean by financial risk as opposed to financial volatility? Financial risk refers to the possibility of gain or loss to net worth due to unexpected price changes. Exposure to financial risk can differ between agencies and agents, and the accepted methods of risk management include insurance, asset/liability management and hedging. Many analysts also refer more explicitly to price risk as the potential for prices to deviate from their expected level. The main point of making the distinction between volatility and risk is

Stock market volatility measured by percentage price change; July
1973–December 1994

Stock market	Normal volatility	Extreme volatility
	Monthly percentage change	
FTSE	−2.52 – 4.22	−9.59 – 10.51
CAC	−4.00 – 5.00	−10.10 – 13.21
FAZ	−2.13 – 3.62	−7.62 – 8.28
MilanBC	−3.17 – 5.51	−11.01 – 12.59
Nikkei	−1.57 – 3.17	−9.34 – 9.27
Dow Jones	−1.67 – 3.37	−5.96 – 9.21

Normal volatility is defined as that within which 50 per cent
of changes occur. Extreme volatility is defined as that which
occurs 5 per cent of the time. See Engel and Hakkio (1993) for
further details of this approach to defining normal and extreme
volatility.

that the former implies the latter only to the extent that it is unexpected. It is
easy to conceptualise the possibility of frequent, large and fast price changes
(i.e., volatile prices) which are fully expected and which consequently involve
no risk. Generally, however, financial asset prices tend to move in an unpredictable fashion in more or less efficient markets so that volatility generally
implies risk. We shall elaborate on this presently.

Unconditional Volatility

The most basic measure of financial asset price volatility involves looking
at the size of percentage price changes. The larger are these, the greater is
the degree of volatility. Table 1 provides an example of this approach to
measuring the volatility of stock market returns in Britain, France, Germany,
Italy, Japan and the United States over the period July 1973–December 1994
using respectively the FTSE, CAC, FAZ, MilanBC, Nikkei and Dow Jones
indices. Following Engel and Hakkio (1993) who recently used this approach
to describe exchange rate volatility, normal stock market volatility is defined
as that which occurs 50 per cent of the time and extreme volatility is defined
as occurring 5 per cent of the time. The Table shows that normal stock
market volatility is highest in France, followed by Italy, Britain, Germany,
the United States and Japan. Looking at extreme volatility, Italy, France and
Britain have the highest ranking followed by Japan, Germany and the United
States with the lowest level of extreme volatility. Generally, therefore, the

TABLE 2
Stock market volatility measured by standard deviation; July 1973–December 1994

Stock market	Mean	Standard deviation	Minimum value	Maximum value
FTSE	.0066	.0764	−.251 (87:10)	.483 (75:01)
CAC	.0055	.0712	−.289 (81:05)	.222 (78:03)
FAZ	.0072	.0602	−.197 (90:09)	.168 (80:10)
MilanBC	.0021	.0778	−.242 (81:06)	.253 (86:02)
Nikkei	.0093	.0658	−.199 (90:03)	.251 (90:10)
Dow Jones	.0061	.0467	−.257 (87:10)	.140 (75:01)
World	.0066	.0402	−.198 (87:10)	.091 (76:01)
Europe	.0059	.0538	−.191 (87:10)	.091 (76:01)
Japan/ US	.0070	.0419	−.204 (87:10)	.117 (76:01)

Note: All indices are rebased to 1973 = 100. Source is Datastream. The world portfolio consists of the minimum variance Markowitz efficient portfolio of all markets included in the analysis. The European portfolio is constructed similarly from the European markets and the Japan/US portfolio is constructed from the Nikkei and the Dow Jones stock market indices.

rankings in terms of normal and extreme volatility correlate to some degree but not completely. For example, normal volatility in the Nikkei is less than in the FAZ or the Dow Jones, but extreme volatility is larger in the Nikkei than in the FAZ or the Dow Jones.

Although this measure of volatility is useful and insightful, the possible confusion caused by changes in the rankings can be overcome by standardising the price changes around the average price change. This gives the most universally used conventional measure of financial asset price volatility as the variance or (its square root) the standard deviation of price changes. Indeed, the terms volatility and standard deviation are often used interchangeably in finance. Table 2 provides this measure of volatility on the same dataset as in Table 1. It shows that stock market volatility is highest in Italy, followed by Britain, France, Japan, Germany and the United States. Considering all three measures thus far, the high volatility stock markets are in Britain, France and Italy while the low volatility stock markets are in Germany, Japan and the United States. Within these groupings, however, the rankings vary with the measure adopted.

Table 2 also provides the mean return and volatility of three constructed Markowitz-efficient minimum variance portfolios. These are *first*, the world portfolio consisting of all equity indices included in the sample (comprising

–7.33 per cent in the FTSE, –2.71 per cent in the CAC, 19.76 per cent in the FAZ, 7.62 per cent in the MilanBC, 19.82 per cent in the Nikkei and 62.85 per cent in the Dow Jones), *second*, the European portfolio (comprising 17.21 per cent in the FTSE, 13.46 per cent in the CAC, 50.29 per cent in the FAZ and 19.04 per cent in the MilanBC) and *third*, the non-European portfolio (comprising 28.65 per cent in the Nikkei and 71.35 per cent in the Dow Jones). These portfolios are constructed allowing short sales with no riskless borrowing or lending, and they contain the residual undiversifiable risk in the groups of equity markets. As expected, the volatility of these portfolios is less than that of any of their constituent assets because of the benefits of diversification. What is interesting, however, is that in spite of its greater degree of diversification, the volatility of the European portfolio remains 28 per cent higher than that of the non-European portfolio. Furthermore, this greater degree of risk is not compensated for in terms of higher expected return, because the non-European portfolio earns an 18.6 per cent higher expected return.

Conditional Volatility

The simple measures considered thus far are referred to as unconditional measures of volatility because they are made without regard to whether available information is used to predict it. In other words, they are measures of volatility which are unconditional on the available information set. Recent developments in econometrics and finance, however, have lead to the increasing use of more sophisticated measures of volatility which are made with regard to the best use of available information to predict it. These measures are referred to as conditional volatility measures because they are made conditional on the available information.

What is the basic insight behind the new measures of conditional volatility? It is that financial asset prices are partly determined by their volatility. This is embodied in many financial models such as the capital asset pricing model (CAPM) and the Black-Scholes options pricing model. Furthermore, volatility is itself predictable. Indeed, financial market participants frequently make predictions of future volatility on the basis of current and past volatility in order to make decisions about their market behaviour. For example, one of the traditional methods used by financial analysts to predict price volatility is the so-called volatility clustering technique. This involves obtaining data on past standard deviations and predicting current and future standard deviations on the basis of some model derived from the past data. It is frequently found that financial volatility tends to be clustered so that large price changes in any direction tend to be followed by subsequent large price changes which are not necessarily in the same direction. The new measures of conditional volatility are best seen as upgraded versions of the traditional volatility clustering technique.

The simplest of the new measures of conditional volatility is the ARCH (autoregressive conditional heteroscedasticity) model which was pioneered by Engle (1982). This model predicts the conditional variance as a simple weighted average of past squared prediction errors. The inclusion of squared prediction errors encapsulates the fact that volatility clustering implies price changes of either sign. This measure of conditional volatility has been used in numerous studies in economics and finance.

The basic ARCH model has been extended in a number of ways, some of which are worthy of mention here. The GARCH (generalised ARCH) model which was pioneered by Bollerslev (1986) extends the simple ARCH model by allowing past conditional variances to enter the model as well as the past squared prediction errors. The EGARCH (exponential GARCH) model of Nelson (1991) in turn generalises the GARCH model by allowing previous prediction errors of different sign to impact differently on conditional volatility. Many additional extensions have been proposed and used in various ways in the past decade. The interested reader is referred to Bollerslev, Chou and Kroner (1992) and Engle (1993) for more complete and excellent summaries of the relevant literature on ARCH models and their uses in finance.

In what follows we use a simple type of ARCH model pioneered by Schwert (1989) to measure the conditional volatility of the variables used in this analysis. How does it work? Given that our data is monthly, we begin by estimating a 12-th order autoregression of the change in the log of the variable in question, say q, including 12 seasonal dummy variables to capture the seasonal variations in the data. This equation therefore takes the form as shown below.

$$\Delta \log q_t^i = \sum_{j=1}^{12} \alpha_j^i \Delta \log q_{t-j}^i + \sum_{m=1}^{12} SD_{mt} + \varepsilon_t^i. \tag{1}$$

The next step involves calculating the absolute value of the errors from equation (1). We then estimate another 12-th order autoregression on these absolute errors including as before 12 seasonal dummy variables to capture the seasonal variations in the standard deviations of the variable q. This equation therefore takes the form as shown below.

$$/\varepsilon_t^i/ = \sum_{j=1}^{12} \alpha_j^i /\varepsilon_{t-j}^i/ + \sum_{m=1}^{12} SD_{m,t} + \mu_t^i. \tag{2}$$

We complete the construction of our measure of conditional volatility by noting that the dependent variable in equation (2) is our prediction of the standard deviation of changes in the variable q. The fitted values from this equation therefore measure the conditional standard deviation of q.

It is worth noting that this measure of conditional volatility represents a generalisation of the 12-month rolling standard estimator used by Officer (1973), Fama (1976) and Merton (1980) to measure stock market volatility, because it allows the conditional mean to vary over time in equation (1) while also allowing different weights to apply to the lagged absolute unpredicted changes in q in equation (2). This measure has been used by Schwert (1989) to examine the relationship between stock market volatility and underlying economic volatility. It is similar to the ARCH model of Engle (1982) which, in its various forms, has been widely used in the finance literature. Davidian and Carroll (1987) argue that the basic specification in equation (1) based on the absolute value of the prediction errors is more robust than those based on the squared residuals from the simple ARCH model.

The Conditional Volatility of Financial and Economic Variables

Table 3 presents the conditional volatility of financial asset prices (the stock market, interest rates and exchange rates) and economic variables (inflation and industrial production) for the same set of countries considered above over the period January 1976 - December 1994 using the methodology just described. The data is also depicted in Figures 1–5. It consists of end-of-month observations on all variables and the source is Datastream. The interest rates are on call money, the exchange rates are SRD rates, inflation is the change in consumer prices and industrial production is the monthly volume index.

Before examining this data, it is useful to recall that the prices of financial assets are fundamentally interlinked with each other as well as being determined by events that unfold in the real sector of the economy. For example, the expected price of equity at any point in time is equal to the discounted present value of expected future cash flows (including capital gains and dividends) to stockholders. These cash flows are themselves influenced by developments in the financial sector (such as changes in the discount interest rate and in

TABLE 3
Summary statistics of conditional volatility of financial and economic variables

Variable	Mean	Standard deviation	Minimum value	Maximum value
Stock Markets				
FTSE	.0404	.0123	.003 (88:04)	.072 (90:09)
CAC	.0452	.0115	.008 (75:11)	.090 (88:02)
FAZ	.0353	.0129	.000 (88:01)	.091 (90:09)
MBCI	.0497	.0152	.011 (94:12)	.088 (86:06)
Nikkei	.0346	.0189	.002 (79:07)	.127 (90:10)
Dow Jones	.0306	.0108	.004 (87:12)	.115 (75:10)
Interest Rates				
Britain	.0883	.0378	.0161 (88:02)	.2475 (78:07)
France	.0353	.0186	.0057 (75:12)	.1464 (92:10)
Germany	.0497	.0241	.0084 (92:06)	.1714 (75:09)
Italy	.0289	.0190	.0000 (83:08)	.1113 (92:10)
Japan	.0364	.0141	.0045 (83:06)	.0853 (86:04)
US	.0433	.0182	.0092 (84:03)	.1430 (80:06)
Exchange Rates				
Britain	.0168	.0049	.0043 (93:05)	.0333 (81:03)
France	.0128	.0042	.0033 (83:06)	.0253 (83:03)
Germany	.0130	.0032	.0053 (91:08)	.0220 (92:01)
Italy	.0132	.0052	.0000 (84:08)	.0339 (92:11)
Japan	.0164	.0049	.0037 (93:08)	.0327 (78:11)
US	.0124	.0035	.0050 (77:08)	.0212 (92:11)
Inflation				
Britain	.0028	.0013	.0000 (80:03)	.0137 (79:08)
France	.0015	.0005	.0000 (76:03)	.0033 (76:07)
Germany	.0014	.0004	.0005 (93:05)	.0028 (82:07)
Italy	.0022	.0014	.0001 (92:11)	.0085 (77:02)
Japan	.0031	.0009	.0009 (89:03)	.0066 (76:04)
US	.0016	.0005	.0005 (76:04)	.0041 (76:01)
Industrial Production				
Britain	.0206	.0132	.0000 (93:10)	.0893 (79:09)
France	.0143	.0047	.0034 (89:02)	.0355 (75:09)
Germany	.0187	.0091	.0033 (85:01)	.0524 (85:07)
Italy	.0239	.0154	.0000 (80:02)	.0786 (78:08)
Japan	.0123	.0052	.0020 (81:12	.0353 (88:09)
US	.0069	.0021	.0029 (85:08)	.0162 (76:02)

Note: The stock market indices are in national currencies, interest rates
are on call money, exchange rates are SRD rates, inflation is the change
in consumer prices, and industrial production is the monthly volume
indices, all over January 1976–July 1994.

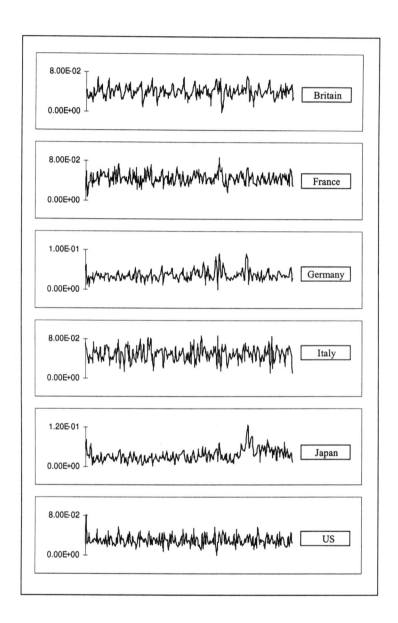

Fig. 1. Conditional volatility of the stock market, January 1976–December 1994.

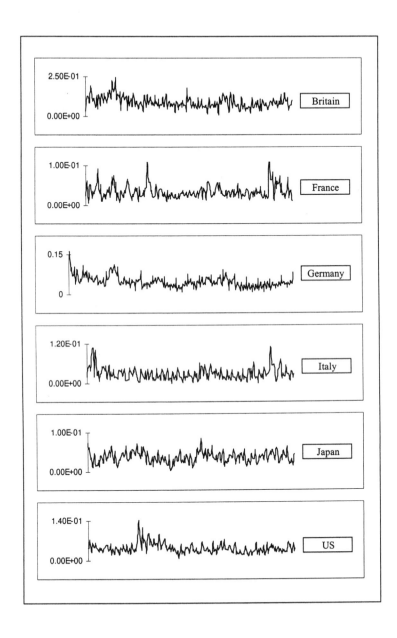

Fig. 2. Conditional volatility of interest rates, January 1976–December 1994.

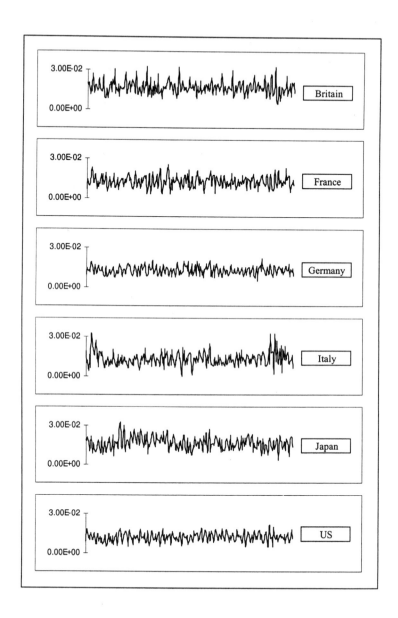

Fig. 3. Conditional volatility of exchange rates, January 1976–December 1994.

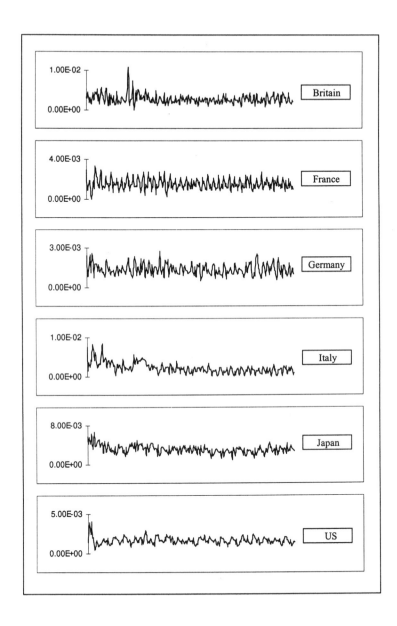

Fig. 4.   Conditional volatility of inflation, January 1976–December 1994.

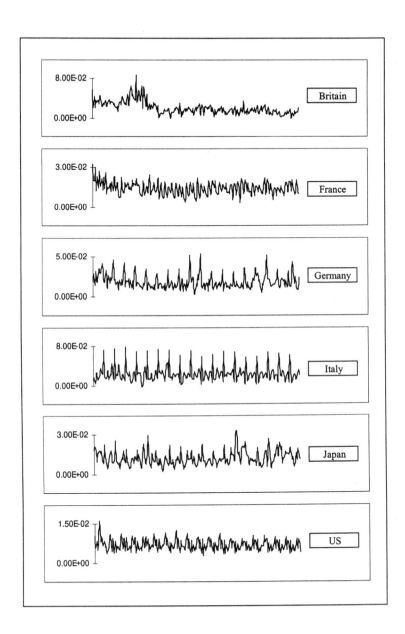

Fig. 5.   Conditional volatility of industrial production, January 1976–December 1994.

the exchange rate) as well as in the macroeconomy (such as the level of economic activity and the rate of inflation). This example can be replaced with others using more or less the same set of variables together with alternative causalities. For example, developments in the stock market will influence real economic activity, inflation, interest rates and the exchange rate. The basic conclusion is that the financial and economic variables are all co-determined within a general causal framework.

It follows from this that the variance of financial asset prices depends on the variances of other financial asset prices and economic variables as well as on the covariances between them. This raises the question of whether volatility in some part of the system can be used to predict subsequent volatility elsewhere. For example, what determines stock price volatility and can the latter anticipate future volatility in economic variables such as income and prices? This issue has been recently examined by a number of authors including Schwert (1989) and Najand and Rahman (1991) with mixed results. In the European context, does the volatility in exchange rates which is particularly extreme around the time of EMS realignments get predicted by or relayed to the volatility of European interest rates and stock prices?

Perhaps the first interesting finding from Table 3 concerns the ranking of variables according to their relative conditional volatilities. Interest rates have the greatest conditional volatility on average across countries with a mean conditional standard deviation of .022. This is followed by the stock market with an average conditional volatility of .014, industrial production with .008, the exchange rate with .004 and inflation with .001. This ranking of conditional volatilities over all the countries included in the sample is mostly replicated at the individual country level. For example, interest rates are the most volatile variable in all countries except Japan where it ranks second behind the stock market. The stock market itself is ranked second in all the other countries except Britain and Italy where it is ranked third. Industrial production is ranked second in Britain and Italy, and third in all other countries except the United States where it is ranked fourth. The exchange rate and inflation are ranked fourth and fifth in all countries except the United States where the ordering is reversed.

Figure 1 depicts the stock market volatilities which are summarised in Table 3. It is useful to consider the Figure in conjunction with the Table. The Italian market shows the greatest volatility followed by France, Britain, Germany and Japan with the United States being the least volatile. The range of cross-country experience with stock market volatility is quite wide, with Italy's volatility being over 60 per cent greater than that of the United States. The four European stock markets are all more volatile than the non-European stock markets included in this sample. The average volatility of the four European stock markets is just over 30 per cent higher than the average of the Nikkei and the Dow Jones. Inspection of the Figure reveals that there have been some notable changes in the level of stock market volatility over time, particularly during the 1987 stock market crash and during the early 1990s in the Nikkei which is associated with the rising political uncertainty in Japan at the time.

Figure 2 depicts the interest rate volatilities. Britain has the most volatile interest rates, followed by Germany, the United States, Japan, France and Italy. The range of cross-country experience with interest rate volatility is very wide, with Britain's volatility being over 300 per cent greater than that of Italy. The average volatility of European interest rates is 27 per cent higher than the average of Japan and the Unted States. These findings are not surprising insofar as the European countries have used interest rate policy to assist with the achievement of exchange rate stability as required by the EMS. In addition, Britain and Germany have aggressively pursued tight monetary policies with interest rates as policy instruments while relying less on capital controls than the other European countries. By contrast, the countries with the lowest interest rate volatility, France and Italy, have used capital controls to considerable degrees. The Figure also reveals that there have been some notable changes in the level of interest rate volatility across the countries under consideration, particularly in the late 1970s in Britain and in the early 1980s in the United States which is associated with the monetarist policies of the then Prime Minister Thatcher and President Reagan respectively. These are not isolated episodes, however, as inspection of France and Italy also reveals significant changes in interest rate volatility in the late 1970s and early 1990s.

Figure 3 depicts the exchange rate volatilities. It is important to note that the SRD rates used here do not emphasise intra-European EMS exchange rate volatilities. Nevertheless, the measure is interesting from a more international perspective. The Table reveals that Britain has the most volatile exchange rate followed by Japan, Italy, Germany, France and the United States. The conditional volatility of the most volatile foreign exchange market in Britain is 35 per cent higher than that in the least volatile market in the United States. The four European countries in this sample have a mean conditional exchange rate volatility which is only marginally less than the average of the non-European countries in the sample. The evidence is consistent with that of Bewley and Kearney (1990) that the EMS system has succeeded in reducing intra-European exchange rate volatility without reducing the volatility of the EMS as a whole with non-EMS currencies

Figure 4 focuses on the volatility of inflation. The Table reveals that Japan has the highest conditional volatility of inflation followed by Britain, Italy, the United States, France and Germany. The range of cross-country experience with inflation volatility is wide with the Japanese volatility being just over 220 per cent greater than the volatility of German inflation. This data is consistent with the frequently cited generalisation that high inflation tends to be associated with high variance of inflation, because the country with the lowest inflation, Germany, has the best record in terms of low levels of inflation. The Figure reveals some changes over time such as in Britain during the early 1980s, while Italy reveals a tendancy towards decline which may reflect some benefits of EMS membership.

Figure 5 turns the focus of attention to the volatility of industrial production. This is highest in Italy, followed by Britain, Germany, France, Japan and the United States. The range of cross-country experience with industrial production volatility is very wide indeed, with Italy's volatility being over 340 per cent greater than that in the United States. This partly reflects the size of the economies in question, with the larger economies tending to have lower industrial production volatilities due to the greater degree of diversification in their production. The average volatility of industrial production in the European economies included in this study is just over 200 per cent greater than the average of the non-European countries, although there is considerable variation across individual countries.

Related work on the convergence in the volatility of industrial production in Europe over the period from January 1976–December 1994 by Jacobson and Kearney (1995) divides the EC economies into two groups called the Core economies (Belgium, Britain, Denmark, France, Germany and the Netherlands) and the PIIGS economies (Portugal, Ireland, Italy, Greece and Spain). The average growth rate for the Core economies over this time period is 1.73 per cent per year compared to an average for the PIIGS economies of 4.34 per cent per year, which confirms the noted evidence towards convergence in the level of economic activity within the EC.

Concerning the conditional volatility of industrial production, however, the story is quite different. Dividing the sample into the pre-EMS (1964:2 - 1979:3) and post-EMS (1973:4 - 1994:6) periods, the conditional standard deviation of the overall EC industrial production index declined slightly by 1.62 per cent between the pre- and post-EMS periods. Within the Core economies, however, the mean conditional standard deviation of industrial production declined by 5.32 per cent, while it declined in the PIIGS economies by 3.62 per cent. Putting this another way, the conditional volatility of the PIIGS economies is more than 45 per cent higher than for the Core economies over the whole 30 year data period. When broken up into the pre- and post-EMS periods, this figure has risen (by almost 6 per cent) from being 44.72 higher in the earlier period to being 47.32 per cent higher in the latter period.

Some countries seem to be inherently more volatile than others. Britain has the highest interest rate and exchange rate volatility, the second highest volatility in inflation and in industrial production and the third highest stock market volatility. Italy has the highest volatility in industrial production and in the stock market, and the third highest volatility in inflation and exchange rates. By way of contrast, the United States has the lowest volatility in its industrial production, its stock market and in its exchange rates, coupled with the third lowest volatility in its inflation. Using an equally weighted average of the variables included in this study. the overall rankings in terms of country volatilities are (from highest to lowest) Britain, Italy, Japan, Germany, France and the United States. These findings are of considerable interest to financial market participants, policymakers and researchers. They beg consideration of the causes of the underlying volatilities, how they are related to each other, how they are transmitted across political frontiers and what scope exists for policymakers to exert influence. The two sections which follow focus in turn on each of the last two issues.

3. THE TRANSMISSION OF FINANCIAL VOLATILITY ACROSS INTERNATIONAL STOCK MARKETS

The major causes of financial volatility which were isolated in the previous section included institutional change, deregulation and innovation, technological developments and the ongoing tendancy towards globalisation. In this section, we turn our attention to the transmission of financial volatility from one country to another. More specifically, we illustrate the international transmission of financial volatility by focusing on the stock market as an example. A number of studies have examined this issue using high frequency (mostly daily) data. For example, Hilliard (1979) examined the contemporaneous and lagged correlation of closing stock market returns across 10 of the world's leading stock markets, Goodhart (1988) examined intra-daily movements in 3 national markets, Eun and Shim (1989) examined stock market returns across 9 national stock markets and Barclay, Litzenberger and Warner (1990) examined price volatility and volume for common stocks on the New York and Tokyo stock exchanges. The analysis in this section compliments this research by focusing on the low frequency (monthly) data.

The model is specified by grouping the conditional volatilities of the 6 stock market indices into a vector, and the relationship between them is estimated using the vector autoregressive model in equation (3).

$$Z_t = A(L)Z_t + e_t \tag{3}$$

with Z being a vector of the conditional volatilities of the 6 stock market indices, and the e vector consisting of mutually independent and serially uncorrelated white noise innovations.

Table 4 presents the results. The equations are well determined with over half (57 per cent) the variation in the conditional variance of the stock markets being explained by the model on average. This varies, however, from a high of two thirds for the Japanese stock market to a low of two fifths for the German stock market. For each equation, the Table first presents the R2's, the standard errors of the regressions and the DW statistics. This is followed by the constant term and the summary of the lags of each coefficient (with its associated t-statistic in brackets). This is then followed by the F-test statistic for the joint exclusion of all lags of a variable in each regression equation.

The constant term is positive in each equation and is strongly statistically significant in each stock market except the MilanBC and the Dow Jones. Consider the exclusion tests. Looking firstly at the rows of the Table, we see that the FTSE's volatility causes variations in the MilanBC's, the CAC causes the FTSE, the Nikkei and the Dow Jones, the FAZ causes all except the FTSE, the MBCI causes all except the FAZ, the Nikkei causes the CAC, the FAZ and the Dow Jones, and the Dow Jones causes all except the FAZ. Looking now at the columns of the Table, we see that the FTSE's stock market volatility is caused by the volatility of the CAC, the MilanBC and the Dow Jones; the CAC, the Nikkei and the Dow Jones is caused by all except the FTSE, the FAZ is caused only by the Nikkei, and the MilanBC is caused by the FTSE, the FAZ, and the Dow Jones.

In summary, these F-tests for the joint significance of all lags in the vector autoregressive model indicate a strong degree of international transmission of stock market volatility. The strongest effect is from the Dow Jones to the other stock markets. In this case the effect is strong to all other markets except the MilanBC, and the sum of coefficients at the top of the Table indicates that the effect is statistically significant in many cases. This result is replicated to a lesser extent for the FAZ, the Nikkei, the MilanBC and the CAC in that order. By contrast, volatility in the FTSE determines only the MilanBC. These exclusion tests indicate that the Dow Jones stock market is the most open to international influence, followed by the FAZ, while the FTSE is the

TABLE 4
Vector autoregression model for the international transmission of stock market volatility

	FTSE	CAC	FAZ	MBCI	Nikkei	Dow Jones
R2	.54	.66	.39	.58	.67	.59
SEE	.0095	.0080	.0102	.0102	.0132	.0073
DW	1.96	2.10	2.07	1.95	1.85	1.91
Constant	0.037	0.038	0.015	0.180	0.066	0.008
	(2.02)	(2.44)	(0.78)	(9.14)	(2.58)	(0.54)
Sums of Coefficients:						
FTSE	−.038	0.344	0.193	−0.492	0.251	−0.112
	(0.22)	(2.30)	(1.02)	(2.65)	(1.02)	(0.85)
CAC	0.214	0.288	0.022	−0.107	−0.254	0.009
	(1.75)	(0.16)	(0.16)	(0.80)	(1.44)	(0.09)
FAZ	.099	0.361	0.122	0.128	0.199	0.172
	(0.57)	(2.38)	(0.63)	(0.68)	(0.80)	(1.28)
MBCI	0.095	−0.368	0.542	−0.884	−0.392	0.717
	(0.46)	(2.03)	(2.34)	(3.92)	(1.31)	(4.48)
Nikkei	−0.035	−0.149	0.108	−0.045	0.777	−0.014
	(0.60)	(2.90)	(1.65)	(0.70)	(9.21)	(0.31)
Dow Jones	−0.091	−0.104	−0.708	−2.000	−1.712	−0.604
	(0.32)	(0.41)	(2.21)	(6.39)	(2.83)	(2.71)
Exclusion Tests:						
FTSE	8.92	1.47	1.12	4.39	0.60	1.54
	(0.00)	(0.19)	(0.35)	(0.00)	(0.73)	(0.17)
CAC	5.19	19.00	1.23	0.53	2.16	4.53
	(0.00)	(0.00)	(0.29)	(0.78)	(0.05)	(0.00)
FAZ	0.70	6.35	3.07	4.24	2.90	2.28
	(0.65)	(0.00)	(0.01)	(0.00)	(0.01)	(0.04)
MBCI	3.43	4.53	1.42	7.78	2.39	4.10
	(0.00)	(0.00)	(0.21)	(0.00)	(0.03)	(0.00)
Nikkei	1.60	3.69	3.83	0.94	17.43	3.30
	(0.15)	(0.00)	(0.00)	(0.46)	(0.00)	(0.00)
Dow Jones	2.73	4.74	1.20	12.22	13.71	4.39
	(0.01)	(0.00)	(0.31)	(0.00)	(0.00)	(0.00)

Note: The numbers in brackets in sums of coefficients section of the Table are t-statistics. Those in brackets under the F-statistics for the exclusion tests are marginal significance levels.

least open to international influence on its volatility. The strong findings in this Table have been checked to ensure that they are robust to the currency denomination of the stock markets. Accordingly, the model was re-estimated with the stocks in their own local currencies and the results are very similar.

The implications of this analysis for the international transmission of stock market volatility can be illustrated by presenting the impulse response functions which are derived from the vector autoregressive model. These impulse responses describe how a rise in the volatility of one country's stock market is transmitted across political frontiers to the stock markets in the other countries included in the study. Two examples are presented in Figures 6 and 7. The first of these illustrates the effects of a 1 standard deviation innovation in the volatility of the Dow Jones, and the second does similarly for the Nikkei.

Consider first the effects of a 1 standard deviation rise in the conditional volatility of the Dow Jones which is presented in Figure 6. The initial effects are to cause a rise in the volatility of the CAC and the MilanBC indices together with a decline in the volatility of the FTSE, the FAZ and the Nikkei. Over subsequent months, the volatility of the FTSE rises, the FAZ declines and the others oscillate before all markets eventually settle down. Now compare these results with those from a 1 standard deviation rise in the volatility of the Nikkei which are presented in Figure 7. The initial effects are to cause a rise in the volatility of the FTSE, the FAZ and the MilanBC indices together with a decline in the volatility of the CAC and the Dow Jones. Over subsequent months, the volatility of the CAC shows continuing decline while the others oscillate before all markets eventually settle down.

Closer inspection of these simulations reveal some interesting conclusions about the international transmission of stock market volatility. *First*, the overall power of the Dow Jones to impact upon the volatility of other stock markets is greater than that of the Nikkei. This is shown by the scale of the Figures and is consistent with the estimation results from the vector autoregressive model. *Second*, the two major non-European stock markets tend to have offsetting effects on each other's volatilities, and this is reflected in the other results. This finding is also suggestive of the possibility that there exists a given amount of systemic volatility in the world's stock markets that gets distributed across markets along the transmission lines identified in this analysis. *Third*, the MilanBC index which is the second most volatile stock market behind the Nikkei is the only one whose volatility initially rises in response to a rise in either the Dow Jones or the Nikkei. *Finally*, the volatility of the FTSE and the FAZ both initially decline in response to higher volatility in the Dow Jones and both initially rise in response to higher volatility in the Nikkei, whereas the response of the CAC is in the opposite direction. This

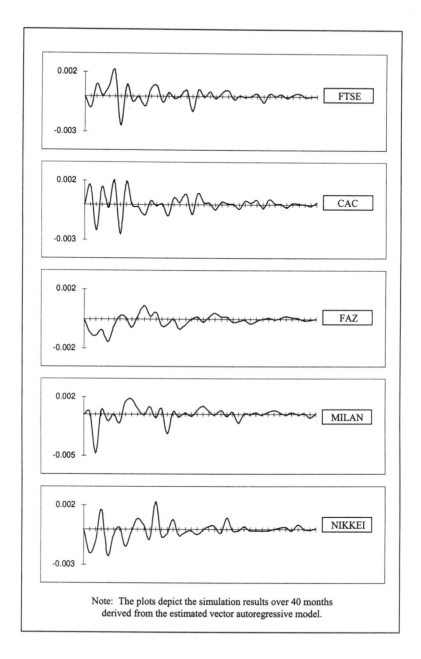

Note: The plots depict the simulation results over 40 months
derived from the estimated vector autoregressive model.

Fig. 6. The effects of a one standard deviation rise in the volatility of the Dow Jones stock
market.

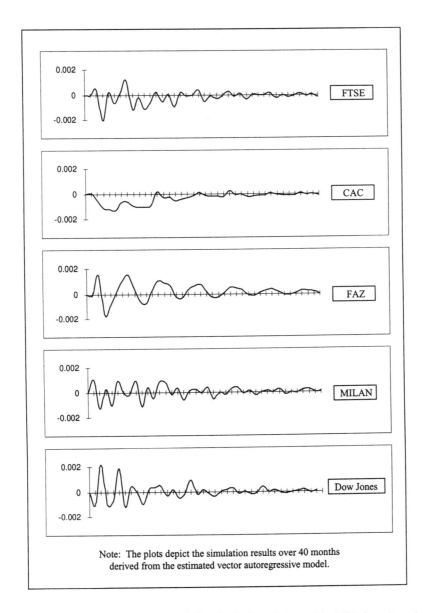

Note: The plots depict the simulation results over 40 months
derived from the estimated vector autoregressive model.

Fig. 7. The effects of a one standard deviation rise in the volatility of the Nikkei stock market.

suggests a degree of 'substitutability' amongst the major European stock markets in terms of their volatilities which is worthy of further investigation.

4. MANAGING FINANCIAL VOLATILITY

Policymakers and regulators who are concerned about financial market volatility must address two important issues. The first issue concerns what level of volatility is excessive. Excessive volatility must be measured relative to some agreed benchmark of acceptable or non-excessive volatility, and this has proved to be very difficult to achieve. In addition, the level of volatility which is considered to be excessive may well differ across different markets. It may well be, for example, that a level of volatility which is considered to be acceptable in the bond markets may be considered to be excessive in the stock markets or in the foreign exchange markets. The second issue concerns what measures can be adopted to reduce financial volatility without impacting adversely upon the efficient workings of the financial markets. The purpose of this section is to summarise current thinking on these two issues.

Researchers have attempted to answer the question about whether financial market volatility is excessive in a number of ways. Scott (1991) provides a useful survey of the relevant literature. The early work on this issue by Shiller (1981) employed the variance bounds technique to examine whether the stock market is excessively volatile. This technique involves comparing the actual levels of stock market volatility with the variance restrictions which are implied by the present value model of the determination of stock prices. Shiller (1981) concluded that the stock market is excessively volatile. This work has been considerably refined by Mankiw, Romer and Shapiro (1985), Campbell and Shiller (1987) and West (1988). The current received wisdom from variance bounds analysis is that the stock markets may be excessively volatile and that the bond markets are not. This type of analysis has not succeeded in reaching a similar degree of consensus regarding the volatility of the exchange rate due to the absence of an agreed theoretical framework upon which to base the variance bounds restrictions.

The interest of researchers in financial market volatility has also led to an emerging and extensive literature on the role of fads, noise traders and speculative bubbles in causing and sustaining financial market volatility. A detailed examination of the relevant literature is beyond the scope of this paper, but the interested reader is referred to the excellent reviews in Black (1986), West (1988) and Camerer (1989). Suffice it here to remark that the existence of fads and speculative bubbles act more as a mechanism which moves financial asset prices away from their equilibrium levels for extended periods of time rather than actually causing or sustaining increased levels of market volatility. Indeed, fads can be usefully interpreted as bubbles which have not yet reached maturity. The same cannot be said of noise traders who actually exist in the markets on the basis of their ability to generate profit from the existence and continuation of volatility. It follows from this that regulators who are concerned about the existence of excessive financial market volatility ought more appropriately be concerned about the effects of the latter rather than the possible existence of fads and speculative bubbles.

Following the October 1987 stock market crash, the United States president appointed the Brady Commission to investigate its causes. The Brady Commission's findings concerning financial market volatility have been the subject of extensive debate during the intervening years. Readers who are interested in a survey of the pro- and anti-Brady Commission views can usefully consult Greenwald and Stein (1988) and Malkeil (1988) respectively. The issues which are raised in this debate are central to the issues which confront would-be regulators of financial market volatility. Specifically, three issues remain to be resolved. *First*, did portfolio insurance cause the volatility associated with the October 1987 crash and if so, could it do so again? *Second*, could the existence of circuit breakers, margin requirements and price halts lead to a sustainable reduction in financial market volatility? *Third*, should inter-market clearing and credit mechanisms be improved and should one regulator oversee the various markets? The prevailing view seems to be that the answer to the first two questions is negative and to the final question is positive. Interestingly, Subrahmanyam (1994) has recently shown how trading halts can actually raise the level of market volatility by inducing market participants to suboptimally advance their trading actions. Overall, the implication of recent research in the European context points to the potential benefits to be gained by more international collaboration in managing financial volatility in markets other than the foreign exchange market.

5. SUMMARY AND CONCLUSIONS

The issue of volatility has become increasingly important in recent times. Concern has been focused upon whether volatility has risen in recent times, whether deregulation and innovation cause increased volatility and risk rather than more efficiently redistributing it, whether global financial integration leads to faster transmission of volatility across frontiers, how financial managers can most efficiently manage risk and what role regulators ought to play in the process.

The purpose of this paper has been threefold. It began by presenting an overview of developments in the measurement of volatility. In doing so, it employed a comprehensive dataset of economic and financial variables for 6 countries (Britain, France, Germany, Italy, Japan and the United States) over the period January 1973–December 1994 to illustrate the traditional and recently developed measures of volatility. A by-product of this included an assessment of the relative volatilities of the economic and financial systems of the countries included in the sample. Section 3 then turned the focus of attention to the international transmission of financial volatility and presented the results of a vector autoregressive model which describes the international transmission of stock market volatility.

Section 4 summarily examined the current issues which are faced by regulators and policymakers who are concerned about financial volatility and its transmission. It pointed to three issues which remain to be resolved. *First*, does portfolio insurance cause financial volatility, *second*, can circuit breakers, margin requirements and price halts lead to a sustainable reduction in volatility and *third*, should inter-market clearing and credit mechanisms be improved and should one regulator oversee the various markets? The prevailing view seems to be that the answer to the first two questions is negative and to the final question is positive. Overall, the conclusion is reached that more international collaboration in managing financial volatility in markets other than the foreign exchange market should be on the European agenda.

REFERENCES

Agmon, T. (1972). "The Relations Among Equity Markets: A Study of Share Price Co-Movements in the United States, United Kingdom, Germany and Japan", *Journal of Finance*, 27, 839-855.

Bailey, M.J., G. Tavlas, and M. Obstfeld (1988). "Trade and Investment under Floating Rates: The US Experience; Reforming the Exchange Rate System", *Cato Journal*, 8;2, 421-449.

Barclay, M.J., R.H. Litzenberger, and J.B. Warner (1990). "Private Information, Trading Volume and Stock Return Variances", *Review of Financial Studies*, 3, 233-253.

Barone-Adesi, G. and B. Yeung (1990). "Price Flexibility and Output Volatility: The Case for Flexible Exchange Rates", *Journal of International Money and Finance*, 9;3, 276-298.

Bewley, R. and C. Kearney (1989). "A Systems Approach to Modelling the EMS Exchange Rate Mechanism", *Economic and Social Review*, 20, 2, 111-120.

Black, F. (1986). "Noise", *Journal of Finance*, 41, 529-543.

Bollerslev, T. (1986). "Generalised Autoregressive Conditional Heteroscedasticity", *Journal of Econometrics*", 31, 307-327.

Bollerslev, T., R.Y. Chou, and K.F. Kroner (1992). "ARCH Modelling in Finance: A Review of the Theory and Empirical Evidence", *Journal of Econometrics*, 52, 5-59.

Brooks, M. (1993), "The Search for a Better Measure of Volatility", *Euromoney*, March, 55-56.

Camerer, C. (1989). "Bubbles and Fads in Asset Prices", *Journal of Economic Surveys*, 3,1, 3-41.

Campbell, J.Y. and R.J. Shiller (1987). "Stock Return Variances: The Arrival of Information and the Reaction of Traders", *Journal of Finance*, 17, 5-26.

Chan, K.C., A. Karolyi, and R.M. Stulz (1992). "Global Financial Markets and the Risk Premium on US Equity", *Journal of Financial Economics*, 32, 137-167.

Chung, K.H. (1989). "The Impact of Demand Volatility and Leverages on the Systematic Risk of Common Stocks", *Journal of Business Finance and Accounting*, 16;3, 343-360.

Cooley, T.F. (1993). "Comment on An Equilibrium Model of Nominal Bond Prices with Inflation-Output Correlation and Stochastic Volatility", *Journal of Money, Credit and Banking*, 25;3, 666-672.

Davidian, M. and R.J. Carroll (1987). "Variance Function Estimation", *Journal of the American Statistical Association*, 82, 1079-1091.

Dornbusch, R. (1976). "Expectations and Exchange Rate Dynamics", *Journal of Political Economy*, 84, 1161-1176.

Engle, R.F. (1982). "Autoregressive Conditional Heteroscedasticity with Estimates of the Variance of UK Inflation", *Econometrica*, 50, 987-1008.

Engle, R.F. (1993). "Statistical Models for Financial Volatility", *Financial Analysts Journal*, 49;1, 72-78.

Eun, C. and S. Shim (1989). "International Transmission of Stock Market Movements", *Journal of Financial and Quantitative Analysis*, 24, 241-256.

Federal Reserve Bank of Kansas City (1988). *Financial Market Volatility*, A Symposium Sponsored by the Federal Reserve Bank of Kansas City.

Finnerty, J.D. (1988). "Financial Engineering in Corporate Finance: An Overview", *Financial Management*, Winter.

Goodhart, C.A.E. (1988). "The International Transmission of Asset Price Volatility", in Federal Reserve Bank of Kansas City, *Financial Market Volatility*, A Symposium Sponsored by the Federal Reserve Bank of Kansas City.

Greenwald, B. and J. Stein (1988). "The Task Force Report: The Reasoning behind the Recommendations", *Journal of Economic Perspectives*, 2,3, 3-23.

Hilliard, J.E. (1979). "The Relationship between Equity Indices on World Exchanges", *The Journal of Finance*, 1, March, 102-114.

Jacobson, D. and C. Kearney (1995). "Convergence in the Volatility of European Industrial Production", Research Paper, Dublin City University Business School, May.

Koch, P.D. and T.W. Koch (1991). "Evolution in Dynamic Linkages across Daily National Stock Indices", *Journal of International Money and Finance*, 10, 231-251.

Malkeil, B.G. (1988). "The Brady Commission Report: A Critique", *Journal of Portfolio Management*, Summer, 9-13.

Malliaris, A.G. and J.L. Urrutia (1992). "The International Crash of October 1987: Causality Tests", *Journal of Financial and Quantitative Analysis*, 27;3, 353-364.

Mankiw, N.G., D. Romer, and M.D. Shapiro (1985). "An Unbiased Reexamination of Stock Market Volatility", *Journal of of Finance*, 40, 677-687.

Marshall, J. and V.K. Bansal (1992). *Financial Engineering: A Complete Guide to Financial Innovation*, New York Institute of Finance, New York.

Najand, M. and H. Rahman (1991). "Stock Market Volatility and Macroeconomic Variables: International Evidence", *Journal of Multinational Financial Management*, 1;3, 51-66.

Peel, D.A., P.F. Pope and P.K. Yadav (1993). "Deregulation and the Volatility of UK Stock Prices", *Journal of Business Finance and Accounting*, 20, 3, 359-372.

Poole, W. (1970). "Optimal Choice of Monetary Policy Instruments in a Simple Stochastic Macro Model", *Quarterly Journal of Economics*, 84, 197-216.

Roll, R. (1989). "Price Volatility, International Market Links and their Implications for Regulatory Policies", *Journal of Financial Services Research*, 3, 211-246.

Schwert, G.W. (1989). "Why Does Stock Market Volatility Change Over Time?", *Journal of Finance*, 54:5, 1115-1151.

Scott, L.O. (1991). "Financial Market Volatility: A Survey", *International Monetary Fund Staff Papers*, 38;3, 582-625.

Shiller, R.J. (1981). "Do Stock Prices Move too much to be Justified by Subsequent Changes in Dividends?", *American Economic Review*, 71, 3, 421-436.

Subrahmanyam, A. (1994). "Circuit Breakers and Market Volatility:A Theoretical Perspective", *Journal of Finance*, 49, 1, 237-254.

Timmermann, A.G. (1993). "How Learning in Financial Markets generates Excess Volatility and Predictability in Stock Prices", *Quarterly Journal of Economics*, 108;4, 1135-1155.

Von Furstenberg, G.M. and B. Nam Jeon (1989). "International Stock Price Movements: Links and Messages", *Brookings Papers on Economic Activity*, 1, 125-179.

West, K.D. (1988). "Bubbles, Fads and Stock Price Volatility: A Partial Valuation", *Journal of Finance*, 43, 639-656.

Volatility, International Trade and Capital Flows

Summary

The purpose of this paper is to find empirical evidence for the interaction between volatility and international transactions in real and financial assets for the Netherlands. The main finding is that this influence depends on the volatility measure chosen. Dutch foreign trade is hampered by short-term exchange rate volatility, reflecting uncertainty due to payment lags. Direct investment for the Netherlands, inward as well as outward, is stimulated by long-term exchange rate volatility, revealing the dominance of production diversification incentives. On the Dutch bond market, short-term exchange rate volatility deters investors leading to repatriation of capital and higher bond volatility. Stock market volatility increases slightly with increasing long-term exchange rate volatility, probably because the exchange rate affects profitability. Our preliminary results suggest that there are no strong arguments in favour of international capital restrictions to reduce volatility.

Ad Stokman studied econometrics at the University of Amsterdam. From 1980 to 1989 he worked in the Balance of Payments Department of De Nederlandsche Bank. He was then appointed a researcher in the Econometric Research and Special Studies Department of the Bank, involved in macroeconometric model building and forecasting. His published works include papers on the information content of the yield curve, applications of game theory, effects of exchange rate risk on international trade and determinants of discount rate policy of the Bundesbank. In March 1995 he received a Ph.D. degree on a thesis about terms of payment in international trade.
Peter Vlaar studied economics at the Free University of Amsterdam. From 1990 to 1994 he worked as a research assistant at the University of Limburg at Maastricht during which he wrote a Ph.D. thesis on exchange rates and risk premia within the European Monetary System. Since then he has worked as a researcher at the Econometric Research and Special Studies Department of De Nederlandsche Bank, involved with volatility analysis, macroeconometric modelbuilding and risk management. Dr Vlaar has published several articles, primarily on European exchange rates and risk premia.

VII. Volatility, International Trade and Capital Flows

AD C.J. STOKMAN and PETER J.G. VLAAR

1. INTRODUCTION

Since the breakdown of the Bretton Woods system, exchange rates have been widely fluctuating in an almost unpredictable way. Recently, the turbulence within the European Monetary System and the real depreciation of the US dollar contributed to increased interest in exchange rate volatility and once again opened the debate on the desirability of exchange rate management. Within the bond market, the sudden rise in volatility in 1994 contributed to the popular belief that financial innovations and international capital mobility increase volatility. Financial innovations were also blamed for the stock market crash of October 1987. These developments have led to questions about the desirability of financial liberalisation.

Despite the continuous interest in volatility, neither the reasons for nor the consequences of volatility are well-documented empirically. The purpose of this paper is to find empirical evidence for the interaction between volatility and international transactions in real and financial assets. This will be investigated for three types of international transactions of the Netherlands. In Section 2 we focus on Dutch foreign trade, in Section 3 on foreign direct investment and in Section 4 on international transactions in Dutch securities (bonds and stocks). Concerning international trade and foreign direct investment, we will consider both short and long-term exchange rate volatility as a source of risk. With respect to securities we will, in addition to exchange rate volatility, include bond and stock market volatility in our analysis.

2. EXCHANGE RATE VOLATILITY AND FOREIGN TRADE

The view that an increase in risk will lead risk-averse individuals to reduce their efforts in higher-risk activities and to shift to lower- risk ones has led many to conclude that exchange rate volatility must in principle have a negative effect on international trade (Cushman, 1983). So far, however, it

117

has remained an open empirical question whether exchange rate variability has the presumed negative effects (IMF, 1984). According to modern theory of production and consumption under risk, clear-cut conclusions about the effects of risk cannot easily be drawn, as increased uncertainty leads to a fundamentally ambiguous effect on trade: greater profit opportunities attract individuals, greater risk discourages risk-averse individuals (De Grauwe, 1988). Notwithstanding the diverse outcomes of theoretical studies and the inconclusiveness of empirical studies, business surveys provide strong evidence that, despite the possibility of hedging, which is in itself costly, foreign exchange risk is still considered a major obstacle to trade and investment (European Commission, 1990).

Concerning the empirical investigation of exchange rate risk, several methodological issues arise. First of all, a distinction must be made between exchange rate *volatility and misalignment* (Williamson, 1985). Volatility is a high-frequency concept referring to movements in the exchange rate over relatively short periods of time. Misalignment, on the other hand, refers to the fact that an exchange rate may not be in line with its fundamentals (however defined) over a longer period of time. Both concepts have been applied throughout this paper. Second, volatility can be measured by using either *nominal* or *real* exchange rates. There is no unambiguous conclusion in the literature as to whether variability in the real or in the nominal exchange rate is the appropriate proxy for exchange rate risk (Thursby and Thursby, 1987). For the high-frequency measure, nominal exchange rate variability is probably the appropriate measure since prices are almost fixed in the short run. As far as misalignment is concerned, price differentials cannot be disregarded so real exchange rate variability is the relevant measure.

The exchange rate risk measures we use are defined as the root mean squared percentage change in *nominal daily* trade-weighted exchange rates during a quarter (denoted as $vole^s$) and *real monthly* trade-weighted exchange rates during two years (denoted as $vole^l$), respectively.

Consumer price indices are used as deflator since other deflators were not available on a monthly basis. We consider the following currencies: the US Dollar, the British Pound, the German Mark, the French Franc, the Italian Lira and the Belgian Franc. Figure 1 gives an illustration of the overall development of these two indicators of volatility.

Following Hooper and Kohlhagen (1978), we assume that exchange rate risk is the only source of risk in the economy. Unexpected variations in the spot exchange rate affect the unhedged profits of firms because of the time lag between the contract and the date of payment. This theory reflects the importance of *short-term* volatility. A representative risk-averse importer

per cent per year

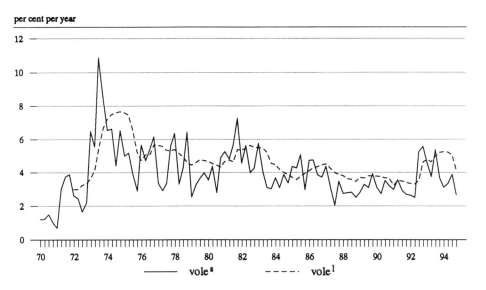

Fig. 1. Short- and long-term volatility for the Netherlands effective exchange rate.

maximizes his utility, which depends positively on the expected value of profits and negatively on its standard deviation. Furthermore, the importer is assumed to take import prices as given, and to set the domestic price of the imported goods taking into account the demand curve faced in the domestic market. In the model, the proportion of contracts hedged through the forward market and that denominated in the domestic currency are exogenous.

The influence of *long-term* exchange rate risk on foreign trade can be explained by sunk entry and exit costs (Baldwin and Krugman, 1989, Dixit, 1989). According to this theory, firms have to invest before they can export their goods to a country. These investments include, for instance, a distribution system and marketing activities. The costs of these investments cannot be retrieved if the firm decides to stop the export activities to this country. The firm has to be sure that the costs of this initial investment are recovered before exports to this country are no longer profitable, for instance because the real exchange rate has changed. As the exchange rate becomes more volatile, firms will tend to wait longer, widening the interval in which neither entry nor exit occurs. Therefore, long-term real exchange rate variability might also hamper foreign trade.

In addition to exchange rate volatility, foreign trade is expected to be influenced by price ratios, industrial production and capacity utilisation rates.

The industrial production in the Netherlands (y^{nl}) and a trade-weighted foreign country (y^{cc}), respectively, serve as scaling variable for imports (m) and exports (x). The price ratios are measures of price-competitiveness. A rise in Dutch export prices (p_x^{nl}) relative to foreign competitors (p_x^{cc}), which is equivalent to a loss of competitiveness for Dutch exporters, will negatively affect sales. A rise in Dutch import prices (p_m^{nl}) relative to prices of total demand in the Netherlands (p_d^{nl}), which indicates an improvement of competitiveness of Dutch producers relative to foreign suppliers of goods and services with the Netherlands as their destination, will result in a smaller demand for imports. The capacity utilization rate in the Netherlands (q^{nl}) is included to capture spillover disequilibrium responses from domestic to foreign markets and vice versa. When capacity utilization is low, Dutch producers will have an incentive to sell more abroad. With capacity utilization ratios going up, this incentive wanes. In the case of imports, high utilization rates in the Netherlands will spill over to higher demand for foreign products.

Both equations have been estimated over the period from 1970:I up to 1991:IV. More recent years have not been included because of deteriorating quality of the trade data, due to changes in the reporting system. In order to distinguish between long-run equilibrium relations and short-term dynamics, the equations have been put in an error-correction framework. The estimation results are shown below, disregarding the constant and seasonal dummies.

$$\Delta \ln x = \underset{(3.7)}{1.22} \cdot \Delta \ln y - \underset{(1.9)}{0.21} \cdot \Delta \ln(p_x^{nl}/p_x^{cc}) + \underset{(0.9)}{0.011} \Delta \ln \text{vole}^s$$

$$- \underset{(2.0)}{1.06} \Delta q^{nl} - \underset{(4.7)}{0.37} (\ln x_{-1} - \underset{(13.4)}{2.00} \cdot \ln y_{-1}^{cc}$$

$$+ \underset{(3.1)}{0.68} \cdot \ln(p_x^{nl}/p_x^{cc})_{-1} + \underset{(1.3)}{0.029} \cdot \ln \text{vole}_{-1}^s + \underset{(2.5)}{1.13} \cdot q_{-1}^{nl}) \qquad (1)$$

Period of estimation: 1970:I–1991:IV.

$\bar{R}^2 = 0.58, \quad \text{SE} = 0.034, \quad \text{DW} = 2.38,$
$P(Q(1)) = 0.06, \quad P(Q(12)) = 0.41.$

$$\Delta \ln m = \underset{(2.8)}{0.70} \cdot \Delta \ln y^{nl} - \underset{(3.3)}{0.78} \cdot \Delta \ln(p_m^{nl}/p_d^{nl}) - \underset{(1.7)}{0.019} \Delta \ln \text{vole}^s$$

$$+ 0.45\Delta q^{nl} - 0.72(\ln m_{-1} - 1.15 \cdot \ln y^{nl}_{-1}$$
$$ (0.9) \qquad (6.3) \qquad\qquad (8.0)$$

$$+ 0.84 \cdot \ln(p^{nl}_m/p^{nl}_d)_{-1} + 0.028 \cdot \ln \text{vole}^s_{-1} - 0.62 \cdot q^{nl}_{-1})$$
$$ (3.9) \qquad\qquad\qquad (2.0) \qquad\qquad (2.2) \tag{2}$$

Period of estimation: 1970:II-1991:IV.

$$\bar{R}^2 = 0.66, \quad SE = 0.033, \quad DW = 1.81,$$
$$P(Q(1)) = 0.34, \quad P(Q(12)) = 0.95.$$

All parameters of equations (1) and (2) have the expected sign. Long-term parameters with respect to production are bigger than 1, and for exports are even close to 2, which reflects the process towards integrating national markets. Both exports and imports are sensitive to price competitiveness, with elasticities not different from 1 (at a 95 per cent confidence level), a value regularly found in other empirical studies. Disequilibrium effects, measured by the capacity utilization rate, are found to be significant in both equations.

According to our results, only short-term exchange rate volatility hampers trade in the long run. The coefficients for exports and imports are of about the same size, although only that for imports is statistically significant. Adding vole^l or replacing vole^s by vole^l results in negligible effects of long-run exchange rate volatility. This probably means that payment lags are a more important source of exchange rate risk than sunk costs. An explanation for this finding might be that the risks due to payment lags are experienced by all exporting firms whereas sunk costs considerations are only important for newly exporting firms. The exchange-rate-volatility parameters for exports of goods and services are comparable in size to the ones found earlier for intra-EC exports of the Netherlands (Stokman, 1995). In the latter study, which distinguished between various components of foreign trade, exchange rate volatility was found to have a significant damaging effect on trade for four out of five categories of goods distinguished.

3. EXCHANGE RATE VOLATILITY AND NETHERLANDS FOREIGN DIRECT INVESTMENT

Foreign direct investment (FDI) is an increasingly important economic activity in the world. For countries like the Netherlands with its high concentration of large multinational companies headquartered here, direct investment is vital. In this section we will analyse the impact of exchange rate volatility on the patterns of inward and outward direct investment for the Netherlands (FDIM and FDIX, respectively). Beside expected returns on investment, market presence and avoidance of both protectionist measures and exchange rate risks are the predominant incentives for FDI. Exchange rate movements may add uncertainty to the decision to enter a foreign market. Former studies on the relation of direct investment and exchange rate risk reveal that, to the degree that companies are risk-averse, uncertainty about future exchange rate behaviour can be an obstacle to entry (Kohlhagen, 1977, Cushman,1985). By contrast, according to production flexibility arguments, exchange rate variability may actually stimulate investment (Aizenman, 1992). For exporters and importers, foreign direct investment may be considered an effective means to circumvent the potentially adverse effects of exchange rate movements. The stronger the domestic currency and the higher its volatility, the bigger the necessity for investments abroad to diversify risks. Moreover, FDI is cheaper and thus more profitable, if one's currency is currently overvalued. From this point of view, direct investment may be a substitute for international goods trade. Some types of foreign direct investment activities, however, are complementary to international trade in goods, as is the case for direct investment in distribution systems and marketing needed to support and start export activities (export promotion). Such activities, which form a substantial part of FDI of the Netherlands, are negatively influenced by both a strong currency and exchange rate volatility. Beside these categories of physical investments, FDI data also include international financial transactions within firms. The influence of exchange rates on these transfers is not self-evident since they can be used for both speculative and hedging activities.

Thus, the overall net effect of both the level and the volatility of the exchange rate on aggregate foreign direct investment may be either positive or negative. This is possibly the reason why the empirical literature only provides rudimentary insight into the link between exchange rate variability and FDI. Goldberg (1993) shows that — under a restrictive set of assumptions — increased exchange rate volatility tends to stimulate US bilateral FDI flows, thus supporting the production diversification motive. In contrast, Campa (1993) finds that exchange rate volatility is negatively correlated with the number of foreign investments in the US wholesale market during the 1980s. Concerning actual real exchange rates, Campa and Goldberg (1995) reveal that these tend to have little or no effects on direct investment in high mark-up sectors which absorb much of the actual exchange rate changes in their mark-ups, whereas the reverse holds for low mark-up industries.

For the Netherlands, we have analysed the stock of outstanding direct investment (FDIX) abroad and the stock of inward direct investment (FDIM), both deflated by the Dutch consumer price index (p_c). Several explanatory variables have been investigated. The first is a measure of the world trade volume relevant for the Netherlands (m_w), which is a proxy for both the wealth of foreign investors and the size of the sales area which can be covered from the Netherlands. The second is the long-term and short-term exchange rate volatility measure. The third variable is the long-term interest rate in the Netherlands relative to the rest of the world ($r_l^{nl} - r_l^{wo}$) as a measure for the influence of portfolio investment elements of FDI-intragroup financial transactions. Concerning FDIX we also introduced a measure of relative tax burden in the Netherlands, defined as taxes on profits relative to GDP (tax_{gdp}^{nl}), because they are supposed to have a positive influence on direct investment. Other factors like the level of real exchange rates, labour income rates and so on have also been included in our analysis without notifiable or with wrong-signed effects and have, therefore, been excluded. The relations for FDIM and FDIX are specified in an error-correction form:

$$\Delta \ln(\text{FDIM}/p_c) = 0.16\Delta \ln m_w + 0.08\Delta \ln \text{vole}^l + 0.02\Delta(r_l^{nl} - r_l^{wo})$$
$$\quad\quad (0.54) \quad\quad\quad\quad (2.38) \quad\quad\quad\quad 2.83$$

$$- 0.18(\ln(\text{FDIM}/p_c)_{-1} - 1.30 \ln m_w {}_{-1} - 0.20 \ln \text{vole}^l_{-1}$$
$$\quad (3.60) \quad\quad\quad\quad\quad\quad (15.60) \quad\quad\quad (2.36)$$

$$- 0.07(r_l^{nl} - r_l^{wo})_{-1}).$$
$$\quad (3.31) \quad\quad\quad\quad\quad\quad\quad\quad\quad\quad\quad\quad (3)$$

Period of estimation: 1980.I–1994.IV.

$\bar{R}^2 = 0.38$,   SE $= 0.014$,   DW $= 2.24$,
$P(Q(1)) = 0.22$, $P(Q(12)) = 0.37$.

$$\Delta \ln(\text{FDIX}/p_c) = 0.02\Delta \ln m_w + 0.05\Delta \ln \text{vole}^l + 0.04\Delta \ln \text{tax}_{gdp}^{nl}$$
$$\quad\quad (0.12) \quad\quad\quad\quad (2.53) \quad\quad\quad\quad (3.47)$$

$$- 0.32(\ln(\text{FDIX}/p_{c-1}) - 1.18 \ln m_w {}_{-1} - 0.09 \ln \text{vole}^l_{-1}$$
$$\quad (3.05) \quad\quad\quad\quad\quad\quad (5.81) \quad\quad\quad\quad (2.73)$$

$$- 0.09 \ln \text{tax}_{gdp}^{nl} {}_{-1} - 0.01t) - 0.28\Delta \ln(\text{FDIX}/p_c)_{-4}$$
$$\quad (2.91) \quad\quad\quad\quad (3.91) \quad (2.36) \quad\quad\quad\quad\quad (4)$$

with t: time trend. Period of estimation: 1980.I–1994.IV.

$$\bar{R}^2 = 0.66, \quad \text{SE} = 0.008, \quad \text{DW} = 2.16,$$
$$P(Q(1)) = 0.45, \quad P(Q(12)) = 0.40.$$

Regarding these results, the following conclusions can be drawn. Both outward and inward direct investment are closely related to developments in world trade with an elasticity of above one, reflecting the globalization of production. For FDIX this is also expressed in the time trend. Furthermore, a relatively high tax burden causes pressure for shifting production from domestic to foreign locations. The impact of exchange rate volatility on direct investment is positive for FDIM as well as for FDIX. The higher the long-term exchange rate volatility, the more direct investment increases. The short-term measure of exchange rate volatility does not turn out to be significant, which is what one would expect from FDI activities as they are related to long-run decision-making. These results indicate that the production diversification motive dominates FDI. Surprisingly, no significant effect of the level of the exchange rate could be found. A possible explanation for this might be that the parts of FDI that are complementary to international trade compensate exchange rate level effects on FDI in production diversification without being harmed as much by exchange rate volatility. A reason why such activities might be less vulnerable to exchange rate volatility is that these activities are more flexible than production, that is, a higher proportion of the costs is variable instead of fixed. That FDI in distribution, export promotion and so on is indeed less sensitive to long-term exchange rate volatility, is confirmed by our findings in the previous section, which revealed that foreign trade is not significantly affected by long-term exchange rate volatility.

4. Volatility and Portfolio Investment

Here we investigate the relationship between volatility and both the level of and the changes in the stock of Dutch securities in foreign hands. This subject has become increasingly popular as international capital flows are held partly responsible for volatility on both bond and foreign exchange markets. This belief has even induced politicians to propose limitations on international capital flows, for instance by means of a Tobin tax.

From a theoretical point of view, however, the causality between international capital flows and volatility is far from unambiguous. On the one hand, volatility might deter risk-averse foreign investors and therefore induce capital flight. On the other hand, volatility patterns on the Dutch bond and stock markets might change with the globalisation of capital markets due to at least three reasons. First, the entry of foreign traders into the domestic market increases the total number of traders and therefore improves the thickness of the market, leading to lower average volatility. Second, foreign traders are likely to have different preferences as their utility is expressed in a different currency. Therefore, if foreign exchange risk is not fully hedged, foreign exchange volatility might spill over to the bond or stock markets due to capital flows. Third, globalisation of financial markets increases the number of investment opportunities as investors are no longer restricted to investing in domestic securities. For these reasons, differences in economic performance between countries might induce international capital flows leading to higher volatility.

In Figure 2 the volatility of bond prices, stock prices and exchange rates is shown. The measures are computed as the standard deviations of daily growth rates within one month. The exchange rate volatility measure is a weighted average of bilateral exchange rate volatilities with weights related to the ownership of Dutch securities. Stock market volatility is always much higher than exchange rate volatility, which is in turn higher than bond market volatility. Therefore, foreign exchange risk is more likely to deter foreign investors, leading to capital flight and volatility, on the bond market than on the stock market as the influence of exchange rate volatility on the risk-return trade-off of foreign investors is more important there.

In order to determine the interrelationship between volatility and capital flows for the Netherlands, equations were estimated for both directions. An empirical problem emerges about the timing of possible causal connections. As the influence of capital flows on volatility, or vice versa, is likely to be immediate rather than with a time lag of one month (the time frequency considered here), Granger causality tests do not detect the true causal relationships. Therefore, the dependencies are modelled in a simultaneous model, including volatility and capital flow measures as well as macroeconomic variables.

Theoretically, stock prices represent the discounted flow of expected future dividends whereas bond prices depend on future short-term interest rates. Empirically, there is not much support for these theories, however. Stock prices are much too volatile compared to changes in macroeconomic conditions. For a period of over one hundred years Schwert (1989) compared US stock market volatility with the volatility of macroeconomic series but could not find any close relationship. Fortune (1989), on the other hand, did find a significant influence of monetary variables, which may influence future

per cent per year

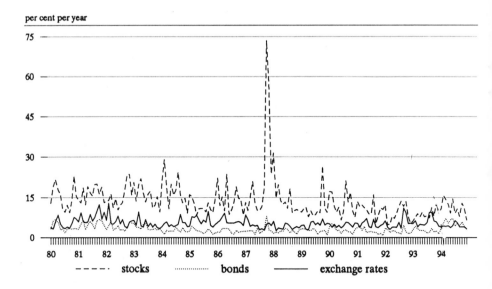

Fig. 2.   Volatility measures for stocks, bonds and exchange rates.

short-term interest rates, on the volatility of bills and bonds and of 'business health variables', which are likely to influence future dividends on stocks. By far the most popular empirical research topic on volatility concerns its autocorrelation, which can be modelled by means of an ARCH specification (Engle, 1982) or one of its generalisations. These studies do not, however, explain the differences in volatility over time. Another hot topic concerning volatility is the influence of financial innovations, such as options and futures. Contrary to popular belief, empirical results usually indicate that these innovations decrease volatility (see, for instance, Robinson, 1993), although some studies indicate an increasing effect of option expiration. We will not include these effects, primarily because of a lack of appropriate data as most derivative contracts on Dutch securities, especially on bonds, are traded 'over the counter'. Overall, the understanding of volatility is far from complete. Psychological factors seem to be the most important, but these are hard to quantify. The October 1987 stock market crash, for instance, can probably only be explained by herd behavior of market participants (Shiller, 1988). Other obvious candidates for the description of the volatility of Dutch securities are the foreign counterparts. These are not included as the inclusion of, for instance, German volatility would merely shift the causality question to the German market. Macroeconomic conditions in both countries can be expected to be more or less the same. Moreover, the main channels by which foreign volatility affects volatility on Dutch markets are international capital flows, which are included.

As to the understanding of foreign ownership of domestic financial assets, things do not look much better. Theoretically, these flows can be explained by international portfolio diversification. This might be affected by changes in expected risk and return characteristics, of which exchange rate volatility is one important element. Empirical results usually indicate that — from a theoretical point of view — investors hold too little of their financial wealth in foreign securities, however (see, for instance, French and Poterba, 1991).

Our results for the bond market are shown in equations (5) and (6). The models are estimated by three-stage least squares.[1] Here fl(bond^f) measures capital flows due to transactions in Dutch bonds between foreigners and Dutch residents. This measure is preferred to growth rates of stocks of bonds because these include in addition to capital flows also revaluations of the remaining stock.

$$\text{volb} = 3.34 - 19.03\text{fl}(\text{bond}^f)/\text{bond}^f{}_{-1} - 0.41\ln(\text{bond}^f/p_c^{nl})_{-1}$$
$$\phantom{\text{volb} = }(2.12)\ (2.01) (2.17)$$

$$+\ 0.06\ddot{p}^{nl} + 0.08|\Delta\ddot{y}^{nl}|_{-2} + 0.19\text{vole}^s + 0.61|\Delta r_s^{nl}|$$
$$(1.45)(1.88)(1.68)(1.93)$$

$$+\ 0.96\Delta r_l^{nl} + 0.29\text{volb} + 4.80\text{dum}_{87.10} + 1.95\text{dum}_{94}$$
$$(2.26)(4.57)(5.01)(5.14) \tag{5}$$

Period of estimation: 80:02–94:12.

$$\bar{R}^2 = 0.52, \quad \text{SE} = 1.003, \quad \text{DW} = 2.00,$$
$$P(Q(1)) = 0.89, \quad P(Q(12)) = 0.36.$$

$$100 * \text{fl}(\text{bond}^f)/\text{bond}^f{}_{-1} = 2.87 - 0.17\text{volb} - 0.28(\ddot{p}_c^{nl} - \ddot{p}_c^f) - 2.52\Delta r_l^{nl}$$
$$\phantom{100 * \text{fl}(\text{bond}^f)/\text{bond}^f{}_{-1} = }(3.26)\ (1.08)(3.58)(3.25)$$

$$-\ 0.37\text{vole}^s$$
$$(1.95) \tag{6}$$

Period of estimation: 80:02–94:12.

$$\bar{R}^2 = 0.07, \quad \text{SE} = 2.056, \quad \text{DW} = 1.69,$$

$$P(Q(1)) = 0.06, \quad P(Q(12)) = 0.46.$$

According to our results, capital flows significantly influence bond market volatility (volb), whereas the opposite cannot be detected. When split up, the signs of the coefficients of capital outflows and capital inflows on volatility are the same, although only the former is statistically significant. This means that capital outflows increase volatility whereas capital inflows decrease volatility. A possible explanation for this phenomenon might be that foreigners buy Dutch securities when bond prices are rising (see equation 6) while volatility is lower under these circumstances (equation 5). Since the hypothesis of equal coefficients could not be rejected, the distinction between capital in- and outflows was not pursued. An increase of the real value of Dutch bonds in foreign hands (bond$^f/p_c^{nl}$) decreases bond market volatility, probably as a result of the improved thickness of the market. Overall, the results do not provide strong arguments in favour of international capital restrictions. Although capital outflows increase bond market volatility somewhat, capital inflows have the opposite effect. Moreover, restrictions are likely to discourage foreign demand for Dutch securities, thus reducing the liquidity of the market and thereby increasing bond market volatility.

As to the other determinants of bond market volatility and international capital flows, the following can be said. The influence of inflation ($\dot{p}^{nl}$) on bond volatility is just not significant. Higher domestic than foreign inflation rates do cause capital outflows, however. Changes in the industrial production growth rate ($\dot{y}^{nl}$), either positive or negative, increase bond volatility. Both inflation and changes in the business cycle increase uncertainty about future monetary policy. That monetary policy matters can be deduced from the significant effect of absolute changes in short-term interest rates (r_s^{nl}) on volatility. Short-term exchange rate volatility (vole^s) increases bond volatility as well, probably because it induces foreigners to sell Dutch bonds (equation 6). Leverage effects are clearly present in the bond market as increases in the long-term interest rate (decreases in bond prices) increase bond volatility. They also lead to capital outflows, indicating bandwagon behaviour of foreign investors. The dummy variable for October 1987 was included to accommodate the consequences on the bond market of the stock market crash. The dummy variable for 1994 was included since statistical tests indicated a structural break in that year. The reasons for the high volatility in 1994 could hardly be explained by the variables investigated. German monetary policy might have been less predictable since the (unexpected) economic recovery started when interest rates were already high and inflation was declining. For a long time, both increases and decreases in official interest rates were possible, depending on the economic indicator investigated. Whether the increase in volatility is only temporary or structural is still an open question. At the end of 1994 volatility was declining, but the level was still higher than in 1993.

According to the estimation results in (7) and (8), the direction of causality between volatility and capital flows on the stock market is opposite to that on the bond market. An increase in stock volatility (vols) leads to capital outflow ($\text{fl}(\text{stock}^f)$) whereas capital flows do not seem to influence stock volatility. Also when split up, no significant effect of either capital inflows or outflows on volatility could be detected. As for the bond market, more stocks in foreign hands reduce average stock volatility. This means that as far as volatility is concerned, there are even fewer reasons for restrictions on international financial transactions on the stock market than on the bond market.

$$\text{vols} = 16.64 - \underset{(0.44)}{57.10}\text{fl}(\text{stock}^f)/\text{stock}^f_{-1} - \underset{(2.07)}{1.93}\ln(\text{stock}^f/p_c^{nl})_{-1}$$
$$\phantom{\text{vols} =} \underset{(2.13)}{}$$

$$+ \underset{(3.05)}{0.32}\dot{y}^{nl}_{-2} + \underset{(2.18)}{0.87}\text{vole}^l + \underset{(2.18)}{2.93}|\Delta r_s^{nl}| + \underset{(4.71)}{0.26}\text{vols}_{-1}$$

$$+ \underset{(14.19)}{57.52}\text{dum}_{87.10} + \underset{(5.21)}{28.17}\text{dum}_{87.11} \tag{7}$$

Period of estimation: 80:03–94:12.

$$\bar{R}^2 = 0.70, \quad \text{SE} = 4.033, \quad \text{DW} = 2.06,$$
$$P(Q(1)) = 0.63, \quad P(Q(12)) = 0.70.$$

$$100 * \text{fl}(\text{stock}^f)/\text{stock}^f_{-1} = 0.02 - \underset{(1.68)}{0.01}\Delta\text{vols} - \underset{(1.82)}{0.06}\text{re}\dot{\text{x}}\text{r} + \underset{(3.74)}{0.05}\dot{p}_{\text{stock}}$$
$$\phantom{100 * \text{fl}(\text{stock}^f)/\text{stock}^f_{-1} =} \underset{(0.64)}{}$$

$$+ \underset{(0.54)}{0.34}(100 * \text{fl}(\text{stock}^f)/\text{stock}^f_{-1})_{-1} \tag{8}$$

Period of estimation: 80:03–94:12.

$$\bar{R}^2 = 0.35, \quad \text{SE} = 0.400, \quad \text{DW} = 1.94,$$
$$P(Q(1)) = 0.72, \quad P(Q(12)) = 0.79.$$

High industrial production growth rates increase stock volatility, which might be explained by more uncertainty about dividends. Short-term exchange rate volatility is not important for the stock market. Given the relatively small magnitude of exchange rate volatility relative to stock volatility, this is not surprising. Long-run exchange rate volatility does increase stock volatility, however. The most likely reason for this finding is the influence of the exchange rate on the profitability of Dutch firms. A real appreciation of the Dutch guilder (rexr > 0) results in capital outflows. This probably also reflects the reduced profitability of Dutch firms. As in the bond market, bandwagon behaviour is highly significant in the stock market, as a rise in stock market prices induces foreign investors to buy Dutch stocks. We could not find leverage effects in the stock market, however. A possible reason for this lack of empirical evidence for asymmetric effects of price movements on volatility might be the inclusion of the dummies for the October 1987 crash. Changes in short-term interest rates significantly increase stock volatility, whereas long-term interest rates have no effect. This is in accordance with the results of Fortune (1989) and suggests that investors adopt short time horizons in assessing the value of stocks.

5. CONCLUSIONS

The main conclusions of this paper are:

1 Exchange rate volatility does affect international goods and capital flows in a significant manner. The influence depends on the volatility measure chosen.

2 Foreign trade is hampered by short-term exchange rate volatility, reflecting uncertainty due to payment lags, whereas long-term volatility, reflecting risk due to fixed entry and exit costs, has no significant influence.

3 Foreign direct investment for the Netherlands, inward as well as outward, is stimulated by long-term exchange rate volatility, revealing the presence of production diversification incentives. Short-run exchange rate volatility does not affect foreign direct investment in a noticeable way, reflecting the notion that foreign direct investment primarily relates to long-run decision-making.

4 On the Dutch bond market short-term exchange rate volatility deters foreign investors, leading to capital flight and higher bond volatility. Stock market volatility is slightly increased by an increase in long-term exchange rate volatility, probably because the exchange rate affects the profitability of firms.

5   Other factors relevant for volatility are short-term interest rate changes, growth in industrial production and inflation rates (only for the bond market).

6   Capital flows are primarily characterised by bandwagon behaviour. If prices rise, foreigners buy Dutch securities.

7   The relationship between financial market volatility and capital flows differs between the stock market and the bond market. On the bond market capital flight increases volatility whereas the reverse is true in the stock market. These preliminary results indicate no strong arguments in favour of international capital restrictions to reduce volatility as even the increasing effect of capital outflows on volatility on the bond market was compensated by a reducing effect of capital inflows. Moreover, capital restrictions are likely to discourage foreign ownership of Dutch securities, leading to higher volatility on both markets.

NOTES

1. As instruments for exchange rates and interest rates, the German counterparts were chosen. For the other unlagged variables, the lagged variable was used. The volatility and the captital flow equations were estimated with the same set of instruments. This methodology was also used for the stock market.

REFERENCES

Aizenman, J. (1992). *Exchange Rate Flexibility, Volatility, and Domestic and Foreign Direct Direct Investment*, IMF Staff Papers, pp. 890–922.

Baldwin, R.E. and P.R. Krugman (1989). Persistent Trade Effects of Large Exchange Rate Shocks, *Quarterly Journal of Economics* 104, pp. 635–654.

Campa, J.M. (1993). Entry by Foreign Firms in the United States under Exchange Rate Uncertainty, *The Review of Economics and Statistics* 75, pp. 614–622.

Campa, J.M. and L.S. Goldberg (1995). *Investment, Pass-through and Exchange Rates: A Cross-Country Comparison, NBER Working Paper* 5139.

De Grauwe, P. (1988). *Exchange Rate Variablility and the Slowdown in Growth of International Trade*, IMF Staff Papers, pp. 63–84.

Dixit, A.K. (1989). Hysteresis, Import Penetration and Exchange Rate Pass-through, *Quarterly Journal of Economics* 104, pp. 205–228.

Engle, R. (1982). Autoregressive Conditional Heteroskedasticity with Estimates of the Variance of United Kingdom Inflation, *Econometrica* 50, pp. 987–1007.

Fortune, P. (1989). An Assessment of Financial Market Volatility: Bills, Bonds and Stocks, *New England Economic Review*, pp. 13–28.

French, K. and J. Poterba (1991). International Diversification and International Equity Markets, *American Economic Review* 81, pp. 222–226.

Goldberg, L.S. (1993). Exchange Rates and Investment in United States Industry, *The Review of Economics and Statistics* 75, pp. 575–588.

Hooper, P. and S.W. Kohlhagen (1978). The Effect of Exchange Rate Uncertainty on the Prices and Volume of International Trade, *Journal of International Economics* 8, pp. 483–511.

International Monetary Fund (1984). The Exchange Rate System: Lessons of the Past and Options for the Future, *IMF Occasional Paper* 30.

Robinson, G. (1993). The Effect of Futures Trading on Cash Market Volatility: Evidence from the London Stock Exchange, *Bank of England Working Paper Series* 19.

Schwert, G.W. (1989). Why does Stock Market Volatility Change over Time, *The Journal of Finance 44*, pp. 1115–1154.

Shiller, R.J. (1988). Causes of Changing Financial Market Volatility, *Financial Market Volatility*, Federal Reserve Bank of Kansas City.

Stokman, A.C.J. (1995). Effects of Exchange-Rate Risk on Intra-EC Trade, *The Economist* 143, pp. 41–54.

Thursby, J.G. and M.C. Thursby (1987). Bilateral Trade Flows, the Linder Hypothesis, and Exchange Rate Risk, *The Review of Economics and Statistics* 69, pp. 488–495.

Williamson, J. (1985). *The Exchange Rate System*, Policy Analyses in International Economics 5, Institute for International Economics.

Part C

Institutional Issues and Practices

Institutional Investors, Unstable Financial Markets and Monetary Policy

Summary   611

This article focuses on the issues which may arise for central banks in the pursuit of *monetary stability* in the context of *asset price volatility*, and the impact thereon of *growth of institutional investors* such as pension funds, life insurers and mutual funds. The evolving pattern of volatility is considered to have entailed a major shift in the stability of central banks' environment and poses difficulties for monetary policy. The article first seeks to outline the reasons why institutions may destabilise financial markets, drawing on the economic literature and the outcome of recent discussions of the author with major institutional players, and supplemented by indications of their growing size and activity. Then it outlines four periods of market volatility, where institutions were heavily involved, and that raised concerns for monetary stability, namely the stock market crash of 1987, the ERM crises of 1992–3, the bond markets in 1993-4 and the Mexican crisis of 1994–95. The paper concludes that the following features recur intermittently in international financial markets; irresistible and rapid price shifts, in both directions; heavy involvement of institutional investors in both buying and selling waves; bank lending playing a rather subordinate role; international investment; signs of overreaction to the fundamentals and excessive optimism prior to the crisis; at times, inappropriate monetary policies; a shock to confidence which precipitated the crisis, albeit not necessarily sufficient in itself to explain the scale of the reaction; and rapid and wholesale shifts between markets, often facilitated by financial innovations. There is a range of policy implications. In particular, monetary policymakers generally will have to take increasing account of the actions, views and expectations of institutional investors concerning their monetary policy and economic developments. There is also a rich agenda for further research in this area.

E. Philip Davis has worked at the Bank of England since leaving Oxford University in 1980, except for two spells on secondment: to the Bank for International Settlements in 1985–87, and, currently, to the European Monetary Institute. He is also a research associate of the Financial Markets Group at the London School of Economics. He has published widely in the fields of institutional investments, euromarkets, banking, corporate finance, financial regulation, and financial stability.

VIII. Institutional Investors, Unstable Financial Markets and Monetary Policy

E. PHILIP DAVIS*

INTRODUCTION

The concerns of central banks in monetary policy setting — maintenance of the value of the currency (monetary stability) and protection of the financial system against the possibility of a systemic collapse (financial stability) — are being pursued in the context of a rapidly changing financial environment. Financial liberalisation and deregulation, abolition of exchange controls, financial innovation, institutionalisation and growth of euromarkets constitute important components of recent financial change. These have entailed, for example, a decline in credit rationing, and hence a need for a more market-based approach in policy execution, as well as heightened instability of prices and flows in financial markets. In this context, the specific focus in this article is the pursuit of *monetary stability* in the context of *asset price volatility*, and the impact thereon of *growth of institutional investors* such as pension funds, life insurers and mutual funds. The evolving pattern of volatility, which involves not merely day-to-day fluctuations but also may at times entail medium term deviations from levels consistent with fundamentals, is considered to have entailed a major shift in the stability of central banks' environment and poses difficulties for monetary policy.[1]

The paper is structured as follows. First, it seeks to outline the reasons why institutions may destabilise financial markets, based on the current state of the art in this field in the economic literature, informed by the outcome of recent discussions of the author with major institutional players, and supplemented by indications of their growing size and activity. Then it outlines four periods of market volatility, where institutions were heavily involved, and that raised concerns for monetary stability, namely the stock market crash of 1987, the ERM crises of 1992–3, the bond markets in 1993–4 and the Mexican crisis of

*The author thanks E. Gnan, J. Priesemann, J. Frijns and G. Rich for helpful comments. Views expressed are those of the author and not those of the EMI, Bank of England or Markets Group.

1994–95. The paper concludes by considering features of these crises in the light of the theory, addressing economic and monetary policy issues raised by such instability and suggesting further research.

1. INSTITUTIONAL INVESTORS AND ASSET MARKET INSTABILITY

In assessing whether behaviour of financial markets may be affected by the presence of the various types of institutions, a starting point is to consider the *aims of institutional investors*, and how structural features may lead their behaviour to differ from those of an individual, value-maximising investor. The relevant comparison to be made is with the theoretical paradigm of *rational investors or speculators*, where, following Friedman (1953), such rational investors would seek to use all relevant information in an efficient manner (and if possible gain information others do not have), buy when prices are below fundamentals and sell when they are above, and thereby efficiently stabilise markets at levels consistent with the fundamentals.

Fund management, for example of a pension fund or mutual fund, is a service involving management of an investment portfolio on behalf of a client. Such delegation raises *principal-agent problems*, as unless the manager is perfectly monitored and/or a foolproof contract drawn up, he may act in his own interests (e.g. in generating excessive commission income) and contrary to those of the fund. One can suggest *a priori* that such monitoring will be costlier when managers lack reputation or relationships, which otherwise constitute assets that would depreciate in the case of opportunistic behaviour. Various features of fund management can be seen as ways to reduce principal-agent problems. For example, pension fund managers are offered short (3-year) mandates, with frequent performance evaluation;[2] fees related to the value of funds at year-end and/or performance related fees. Open-ended mutual-fund and insurance managers will suffer loss of new business if they underperform, while closed-ended mutual funds may be taken over.

These means used to resolve the principal-agent problems in the fund management relation give rise to institutional behaviour which *could* induce capital market volatility. One is the *desire of managers to show they are of good quality*, for example in the context of short mandates. In the model of Scharfstein and Stein (1990),[3] herding — whereby all managers move in the same direction to buy or sell assets — occurs because the market for fund management skills takes into account both the success of investment strategies and the similarity to others' choices. The first piece of evidence is not used exclusively, since there are systematically unpredictable components of investment, while good managers are expected to receive correlated signals (they all observe the same relevant pieces of information); hence all good managers may be equally unlucky. On the other hand, a manager who alone makes a good investment may be a lucky but poor quality manager. So mimicking others is the best way to show quality. A related factor that could induce volatility is the above-mentioned *regular performance checks against the market* (as frequently as monthly in the United States, but less in the United Kingdom). As above this may induce similar behaviour, and hence 'herding' to avoid performing significantly worse than the median fund.[4] As a consequence, funds may, for example, adopt similar portfolios even if their own information suggests a different pattern could yield better returns. This may in turn amplify shocks to prices.

Short time horizons may affect *information acquisition* and hence market dynamics (Froot et al., 1992). This is contrary to the traditional view that there can be no distinction in behaviour between those with short and long time horizons, because an investor desiring to hold an asset for five minutes cares about the expected price then, which in turn depends on the expected price five minutes later, in an infinite regress which ensures behaviour remains in line with the long term fundamentals. The argument is, that whereas if assets were to be held forever, it would be rational to seek to gain information not held by others, it may be rational for fund managers with a short time horizon — for reasons as above — to concentrate on the same information as others, which may even be information extraneous to fundamentals. This is because the larger the number of investors who study the information, the more quickly it enters the market, and the greater the benefit from early learning. Use of chartism may be a case in point.

But these specific mechanisms are not the only possible reasons for institutional herding. A simpler mechanism may underlie sharp movements by open-ended mutual funds, namely simple *purchases and sales of units* by households, which oblige the manager to liquidate assets immediately in order to redeem the units. This may be a powerful mechanism if households are risk adverse and subject to major shifts in sentiment. It may be increased by the shift to defined contribution pension funds; such as the so-called 401(k) funds in the US; these assets are typically held in such mutual funds and their disposition is often at the discretion of the individual investor. Risk averse investors may sell funds in response to short run moves, contrary to appropriate long-run time horizons of their (retirement) assets. Or mutual fund managers may *transact repeatedly* to generate commission income, thus generating market volatility. Other reasons for herding by institutions could include institutions' *inferring information from each others' trades*, about which they are relatively well informed, and herding as a result (Shilller and Pound (1989)). Moreover, they may be *reacting to news*, which they all receive simultaneously, in a similar manner; such news may cause sizeable portfolio shifts in a world characterised by *uncertainty*[5] and not merely *risk*, if it causes funds to change their views about the future.

The main focus of the section above is on information, but the *risk management framework* may also play a role. If defined benefit pension funds have strict minimum solvency limits, they are subject to heightened shortfall risk if asset values decline (Davis, 1995a). This may encourage 'herding' either via direct sales of equities for bonds or by the effects of hedging in so-called contingent immunisation or portfolio insurance strategies on market prices (see below). More generally, as shown by Frijns et al. (1995), tighter solvency requirements will shorten time horizons, with possible consequences as noted in this section. Defined contribution funds are less subject to these effects, but as noted above may be vulnerable to changes in investor sentiment.

Herding by institutions need not always be destabilising, indeed it may speed the market's adjustment to a new equilibrium price, for example when there are tax changes, or offset irrational shifts in behaviour by other investors such as individuals and foreigners, or in response to monetary policy errors which result in overvalued exchange rates. What is needed is for institutions also to follow strategies which may be contrary to fundamentals and profit maximising — buying high and selling low — so-called *positive feedback trading*. Cutler et al. (1990) suggest that institutions may *themselves* act in this manner. This may be a consequence of biases in judgement under uncertainty by fund managers, which leads to extrapolative expectations or trend-chasing rather than focus on fundamentals. Certain investment strategies may also induce such behaviour, such as stop-loss orders, purchases on margin and dynamic hedging strategies. These may be common when there are minimum funding limits. Institutions may also seek *indirectly* to provoke positive feedback trading (De Long et al., 1990), since in the presence of irrational investors such as households it is rational for institutions (such as hedge funds) to buy in the knowledge that their own trades will trigger further feedback trading by irrational investors, thus amplifying the effect.

There was evidence of positive feedback behaviour in the stock market (Shiller, 1988), where investors' reasons given to sell in the wake of the 1987 Crash were often merely that prices had fallen, in expectation of further price falls. Also in forex markets (Frankel and Froot, 1988), forecasters persistently urged institutions to buy dollars during the "bubble" of the early 1980s although admitting that the dollar was overvalued. Circumstantial evidence is provided by the correlation of stock returns at short time horizons, and negative correlation at long horizons, contrary to the random walk anticipated by efficient markets (Fama and French, 1988, Lo and McKinlay, 1988). Lakonishok et al. (1991) examine the evidence for herding, positive feedback trading or other forms of potentially destabilising behaviour for a sample of 341 US money managers' quarterly investments in individual stocks. Their conclusions were that there was weak evidence of such behaviour for smaller stocks, but not for large ones. However, they could not rule out market-wide herding, for example if money managers follow each other in market timing, or herding in individual stocks at a higher than quarterly frequency. It is market-wide and cross-market herding which is the main cause for concern for central banks. Indeed, an important phenomenon in recent years is that institutions increasingly "trade markets" and not stocks, reflecting profit opportunities.[6]

In principle, investors following positive-feedback trading strategies should make losses that may lead them to withdraw from the market. But in practice patterns of positive-feedback trading may persist if, for example each episode looks rather different so learning from previous mistakes is limited; or if the errors made by positive feedback traders lead them to accept higher market risk, and hence to gain higher returns. And historical evidence suggests it may occur over both short and relatively long horizons.

Linked to performance evaluation and herding is the *persistence of active management of institutional funds* instead of forms of indexation, despite the fact that the evidence is almost uniformly contrary to the efficacy of active management of funds within asset categories.[7] Obviously active management is needed for the patterns above to arise. The superior performance of indexation is in line with the efficient markets hypothesis, which suggests that, given prices already incorporate all available information, there is no net benefit from spending extra cash to try to beat the index.[8] Active management by *mutual funds* may be explicable in terms of desire to generate fee income. Lakonishok et al. (1992) suggest that the persistent use of active management by *pension funds* despite such evidence is related to further agency problems. In particular, they suggest that these may arise within the management structure of the sponsor of a pension fund; corporate treasurers seek to bolster their own positions vis-à-vis their managers, and hence seek fund managers that can offer good excuses for poor performance, clear stories about portfolio strategies and other services unrelated to performance. They avoid indexation, as this would reduce their own day to day responsibilities, as well as internal asset management, as this would give them too great a responsibility for errors. The authors suggest these agency costs are additional to the difficulties (as noted above) which arise between a (rational profit-maximising) sponsor and the fund manager. However, an alternative explanation may be that active market-selection (as opposed to asset selection within a market) still provides value-added compared to global indexation. Moreover, the points made in this sector should not be exaggerated since some shift to passive management does appear to be underway, particularly within markets ("stock selection" as opposed to "asset allocation"). 30 per cent of UK pension funds' domestic equities may be indexed at present.

The above literature, which is largely centred on herding[9] by institutions in securities markets, may be linked to the considerable research on foreign exchange markets, albeit usually focused on traders in banks rather than institutions per se, which has found similar behaviour patterns to these. Such research on herding is often based on the idea, which originated with Keynes (1936), of two groups of investors or traders in the market, one the professional investors, fundamentalists or informed traders who act in the light of economic theory, and the other being speculators, chartists or noise traders, who seek merely to profit from day to day movements. The analysis of authors such as Dornbusch (1990) suggests institutional investors may act in either capacity; they need not always be the informed traders. Following the discussion above, he highlighted the importance in an international context of performance assessment of fund managers over a short time horizon in relation to the median fund manager, which means that managers cannot afford to ignore a general shift in opinion regarding a foreign equity market or exchange rate, even if the movement is considered to be short term and reversible. Similar opinions were expressed by fund managers interviewed by the author, who talked of a "massive consensus that certain currencies should not be held" in early 1995. Note also that exchange rate risk and market risk can be dissociated by hedging, and in some fund managers are run as separate profit centres.

Institutions may also be susceptible to herd behaviour in foreign markets owing to *home asset preference*. Besides structural and regulatory reasons, a key economic factor seems to be scepticism regarding purchasing power parity holding, even in the very long term (Beenstock, 1986); long term shifts in real exchange rates mean currency mismatching can involve risk, especially for a mature pension fund or one subject to strict solvency regulations, as assets may fall short of liabilities. Besides low foreign asset holdings relative to a "global portfolio" (Davis, 1995a), such preferences may induce shifts to domestic markets at times of asset price volatility.

As regards the dynamics which may be induced by such behaviour, Evans and Lewis (1993) show there are persistent excess returns in spot and forward currency markets, and in bond markets. They suggest that "informed traders"

TABLE 1
Banks' relative importance in the financial sector

	1980	1993
UK	0.62	0.54
US	0.33	0.24
Germany	0.83	0.82
Japan	0.60	0.48
France	0.86	0.73

Bank assets as a proportion of assets of all financial institutions

are more risk averse than "noise traders" and hence are unwilling to take large positions even when currencies are far from equilibrium. Alternatively, there may be a range of values of the exchange rate within which a precise equilibrium is not defined, and within which sharp movements can occur in response to "herding", as the influence of noise traders predominates, but also margins beyond which the rate is definitely considered contrary to the fundamentals, and the judgements of informed traders prevail (De Grauwe, 1989). Clearly, the width of the range may itself change as uncertainty increases. In a fixed rate system, such heightened uncertainty may ultimately shift the range of plausible values beyond the bands that the authorities seek to defend. Following these ideas, Carpatanis (1993), favours an explanation of heightened volatility based on an initial situation of dispersed expectations and heightened uncertainty, perhaps caused by divergent views on the appropriate macroeconomic policy of a government. This increases the weight of noise traders relative to informed traders, as *informed traders, lacking confidence in their own judgement, find it rational in such circumstances to follow the rest of the market*. In such a situation a loss of credibility by the authorities — for whatever reason — may lead to a crisis, with all market opinion converging, and a rapid shift in the rate, overcoming any resistance by authorities.

Such patterns as outlined are clearly long established features of investment and fund management; why should they come to the fore now? Basically, it is because the *size and activity of institutions has increased sharply*. The rapid expansion of the balance sheets of institutional investors is well documented. It underlies the widespread decline in the share of banks in financial assets (Table 1) as well as being apparent in the size of institutions' portfolios relative to GDP (Table 3). Growth has also been impressive; the 300 largest US institutions held assets equivalent to 30 per cent of GDP in 1975 ($535 billion) but in 1993 were 110 per cent ($7,250 billion) although there has

TABLE 2
Government bonds held by foreign investors (% of total)

	1979	1992
UK	11.4	12.5
US	18.5	20.4
Germany	5.0	25.9
Japan	2.3	5.6
France	0.0	31.8
Italy	1.2	6.1
Canada	15.0	27.7

Source: IMF (1995)

also been a more general growth of the financial assets/GDP ratio. Factors underlying such growth of institutional investors include the ageing of the population in OECD countries, which has led to increased saving for old age, notably given the pressures to which state social security schemes are subject (Davis 1995a); advances in technology, which enable funds to be managed at relatively low cost, and with correspondingly high yields for investors; and the mutually reinforcing development of securitisation, which has provided a ready supply of assets in which to invest.

Besides size per se, evolving patterns of behaviour and related technology are important to the influence institutions may exert on financial markets. A key feature is the increasing *international investment* of these institutions, whereby cross border equity holdings rose from $800 billion in 1986 to $1,250 billion in 1991, while total cross border ownership of equities plus bonds was $2,250 billion. This is reflected in foreign holdings of bonds (Table 2). This internationalisation has been accompanied by an increasingly *active approach to portfolio investment* on behalf of institutions. Whereas in 1982 UK pension funds held foreign equities for 2 years on average, in 1994 the average holding period was under 6 months (WM, 1995), while the stock of foreign equities held by UK pension funds had risen from around $20 billion to $150 billion. As noted in Howell and Cozzini (1991), the *rise of global asset allocation* as a tool of fund management, and the *development of derivatives markets* such as those for stock index futures have stimulated and facilitated massive increases in short-term cross border flows. One equity transaction in three in Europe now involves a foreign transactor; and trading in index futures often far exceeds trade in the underlying. Although investors desire by adopting such strategies to reduce risk, the *focus of funds on a small*

TABLE 3
Assets of Pension Funds 1991

	Narrow definition[1]			Broad definition[2]		
	Stock of assets (end-1991) $ bn	% of personal sector assets	% of GDP	Stock of assets (end-1991) $ bn	% of personal sector assets	% of GDP
United States	2,915	22	51	3,780	29	66
United Kingdom	643	27	60	786	33	73
Germany	59	3	3	80[3]	4	4
Japan	182	2	5	303[3]	3	8
Canada	187	17	32	205	19	35
Netherlands	145	26	46	242	43	76
Sweden	39	–	16	126	–	49
Denmark	22	–	16	82	–	60
Switzerland	173	–	–	–	–	–
Australia	62	19	22	110	34	39
France	22	–	2	41	–	5
Italy	50	–	6	–	–	–

[1] Includes only independent (private and public sector) funded pension schemes. [2] For the United States, Australia, Canada and Denmark includes data for pension reserves of life insurers; for the United Kingdom and Japan includes estimates of life insurance companies' pension fund reserves; for Denmark includes funds managed by banks; for Sweden includes social security (ATP) scheme; for the Netherlands includes the Civil Service Pension Fund (ABP); for France includes ARRCO/AGIRC reserves. [3] In Germany and Japan there are large reserve funded (or "booked") pension plans with assets held directly on the sponsoring firm's balance sheet. The value of these in 1991 was $150 billion in Germany and an estimated $120 billion in Japan. Source: Davis (1995).

number of leveraged instruments often leads to market destabilisation and sharp price swings.

Nor need the behaviour be confined to securities markets. Besides the fact that flows of securities themselves have a direct effect on the exchange rate, there is broader evidence of institutionalisation of the foreign exchange markets, reducing the relative importance of banks. As recorded by IMF (1993), new players include *hedge funds* — themselves a form of institutional investor — and the increasing sophistication of *corporate treasury operations*. But most important was seen to be the effects on foreign exchange markets of internationalisation of portfolios of *pension funds, mutual funds and life insurers*, which combined with their absolute size, willingness to turn over investments and use derivatives gave them considerable leverage (see Section 2.2 below).

In the next section we outline four "case studies" of asset market fluctuations in which institutions played a major role, and note the difficulties they pose for monetary policy. Basically, we are investigating whether behaviour can be seen at a macro level consistent with the theory. Given lack of precise data on balance sheets and of individual transactions, the descriptions are largely qualitative.

2. CASE STUDIES

2.1. Equity Markets in 1987

Whereas popular accounts tend to focus on October 19–20, focus on the Crash itself abstracts from the need for an explanation why the market rose so much prior to the Crash. Davis (1995b), summarising available accounts, suggests that there was a deviation between fundamentals and prices — a form of speculative bubble — which was reflected in historically unprecedented yield ratios between bonds and equities. Such a situation leads to a suspicion of forms of trend-chasing, led by institutions fearing to perform worse than their peers. Indeed, in line with the theory above, there is anecdotal evidence that fund managers felt under pressure from performance appraisal not to sell, even if they all individually agreed prices were too high, as they feared being left out in a further rise, while being comforted in the event of a fall that they would not be alone (Scharfstein and Stein, 1990). Market technology may also have played a role, as lower transactions costs, combined with the spread of dynamic hedging techniques sold to institutions as "portfolio insurance", fostered an impression of high liquidity and led funds into the illusion that they could exit before prices fell sharply (Brady, 1989). But only in the US was portfolio insurance used to a significant extent, whereas markets collapsed world-wide. And clearly many "fundamental" factors also played a role in generating buoyant expectations, such as the merger wave in many countries, falling interest rates over 1987, buoyant economic prospects and rapid monetary growth.

As regards the immediate causes of the collapse, since it relies on continuously rising prices, a bubble can be burst by any form of adverse news; in practice, factors underlying the crisis itself may have included current account imbalances between the US, Germany and Japan, which led to fears of a falling dollar and caused rises in long term US interest rates in the week prior to the crash. Also, tensions in the policy coordination process between those countries may have played a role in triggering the crisis. Evidence supportive of the bubble hypothesis is that none of these items could in themselves justify a price adjustment of the magnitude observed (Fortune, 1993).

Some commentators in the United States also blamed the interaction between institutional investors' portfolio insurance and index arbitrage[10] strategies for causing volatility at the time of Crash itself. Basically, it was considered that computer-driven sell orders for futures, which are a normal feature of portfolio insurance (or 'dynamic hedging') strategies when prices fall, helped drive the market down much faster than would otherwise have been the case. The initial wave of selling of futures is thought to have driven futures to a discount to the market (known as backwardation) as well as reducing stock prices themselves and triggering further portfolio insurance-related sales of futures. The backwardation encouraged index arbitrageurs to sell stocks and buy futures, thus leading to a so-called cascade effect or accelerating price decline (Brady, 1989). The view of the Crash itself as dominated by portfolio insurance is, however, disputed (for a survey see Fortune (1993)).[11] What is less disputed is that institutions were heavily involved in the selling wave that accompanied the crash, with a particular tendency to dispose of cross border holdings, showing home asset preference. Such sales helped to generate the contagion across national markets, which was such a feature of October 1987 (Bertero and Mayer, 1989).

The crash posed major issues for monetary policymakers in both the short and medium term. In the short term the major concern was to avoid systemic risk arising from failure of investment banks, which was combated by an easing of liquidity and moral suasion on banks to lend. Such easing was continued, however, owing to fears that there would be a "Great Depression" due to effects of lower equity prices on consumption and investment in the wake of the crash. In fact the latter fears seem not to have been justified, and the easing of monetary conditions foreshadowed inflation in a number of countries.

2.2. *The ERM Crisis of 1992–3*

In assessing the effect of institutions on the operation of the ERM, it is important first to note that the success of the ERM had been built at times when a number of participants had exchange controls, thus limiting speculative pressures (though not eliminating them, see Gros (1992)). The disadvantages of such controls, for example in terms of higher risk premia (Cody, 1989), and corresponding restricted access to international capital markets, made them unattractive (as well as being contrary to the EU Single Market). But there is a cost. It is widely acknowledged that in the absence of such controls, the need in a fixed rate regime for identical monetary policies, for similar inflation performance (ensuring alignment of real exchange rates) and for similar cyclical performance per se, becomes more urgent. It also puts greater weight on intervention and the level of interest rates as means of counteracting speculative pressures.

Second, the overall volume of transactions in the foreign exchange market had risen rapidly over the 1980s and early 1990s, tripling between 1986 and 1992 to reach $1,000 billion, hence growing at a rate far beyond the growth rate in official reserves, which in 1992 totalled around $500 billion[12] (although note that the ERM included rules for limited sharing of reserves during periods of speculative pressure).

Third, as noted above, participants have become more diverse. *Banks and securities houses*, the traditional participants, can take positions against currencies particularly within a trading day, but these are limited by prudential requirements as well as internal risk-management rules; banks reportedly tended in 1992–3 to focus on their role as intermediaries in the foreign exchange markets, providing liquidity, innovative portfolio strategies and advice to customers. *Hedge funds* — a form of institutional investor — seek to profit from movements in exchange rates and interest rates by leveraged investments, either selling vulnerable currencies forward, using their capital to finance margin requirements, or by establishing interest-rate positions via futures to profit from an interest rate decline after the crisis. But analysts suggest that their relatively small size means that their direct influence should not be exaggerated; they may be more important for leading institutions and companies to re-examine their assumptions regarding a currency.[13] *Corporate treasury operations* enable non-financial firms to fund themselves in the cheapest markets and cover themselves by use of currency swaps, and to hedge future earnings against currency shifts, as well as taking open positions in their own right.

But perhaps most crucial was the consequences of internationalisation of the portfolios of *institutional investors* such as pension funds, mutual funds and life insurers - in countries where regulations permit such diversification.[14] Commentators such as IMF (1993) and BIS (1993) suggested that institutional involvement was both the most novel feature of crises and also the reason why speculative pressures rapidly increased. International diversification meant such institutions would inevitably be affected by exchange rate turbulence; and as noted they are becoming increasingly willing to turn over investments rapidly and change the currency composition of their portfolios, given falling transactions costs and development of derivatives; as outlined, managers are exceptionally sensitive to any losses that could make their own funds perform badly relative to the rest of the market, thus encouraging adoption of similar strategies; they often separate exchange rate and investment risk for investment management purposes by hedging, thus encouraging focus on exchange rates; and the resources available to pension funds and life insurers far exceed national foreign exchange reserves, so that relatively small proportionate portfolio shifts could lead to major pressures on exchange rates. In 1992 UK pension funds alone had assets of $700 billion whereas in August 1992, the French reserves were $28 billion, British $40 billion, Italian $20 billion and Swedish $20 billion.

There are two further reasons why institutions should be *particularly* singled out for making the ERM vulnerable in 1992–3. One factor is the existence of *convergence plays*. The drive to EMU, as long as it was considered credible, led to large potential profits from holding assets in the weaker, higher yielding currencies. So long as the fixed exchange rate was expected to hold, or even with small realignments prior to EMU, large capital gains could be anticipated as yields on bonds denominated in such currencies converged with German ones. Such so-called convergence plays grew to extremely large volumes, as evidenced by portfolio inflows to countries such as Spain, France and Italy over 1989–91. UK pension funds, for example, built up foreign bond exposures quite considerably over this period, from 0 per cent of their portfolios in 1986 to 4 per cent in 1991 (Source: WM (1993)). The IMF (1993) suggest the total value of such investments prior to the crisis was $300 billion. Note also that governments sought to encourage such international investment, as a means to reduce the cost of fiscal deficits and avoiding monetary financing, as well as improving access of domestic firms to equity finance and improving the competitiveness of their financial centres; the success of such approaches is apparent in Table 2.[15] Reflecting confidence over convergence, US pension funds and corporations in the high-yield currencies would often content themselves with hedging against the DM, i.e. in the most liquid derivatives market. Not that institutional investors were the only convergence players. In addition, non financial and financial companies in the high-yield currency countries often sought to fund themselves in DM or Guilders.

Given the scale of the exposures involved, the unwinding of such "convergence based" exposures, or at least increased hedging, in the wake of the Danish referendum, could clearly have been an important component of pressure on the system. This reaction within the ERM was likely to be particularly strong since confidence — in a process such as EMU — is rarely measured in terms of gradations (as is the case of most forms of *risk*). Either there is confidence, or there is not (a characteristic of *uncertainty*). As noted by Raymond (1990), credibility may be binary in the ERM, either complete or low. The importance of confidence meant that any stimulus such as a data item perception of policy conflict or inconsistency in an economy that would lead markets to revise their opinions could have consequences seemingly totally out of line with the scale of the event in question, as it would lead the market to question not merely its current decisions but the processes and assumptions underlying such decisions. Evidence from market participants shows that pressure arose from unwinding of convergence plays in a number of ways. In order to protect the value of their investments, institutions sold their foreign assets, hedged their exposures and sold the vulnerable currencies short, while non-financial companies in countries such as Italy, which had arranged "convergence" financing in DM, undertook massive hedging to cover their exposures, and US corporations and investors that had hedged high-yield currencies with the DM sought to unwind their hedges.

A second feature linked to institutions (albeit also used by banks to hedge their over-the-counter derivative positions) is techniques developed for institutional investors seeking to protect the value of their foreign currency securities (or of options they have written on their assets), so-called *dynamic hedging*. These involved the construction of synthetic put options on a currency by a combination of a short position in one currency and a long position in another, and adjusting the ratio continuously in line with the exchange rates, interest rates and expected volatility. There are strong parallels with portfolio insurance during the Crash. Such instruments could exert increasing pressure on currencies when central banks raise their discount rates, contrary to the authorities' expectations, because they require the short position in the currency in question to be made shorter when the spread between the attacked currency's interest rate and domestic interest rates rises. In addition, according to the IMF, illiquidity in the cash and derivatives markets, by making such dynamic hedging strategies less viable, would often lead portfolio managers to shift to 100 per cent hedged positions using futures, which would entail further selling of weak currencies.

The issue for monetary policy raised by the crisis was the need to raise interest rates sufficiently to offset speculative pressures, at a time when economies were often undergoing a recession, so as to retain the ongoing counter-inflationary benefit of a currency peg. The UK, Italy and the Nordic countries proved unable to retain their pegs, while the ERM bands had to be widened for all the remaining ERM currencies except the Netherlands. Notably for the latter group, the degree to which fundamentals such as the misalignment of real exchange rates warranted pressures on nominal exchange rates is open to doubt.

2.3. Bond Markets in 1994

In early 1994, as a consequence of a wave of one-way selling, bond yields rose sharply — albeit not by identical amounts — in all major countries, after having declined to historically low levels in 1993. An important trigger was the rise in US interest rates that took place in early 1994, and which was seen as the turning point in the interest rate cycle; also monetary growth in Germany was well above target at this point, and evidence was emerging of a more rapid recovery in Europe than had been previously anticipated. This sharp adjustment in bond prices shared a number of the features outlined in Section 2.2 above. The players were similar to the ERM crisis, in that hedge funds, investment banks and institutional investors from outside the countries concerned had built up large open positions and were the main sellers of government bonds during the adjustment. Foreign holdings of bonds stood at high levels (Table 2). Trading volumes were atypically large. Furthermore, there was felt to be an important role for derivatives markets (due to proxy hedging) in helping to drive bond markets down together, including those where the fundamentals were relatively favourable but which had liquid futures markets. Leveraged positions taken through the derivatives markets may have been one reason for rapid selling, although most open positions were not leveraged. Stop-loss orders, often driven by the risk management systems of securities houses' trading desks, also played an important role.

Most crucially, prior to the adjustment the market had adopted strong views regarding future trends in exchange rates and interest rates, generating historically low levels of bond yields prior to the crisis. The low level of US interest rates may have contributed to this. But also as noted by EMI (1995), "bond prices can become detached from underlying fundamentals as extrapolative or "chartist" expectations of future decreases in bond yields became self-fulfilling". The correction of these expectations, as in the case of the convergence plays, unleashed a wave of selling, notably by cross border investors and leveraged players (including some mutual and hedge funds) which induced a major price adjustment. As noted by BIS (1995), "it is not clear that the arrival of new information was sufficient to justify the average intensity of the response". A major role was also reportedly played by retail investors operating via mutual funds, which bought heavily in 1993 and sold in the downturn of the market.

The bond market adjustment was considered to be of major relevance as a signal of market concern over fiscal policy, of lack of credibility of monetary policies and in some countries as a signal of actual inflationary pressures. But there was widespread recognition that the quality of such signals may have been adversely affected by the previous overvaluation of bonds. The rise in yields also in itself entailed a tightening of monetary conditions, that may have helped to slow output growth.

2.4. The Mexican Crisis of 1994–5

The collapse of the Peso exchange rate in late 1994 and the severe financing difficulties undergone afterwards by the Mexican authorities have also been traced back partly to the behaviour of institutional investors. In common with many other developing countries, Mexico was the recipient of major capital inflows during the late 1980s and early 1990s. Most of these were in the form of portfolio investment[16] and direct investment rather than bank loans. Inflows were encouraged by prudent macroeconomic policies (which reduced inflation and the government deficit and stabilised the exchange rate), privatisation, structural reform and improved economic prospects as a consequence of the North American Free Trade Agreement (NAFTA). However, the large capital inflows, in the context of a quasi fixed exchange rate regime[17] and inability to sterilise the effects of the inflows on domestic monetary conditions, led to an appreciation of the real exchange rate and an increase in the current account deficit. Much of the latter was related to increased consumption and lower saving.

An output slowdown in 1993 — related to restructuring of firms in manufacturing, uncertainty about NAFTA and tightening of credit conditions — did not interrupt capital flows unduly nor threaten the exchange rate regime. Indeed the fall in bond yields in the US and other OECD countries led to a growing willingness by mutual funds to pour funds into countries such as Mexico — seeking a higher risk/return trade-off. As noted by Reisen

(1995), such funds must publish valuations daily and have sufficient cash to repay holders at times of crisis so are potentially unstable holders. Potential longer term investors such as pension funds often limited their investment in countries such as Mexico owing to low credit ratings.

In 1994 a degree of fiscal expansion was envisaged, while not threatening balance in the public sector. Approval of NAFTA was expected to lead to growing foreign direct investment as well as stimulating exports. Growth resumed and inflation fell to the lowest — 7 per cent — for many years, although the external deficit expanded, along with imports and private sector expenditures. But the year was marked by growing financial turbulence ending in a balance of payments crisis in November. A key factor was the strong growth in the US, as well as recovery in other industrial countries, which increased the global demand for investment funds, and the partly-related rise in bond yields noted in Section 2.3 above. This made international investors reassess emerging markets. Mexico suffered particularly because of domestic political unrest. The assassination of the Presidential candidate Colosio in March led to a cessation of capital inflows and drain on reserves; pressure on the exchange rate was combated by allowing the interest rate to rise sharply, as well as a credit line from the US and Canada. Peso denominated bonds were in the ensuing months swapped for Tesobonos, short term bonds indexed to the US Dollar but repayable in Pesos. Private credit increased sharply. After an election in November, rumours of a new exchange rate regime and knowledge that Tesobonos were due for rollover provoked a flight from the currency and massive loss of reserves, while the interest rate was *not* increased; finally the rate was allowed to float on 20 December. Rating agencies downgraded the country. These led to a loss of confidence both in the currency and in Mexico's willingness to service its external debt. Private sector borrowers were also badly affected. By end-January, when the exchange rate had fallen 40 per cent despite very high interest rates, the international community agreed a rescue package to forestall default on Tesobonos.[18]

According to IMF (1995), domestic and external shocks contributed to the crisis, by leading investors to question aspects of the overall situation they had hitherto chosen to ignore. But this was exacerbated by accommodating monetary policy that proved incompatible with the exchange rate. These together led institutions to consider the current account unsustainable, a concern that may be warranted in the light of the large capital inflows since 1990 having financed consumption rather than investment, as evidenced by the fall in national saving. Such concerns on the part of fund managers were aggravated by the scale of redemptions by retail investors in mutual funds (including personal pension assets in "401(k)" accounts). As an example, a major mutual fund cut its exposure from $9 billion to $250 million during the crisis, before beginning to buy in March. Many funds were obliged to sell assets in other unrelated markets, thus spreading contagion elsewhere.

The policy implications of the crisis were considerable, not merely for the inflationary and funding risks to the Mexican economy, but also for leading to concern that there would be a domino effect on emerging economies which were also reliant on capital inflows, although this was disputed. This concern was the basis for the international loans advanced to Mexico in early 1995, as well as the extension of IMF "early warning" surveillance and own-funds. It also led to deeper consideration of the usefulness of temporary controls on capital inflows.

3. CONCLUSIONS

It is suggested that the events outlined above, whose effects are consistent with theory, have a number of common features, consideration of which may enable similar patterns in the future to be more easily detected, to offer clues about the appropriate response of the authorities, and provide a background for future research. These included:

- heavy involvement of institutional investors in both buying and selling waves
- bank lending played a rather subordinate role
- international investment
- signs of overreaction to the fundamentals and excessive optimism prior to the crisis
- at times, inappropriate monetary policies
- a shock to confidence which precipitated the crisis, albeit not necessarily sufficient in itself to explain the scale of the reaction
- rapid and wholesale shifts between markets, often facilitated by financial innovations.

This paper does not seek to argue that markets are *always* subject to excess volatility and deviations from fundamentals (indeed, *average* day to day volatility shows no tendency to increase). Nonetheless, these features suggest that the stylised forms of behaviour outlined in Section 1, and empirically tested thus far in rather restricted market situations, are now *intermittently-recurrent* characteristics of a globalised financial market dominated by institutional traders. There seems to be little evidence of "learning" that might make such events less common in the future.

This section now goes on to seek to draw tentative policy conclusions for monetary policy. Policymaking in an institutionalised and globalised environment is clearly a more difficult and uncertain process than in a purely domestic and retail/bank based setting. Notably for countries defending exchange-rate pegs, the rapidity with which markets are able to react to news shortens the reaction times required of central banks, and necessitates action on the basis of less complete information. Reserves are likely to be wholly inadequate against the scale of transactions that institutions can undertake; hence greater stress is placed on the interest rate weapon in defending the currency, which may have adverse repercussions for the economy, and may be counterproductive if considered by markets to be unsustainable.

Bond-market globalisation, and the consequent tendency for foreign yields to have a greater influence on domestic bond markets, reduces the influence of domestic inflation expectations and short term interest rates on domestic long rates, and hence may diminish the leverage of domestic monetary policy over the economy. On the other hand, the sensitivity of bond yields to lax monetary and fiscal policy may be seen as a useful discipline, which may buttress central bank arguments for monetary stringency and fiscal consolidation vis-à-vis politicians. Third, the possibility of overshooting and movement for non-fundamental reasons reduces the clarity of the signals that may be derived from bond yields. Conventionally these are seen as composed of three components, real yields, inflation expectations and uncertainty, where the use of index linked bond yields and volatility of options prices enable an idea to be obtained of the size and movement of the inflation component. But the possibility of overshooting makes this approach potentially inaccurate.

To the extent that equity, foreign-exchange and bond-market adjustments become recurrent features of international capital markets, monetary policymakers generally will have to take increasing account of the views and expectations of the global financial markets concerning their monetary policy and economic developments. Policy actions which are not well explained may generate heightened volatility. Talking to both domestic and foreign institutions on a regular basis may be warranted. Policymakers will need to be aware that, whereas markets may at times work on the basis of fundamentals and hence impose useful discipline on policymakers, at other times they may be subject to bubbles or trend chasing "amplifying the disruptive implications of collective misjudgements" in the words of BIS (1995). Massive and undetected overhangs of open positions may develop in markets, to be sharply unwound when the underlying market assumptions are proved incorrect. These issues make convergence of economies — notably in adopting fiscal consolidation, but also low inflation and provision of a "nominal anchor" — and cooperation between authorities yet more important. They may also present major dilemmas to the authorities when there is a potential conflict between growth and counter-inflation objectives, or indeed between monetary and financial stability more generally. They imply a need for improved capital account statistics to detect movements at an early stage and also data on distribution of shares and bonds across the household[19] and institutional sectors to calibrate wealth effects of market-shifts.

Some analysts would go further and criticise the "asymmetric" behaviour of the authorities themselves, which may worsen instability. They may be excessively willing to claim credibility as a consequence of falling bond yields rather than conceding that yields have undershot. Equally, there is rarely concern over rising share prices, and real misalignments in exchange rates are often disregarded as long as spot rates remain stable. Convergence plays were seen as votes of confidence in the respective economies.

The broader issue of *capital controls* for all transactions remains a potential response to exchange rate instability, but most OECD countries have concluded that the benefits of open international capital markets, in terms of cost and efficient allocation of funds, for finance of economic development, budget and trade deficits is too valuable to be cast aside. Practice with controls showed they were often circumvented or subject to loopholes. Moreover, temporary introduction of exchange controls in a crisis would probably raise the risk premium on assets denominated in the currency concerned for a considerable period, and lead markets to anticipate their introduction in advance during the next crisis, thus aggravating the situation.

Others have revived the issue of the so-called *Tobin tax* on gross foreign exchange transactions to slow the response of financial markets to news (Eichengreen, Tobin and Wyplosz, 1995); others point out the well known shortcomings of this suggestion (Garber and Taylor, 1995), notably that a country imposing such taxes unilaterally would face disintermediation. Moreover, a tax imposed globally could still be avoided by undertaking of separate positions and transactions to mimic a foreign exchange deal, particularly via use of derivatives, necessitating application to an ever-wider range of instruments. And since success of such a tax would likely entail a decline in liquidity, and liquidity tends to be stabilising, it might have directly counterproductive effects on volatility.

A further point of major debate in the wake of the Mexican crisis was whether an *international lender of last resort for countries* is also needed. As noted, the IMF's funds have been increased to help it play such a role.

It is important to add in conclusion that internationalisation of portfolios is still in its infancy, while institutions themselves continue to show rapid growth, so these problems for policymakers are unlikely to recede. Moreover, the internationalisation of holdings of domestic securities such as government bonds seems likely to persist. These make further empirical investigation of the behaviour of global capital flows and the decision making processes of institutions all the more important. In our view, the following may inter alia prove fruitful avenues of research: interview surveys of fund managers' views on the constraints and pressures to which they are subject, pinpointing the precise forms of behaviour adopted; monitoring trades of a selection of managers in a global, cross-market context to detect "cross market herding"; and tests of whether deviations of prices from fundamentals actually *do* become more common when markets become pervaded by institutional traders (the evidence on day-to-day volatility at least would seem to be contrary to this expectation).

NOTES

1. It is not of course denied that the patterns illustrated may also have adverse consequences for financial stability and allocational efficiency more generally, see Davis (1994, 1995a and b).

2. Note that performance evaluation over a short period contrasts sharply with the nature of liabilities, whose maturity may extend to 25 years or more for life insurers and pension funds.

3. See also the related papers by Welch (1992) and Banerjee (1992), which assess rational herding, sequential decisions and so-called information cascades, where each decision maker takes into account the decision of previous decision makers in his or her choices, ignoring private information. Note, however, these are not applied specifically to institutions in the way Scharfstein and Stein and Froot et al. are.

4. See Davis (1995a), who, after interviewing 12 fund managers on international investment strategies in London in 1991-93 found "Most of the managers, but particularly those who are external managers, felt some pressure not to underperform relative to their peers, for fear of losing the management contract. Indeed some trustees set an explicit objective to managers not to underperform the median fund — but obviously impossible for all managers. (In contrast, overperformance is not rewarded commensurately — i.e. there is a strong asymmetry in outcomes.) Such behaviour is reinforced by frequent use of bench-marks such as the CAPS median performance indicator (for small funds). This would in turn induce similar behaviour to other managers in terms both of bench-mark level of international investment and choice of market. Managers who could afford to act more freely, perhaps because of their firm's reputation, still felt a need to know the consensus in order to act in a contrarian manner."

5. That is, characterised by events such as market crashes to which probability analysis cannot be applied.

6. See Howell and Cozzini (1992), Davis (1995a).

7. As an example of recent evidence, Lakonishok et al. (1992) show that most US investment management is active, but fund managers consistently underperform the market, for example the equity proportion of US funds (excluding the management fee) underperforms

the S&P 500 index by an average of 1.3 per cent pa over 1983–9, or 2.6 per cent if returns are value weighted. Overperform in some periods is virtually never sustained.

8. Nevertheless, as noted by Grossman and Stiglitz (1980) and Cornell and Roll (1981), the efficient markets hypothesis does not rule out small abnormal returns as an incentive to acquire information, but those acquiring costly information should have only average net returns after the costs of acquiring information are taken into account. In practice, active managers underperform.

9. Abstracting from herding, Blake (1992) notes that volatility may increase with maturity of pension funds, as it implies less inflows, and the need for large and potentially destabilising portfolio shifts to adjust from equities to bonds.

10. Index arbitrage involved buying and selling simultaneously a stock index futures contract and the underlying stocks, so as to profit from any discrepancy (known as spread or basis) between them.

11. On the one hand, any form of strategy which aimed to lock in current values, such as stop-loss selling of equities (selling when the price had fallen to a pre specified level), would equally have induced a rush of sales when the market fell; and this was probably the more prevalent strategy. Also Fortune (1993) suggests that discounts between stock index and futures prices were in fact illusory, resulting from such cash market phenomena as delays in reporting of individual share prices, late openings or trading halts for individual stocks. Moreover Grossman (1988), examining US daily transactions data for 1987 as a whole, found no link from stock market volatility to programme trading.

12. Actual sales of DM by central banks to protect ERM currencies in the second half of 1992 totalled DM 188 billion ($118 billion) (IMF, 1993).

13. Compare De Long et al. (1990) outlined in Section 1.

14. Both life insurers and pension funds in a number of EU countries remain heavily restricted in their international investment.

15. Note in this context that internationalisation of portfolios may have an effect on exchange rates independent of the volume of assets outstanding only when international investors behave differently to those who are domestically based owing to home asset preference.

16. Personal contacts of Mexican officials to fund managers were reportedly an important aspect.

17. The rate was fixed in 1988 then allowed to depreciate at a preannounced rate.

18. Sachs et al. (1995) note strong parallels to a bank run.

19. The implications of large losses to a few rich individuals will differ from a more widely distributed effect, while indirect holdings via pension funds may mean short-term fluctuations are seen as irrelevant to ultimate beneficiaries.

REFERENCES

Bank for International Settlements (1993). *63rd Annual Report*, BIS Basle.
Bank for International Settlements (1995). *65th Annual Report*, BIS Basle.
Banerjee, A. (1992). A simple model of herd behaviour, *Quarterly Journal of Economics*, 57, 797-817.

Bertero, E. and C. Mayer (1989). Structure and performance: global interdependence of stock markets around the crash of October 1987, Discussion Paper No 307, Centre for Economic Policy Research, London.

Blake, D. (1992). *Issues in pension funding*, Routledge, London.

Brady, N. (1989). Report of the presidential task force on market mechanisms, US Government Printing Office, Washington DC.

Cartapanis, A. (1993). Le rôle déstabilisant des mouvements de capitaux sur le marché des changes: une question de contexte, paper presented at the XIIIème Colloque Banque de France-Université, November 1993.

Cody, B.J.(1989). Imposing exchange controls to dampen currency speculation, *European Economic Review*.

Cornell, B. and R. Roll (1981). Strategies for pairwise competitions in markets and organisations, *Bell Journal of Economics*, 12, 201-3.

Cutler, D., J. Poterba and L. Summers (1990). Speculative Dynamics and the role of feedback traders, *American Economic Review*, 80, Papers and Proceedings.

Davis, E.P. (1994). Market liquidity risk, in eds. Fair, D. and R. Raymond, *The Competitiveness of Financial Institutions and Centres in Europe*, Kluwer Academic Publishers.

Davis, E.P. (1995a). *Pension funds, retirement-income security and capital markets - An international perspective*, Oxford University Press.

Davis, E.P. (1995b). *Debt, financial fragility and systemic risk, revised and extended version*, Oxford University Press.

De Grauwe, P. (1989). *International money; post war trends and theories*, Clarendon Press, Oxford.

DeLong, J.B., A. Shleifer, L. Summers, and R. Waldman (1990). Positive feedback investment strategies and destabilising rational speculation, *Journal of Finance*, 45, 379-95.

Dornbusch, R. (1990). It's time for a financial transactions tax, *International Economy*.

Eichengreen, B., J. Tobin, and C. Wyplosz (1995). Two cases for sand in the wheels of international finance, *Economic Journal*, 105, 162-72.

EMI (1995). *Annual Report 1994*, European Monetary Institute, Frankfurt.

Evans, M. and K.K. Lewis (1993). Trends in excess returns in currency and bond markets, *European Economic Review*.

Fama, E.F. and K.R. French (1988). Permanent and temporary components of stock prices, *Journal of Political Economy*, 96, 246-73.

Fortune, P. (1993). Stock market crashes; what have we learned from October 1987, *New England Economic Review*, March/April,

Frankel, J.A. and K.A. Froot (1989). Chartists, fundamentalists, and the demand for dollars, in Anthony Courakis and Mark Taylor, eds.: *Policy Issues for Interdependent Economies*, MacMillan, London.

Friedman, Milton (1953), The case for flexible exchange rates, in Milton Friedman, ed.: *Essays in Positive Economics*, University of Chicago Press, Chicago, IL.

Frijns, J., R. Kleynen and F. Quix (1995). *Risk management from the perspective of the economic functions of different financial institutions.*

Froot, K.A., D.S. Scharfstein, and J.C. Stein (1992). Herd on the Street: Informational Inefficiencies in a Market with Short-Term Speculation, *The Journal of Finance*, 47, 1461-84.

Garber, P. and M.P. Taylor (1995). Sand in the wheels of foreign exchange markets, a sceptical note, *Economic Journal*, 105, 173-80.

Gros, D. (1992). Capital controls and foreign exchange crises in the ERM, *European Economic Review*.

Grossman, S. (1988). Program trading and market volatility; a report on interday relationships, *Financial Analysts Journal*, July-August, 18-28.

Grossman, S. and J.E. Stiglitz (1980). On the impossibility of informationally efficient markets, *American Economic Review*, 70, 393-408.

Howell, M. and A. Cozzini (1991). *Games without frontiers; global equity markets in the 1990s* , Salomon Bros., London.

Howell, M. and A. Cozzini (1992). *Baring Brothers' Capital Flows 1991/2 Review* , Baring Brothers, London.

IMF (1993). *International Capital Markets Part I. Exchange rate management and international capital flows*, International Monetary Fund, Washington DC.

IMF (1995). *World Economic Outlook*, IMF Washington.

Keynes, J.M. (1936). *General theory of employment, interest and money*, MacMillan, London.

Lakonishok, J., A. Schleifer and R.W. Vishny (1991). Do institutional investors destabilize share prices: Evidence on herding and feedback trading, Working Paper No. 3846, National bureau of Economic Research.

Lakonishok, J., A. Schleifer and R.W. Vishny (1992). The structure and performance of the money management industry, *Brookings Papers: Microeconomics* 1992, 339-91.

Lo, A. and C. MacKinlay (1988). Stock prices do not follow random walks: Evidence from a simple specification test, NBER Working Paper 2168.

Raymond, R. (1990). Conduite d'une politique monétaire nationale au sein d'une zone monétaire, *Cahiers Économiques et Monétaires de la Banque de France,* 30.

Reisen, H. (1995). Managing Temporary Capital Inflows, Lessons from Asia and Latin America, Mimeo, OECD Development Centre.

Sachs, J., A. Tornell and A. Velasco (1995). The collapse of the Mexican Peso, what have we learned, Working Paper No. 5142, National Bureau of Economic Research.

Scharfstein, D.S. and J.C. Stein (1990). Herd behaviour and investment, *American Economic Review*, 80, 465-79.

Shiller, Robert (1988). Portfolio insurance and other investor fashions as factors in the 1987 stock market crash, NBER Macroeconomics Annual.

Shiller R.J. and J. Pound (1989). Survey evidence of diffusion of interest and information among institutional investors, *Journal of Economic Behaviour and Organisation*, 47-66.

Welch, I. (1992). Sequential sales, learning and cascades, *Journal of Finance*, 47, 695-732.

WM (1995). *WM UK pension fund service annual review, 1994*, The WM Company.

Internal Organisation of Risk Control and Management in a Bank with Large International Operations

Summary

Transacting interest rate and foreign exchange products with customers and banks expose a bank to fluctuations in market rates. The author demonstrates how the risk implications of such exposures can be measured and how an internal control system has to be designed and implemented in order to protect a bank against serious losses.

The development of trading organisations in banks in the last ten years shows a clear trend towards risk orientation. Furthermore globalisation and complex financial products require a high level of technical and mathematical skills for risk managers. The focus is on processes of managing and controlling market risk.

The ability to quantify market risk is a prerequisite for risk management and risk control. Much research remains to be done in this area. Nevertheless, applying the right pragmatic approaches allows a bank to set up an effective risk control organisation. Risk control is not only a methodological challenge, its implementation also requires significant education on all hierarchical levels and may very well affect the way the overall trading business is managed.

The information provided by risk control leads to further decisions being taken by senior management (e.g. defining the maximum market risk that a firm is willing to take). Such decisions require close co-operation between risk control and top management.

Some of the control functions are to be included in the operations area (especially in settlements and financial control). Besides segregation of duties, a quality-oriented design of the processes in operations and well-trained personnel play an important role in a trading organisation.

Robert S. Gumerlock is head of Operations and Control at SBC Warburg, a Division of Swiss Bank Corporation. He is a member of the Executive Board of SBC Warburg. After his studies at the University of Notre Dame, South Bend (Indiana) in 1975, he obtained a Masters Degree in Mathematics from Northwestern University, Evanston (Illinois) in 1978. He then took up employment with O'Connor & Associates, a Chicago options-trading boutique, where he had various responsibilities, including mathematical research, trader recruiting and education, floor trading in San Francisco and business management in the London subsidiary. With the acquisition of O'Connor & Associates by Swiss Bank Corporation in 1992, he moved to Zurich to direct the centralisation of market risk control across all of the bank's trading operations including Capital Markets, Treasury and Derivatives. In 1994 he became head of Financial Control as well, and since 1995 he has been also responsible for Operations and Services at SBC Warburg world-wide.

IX. Internal Organisation of Risk Control and Management in a Bank with Large International Operations

ROBERT S. GUMERLOCK

1. RISK MANAGEMENT ORGANISATION

1.1. The Development of Trading Organisations Towards Risk Orientation

Comparing a typical organisation structure of a trading organisation of today and of ten years ago, we observe several significant differences.

Today's trading organisations are typically organised around the three major classes of market risk, namely foreign exchange, interest rates, and equities. This structure has also been recommended by the regulatory authorities. Ten years ago, a bank's trading organisation may have distinguished between foreign exchange/money markets, primary markets and secondary markets.

Whereas in the past an organisation may have been subdivided into treasury services, cash securities, futures and options, today the preference lies in organising the business along risk sub-categories (e.g. a currency pair or a particular equity market). Synergies can be achieved by managing derivatives together with their underlying instruments.

In the past, many banks were organised regionally, today a specific market risk is preferably managed centrally in one global book. The advantages of a concentration with respect to (round-the-clock) risk management and risk control easily compensate the disadvantages of decreased risk-diversification and potential tax problems.

Furthermore, in the past, settlement, middle and back office functions were often allocated to the trading areas, whereas today the concept of segregation of duties requires separate management.

This development in internal organisation structures reflects the development in the financial markets. Globalisation and the need for sophisticated exposure management techniques, especially for derivative products created the need for the function "risk management", for "risk managers", and — after some unsuccessful experiences — for an elaborate risk control.

We are aware of the many different types of risk that occur in trading, however, in the sequel the emphasis is on market risk.

1.2. Risk Management – A Definition

The function of risk management is to ensure that the exposures entered into are consistent with the objectives of each trading area and that unwanted risks are hedged or closed out. Risk management is the responsibility of the head of a trading area. Head traders are sometimes also called risk managers, a term which emphasises their central place in protecting the institution against risk as well as the very active nature of their particular role.

We distinguish between risk management and risk control. Risk control is responsible for ensuring that the risks entered into are consistent with the limits and authorities which have been delegated to the trading areas. It also advises management on new risks which may not have been foreseen within the limit structure and it suggests new controls as they are required. Risk Control does not guarantee that no money will ever be lost in trading (which is impossible to achieve), but it does ensure that risks taken are within pre-set parameters (loss limits).

2. QUANTIFICATION, AGGREGATION AND LIMIT STRUCTURES

2.1. Market Risk Quantification

To manage and control market risk, we have to be able to quantify it. In its recommendations "Derivatives: Practices and Principles", the Derivatives Study Group of the Group of Thirty suggests use of a value-at-risk concept to measure market risk.

Measuring Market Risk (G30 recommendation #5)
Dealers should use a consistent measure to calculate daily the market risk of their derivatives positions and compare it to market risk limits.

i) Market risk is best measured as value at risk using probability analysis based upon a common confidence interval (e.g., two standard deviations) and time horizon (e.g., a one-day exposure).

ii) Components of market risk that should be considered across the term structure include: absolute price or rate change (delta); convexity (gamma); volatility (vega); time decay (theta); basis or correlation; and discount rate (rho).

Without going into detail, market risk measurement can be subdivided into value-at-risk, model risk, and stress event risk. Value-at-risk is based on an assumed or observed distribution of revenues; it is thus the probability-based component quantifying a loss that will not be exceeded within a given time period and with a predefined probability. It is based on the assumption that future market dynamics (volatilities and correlations) behave the same as in the past. The accuracy of this risk measure, given an "un-stressed" market environment, depends on the quality of a firm's value-at-risk implementation. Key issues are the selection of risk factors, the model and the aggregation techniques within a product class (e.g. equities).

Value-at-risk, then, is a firm's baseline risk measure which reflects the integrity of its internal methods. Recognising that no model is perfect, an adjustment to this estimate is necessary to account for modelling imprecision. We label this source of uncertainty "model risk". Since value-at-risk is a probability-based measure, the general level of model risk is quantifiable, over time, by measuring how well the value-at-risk estimates describe the actual profit and loss distribution. A well devised back-testing methodology provides the mechanism for this assessment and should be used as the basis for calculating an appropriate model risk adjustment factor.

2.2. Stress Testing

This adjusted value-at-risk estimate captures the risk of statistically predictable market events which include extremes of the order of two to three standard deviations, but not the outliers that result in times of market distress. These market conditions are characterised by illiquidity, risk factor moves well beyond three standard deviations, and a complete breakdown in correlations. Stress testing is designed to measure the potential size of this risk, which we refer to as "stress event risk". This risk is largely subjective, and the key to its measurement is to identify the scenarios that represent "the rare event".

Stress Simulations (G30 recommendation #6)

Dealers should regularly perform simulations to determine how their portfolios would perform under stress conditions.

2.3. Aggregation

An overall stress scenario can be characterised by risk factor moves within a predefined holding period and by the correlations applied for aggregation. Assuming a correlation of zero will most likely underestimate the aggregate risk, using a correlation of one will most certainly overstate it, although this case covers the risk of unstable correlations. Furthermore, since stress tests are based on an unchanged portfolio, which means that the stress scenario assumes that no additional trades are done during a market shock, one can argue that stress testing also covers the market liquidity risk, at least for the underlying holding period.

Stress testing can be considered as a robust pragmatic approach for quantifying market risk.

2.4. Relation to the Regulators

Risk quantification also provides the basis for any attempt to underlie market risk with capital. Besides the classic static measurement systems that are already used to define the capital adequacy requirements, the BIS alternatively includes a model approach in their recommendations. It can be considered a "quantum leap" in regulations to let banks measure their market risk for capital adequacy purposes according to their own model provided that the model suffices to a certain standard; and the primary question should not focus on whether an institution's internal models can be used, but rather at what level of confidence risk should be measured.

This is also a step towards decreasing the gap between regulations and the "economic reality" recognised for managing the firm. Perhaps this even means an end to the interminable discussions on return on regulatory capital versus return on risk-adjusted capital.

3. RISK CONTROL

Risk control is, in short, the oversight of activities of management who evaluate, monitor, and, when necessary, contain the risk management of the firm.

3.1. Another Demarcation to Risk Management

As practised in the major institutions, risk control grew to supplement the expertise of traders and the risk managers. Risk managers can react very quickly in liquid markets, therefore they can afford a short term view and hence tend to be concerned with portfolio simulations whose range is only a few tics. In their view any broader simulation like stress testing seems unrealistic, because it does not include the trades that would have been done while the market moves to a new level. This "assumption of liquidity" is perhaps the major axiomatic difference in outlook between risk managers and risk controllers.

Risk control is a decidedly more passive endeavour than risk management and supplements the primarily short term view of the risk manager. Risk control considers wider moves in market factors ("market shocks") than traders. Risk controllers generally apply the stress testing to the portfolio as it presently stands and make no attempt to project what additional trades might have been done.

A risk control professional has to mediate between the firm's board and the traders, assessing risk tolerance of the board and translating that into quantitative constraints that are relevant to traders on their own terms.

3.2. The Function

The responsibilities of a risk control group can be summarised as follows:

– to recommend to the group board and, if approved, to the board of directors, a risk limit structure that ensures the level of risk being taken by the trading businesses is commensurate with its "risk appetite" and capital structure;

– to monitor actual risk exposures by business line daily (sub-analysed by risk type) and report consolidated global exposures to senior management of both general and trading management. All excesses over approved limits are detected and investigated daily and must be approved by senior management. Prompt action is taken to ensure that all limit excesses are either rectified or approved at the appropriate level of authority;

– to monitor daily movements in reported profit and loss and review these against the reported risk exposures to ensure that the two are consistent. Apparent inconsistencies are investigated and reported;

– to review the adequacy of the limit structure and recommend improvements as and when necessary. In particular, the effectiveness of the limit structure is reviewed following any major market movement to assess its effectiveness in predicting the effect on the firm's positions;

– to provide the senior management with a daily report on market risks and the resulting profit and loss, and to produce more detailed weekly and monthly reports for the attention of the board. It also establishes analyses which help senior management to understand better where and how revenues are being earned.

3.3. The Organisation

The organisation of a global risk control has to be in line with the underlying corporate philosophy. The two extreme solutions are

- having a group that does risk management and aggregation across the businesses, monitors and controls risk limits and performance targets, performs stress testing and does further development, and
- having a small group that receives data in a specified format, which is restricted to aggregate and check risk limits. This approach might not work in a hierarchical environment.

Fundamental to the risk control process is its independence from the origination, sales and trading groups of the different businesses. At Swiss Bank Corporation, the risk control function is performed by a global team of 40 people with functional managers in each time zone. The link between risk control, trading and senior management is performed by a risk management committee where issues like trading policy, limits system, methodology, reporting structure and planning as well as recent events are discussed.

3.4. Skills Required

To be a good market risk controller, trading experience is necessary. Somebody who is not familiar with the trading areas will possibly neither be able to perform a control function nor be accepted by the traders. He might not succeed in obtaining the necessary information. A trader's day consists of profits and losses, and he or she is reluctant to share information about losses. However, under our existing value system it is difficult to convince someone who has the skills and knowledge to be an excellent trader or even risk manager of "high tech" products not to trade but to do risk control. The culture of the bank, the remuneration system and the career plans have to provide material support in this regard.

3.5. Independent Market Risk Control

Following the "Barings incident", the principle of segregation of duties, of an independent market risk control function is not subject to discussion anymore.
Independent Market Risk Control (G30 recommendation #8)
Dealers should have a market risk control function, with clear independence and authority, to ensure that the following responsibilities are carried out:
   i) The development of risk limit policies and the monitoring of transactions and positions for adherence to these policies.
   ii) The design of stress scenarios to measure the impact of market conditions, however improbable, that might cause market gaps, volatility swings, or disruptions of major relationships, or might reduce liquidity in the face of unfavourable market linkages, concentrated market making, or credit exhaustion.

iii) The design of revenue reports quantifying the contribution of various risk components, and of market risk measures such as value at risk.

iv) The monitoring of variance between the actual volatility of portfolio value and that predicted by the measure of market risk.

v) The review and approval of pricing models and valuation systems used by front- and back-office personnel, and the development of reconciliation procedures if different systems are used.

However, it is one thing to design independence on the organisation chart, to maintain independence in daily business is quite different. Having a powerful and skilled risk control, this knowledge potential will probably not only be used for control, but also for education and consulting. Since there needs to be a close contact between risk control and trading, there is a tendency that risk controllers are being involved in business by the traders through in advance approval of methods, transactions or new products.

3.6. Setting Up a Control Process

Setting up a risk control function requires a clear concept on the methodological approach and a risk control organisation. The latter may not be underestimated. Hiring and training the local teams, a satisfactory information flow from the trading area, the infrastructure for establishing and transmitting the risk profiles for each book on a daily basis, and the implementation of quality checks tend to be very time consuming, and the risk control teams need to get acceptance from the trading areas.

While it is relatively easy to get approval for a limit system, it may be a lengthy process to quantify and allocate sublimits to businesses. Once business restrictions are quantified, there is not much room left for interpretation. Such quantification processes are in fact very often processes of working out an in-depth agreement on how a business is managed and on the responsibilities, authorities, measures and goals.

4. SENIOR MANAGEMENT

Senior management is the most important customer of market risk control. The rise of risk control as an independent function mediating between risk managers and board-level senior management is a recent phenomenon. It may relate to the concern of senior management to ensure that it is represented by someone with the same skills in mathematics as traders.

The Role of Senior Management (G30 recommendation #1)

Dealers and end-users should use derivatives in a manner consistent with the overall risk management and capital policies approved by their boards of directors. These policies should be reviewed as business and market circumstances change. Policies governing derivatives should be clearly defined, including the purposes for which these transactions are to be undertaken. Senior management should approve procedures and controls to implement these policies, and management at all levels should enforce them.

Besides determining the strategic direction, senior management has to decide on an overall risk limit and to include the quality of revenues in their considerations.

4.1. The Quality of Earnings and Profits

A quality criterion for earnings is stability. Customer related earnings tend to be less volatile than profits from proprietary trading. The management information systems thus have to provide an answer to the question of how the revenues are earned. The quality of the profits additionally takes into consideration the cost base.

Identifying Revenue Sources (G30 recommendation #4)

Dealers should measure the components of revenue regularly and in sufficient detail to understand the sources of risk.

4.2. The Risk Limit

When using stress testing, the risk measure and therefore also the risk limit is related to a stress scenario. What can be considered a sound risk limit, what is a reasonable "risk appetite" for a bank? Classical approaches set the risk limit in relation to capital or revenues. To intuitively compare a deterministic figure like capital with a stochastic value like risk at least creates a feeling of uncertainty. This is an area where risk control and senior management have to work together closely.

When setting a risk limit in relation to revenues, we have to take into consideration the quality of these revenues. A bank with a high percentage of "stable" earnings can afford a higher risk appetite than a bank whose earnings primarily result out of proprietary trading.

5. SYSTEMS AND OPERATIONS

In addition to the market risk control group, there are a number of other organisational units involved in the overall control process. These include operations, financial control, internal audit, and compliance. Therefore, strict segregation of duties is maintained so that in no instance a trader or salesman can exert any influence over the operational and financial control process.

Operations and financial control have specific responsibilities for ensuring the integrity of data in the various systems in use. A number of controls and reconciliations have to be performed daily or periodically to ensure integrity of data in the front office risk management systems used by both the traders and risk control.

Furthermore, valuations, especially of over-the-counter products where there is no listed price, have to be checked.

This again requires well-trained people in the operations areas. We believe that a continuing commitment to education is vital in a business where product complexity and innovation are almost constantly changing. Swiss Bank Corporation, e.g., has its own dedicated Education Department staffed by experienced professionals with a wide knowledge of risk management techniques and products. A key objective of the education program is that the staff in the control and operational areas attends the same education programs as the sales and trading staff. This focus on training and development of support staff ensures that there is a good understanding of the products and businesses of the bank and that the support areas are able to keep pace with the variety and complexity of business being undertaken.

Professional Expertise (G30 recommendation #16)

Dealers and end-users must ensure that their derivatives activities are undertaken by professionals in sufficient number and with the appropriate experience, skill levels, and degrees of specialization. These professionals include specialists who transact and manage the risks involved, their supervisors, and those responsible for processing, reporting, controlling, and auditing the activities.

Besides the mathematical and technical challenges, the process towards a risk management and risk control organisation is also a process of working out a well defined management environment and a process towards an in-depth understanding of the business.

Currency Exposure Management within Philips

Summary

It is a major challenge to embed modern financial technology in the continuously changing organisational structure of a multinational company. The processes generating cash flow are to be controlled and proper forecasting models are to be implemented. Based on quarterly rolling forecasts the basic information for managing transaction exposures is provided. Clear guidelines from the "internal bank" and involvement of its financial experts in formulating currency policies at a decentralised Products Division level are key success factors in increasing awareness and knowledge at the level where the business decisions are taken.

The risks pertaining to the use of financial instruments are limited by defining the "internal bank" as the sole interface to the external financial institutions and by imposing limits.

The use of statistical analyses indicating the "normal variation" in currency movements is a powerful tool for increasing knowledge about risk. By adopting the use of multi-currency confidence intervals for a portfolio, the business risks can be made visible, and cost-effective policies for protecting margins can be implemented.

Arjen Eelke Ronner graduated from the University of Groningen and he worked there as assistant professor. In 1984 he joined Philips as a senior consultant Statistics and Quality Control and in 1994 was appointed director of the Insurance and Risk Management Department of Philips Finance. He is Professor of Financial Econometrics at the Free University in Amsterdam, where he lectures on financial instruments (derivatives).

Dirk A.M. Trappeniers graduated from the University of Leuven (International Economics). In 1989 he joined Philips and worked mainly at the Centre For Manufacturing Technology (optimization of production lines). In 1994 he joined Philips Finance as Financial Consultant. In 1995 he graduated as Master in Financial Economics from the University of Tilburg.

X. Currency Exposure Management within Philips

ARJEN E. RONNER and DIRK A.M. TRAPPENIERS

> "There is no sphere of human thought in which it is easier
> to show superficial cleverness and the appearance of superior
> wisdom than in discussing questions of currency and exchange."
> *Sir Winston Churchill, 28 September 1949.*

1. INTRODUCTION

As part of risk management, currency exposure management is of major importance to multinational companies. The traditional risks related to international business can be managed more professionally by using advanced financial instruments. Paradoxically, these instruments seem also to enlarge the business risks if their use is not properly controlled. This paper describes current developments in managing currency exposures within the Philips group. In our view, risk management is an integral part of the company's strategy. Increasing the value of the company requires knowledge of the currency exposures, definition of responsibilities, policies and proper control of the processes.

Philips is a multinational company with sales and costs spread all over the world. Accordingly, currency movements are of great importance to the company. A few examples:

- In 1994 approximately 40 per cent of Philips' net sales were in US Dollar or were US Dollar-related, while 32 per cent of costs were in that currency.
- Within five years' time Philips expects a substantial increase in net sales from the Far East region.

Currency exposure management is obviously not a new phenomenon for a multinational company. It has always been a major concern of Philips. For instance, the annual report of 1920 noted:

> "Despite the fact that foreign currencies can fluctuate considerably and surprises are still possible in our foreign production centres — where protection of the internal industry is very high — we are looking to a bright future thanks to significant depreciation of the guilder and the strong cash position of our company."

This paper is structured as follows. In Section 2 the organisation of currency management at Philips is described. In Section 3 definitions are presented for the different exposures (translation, transaction and economic), while Section 4 deals with the various phases of risk management (exposure identification, risk measurement, risk management and transaction execution).

In Section 5 an example of hedging a business exposure is given. An approach for the use of confidence intervals as an indication of values-at-risk is dealt with in Section 6. This approach can play a role in increasing awareness of the currency risks in all parts of the organisation. It provides a yardstick for the measurement and management of the currency risks. Conclusions are presented in Section 7.

2. ORGANISATION OF CURRENCY MANAGEMENT AT PHILIPS

Since the Centurion restructuring process started in 1990, more responsibilities have been decentralized to Product Divisions and Business Groups, independent units in the Product Divisions.[1] Henceforth the abbreviation PD will be used. Management of the PDs is responsible for, among other things, results on currency transactions. The framework for currency management is provided by Philips Finance, the "internal bank". Philips Finance is the sole interface between the PDs and the external financial institutions. Important company values have been formulated and serve as guidelines for internal and external communication. We mention the company values which have been instrumental in defining a currency policy.

- Delight customers.
- Value people as our greatest resource.
- Deliver quality and excellence in all actions.
- Achieve premium return on equity.
- Encourage entrepreneurial behaviour at all levels.

The values in themselves might seem general, but they are a challenge to the "internal bank" to provide the PDs as internal customers with customer-friendly solutions which add value to the company.

Philips Finance operates as an internal bank. It has an operational mandate to be active in financial markets. It is responsible for global funding, treasury management and risk financing and is a profit-oriented cost centre.[2] In this framework Philips Finance defines the financial strategies and policies of the group and supports the PDs in implementing these. The centralization of bank contacts allows economies of scale, greater efficiency and standardization of the policy to be realised.

Currency management is part of doing business, which is why the responsibility for currency management is delegated to the different PDs within Philips. The PDs are responsible for setting up their currency exposure strategy, for organising it, for their risk management.

Despite the fact that the PDs have the main responsibility in their currency exposure management, the role of Philips Finance is such that it guides and monitors the different policies and actions of the PDs. Philips Finance issues guidelines for definitions of exposures, sets limits, gives advice in setting up the exposure management organisation in the PDs, gives advice in the transaction execution part, executes transactions, organizes workshops on the subject and gives presentations.

The execution of the policy, e.g. concluding contracts, is done via the internal bank's local branch offices in the National Organisations (NOs). This network covers more than 60 countries where Philips conducts business activities. The PDs discuss their currency exposure management with the NOs. Finally, the NOs integrate the different policies of the PDs, so that they can give advice and execute the policies accordingly. Philips Finance has the possibility to "net" exposures within company limits and hence add value.

3. DEFINITION AND CALCULATION OF EXPOSURES

Translation Exposure

Translation exposure results from the fact that a foreign affiliate of the holding company has to report and consolidate its financial results in the currency of the "home country" of the holding company. Philips uses the "current rate method" to translate its assets/liabilities. These effects are partly hedged via local financing arrangements and will not be discussed further in this paper.[3]

Transaction Exposure

Transaction exposure results from the fact that transactions were concluded in a foreign currency and that this currency can fluctuate, thereby influencing home currency margins. The currency of denomination/invoicing is of relevance here. This exposure is of importance in the short term (for a period of about one year).[4] The exposure is often hedged via financial instruments because in the short term "real" production changes/movements are mostly not possible.

Economic Exposure

Economic exposure reflects the influence of currency movements on the "value" of the company. The currency of determination is relevant. This is a long-term exposure. Internal hedging/strategic decisions are based on this exposure. Despite the fact that it is very difficult to measure and the variability of the exposure is very large, it gives a first indication and can help reach strategic decisions.

The market value of company X is equal to the discounted figure (discounted by the Weighted Average Cost of Capital) of all expected cash flows in all currencies (currency i; time frame t).[5]

$$\text{Market value } X = \sum_{t=0}^{\infty} E(\text{CF})t/(1 + \text{WACC})$$

$$= \sum_{t=0}^{\infty} \sum_{i=0}^{n} E(\text{CF}^{\text{FC}(i)}) * E(S_{ti})/(1 + \text{WACC}),$$

where $\text{FC}(i)$: Foreign Currency i, $E(S_{ti})$: Exchange Rate of currency i at time t.

Transaction exposure and economic exposure are hedged within Philips via financial instruments or through structural hedging techniques. This will be dealt with below. The relation between the different exposures is presented in Figure 1.

4. RISK MANAGEMENT

There are four main stages in currency risk management: firstly, exposures are to be defined and cash flows in foreign currencies are to be forecast; secondly, risks are to be measured; thirdly, the measured risk is to be managed: and fourthly, decisions have to be executed (see Figure 2). In our experience, exposure identification takes about 60 per cent of the total invested time; risk measurement and management take about 30 per cent of the total time, while transaction execution (plus the follow-up) takes the remaining 10 per cent. A part of the total currency management process has to be done only once (for example, issuing the procedures, defining the reporting and control systems), but a large part has to be done periodically: each period exposures are to be identified, the strategy can be redefined, the authorization file has to be updated and forecasts are to be evaluated.

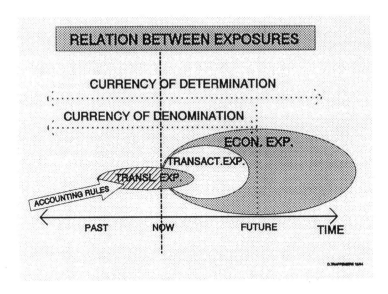

Fig. 1. Relation between exposures

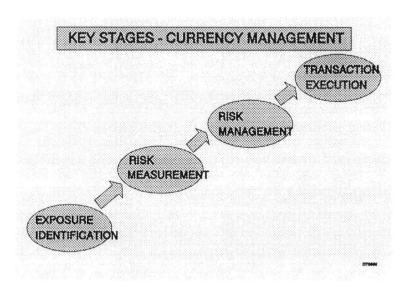

Fig. 2. Key stages - currency exposure management.

In identifying the exposures every quarter the PD calculates cash flow forecasts for the next four quarters (Quarterly Rolling Forecast). This is done by every organisation in the PD, e.g. a sales organisation or a factory. This rolling forecast process started recently, and it is recognized that forecasting requires a continuous process of improvement. We distinguish two types of challenge for improving the cash flow forecasting process: one relates to the knowledge of the business, the other to the finance and accounting systems. On the one hand, business uncertainty makes the forecasting of cash flow difficult. Control of working capital is one of the problems in the accuracy of determining the cash flows.[6] Another difficult item is the translation of the different exposures into the currency of determination. To give an example: a large part of the transactions at Semiconductors are denominated in European currencies, while the currency of determination in most cases is the USD. Currency aspects of divestments and acquisitions also require special attention. On the other hand, the finance and accounting systems are not geared towards cash flow analysis. In Ronner[7] we indicated the importance of proper cash flow analysis and challenges for achieving adequate cash flow analysis in a multinational company: "One of the obstacles to implementing a cash flow- oriented approach and hence improving the cash flow forecasting is that ex-post cash flow analysis is rather limited."

The relatively modest attention devoted to the cash flow in the analysis and interpretation of financial figures is in contrast to the attention devoted to the cash flow in the ex ante investment analysis. The expected cash flow of an investment plan determines to a large extent whether the plan can be financed. In the post-calculation, however, the usual financial ratios from the profit and loss account and balance sheet are often used. As Kaplan[8] states: "In investment decisions, the primary focus is on cash flows. In performance evaluation, however, the emphasis shifts to earnings or earnings-based measures". This discrepancy could be reduced somewhat by measuring after the investment the same variables as are considered to be the yardstick ex ante: the cash flow in relation to (net) assets employed (cash flow from the operation as a percentage of net assets employed). Making a number of assumptions, norms for the long term can be formulated: in a stable situation this percentage could be around the level of the company's cost of capital. Such a ratio emphasises that the investments must be recovered from the cash flow.

Until recently, currency risks at Philips were measured as the absolute value of the net exposure per currency combined with the volatility of the currency. Most attention was given to the major exposures (often split up into three currency blocs: the DEM bloc, the USD bloc and the JPY bloc). In Section 6 we shall deal with a multicurrency portfolio approach.

As a third stage the risks are to be managed at PD level. Policies are to be written, authorization given, procedures set up, strategies defined, limits set, performance measures installed. The organization is to be prepared for the implementation of the currency exposure management.

Most of the short-term transaction exposures are identified in relation to the Rolling Quarterly Forecast. Financial measures are used to protect the short-term currency fluctuations. In Section 5 an example is presented. Strategic review plans have a longer-term horizon and deal with the economic exposure. Structural measures are taken to protect longer-term currency fluctuations; strategic choices often exceed a time frame of ten years. Because of the complexity of the investment decision in addition to standard net present value models, an option-type analysis (real options) can be used. However, the business knowledge should not be lost by applying mathematical models as a black box. In this real-option approach a "platform" is constructed, and when there is an opportunity this platform is expanded.[9] Managers have to take these investment decisions with a large degree of uncertainty. They do not know whether the changing of currency rates is due to the fact that this is only an occasional or a structural change. A certain period of time will pass before the policy is adapted to the currency changes.[10] Figure 3 presents the relation between short and long-term currency problems and the hedging via either the financial markets or the structural adjustments.

In the next stage of risk management, transactions have to be executed. If the policy is well defined this step should not be very complicated for the financial experts. The total portfolio together with the hedge portfolio is to be monitored constantly by marking to market.

The financial instruments available internally are for practical reasons limited to forward contracts, options, combinations of options (often zero-cost constructions like range forwards and participating forwards). Externally, a large range of financial instruments is available.

5. AN EXAMPLE OF A HEDGING STRATEGY

Sensitivity analysis is a very important tool for studying the impact of currency movements on the business, and what actions are needed to reduce this sensitivity. PDs report short-term sensitivity to currency movements. The complexity of the problem should not be underestimated by the financial experts. Sensitivity analysis takes, among other things, the following aspects into account: price agreements, demand elasticities, reactions of competitors, the time-lag needed for price adjustments and for production/capacity adjust-

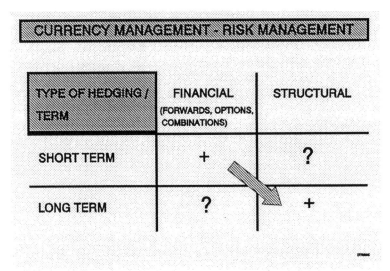

Fig. 3. Financial versus structural hedging.

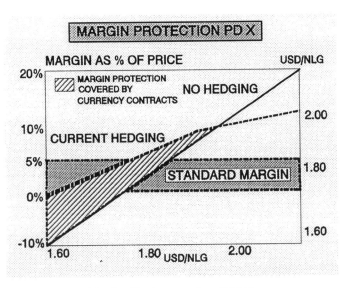

Fig. 4. Margin protection of PD X.

ments, price leader versus follower, the purchasing strategy, subcontracting, the possibility to move to another production location, the predictability of cash flows, the unpredictability of currency movements or stress tests (worst-case scenario). Cooperation between "business" and "finance" is required in order to formulate a suitable business currency strategy.

Depending on the business profiles, the elements of the currency policy are to be determined.

In our view a currency strategy should deal with, among other things, the following questions:

- What is the exposure, how is it measured?
- What are acceptable values of future currency rates, or to phrase it nega-tively, against which rates is cover mandatory?
- What is the volatility, risk profile of the currency portfolio?
- Which period is to be taken into account?

The following example deals with a fairly stable business in which the transaction exposure for a period of approximately one year was discussed with management. The main concern was margin protection, and based on then-prevailing NLG/USD rates of approximately 1.90 NLG/USD a combi-nation of forward contracts, short calls and long puts is presented in Figure 4, which also serves as the basis for a sensitivity analysis.

The strategy was to protect the "standard margin" (assumed to be 5 per cent here). Therefore an acceptable business level exchange rate was set. Furthermore, targets and the level of acceptable risk were agreed. Dynamic monitoring of the position is required in order to protect the value of the portfolio.

6. CONFIDENCE INTERVALS AND VALUE-AT-RISK

Based upon the standard assumptions of e.g. the Black Scholes analysis we can indicate confidence intervals for multicurrency cash flows. We are of the opinion that statistical analysis is also of great value for understanding the impact of currency fluctuations, notwithstanding the fact that the statistical models are not perfect.

Despite all the criticism that can be made of modelling of exchange rates, it should be noted that the pricing of conventional currency options is based on a probabilistic model. I would like to argue on these somewhat pragmatic grounds for the application of this probabilistic model to decisions upon con-fidence intervals for currency flows. A multinational company can attempt in this way to indicate the uncertainty in the total cash flows and to take measures in the financial sector to avoid undesirable effects on the cash flow. Implementation can be relatively simple, as the uncertainties, the so-called volatilities, and interest rates are known for all relevant currency combinations, which is necessary for estimating the confidence intervals within relevant assumptions.

A recent study of the applications of financial instruments within 30 large companies emphasises the importance of quantitative methods.[11]

One of the recommendations was to apply risk concepts in valuing financial entities: "Use probability theory and the usual confidence intervals, volatilities, correlations, normal and lognormal distributions". The study also identifies a need for investment and financing forecasts: "Cash flow forecasts should be made. The translation of cash flows into a value should be made by an expert (dealer)."

Philips is investigating implementing the confidence interval approach in order to define "values at risk". The statistical input needed can be based on historical data, on "implied data", or even on own estimates. All cash flows are broken down into interest rate and foreign exchange risk positions. Correlation between the different foreign exchange and interest rates is taken into account to calculate the risk on the "currency portfolio". The portfolio manager (currency risk manager) has the task of updating the statistical market input and taking the appropriate action. He takes into account the effects of possible hedge actions on the total position.

This statistical approach quantifies, in a way that is in conformity with the market, the risk associated with currency exposures. Besides quantifying the risk, other advantages of the method are:

- It gives the possibility of showing in a uniform way the values at risk.
- Sensitivity analysis is possible by means of simulation; different scenarios can be calculated quickly, by using the same statistical assumptions as in the financial markets.
- Exposures are marked to the market.

7. CONCLUSIONS

It is a major challenge to embed modern financial technology in the continuously changing organisational structure of a multinational company. The processes generating cash flow are to be controlled and proper forecasting models are to be implemented. Based on quarterly rolling forecasts the basic information for managing transaction exposures is provided. Clear guidelines from the "internal bank" and involvement of its financial experts in formulating currency policies at a decentralised PD level are key success factors in increasing awareness and knowledge at the level where the business decisions are taken.

The risks pertaining to the use of financial instruments are limited by defining the "internal bank" as the sole interface to the external financial institutions and by imposing limits.

The use of statistical analyses indicating the "normal variation" in currency movements is a powerful tool for increasing knowledge about risk. By adopting the use of multi-currency confidence intervals for a portfolio, the business risks can be made visible, and cost-effective policies for protecting margins can be implemented.

NOTES

1. There are 14 PDs: for example, Lighting, Sound & Vision, PolyGram, Philips Media, Domestic Appliances and Personal Care (DAP), Communication Systems, Semiconductors, etc.

2. It is not the purpose of our Treasury to make profits; this could induce too much risk for the company. See also The Economist, June 4, 1994, p.15: "The problem arises from the pattern of incentives within companies. Setting profit targets for the treasury departments can create a moral hazard if it rewards the treasurer for making money but not for reducing the risks associated with the company's core business. A treasury that is losing money may make even riskier bets in a bid to meet its profit target."

3. See also J.J. Choi, "A model of firm valuation with exchange exposure" in: *Journal of International Business Studies*, Summer 1986, p. 153–160. Hedging or not hedging translation exposure is not completely irrelevant for the "value" of the company. Examples are: tax effects, hedging decisions are sometimes based on existing reports, shareholders/banks often take into consideration the book results of companies.

4. In principle it is that period for which the expected cash flows can be predicted with a high degree of certainty, or that period for which fixed price agreements were made.

5. See also M.H. Moffet and J.K. Karlsen, "Managing Foreign Exchange Rate Economic Exposure", in *Journal of International Financial Management and Accounting*, 5-2-1994.

6. See also L.M. Austin and M.E. Bradbury, "The Accuracy of Cash Flow Estimation Procedures", *Accounting and Finance*, May 1995. "The results indicate that mechanical rules provide poor estimates for reported cash flows. We also show that the errors between cash flow estimates and reported cash flows can be reduced by adjustments made from footnote disclosures. However, large errors remain, even after adjustments are made from footnote disclosures. These remaining errors are correlated with firm-specific characteristics such as sales (firm size), extraordinary items, foreign currency gains and losses, and changes in inventory."

7. A.E. Ronner, *Kasstromen in een multinationale onderneming*, VU, 1994.

8. R.S. Kaplan, *Advanced Management Accounting*, Prentice Hall, 1983.

9. "A firm with adjustable cash flows essentially owns an option. If the firm is currently using the domestic strategy, it has the opportunity to switch to the foreign strategy as soon as future real exchange rate developments make this profitable. This opportunity is comparable to a *call* option, since in effect the firm pays a fixed "exercise" price, i.e. the adjustment costs, to obtain the foreign strategy. If the firm currently uses the foreign strategy, it basically owns a *put* option. Finally, it should be emphasized that a firm does not always get these "switching options" for free. As is argued below, it often has to make an investment in flexibility first. The investment expenditure can then be seen as the price that is paid to acquire the option.", J.J. Capel, *Exchange Rates and Strategic Decisions of Firms*, 1993, p. 57.

10. See also P. de Grauwe, "Costs of Exchange Rate Variability", in *International Money*, 1989, pp. 217–242. "... the distinction between the temporary and permanent nature of exchange rates matters. ... such movements in the exchange rates will lead to relatively small price changes and will have a small effect on trade flows."

11. Global Derivatives Study Group, *Derivatives: Practices and Principles*, Group of Thirty, July 1993.

REFERENCES

L.M. Austin and M.E. Bradbury, May 1995. The Accuracy of Cash Flow Estimation Procedures, *Accounting and Finance*.

J.J. Capel, 1993. *Exchange Rates and Strategic Decisions of Firms*, p. 57.

J.J. Choi, Summer 1986. A model of firm valuation with exchange exposure, in: *Journal of International Business Studies*, p. 153-160.

The Economist, June 4, 1994, p. 15

Global Derivatives Study Group, July 1993. *Derivatives: Practices and Principles, Group of Thirty*.

P. de Grauwe, 1989. Costs of Exchange Rate Variability, in *International Money*, pp. 217–242.

R.S. Kaplan, 1983. *Advanced Management Accounting*, Prentice Hall.

M.H. Moffet and J.K. Karlsen, 5-2-1994. Managing Foreign Exchange Rate Economic Exposure, in *Journal of International Financial Management and Accounting*.

A.E. Ronner, 1994. *Kasstromen in een multinationale onderneming*, VU.

Measuring Value-at-Risk for Mortgage Backed Securities

Summary

G21

This paper investigates the computation of Value-at-Risk (VaR) measures for mortgage backed securities (MBSs) using data for the Danish MBS market. The current RiskMetrics proposal from J.P. Morgan is used as a reference point throughout, but the study diverges somewhat from their proposal, especially with respect to the estimation of zero coupon yield curves as well as in the choice of mapping techniques.

The MBS-valuation is done by a model developed in Jakobsen (1992,1994), which includes burn-out effects without the need for Monte Carlo simulation. The mapping of delta-equivalent cash flows uses the mapping technique proposed by Ho (1992). The resulting procedure can be employed even for large portfolios of MBS issues with the use of standard computing equipment.

The paper compares the MBS VaR estimates for a daily horizon to actual profits and losses for the period January 1993 to March 1995. The results seem to indicate that our method underestimates the variance of actual returns. However, as discussed in the paper this might be due to the fact that the correlation structure of zero coupon rates was estimated without any a priori restrictions. A study which uses the correlations provided in the RiskMetrics dataset might yield better results.

Svend Jakobsen is Associate Professor, Ph.D., at the Department of Finance, The Aarhus School of Business, Denmark. He has written several papers on problems concerning the estimation of zero coupon yield curves and the development and practical implementation of models for the valuation and risk management of mortgage backed securities.

XI. Measuring Value-at-Risk for Mortgage Backed Securities

SVEND JAKOBSEN*

1. Introduction

Value-at-Risk is fast becoming a standard for the measurement of portfolio risk with official endorsement in the 1993 proposal from the Basle Committee as well as in the Capital Adequacy Directive from the European Commission. The implementation of VaR models has been eased considerably by J.P. Morgan s RiskMetrics initiative.[1] The research staff at J.P. Morgan have worked out detailed description of VaR-calculations for a large class of securities, but even more important they make daily updates of the necessary spot, volatility and correlation data freely accessible through the Internet. This availability of more than 460 high quality data series covering important asset markets in 22 countries has put J.P. Morgan and their RiskMetrics methodology at the centre of future discussions.

This paper discusses the measurement of VaR for mortgage backed securities (MBSs). Mortgage backed securities exist in many countries, but the paper will concentrate on the long-term, fixed-rate, prepayable MBS's primarily found in the US and the Danish bond markets. In Denmark more than 2,200 individual MBS issues are listed at the Copenhagen Stock Exchange with a value of 125 billion USD or roughly 42 per cent of the total bond market.[2] Each MBS issue is backed by a pool of thousands of individual mortgages and the interest and repayment on principal for these mortgages are passed through to the MBS investors on a pro rata basis. In the absence of prepayment each individual mortgage is typically a 20–30 year fixed rate annuity loan, and the MBS issue could therefore be valued as a standard non-callable annuity bond.

The complicating feature of MBS valuation is that each individual borrower has the right to prepay his mortgage at par at any time until maturity. In case

The author wishes to thank Bo Wase Petersen, Carsten Tanggaard and Thoms Øyvind for valuable help and comments. All computations have been done with software developed by Carsten Tanggaard and the author.

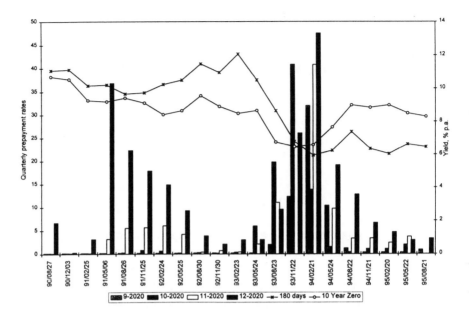

Fig. 1. Quarterly conditional prepayment rates for four different Danish MBS issues in the
period 1990–1995 together with 180 days and 10 years zero coupon rates.

of prepayment the remaining principal on the mortgage is passed through to
the investors thereby shortening the average time to maturity of the MBS
issue. A MBS issue is thus comparable to a portfolio consisting of a large
number of callable bonds each of which can be independently exercised. As
borrowers tend to prepay, when market rates fall below the coupon rate, this
means that MBS cash flows will depend on the level of interest rates.

Figure 1 shows quarterly prepayment rates for 4 Danish MBS's in the
period January 1990 to August 1995. All bonds are of the annuity type with
quarterly payments and an initial time to maturity of 30 years. The figure
shows two periods with a relatively low level of interest rates. In the first
period prepayment occurs only from loans with annual coupon rates of 11 per
cent and 12 per cent while even 9 per cent and 10 per cent MBS issues witness
large prepayment rates in the second period. In some quarters prepayment
rates reach more than 40 per cent, meaning that more than 40 per cent of the
remaining loans are being prepaid. An investor buying the 12 per cent MBS
issue on January 1, 1990 is left with only 5 per cent of the original principal on
October 1, 1995. Without prepayments the remaining principal would have
been 98 per cent of the original principal.

Prepayments are obviously a very important factor in the valuation and risk measurement of mortgage backed securities. Given the option-like feature of prepayments the valuation models for MBS therefore combine an empirical model for the prepayment behaviour of borrowers with a stochastic model for the development of the term structure of interest rates. Most of the current MBS valuation models employ Monte Carlo simulation in order to capture the path-dependent nature of prepayment behaviour. For many of these models a single valuation of a single MBS issue may take several minutes of computer time.

RiskMetrics uses a so-called mapping procedure to represent each security as an equivalent position in one or more of the standard instruments covered by the RiskMetrics dataset. Fixed income securities are mapped into equivalent positions of zero coupon bonds at a fixed set of maturities, individual stocks are mapped to their national stock index according to the beta of the asset etc. Assuming normality, the variance-covariance matrix supplied by J.P. Morgan can now be used to calculate Value-at-Risk for the mapped position. JPM (1994) suggests that options are represented by a mapping of the underlying security multiplied with delta of the option. This delta valuation method, however, implicitly assumes a constant delta and it might lead to biased estimates of VaR for larger changes in the value of the underlying instrument. To remedy this the third edition of the RiskMetrics Technical Document, JPM (1995), recommends that option-like securities should be handled by a structured Monte Carlo approach in which the portfolio is valued for say 10,000 different forecasts of the underlying data-series. Value-at-Risk can then be calculated from the lower 5 per cent cut-off rate in simulated returns.

Mortgage backed securities are not discussed in the latest RiskMetrics proposal, but the computational demands of present MBS valuation models points out a serious problem in their recommendations of structured Monte Carlo simulations. Due to the interaction of prepayment and option payoffs with the return on the ordinary fixed-income securities one has to include the full portfolio in each valuation. Making 10,000 independent valuations of a portfolio which includes say 50 different MBS-issues is simply not practically feasible with the current type of models. To calculate Value-at-Risk for these portfolios one must either use a very simplified MBS-model or alternatively employ the delta valuation approximation.

This paper investigates the calculation of VaR using the delta valuation approximation for Danish mortgage backed securities. We use a so-called mixture distribution valuation model developed in Jakobsen (1992,1994) which contrary to the above-mentioned models allows for very fast calculation of MBS-values. As discussed below our calculation of VaR differs from the

RiskMetrics proposal in some respects, especially with respect to the estimation of zero coupon rates and the mapping methodology. The results should
however be comparable to the results from a more stringent implementation
of the RiskMetrics procedures.

The paper is organised as follows. Section 2 discusses the calculation of
the zero coupon interest rates, volatilities and correlations. Section 3 presents
the MBS-valuation model together with a few valuation results. The mapping
of MBS-securities to delta equivalent positions is discussed in Section 4.
Section 5 compares daily returns on selected MBS-issues with the range
implied by the VaR forecasts. The conclusions are given in Section 6.

2. ESTIMATION OF ZERO-COUPON YIELDS AND VOLATILITIES

Most implementation of VaR-calculations would probably use the volatilities
and correlations supplied in the RiskMetrics dataset. J.P. Morgan calculate
zero coupon rates on a daily basis for more than 22 different countries and
they publish the rates as well. Regrettably the RiskMetrics data available for
the present study did only cover a very limited time period.

To allow for historical comparisons we have therefore estimated the Danish
zero coupon term structure on a daily basis for the period January 1990
to March 1995, a total of 1,300 different business days. We have used a
nonparametric cubic spline yield curve model described in Tanggaard (1995).[3]
The model was estimated on a sample of high liquidity government bonds with
Treasury bills used as a proxy for short-term money market rates. Contrary
to JPM (1995) the estimated zero coupon yield curve was used to calculate
interest rates of all maturities and we have not included any bond specific
spreads in the estimation.

We have finally calculated volatilities and correlations using the exponen-
tially weighted moving average method described in JPM (1995).[4] Table 1
shows the average daily volatility as well as the average correlations between
different maturities. Following RiskMetrics the volatilities correspond to 1.65
times the daily standard deviation of log changes in rates.

Some words of warning should be given with respect to the data presented
above. First of all we have calculated daily volatilities and correlations for
13 different maturities using an estimated curve with approximately four
degrees of freedom. Although the exact statistical properties of such estimates
probably defy any formal analysis it is obvious that the results may reflect the
estimation method chosen at least as much as it reflects the development of
the Danish bond market.[5] Secondly the estimates of daily volatilities are very

TABLE 1

Average price and yield volatilities. Average correlations. Daily data, April 1990 to March 1995

	R030	R180	R360	Z02	Z03	Z04	Z05	Z07	Z09	Z10	Z15	Z20	Z30
Price volatility	0.068	0.187	0.172	0.227	0.354	0.471	0.556	0.698	0.846	0.943	1.775	2.821	5.038
Yield volatility	9.380	4.492	2.136	1.507	1.550	1.530	1.429	1.263	1.183	1.184	1.479	1.761	2.096
Average correlations													
R030	1.000												
R180	0.962	1.000											
R360	0.641	0.807	1.000										
Z02	−0.045	0.118	0.541	1.000									
Z03	−0.058	0.048	0.337	0.859	1.000								
Z04	0.031	0.122	0.349	0.751	0.953	1.000							
Z05	0.083	0.175	0.391	0.708	0.874	0.967	1.000						
Z07	0.101	0.199	0.424	0.677	0.762	0.844	0.923	1.000					
Z09	0.082	0.181	0.407	0.640	0.679	0.722	0.786	0.934	1.000				
Z10	0.070	0.168	0.389	0.610	0.636	0.661	0.710	0.863	0.982	1.000			
Z15	0.018	0.094	0.268	0.424	0.420	0.396	0.395	0.510	0.726	0.833	1.000		
Z20	−0.003	0.060	0.207	0.332	0.316	0.278	0.261	0.360	0.592	0.717	0.980	1.000	
Z30	−0.018	0.034	0.158	0.259	0.234	0.186	0.158	0.246	0.485	0.621	0.944	0.989	1.000

sensitive to outliers and some of the changes in volatility may result from data problems especially for the short-term maturities.

Thirdly and most important we find the correlations between different maturities to be surprisingly low. The estimation method used for this study is extremely good in fitting different segments of the market independently, but given the small sample size, often less than 20 high liquidity bonds, one might suspect, that the correlation estimates are too sensitive to bond specific noise. If correlation estimates are too low, our model will overestimate the diversification gain from investment in bonds or portfolios with a large dispersion of payments. Some evidence of this problem is given below.[6]

According to the description in JPM (1995) our model differs in several respects from the term structure model used to calculate standard RiskMetrics data. The RiskMetrics dataset uses observed money market rates in order to calculate volatilities for 1, 7, 30, 90, 180 and 360 days to maturity. Zero coupon yields of maturities 2, 3, 4, 5, 7, 9, 10, 15, 20 and 30 years are estimated from available data on coupon bonds. JPM (1995) uses a model in which forward rates are approximated by a linear spline with knots at the standard RiskMetrics maturities. The level of forward rates is determined partly by minimising squared price residuals and partly by minimising deviation of forward rates from the Cox, Ingersoll and Ross (1985) one-factor model.[7] The weight given to the CIR-model relative to observed bond prices determines the degree of smoothness of the forward rate curve and also the amount of correlation between maturities. On top of this fairly complicated model JPM (1995) employs bond specific spreads also estimated from historical data.

The weight given to the CIR prior in the RiskMetrics estimation is probably a sine qua non for the RiskMetrics correlation estimates. Judging from a few selected samples their estimates of correlations are also considerably higher than our estimates and probably more realistic when used in a portfolio context.[8] However, a comparison between the two data sets presumably followed by an adjustment of our estimation procedure must wait to a later study.

3. A VALUATION MODEL FOR MBSS

In the last 10–15 years a large number of different valuation models have been developed for the US MBS-market. The typical MBS model includes a prepayment model in which historical prepayment rates are described as a function of a number of exogenous variables. Exogenous variables include proxies for the borrowers, refinancing incentive given the past and present level of interest rates as well as a number of demographic and geographical factors, which capture the effect of household mobility on prepayment rates. Examples of prepayment models can be found in Schwartz and Torous (1989), Richard and Roll (1989) and McConnell and Singh (1991).

Having developed a suitable prepayment model a stochastic term structure model is used to form a consistent sample of future term structure scenarios. Along each scenario the MBS cash flow is found from the estimated prepayment function and priced using standard option pricing techniques.

Solution techniques vary considerably according to the choice of prepayment function. Empirical observations show that mortgage pools which have experienced high prepayment rates for some time tend to get lower prepayment rates as time passes. This so-called *burn-out effect* can be explained by a selection process in which the borrowers most inclined to prepay leave the pool early. Most US prepayment models include the burn-out effect through variables which capture the historical path of interest rates.[9] Valuation models with this type of path-dependency cannot be solved by ordinary backward induction and one has to use a computationally much more demanding Monte Carlo simulation procedure. Depending on the implementation a single valuation of a single MBS issue might take several minutes.

In this paper we use the so-called mixture distribution model proposed in Jakobsen (1992, 1994). Jakobsen (1994) models the heterogeneity among borrowers directly by assuming that each mortgage pool consists of two groups of borrowers, firms and households. Independent prepayment functions are estimated for each of the two groups with prepayment data from the period January 1988 to March 1993. It is shown that prepayment rates for firms are higher than prepayment rates from households for the same level of interest rates. It is furthermore shown that firms, but not households, tend to react to expectations of future interest rates as embodied in the spread between short- and long-term interest rates. A negative spread slows down prepayment from firms, presumably because they postpone prepayments based on an expectation of lower future rates.

The prepayment functions estimated in Jakobsen (1994) do not include any path-dependent variables and the valuation of a single group is done by a very fast backward induction technique. To value the full MBS issue one weights the separate value for each group by its relative share of the pool. Even though individual group behaviour does not show any sign of burn-out the aggregate prepayment rate will display a clear burn-out effect due to the fact that the composition of borrowers changes over time.

In the present paper we use the following simple prepayment models:

(Firms)   CPR = N(−1.8293 + 10.06 ∗ GAIN − 0.0578 ∗ MATURITY),
(Households)   CPR = N(−2.6556 + 9.308 ∗ GAIN − 0.0328 ∗ MATURITY),

where CPR is the quarterly conditional prepayment rate, N is the standard normal distribution function, GAIN is the relative present value gain from prepayment, while MATURITY equals the remaining number of years until maturity. Readers are referred to Jakobsen (1994) for details.[10]

The Danish market for mortgage backed securities has undergone rather large institutional changes in late 1993 and this together with a low level of interest rates has induced very high prepayment rates. It might therefore be appropriate to reestimate the model including prepayment data for the period after April 1993 and using the more detailed data on the composition of borrowers now available from the Danish mortgage institutions. However, the present paper employs the specification above.

For valuation we used the Black, Derman and Toy (1990) (BDT) model using quarterly time steps for a 30 year horizon. For each day in the sample period the model is calibrated to the estimated zero coupon yield curve described above.[11] A single calibration takes approximately 2 seconds. The same calibrated model can be used to value all MBS's on a given business day. A valuation of a thirty-year MBS consisting of two groups of borrowers takes less than half a second on a 486, 66 MHz PC. The derived value of the MBS is referred to as the option-adjusted price (OA-Price) or the estimated value. To compute derived measures like effective duration, option adjusted spread and value-at-risk the calibration and valuation steps will have to be repeated several times.

Figure 2 shows price residuals (option adjusted price less market price) from the model for the period January 1990 to January 1995. The five MBS's shown have quarterly payments and annual coupon rates of 8, 9, 10, 11, 12 per cent respectively with the last payment in year 2020 (9–12 per cent) or 2024 (8 per cent). Despite the relative simplicity of the model it seems to follow market prices well. Figure 3 shows market price and option adjusted price for the 8 per cent bond as well as the effective duration derived from the valuation model. For comparison the figure also shows the theoretical value of a similar non-callable bond. One notes how the rise in market prices flattens out close to par where prepayment risks become imminent. This decrease in price volatility relative to a similar non-callable bond is also reflected in the effective duration estimate, which decreases as prepayment risk increases.

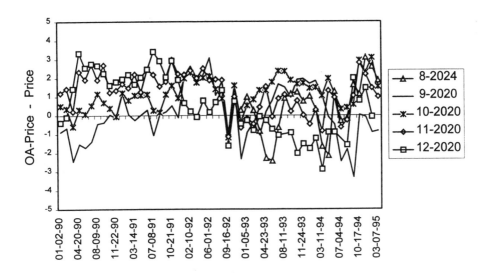

Fig. 2.   Difference between option adjusted price and market price for five different Danish MBS issues. Five weeks interval, February 1990 to February 1995.

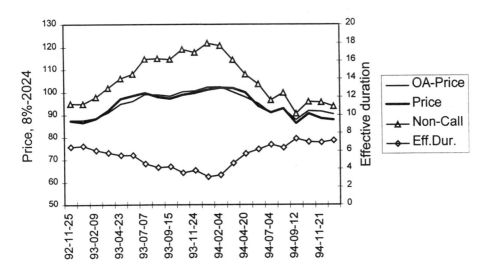

Fig. 3.   Illustration of valuation results for 8 per cent MBS issue. Five weeks interval, February 1990 to February 1995.

4. Mapping of Mortgage Backed Securities

To calculate Value-at-Risk we need to translate the cash flow of individual bonds into the standard maturities on which our volatility and correlation estimates are available. In JPM (1995) this procedure is referred to as mapping. Mapping can be done in a number of ways.

For standard non-callable bonds a popular and very simple method is to distribute each individual payment between the two adjacent standard maturities in such a way that the present value and the duration of the cash flow are kept constant. The RiskMetrics proposal recommends a somewhat different procedure in which each individual payment is distributed so that present value and an approximation to the market risk of the payment is kept constant. Given that the resulting cash flow map is used to derive the total market risk for the bond this seems to be an appropriate procedure.

Bonds with embedded options like callable bonds or mortgage backed securities present a different challenge. They have no single future cash flow, but a multitude of possible cash flows depending on the future path of interest rates. To deal with these securities JPM (1995) proposes to calculate so-called delta-equivalent cash flows (DECF).

The DECF-method assumes the presence of an option pricing model like the one presented in Section 3. One first derives the present value of the bond, P, from the option model with the initial yield curve, $R(t)$, as input. Next the yield curve is shifted locally with a small amount h at maturity T, which should correspond to one of the future payment dates. A new "shifted" price, P_T is obtained and the difference $P - P_T$, between the two prices corresponds to the bond's price sensitivity to changes in T-year rates. To compute the DECF, we note that a T-year zero coupon bond would have a similar price sensitivity of $\exp(-T * R(T)) - \exp(-T * (R(T) + h))$. By computing the ratio between the two price sensitivities we get the DECF at payment time T, i.e. the nominal amount of T-year zeros, which have the same price sensitivity to shifts in the T-year rates as our original bond. Repeating the procedure for each payment date returns the full DECF for the bond. As payment dates rarely coincide with the standard maturities, JPM (1995) recommends that a second step is used to map the DECF as described above.

With quarterly payments a strict implementation of the DECF-procedure would require at least 120 individual calibrations per day and 120 individual valuations for each 30-year MBS. To avoid this amount of computation we have preferred to use an alternative mapping method developed in Ho (1992). The basic idea is similar to the RiskMetrics proposal, but instead of shifting at each individual payment date Ho (1992) computes prices with a number of triangular shift functions successively added to the yield curve. Each shift-function peaks at one of the designated mapping points and it decreases linearly reaching zero at the previous and the following mapping point. Outside this interval the shift-function is zero. The shift-function for the first mapping point adds a constant shift to previous maturities and conversely so for the last shift-function. For payments located at mapping points results will be identical to the RiskMetrics proposal. For intermediate payments the method by Ho will divide the cash-flow between the two adjacent mapping points.

By choosing the standard RiskMetrics maturities 30, 180, 360 days and 2, 3, 4, 5, 7, 9, 10, 15, 20 and 30 years as mapping points in the Ho-algorithm the mapped DECF can be used directly as input to the VaR calculations. The mapping of MBS issues thus requires 13 calibrations of the term structure model per day plus an extra 13 valuations per issue. In the following we have used the Ho-algorithm for non-callable bonds as well although in this case the RiskMetrics mapping procedure would be equally efficient and perhaps more precise.

Figure 4 shows examples of mapped DECF for four Danish mortgage backed bonds on March 17, 1994.[12] In the interpretation of these maps one should note that an upward shift in a specific interest rate affects not only the value of future MBS cash flow, but also the future cash flows themselves. A formal analysis of these effects will be rather complicated, but the following discussion might provide some intuition. To separate the two influences we first define the *present value effect* as the change in MBS value given that prepayment rates and thereby future cash flows are kept fixed. The size of the present value effect for a change in the t-year interest rate reflects the size of the average future t-year cash flow. As prepayment rates increase with the difference between the coupon rate and the market rates, high coupon MBSs should pay back faster on average and for these bonds we will expect relatively large present value effects for changes in short-term interest rates.

Secondly we define the *cash flow effect* as the change in MBS value due to the change in future cash flow given that discount factors are kept fixed. An upward shift in the t-year interest rate will lower the gain from prepayment and thereby the prepayment rates at all settlement dates prior to time t. This will lead to lower instalments on principal and a longer average time to maturity. When coupon rates are above market rates an increase in average time to maturity will therefore increase the value of the bond. The cash flow effect increases with the difference between the coupon rate and the market rate, and a shift in a long-term rate will have a larger influence on cash flows than a shift in a short- term rate.

The DECF maps in Figure 4 show the sum of the present value and the cash flow effect. As expected we find that the present value effect dominates for short-term maturities while the cash flow effect dominates for long-term maturities. This means that an upward shift in short-term rates will lead to a decrease in the MBS value, while an upward shift in long-term rates increases the MBS value. A portfolio of zero coupon bonds able to replicate the interest rate risk of a MBS issue should therefore combine a long position in short-term zero coupon bonds with a short position in long-term zero coupon bonds. The DECF provides us with the exact composition of these hedge portfolios.

According to the model the overall effect of a parallel shift in yields would be to *increase* the value of the 10 per cent MBS, which has a negative effective duration of –0.22.

The calculation of the DECF is highly dependent on the level of interest rates. In Figure 5 DECF of the 10 per cent MBS has been recalculated assuming a 50 and a 100 basis point shift in the yield curve. At the new higher level of yields prepayment intensity decreases and the bond changes from being a substitute for short-term investment to become more dependent on medium-term rates. The overall price sensitivity as measured by effective duration increases from –0.22 to 0.87 and then to 1.98. Most Danish fund managers learned this from hard experience during 1994.

To calculate VaR we first discount the nominal DECF with the zero coupon rates for each standard maturity. The resulting present value map now represents a portfolio of different maturities and the standard deviation of this portfolio is found from the estimated variance-covariance matrix for the business day. We finally multiply the standard deviation by 1.65 to obtain the VaR-forecast for a one day horizon.

The calculation of Value-at-Risk assumes a constant DECF throughout the forecast horizon. One might therefore suspect that VaR calculations based on DECF would underestimate the risk especially in periods of increasing rates. On the other hand one could argue that the DECF should provide a good approximation to actual market risk for short-term horizons. This question is analysed in the next section.

5. THE EMPIRICAL PERFORMANCE OF MBS VaR ESTIMATES

To test the MBS VaR estimates we have made a simple comparison between estimated VaR and the actual profit and loss on each security. The test was

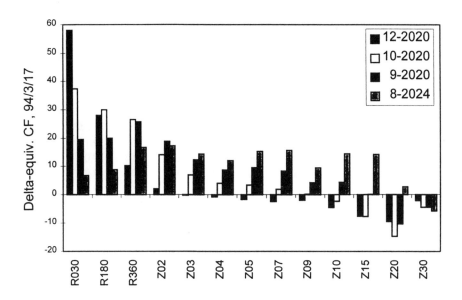

Fig. 4. Delta equivalent cash flows for four Danish MBS issues on March 17, 1994.

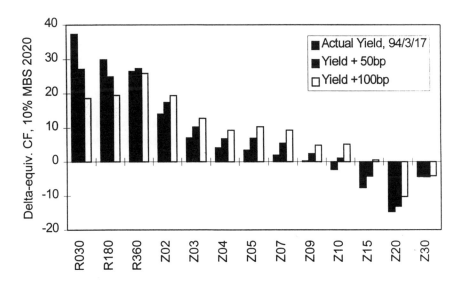

Fig. 5. The effect on the DECF of a parallel shift in the yield curve. 10 per cent 2020 MBS issue, March 17, 1994.

TABLE 2
Daily Value-at-Risk compared to actual profit and loss, January 1993 to March 1995

Bond-Id	Coupon	Type	Issuer	Maturity	Average Observed VaR	Volatility	# Dates	% Out[a]	% Down[b]
9916439	9.00	Bullet	Gov	1995	0.35	0.38	566	7.77	4.95
9917676	9.75	Bullet	Gov	1995	0.27	0.34	529	12.48	7.18
9917759	9.25	Bullet	Gov	1995	0.33	0.37	564	9.57	5.50
9914228	10.00	Bullet	Gov	1996	0.46	0.54	566	21.55*	10.95*
9915035	9.00	Bullet	Gov	1996	0.46	0.77	566	9.19	5.65
9917916	6.00	Bullet	Gov	1996	0.31	0.31	444	9.01	5.86
9918567	6.25	Bullet	Gov	1997	0.26	0.26	191	7.85	5.76
9915548	9.00	Bullet	Gov	1998	0.61	0.62	566	8.13	5.83
9918211	6.00	Bullet	Gov	1999	0.63	0.61	244	4.92*	4.10
9916199	9.00	Bullet	Gov	2000	0.69	0.70	566	9.54	6.36
9917163	8.00	Bullet	Gov	2003	0.76	0.78	566	9.19	5.65
9917833	7.00	Bullet	Gov	2004	0.81	0.82	470	11.70	7.23
9908923	10.00	Serial	Gov	1995	0.24	0.47	545	36.51*	18.53*
9907362	10.00	Serial	Gov	1999	0.44	0.68	566	21.73*	10.25*
9907446	10.00	Serial	Gov	2004	0.58	0.72	566	17.84*	9.01
9717076	10.00	MBS	Nyk	2020	0.40	0.56	565	25.31*	12.92*
9717746	12.00	MBS	Nyk	2020	0.22	0.60	540	24.81*	11.11*
9719445	9	MBS	Nyk	2020	0.53	0.70	566	18.55*	9.19*
9735482	8	MBS	Nyk	2024	0.66	0.71	566	9.72	4.95

[a] * Indicates difference from 10% with 95% significance.

[b] * Indicates difference from 5% with 95% significance.

performed with a one day horizon for the period January 4, 1993 to March 29, 1995, a total of 566 days. For each day the DECF as well as a VaR estimates were calculated for the four MBS issues discussed above as well as for a small number of non-callable government bonds. The latter added only marginally to computation time. Daily profit and loss was calculated as the simple daily change in quoted price not including accrued interest. The results are summarised in Table 2. A selected set of graphs can be found in the Appendix.

For each bond in the sample the table shows the average Value-at-Risk, the observed volatility of daily profit/loss (standard deviations multiplied by 1.65 to compare with VaR estimates), and the number of dates. The column % Out measures the fraction of outliers for each bond. We would expect

10 per cent of all observations to be outside the interval given by VaR and minus VaR. The final column shows the fraction of daily profit/loss which falls below minus VaR. Here we would expect a ratio of 5 per cent. A '*' indicates that the number of outliers deviate significantly from 10 per cent and 5 per cent respectively. According to the table the VaR calculations works nicely for most bullet bonds. The results for the MBS issues are not quite as encouraging. As shown three of four MBS issues have been more risky than predicted by the VaR estimates and only the risk of the 8 per cent bond seems to have been correctly measured by VaR.

The MBS VaR estimates obviously underestimate the true risk involved in MBS-issues. This may be due to the prepayment model, the choice of stochastic term structure model etc. Before improving upon these advanced features it may be worth discussing why the three non-callable Government *serial* bonds in the table fared equally badly.

A serial bond repays equal amounts of principal at each term date. The cash flow from a T-year serial bond is thus equivalent to the cash flow from a portfolio of T ordinary bullet bonds with maturities ranging from 1 to T years. This portfolio interpretation of serial bond cash flow might provide the explanation for our results. In the VaR framework any bond investment is viewed as an investment in a portfolio of standard zero coupon bonds. If prices for these zeros are less than perfectly correlated we should achieve a diversification gain by spreading our investment among different maturities. For a single ordinary bullet bond this diversification effect is minimal as the cash flow is concentrated at maturity. For a single serial bond the diversification effect would be larger, as the cash flow is spread rather evenly in the period up to maturity. However, if correlations are estimated too low, then the real diversification gain will be smaller than expected, i.e. our VaR estimates are too low compared with actual risk.

A high coupon MBS issue will have a composition of DECF which resembles the cash flow from the serial bond. If we have underestimated correlations in general then the VaR estimates for our MBS issues will also be too low. Some evidence of this underestimation especially for the shorter maturities was given in Table 1. This hypothesis is supported by the fact that the number of negative and positive outliers are very similar. The problem does not seem to stem from the option-like features of prepayment at least not with a daily horizon.

6. SUMMARY

In this paper we have investigated the calculation of Value-at-Risk for Danish mortgage backed securities. The results should apply to the huge US MBS market as well. To make results comparable to other studies we have tried to follow the RiskMetrics proposal as much as possible. However, at some points we have had to follow a different route.

We have shown that using the MBS-valuation model proposed in Jakobsen (1994) it is computationally possible to include even large portfolios of mortgage backed securities into the overall estimation of daily Value-at-Risk. However, to obtain an ex ante estimate of VaR one will have to stick with the delta-equivalent valuation techniques and refrain from using the structured Monte Carlo simulation approach suggested in the latest revision of the RiskMetrics document.

The techniques proposed were tested on daily data for a 2.2 year period a total of 566 observations per issue. The results were not entirely successful. On average our model seems to underestimate VaR on high-coupon MBS securities. This could be due to an inadequacy of the MBS model, but a comparison with results from non-callable bonds indicated that the results might also be due to the way in which we have estimated the correlation structure of zero coupon rates. A later study which uses the correlations supplied in the RiskMetrics dataset might provide better results.

Anyway, our study may have pointed out a problem in the current Risk-Metrics proposal. Zero coupon rates for longer maturities are not directly observable and several a priori assumptions are needed in order to obtain the necessary volatilities and correlations. To a certain extend these correlations can be determined independently from actual movements of bond prices by the weight assigned to the estimation prior. As the correlation structure is crucial in the determination of the diversification gains in fixed income portfolios one might wonder how the current level of correlation between zero coupon rates in the RiskMetrics dataset compares with actual experience. This might be a subject for future research.

NOTES

1. RiskMetrics is a registered trademark of J.P. Morgan, New York.
2. Numbers taken from the Monthly Report of the Copenhagen Stock Exchange, June 1995. According to Kau et al. (1993) the value of the US MBS market was 1,400 billion USD or half the size of the US Treasury Bond Market.

3. The paper by Tanggaard (1995) presents a nonparametric approach to the estimation of zero coupon yield curves in which a simple transformation of the yield curve is approximated with a natural cubic spline. Besides smoothness, there are no a priori restrictions on the yield curve and the number of knots and the optimal smoothness can be determined from data. Using Danish data from the period 1985–1994 Tanggaard shows, that based on a GCV-criterion this model outperforms more traditional parametric specifications like the Nelson–Siegel and the CIR-model. For the analysis of this paper we use an iterative estimation technique developed in Tanggaard (1995), which ensures that the smoothness of the curve corresponds to a parametric curve with four degrees of freedom.

4. A starting period of 74 days has been used to calculate an unweighted estimate of volatility and correlation, cf. JPM (1995). This period is not included in the following. Figure A1 in the Appendix shows the estimated zero coupon yields for selected maturities for the full period, while Figure A2 charts estimated daily volatility. Throughout the paper we use the RiskMetrics notation to refer to different maturities, i.e. Rxxx refers to a time to maturity of xxx days, while Zyy refers to a time to maturity of yy years.

5. The RiskMetrics dataset typically provides 22 different interest rate series for each country, but only one data series related to equities. From a risk-management point of view it might be more appropriate to reduce the number of interest series to say 2 or 3 common interest related factors. According to JPM (1995, p. 4) this is currently under review by the RiskMetrics staff.

6. Preliminary investigations with other estimation techniques like the Nelson–Siegel model and a cubic spline with a fixed number of knots indicate similar problems with estimates of low correlation between daily returns although to a lesser degree.

7. In their implementation of the Cox–Ingersoll–Ross (1985) one-factor model JPM(1995) estimates the volatility parameter as well as the sum of the mean reversion and the market risk parameter from historical data. For a given day this procedure leaves only two degrees of freedom, which are used to anchor the CIR model to the zero coupon rates at maturities 2 and 10 years. If full weight was given to the CIR prior the JPM zero coupon yield estimates would amount to a predetermined non-linear interpolation between these two rates.

8. Table A1 in the Appendix shows average daily correlations from the RiskMetrics dataset in August 1995. Note the sharp distinction between the behaviour of observed money market rates (Rxxx) and estimated zero coupon yields (Zyy). As an example the correlation between 1 and 2 year rates (R360–Z02) is 0.664, while the correlation between 2 and 30 years rates (Z02–Z30) is as high as 0.754.

9. One example given in McConnell and Singh (1991) is to let the prepayment function depend on the minimum interest rate experienced in the last 12 months. The idea is that only a rate lower than previous rates will induce some of the remaining borrowers to prepay.

10. Another version, which includes the spread between long- and short-term rates reveals larger differences in prepayment behaviour between firms and households, cf. Jakobsen (1994).

11. As shown above in Figure A2 the yield volatilities change quite dramatically during the 5.5 year sample period and we have therefore used four different volatility structures. The annual volatility, sigma, used for the spot rate t years from now has been given as $\sigma(t) = a + b * \exp(-c * t)$. The values of (a, b) was set to $(0.12, 0.08)$ for 1-Jan-90 to 1-May-91 followed by $(0.12, 0.02)$ until 1-Sep-92, $(0.2, 0.05)$ until 1-Oct-94 and finally $(0.15, 0.03)$ for the remaining period. The parameter c had a value of 0.2 throughout.

12. These graphs correspond closely to the keyrate-duration graph for a US MBS given in Ho (1992).

REFERENCES ·

Black, F., E. Derman and W. Toy, 1990. A one-factor model of interest rates and its application to Treasury bond options, *Financial Analyst Journal*, January 1990.

Cox, J., J. Ingersoll, and S. Ross, 1985. A Theory of the Term Structure of Interest Rates, *Econometrica*, Vol. 53, pp. 363-384.

Ho, Thomas, 1992. Key Rate Durations: Measures of Interest Rate Risks, *Journal of Fixed Income*, September 1992, pp. 29-44.

Jakobsen, S., 1992. Prepayment and the Valuation of Danish Mortgage Backed Bonds, PhD-Thesis, Department of Finance, The Aarhus School of Business.

Jakobsen, S., 1994. A Mixture Distribution Approach to the Valuation of Mortgage Backed Securities, Working Paper, Department of Finance, The Aarhus School of Business, 1994.

J.P. Morgan, 1994. RiskMetrics™–Technical Document, Second Edition, New York, November 1994.

J.P. Morgan, 1995. RiskMetrics™–Technical Document, Third Edition, New York, May 26, 1995.

Kau, J.B, D.C. Keenan, W.J. Muller III and J.P. Epperson, 1993. Option theory and floating rate securities with a comparison of adjustable and fixed-rate mortgages, *Journal of Business*, vol. 26, pp. 646-679.

McConnell, J.J. and M.K. Singh, 1991. Prepayments and the Valuation of Adjustable Rate Mortgage Backed Securities, *The Journal of Fixed Income*, Vol. 1.

Richard, S.F. and R. Roll, 1989. Prepayments on Fixed-Rate Mortgage Backed Securities, *Journal of Portfolio Management*, Spring, pp. 73-82.

Schwartz, E. and W. Torous, 1989. Prepayment and the Valuation of Mortgage Backed Securities, *Journal of Finance*, vol. 44., pp. 375-392.

Tanggaard, C., 1995. Nonparametric Smoothing of Yield Curves, Working Paper, Department of Finance, The Aarhus School of Business.

APPENDIX

Figures A1–A5 and Table A1 are on the following pages.

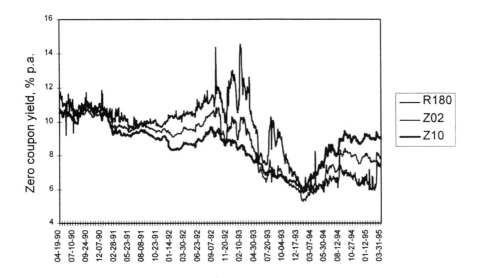

Fig. A.1. Estimated zero coupon yield curves for selected maturities. Daily data, March 1990 to February 1995.

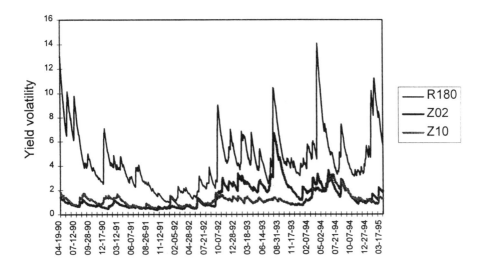

Fig. A.2. Estimated yield volatilities for selected maturities. Daily data, March 1990 to February 1995.

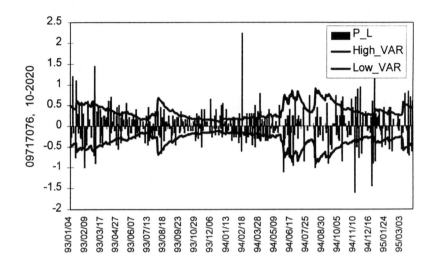

Fig. A.3. Daily profit and loss vs. VaR for 10 per cent 2020 MBS issue, January 1993 to March 1995.

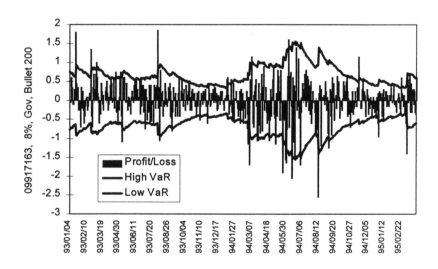

Fig. A.4. Daily profit and loss vs. VaR for 8 per cent 2003 Government bullet bond, January 1993 to March 1995.

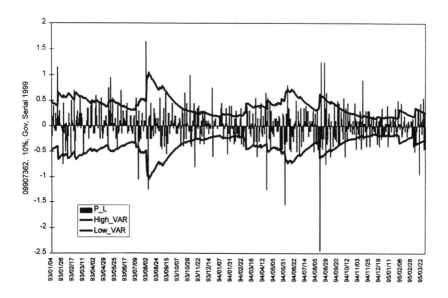

Fig. A.5. Daily profit and loss vs. VaR for 10 per cent 1999 Government serial bond, January 1993 to March 1995.

Svend Jakobsen

TABLE A.1
Average RiskMetrics correlation structure for Danish yields, August 1995. Source: J.P. Morgan, RiskMetrics daily dataset

	R001	R007	R030	R090	R180	R360	Z02	Z03	Z04	Z05	Z07	Z09	Z10	Z15	Z20	Z30
Price volatil.		0.002	0.006	0.017	0.035	0.079	0.161	0.255	0.324	0.401	0.577	0.752	0.821	1.190	1.613	2.61
Yield volatil.	10.604	1.872	1.212	1.124	1.156	1.340	1.334	1.318	1.233	1.163	1.111	1.084	1.058	0.973	0.960	1.02
Average correlations																
R001	1.000															
R007	0.043	1.000														
R030	-0.084	0.691	1.000													
R090	-0.141	0.608	0.835	1.000												
R180	-0.083	0.568	0.776	0.930	1.000											
R360	-0.052	0.474	0.618	0.772	0.780	1.000										
Z02	-0.043	0.209	0.298	0.479	0.487	0.664	1.000									
Z03	-0.050	0.196	0.281	0.434	0.427	0.623	0.955	1.000								
Z04	-0.019	0.216	0.305	0.426	0.425	0.615	0.921	0.980	1.000							
Z05	-0.005	0.181	0.259	0.366	0.370	0.552	0.888	0.947	0.961	1.000						
Z07	0.017	0.090	0.143	0.242	0.242	0.444	0.833	0.890	0.900	0.954	1.000					
Z09	0.033	0.057	0.101	0.188	0.191	0.400	0.797	0.852	0.864	0.919	0.993	1.000				
Z10	0.043	0.063	0.108	0.189	0.195	0.407	0.800	0.854	0.868	0.920	0.986	0.997	1.000			
Z15	0.071	0.100	0.154	0.225	0.238	0.434	0.801	0.837	0.846	0.913	0.949	0.955	0.965	1.000		
Z20	0.081	0.108	0.164	0.228	0.242	0.434	0.780	0.808	0.812	0.887	0.911	0.916	0.928	0.992	1.000	
Z30	0.050	0.045	0.098	0.166	0.175	0.400	0.754	0.798	0.802	0.869	0.931	0.942	0.944	0.944	0.939	1.000

Does the Paris Warrants Market Present a Systemic Risk?

Summary

The first part of the paper is of a statistical nature. It presents the characteristics of the Paris warrants market which are fivefold: a rapidly growing market; an unequal growth among the underlying assets; a large differentiation among assets; a very concentrated market; and whose issuers hold different portfolios.

The second part tries to assess the degree of risk involved in this market. The method is to simulate the behavior of each warrants portfolio of the four largest issuers during an upside and downside shock bearing on stocks and on bonds.

The results show that the regulatory hedging procedures are efficient and the market seems safe. But a systemic risk remains due to the real influence of the hedging operations on the underlying assets.

Bruno Caillet is presently starting his Ph.D. thesis, at the Institut Orléanais de Finance. His research will be in the field of derivatives.

Georges Gallais-Hamonno is Professor at the University of Orléans (France) and Deputy-director of the Institut Orléanais de Finance. His interests are numerous. His latest publications deal with comparisons of performances of private versus government-owned firms (*Journal of Political Economy*, 1994, No. 5) and, in the finance area, with two books, one on mutual funds ("*Sicav et fonds communs de placement, les OPCVM en France*", 1995, Paris, PUF, 2nd édition) and one on options (*Les options négociables*, 1994, Paris, PUF). His current work is on the History of the Paris Stock Exchange during the 19th Century.

XII. Does the Paris Warrants Market Present a Systemic Risk?

BRUNO CAILLET and GEORGES GALLAIS-HAMONNO*

INTRODUCTION

A market for call and put warrants appeared in 1989 at the Paris Stock Exchange. At first, very illiquid, it was a market for institutions. But under the issuers' pressure, market-makers did appear and, since 1993, warrants have been quoted continuously during the Stock Exchange session and have become a quite liquid asset rather actively traded.

Like any negotiable *option*, a warrant is a risky investment and the more so for the issuer because, as seller, he does not know in advance the amount of its potential losses. Moreover, the basic risk is due to the lack of a clearing house. So the warrants market may be faced with two potential systemic risks. One linked with the counterparty's risk; the failure of one issuer unable to pay its exercized warrants leading to a series of failures inside the financial system. The second systemic risk is the possibility for the underlying asset to be destabilized because of the hedging position, thus amplifying the trend, especially a downside one.

Our study is divided into two parts: *the first* describes the present Paris market for warrants in order to measure its size; *the second part* tries to analyse the systemic risks involved and thanks to a simulation, to measure them.

1. THE PARIS WARRANTS MARKET

The call and put warrants are securities traded on a *cash basis*.[1] So, only the issuers are in a short position. The warrants are traded on two different

*The authors thank Nelly Mosseri (Paris-Performance) for having suggested they look at the warrants market. They also thank three professionals for their constructive remarks: J.E. Reymond (Demachy) and two issuers of warrants, M. Denman (Citibank) and M. de Berranger (Crédit Lyonnais). They are also grateful to M. Guyot (Matif SA) for the data he sent and to Mrs Pajaud for improving the written English. Of course, the usual *caveat* holds.

TABLE 1
Number of warrants issued

	1989	1990	1991	1992	1993	1994
Warrants	13	79	105	157	453	578
Annual increases (per cent)	–	+507	+33	+50	+188	+28

markets; on the "organized" market, i.e. the Paris Bourse (Stock Exchange) and on the Over-the-Counter (OTC) market. This OTC market is a real problem. The estimates of its size are rather vague: **from two to nine times the size of the organized one**. But there is no publicly available information on it![2] So, the impossibility of taking it into account severely biased our findings since we are obliged to deal only with the organised market.

These warrants are quoted under the title "international issues" on the official quotation list. Their characteristics are generally the following. They are of the *American* type. In order to limit the risk of quotations manipulations, the *exercise price* usually is an average of the five (sometimes more) last quotations of the underlying asset. For the same reason, the COB only allows as underlying asset those with a very high liquidity. To obviate the delivery problems, the delivery can indifferently be either in cash or in the underlying asset (but only the former seems to effectively take place). In order to prevent "uneducated" individual buyers the minimum quantity to be purchased is rather large: a thousand units for warrants on bonds and a hundred units for the other underlying assets.

We now present the characteristics of this new market.

1.1. A Rapidly Growing Market

Since its inception in 1989, the market for warrants has grown continuously (Table 1). The year 1993 has been the *best* year with an almost trebling of the issues relatively to the preceding year. It should also be noted that it was in 1993 that the market-making started, made either by the issuer itself or by specialized institutions. With the market-making, the warrants are continuously traded, instead of only twice a day (with the noon (12h) and the afternoon (16h 30) fixings).

The sum of all the premiums received by the issuers — under the assumption that the whole issue is sold — is greater than **40 billions Francs**.

The present 1995 year is characterized by a strong decrease of all issues linked with derivative products.[3] And the market for warrants has not been spared.

TABLE 2
Number of warrants issued by type of underlying assets

Number of warrants on	1989	1990	1991	1992	1993	1994
Indices (per cent)	9(70)	46(58)	56(53)	67(43)	127(28)	238(41)
Increase (per cent)	–	+411	+22	+20	+90	+87
Bonds (per cent)	–	22(28)	9(9)	30(19)	111(25)	98(17)
Increase (per cent)	–	–	59	+233	+270	–12
Currency (per cent)	–	–	30(29)	41(26)	129(28)	129(22)
Increase (per cent)	–	–	–	+37	+215	0
Others (per cent)	4(30)	11(14)	10(9)	19(12)	86(19)	113(20)
TOTAL	13	79	105	157	453	578

TABLE 3
Distribution of premiums received according to the underlying assets (for the warrants quoted at the end of 1994)

	Million FRF		
Individual stocks	4.235	11	
Index CAC-40	8.916	22	
Indices other 'general'	3.443	9	} 36
Indices sectoral	2,007	5	
Currencies	1,744	4	
Treasury Bills (BTAN)	7,646	19	} 43
Bonds	9,572	24	
Others	2,671	6	
TOTAL	40,238	100 per cent	

1.2. An Unequal Growth Among the Underlying Assets

All the possible underlying assets have not been favored with the same intensity by issuers (See Table 2).

It seems clear that three types of assets are favoured, indices, bonds and currencies. This statement is based on *the number of issues* — as the COB does (and requests) in its Annual Reports. But it is only part of the story and we believe it to be partly misleading. What matters is the amount of premiums received. As Table 3 shows, the distribution is somewhat different.

It becomes obvious that there are mostly three kinds of warrants: those based on CAC-40; those based on Treasury Bonds and those based on Treasury Bills; the warrants on currencies have "disappeared".

TABLE 4
Number of different underlying-assets (on the warrants quoted at year-end)

	1989	1990	1991	1992	1993	1994
Underlying assets	5	13	14	30	50	85
Increases (per cent)	–	+215	+8	+114	67	70

1.3. A Large Differentiation Among Underlying Assets

Although the underlying assets chosen are only of eight types, the actual assets are very numerous. The growth in issues has been linked with a diversification of the underlying assets — only gold being forbidden (Table 4).

And Table 5 gives some details on the actual distribution at the end of 1994.

The individual stocks chosen are the most liquid and heavily traded on the RM market and generally (but not always) belong to the CAC-40 index. Except Eurotunnel with 6 issues, the 40 other issues are distributed rather evenly among the 20 equities.

The most used indices are naturally those linked with the French market: almost half the issues are based on the CAC-40 index but some issues used the more "general" index SBF-120. Warrants on sectoral indices were issued on 1990 and 1991 but the lack of success let them disappear in 1992 ... before emerging again in 1994. Two foreign indices are used: the Nikkei 225 and above all the Standard and Poor 500 with 26 issues and 14 per cent of all premium received by warrants on indices. Although there is one warrant on the Italian index, there is none on the German DAX-30.

These warrants on indices have an exercise period on average of one year and seven months. The longest one issued by Barclays de Zoete Wedd (BZW) in 1992 has four years and ten months and the shortest one has a little bit less than one year.One can notice that these warrants are direct competitors with the long-term options (18 months) traded on the MONEP (Marché d'Options Négotiables de Paris, the Paris Options' Stock Exchange). This market is led by Société Générale Acceptance and Citibank, representing 68 per cent, followed by BZW with 12 per cent.

The warrants on bonds are mostly on French Treasury Bonds — the "Obligations Assimilables du Trésor" O.A.T.[4] either "strip" or "plain" (95 per cent of the market). The number of individual OAT used is limited to 13 but, due to the "assimilating" mechanism, they are very liquid. They cover the various maturities, from the shortest, 7 years (2002) to the longest, 30 years (2025). The strikes add or not accrued interest. The exercise period is very short;

TABLE 5
Distribution of warrants issued according to the underlying assets
(1994 year-end)

STOCKS			(per cent)
(21) Individual Stocks	46		
Stock portfolios (12 kinds)	21	67	12.2
INDICES			
CAC-40	111		
Other French Indices	37	234	42.5
Foreign indices	38		
Sectoral indices	48		
TREASURY BONDS			
Strip OAT (6 differents)	18		
OAT (7 differents)	77		
TB portfolios	1	100	18.3
Spanish T.B.	1		
US T.B.	3		
CURRENCIES			
FRF/DEM, GBP, JPY	39		
USD/JPY, DEM, FRF, JPY	85	124	22.5
TREASURY BILLS			
Four Kinds	25	25	4.5
		550	100

on average it does not exceed nine and half months. They seem to be used for short-term hedging by buyers. Société Générale Acceptance and Citibank are also the leaders on this TB market with a 71 per cent share, followed by Paribas.

A fifth of the total warrants market is represented by the warrants based on currencies. Only seven are used: three relative to the French Franc and four relative to the US Dollar. If this segment is the second one in terms of number of issues alive at the end of 1994, in terms of volume traded it is the third. They compete with the very active and efficient OTC market made by banks in which options are more flexible. The main advantage of these warrants on currencies is to be open to small investors for speculating and, may be, to small firms for hedging.

TABLE 6
Leading assets: premium received and number of issues (quoted at year-end 1994)

Underlying assets	Premiums received Million FRF	number of issues	per cent of premiums	per cent in the category
Indices				
CAC-40	8,916	111	22	**72**
Bonds				
STRIP OAT 8.50% 2003	325	4	1	3
STRIP OAT 8.50% 2019	109	2	0.3	1
OAT 5.50% 2004	3,759	35	9	39
OAT 6.00% 2025	868	14	2	9
OAT 6,75% 2004	1,974	9	5	21
OAT 8.50% 2023	1,070	5	3	11
Subtotal	8,108	69	20	**85**
Total of the leading underlying assets	17,025	180	42	**78**

But these 85 different kinds of underlying assets can be reduced drastically if one looks at the premiums received instead of the number of issues. (See Table 6).

Although 85 different assets serve as underlyings for warrants, **seven** assets represent 42 per cent of the premiums received.

1.4. A Very Concentrated Market

According to a Bank of International Settlements Report[5] the warrants markets are generally concentrated relatively to the issuers. It is plainly the case in Paris as the Table 6 shows.

In spite of its size, the Paris market is based on only **five** issuers, dominated by Société Générale Acceptance (SGA). The hierarchy somewhat changes according to the criterion used: Goldman Sachs "beats" Paribas with the amount of premium received but has made many fewer issues (26 compared to 38). The Paris market is thus very concentrated.

1.5. The Portfolios of the Largest Issuers Are Very Different

The portfolios of the largest issuers can be analysed from two separate points of view: the kind of assets (Table 8) and the weight granted to the leading assets seen below (See Table 9).

TABLE 7

Distribution of issuers according to the premiums received and the number of issues

Issuer	Premium received Million FRF	per cent	Number of issues
Société Générale Acceptance	13,755	34.16	239
Citibank	7,372	18.31	68
Crédit Lyonnais	2,982	7.41	68
BNP	3,184	7.91	54
Paribas	2,141	5.32	38
Subtotal	29,436	73.11	467
Goldman Sachs	2,552	6.34	26
Indosuez	472	1.17	16
J.P. Morgan	1,371	3.41	15
CS First Boston Frce	461	1.14	10
Bankers Trust	288	0.72	8
Barclays Z.W.	477	1.19	6
J.H. Schroder Wagg	974	2.42	6
Lehman Brothers	251	0.62	6
Merrill Lynch	1,295	3.22	3
Other issues	2,682	6.66	15
Total	40,263	100	578

TABLE 8

Distribution of the kind of assets among the warrants portfolio of the six largest issuers (1994 year-end) (in per cent)

	Société générale	Citibank	B.N.P.	Crédit Lyonnais	Paribas	Barclays ZW
Currencies	29.90	38.30	–	17.80	14.00	–
Treasury Bonds	60.00	15.70	7.30	6.20	10.80	–
Indices	57.90	10.20	4.90	7.80	6.90	12.20

1.6. Concluding Remarks

In Paris, five issuers dominate the market. And although the number of underlying assets is rather large, most of the issues are concentrated on seven of them, the CAC-40 index and six Treasury Bonds (OAT). Consequently, the question of systematic risk appears very relevant: can each of these leading issuers assume the risk brought by its issues? If not, the risk that the failure of one would destabilize the whole financial Paris market is enormous!

TABLE 9
Distribution of the largest issuers' portfolios among the leading underlying assets (1994, year-end, Millions)

	Société Générale	Citibank	Crédit Lyonnais	B.N.P.	Paribas
CAC 40	1,425	1,935	958	516	834
Share[1] (per cent)	(35.70)	(54.66)	(87.32)	(64.49)	(51.89)
Strips OATs	1,300	0	0	0	0
OAT 5.50% 2004	1,774	918	0	429	164
OAT 6.00% 2025	501	0	231	0	0
OAT 6.75% 2004	0	0	225	0	0
OAT 8.50% 2023	0	0	296	0	0
Subtotal Bonds	3,576	918	754	429	164
Share[1] (per cent)	(99)	(61)	(100)	(100)	(80)

[1] Share of the assets in the sub-portfolio of the issuer. P.i. warrants on CAC-40 represent 35.70 per cent of all the warrants on indices issued by SGA and alive at the end of 1994.

2. MEASUREMENT OF THE SYSTEMIC RISK OF THE WARRANTS IN PARIS

On an options market, the security mechanism provided by the clearing house eliminates virtually any risk from a participant's failure, thus eliminating all systemic risk. And this has been empirically proved by the fact that none of the options markets have had security problems during the downside stock-crashes of 1987 and 1990, or the upside shocks of 1991 for stocks and 1994 for bonds. But, as already noted, the warrants do not benefit from a clearing house.

Of course, a prudential system exists which is divided into two parts... On the one hand, an issuer has to receive the formal approval (the "visa") of the COB since it sells to the general public. Moreover the COB makes sure that the total issues on a given asset are not in such an amount as to risk destabilizing the underlying market. On the other hand, an issuer has to be a banking institution submitted to the control of the Commission Bancaire. This latter institution has devised an interesting control mechanism, in order to check that the risk taken is proportional to the issuer's net worth. Each issuer has to have a pricing model for pricing its warrants; it shall compute *daily* its position and its risk exposure and shall daily hedge accordingly. This pricing model has to receive a formal agreement from the Commission Bancaire...[6] But the Commission Bancaire does not control the daily position — it controls them only *monthly*. It is then relevant to try to test the efficiency of such a mechanism.

2.1. Methodology and Data

Our test is to simulate the behavior of the warrants-portfolio of each leading issuer during upside and downside crashes: crashes on stocks and crashes on bonds.[7]

But it is not possible to track down the values of all the warrants belonging to any subportfolio, since it is too well diversified among underlying assets, as it was shown earlier. Luckily the portfolios are also heavily concentrated on a few of them. So, for the sake of simplicity we assume that the content of the "individual stocks and indices" portfolios contain only warrants on *CAC-40 index* and the "bonds and bills" portfolios are only made up of warrants on OAT(s), those belonging to the above-mentioned leading set. Of course, the change in value thus obtained is extrapolated to the total value of the portfolio, assuming that all the underlying assets behave like the one (or the ones) used as yardstick(s). This assumption does not seem very strong because of the "systemic risk" existing in any market and, even, between markets on an international scale (cf. 1987).

These results are finally calculated as a ratio of the issuer's net worth since the aim is to assess *the bankruptcy risk of each issuer*. In order for our test to be as near to reality as possible, we *duplicate the actual past crashes* by starting them on January 11, 1995. This means that we use the actual price variations of every asset, the actual volatilities observed on the warrants market and the actual rates of interest. We also assume that the purchasers of these American-type warrants *do exercise* at the best moment for them (the worst for the issuer), meaning at the end of the crash — although such a behavior is improbable and although there are clauses in the issuing contracts which limit to a given amount the number of warrants which can be exercised at a given time. We also assume that the whole issue was sold — while it is said that, on average, only 70 to 80 per cent is sold. All these assumptions aim to *overestimate the risk of the issuer*.

The duplicated shocks are the following ones.

TABLE 10

Simulated crashes

	Stock and Indices portfolio	Bonds and Bills portfolio
Upside crash	"Desert Storm" January 17, 1991 to March 3, 1991	1994 crash inverted
Downside crash	"Saddam Hussein" July 20, 1990 to August 21, 1990	crash on bonds of 1994

TABLE 11
Results of the simulation of crashes on stocks

Issuer	Upside crash		Downside crash	
	Results	Share Net Worth	Results	Share Net Worth
	Million FF	(per cent)	Million FF	(per cent)
BNP	585	1.16	285	0.59
Citibank	1,762	2.10	121	0.5
Credit Lyonnais	1,063	2.28	855	1.83
Paribas	1,237	3.10	100	0.25
Société Générale	2,924	5.41	**−9,510**	**−17.6**

As far as the bond market is concerned, there has not been any upside crash we have been aware of. So we use the 1994 "downside crash" "upside-down"!! This method overstates the result because an upside crash generally is more diluted over time and smaller in intensity than a downside crash. And especially the implicit volatilities are much smaller. The premiums received are invested at the risk free rate of interest over the average life of the warrants included in each portfolio.

2.2. *The Results on the Stocks Portfolios*

For the two crashes on stocks, the position of each portfolio and its delta-hedging — computed with the Black and Scholes formula — is estimated **daily**.

Generally speaking, the issuers seem to do very well during Stock Exchange crashes since they appear to make profits! (Such a result may come from the unsophisticated delta-hedging!). With one interesting exception: the largest issuer, Société Générale Acceptance, terminates the "1987 crash" with nine and half *billions* of losses, meaning a **17 per cent** loss on net worth.

Whatever the intrinsic quality of our hedging process — and it is hoped that their actual one is more efficient — this clearly means that *Société Générale was on a risky position*, due to non-symetric issues, too many call-warrants and too few put-warrants. Moreover, our results underestimate the true situation of an issuer because its departments — the warrants departments excepted — can also undergo losses from the same shock.

At least, it shows that the question whether there is a systemic risk linked with the warrants market is relevant! There is a second type of systemic risk: is the daily hedging of the issuers not destabilizing the market for the underlying assets, especially during a downside shock? We estimated the daily number

NUMBER OF FUTURES CONTRACTS FOR HEDGING THE WARRANTS
PORTFOLIOS

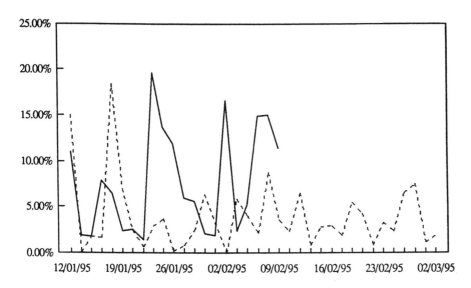

Fig. 1. This graph shows that *there is a systemic risk* in the sense that the hedgers going "with the market" — i.e. buying when the market goes up and selling when it goes down — *will influence the market of the underlying asset.* During the upside crash one day with 15 per cent and another one with 18 per cent of the traded contracts would indubitably disrupt the market which will reach a higher peak! This effect may exist even when their purchases (or sales) are around 7 per cent. And such a situation is more prevalent during a downside crash, really risking making it worse! (— crash 90; - - - crash 91).

of *futures* contracts on CAC-40 on MATIF used by the five issuers to daily hedge their warrants-portfolio and computed the ratio to the actual volume of futures contracts traded during the two crashes.[8]

2.3. The Results on the Bonds Portfolios

Because the 1994 shock on the bond market lasted for the whole year, the hedging positions are only made **monthly.** For the warrants which expired during the simulation we assume that they were exercised at maturity. The hedging ratio is estimated using the Black formula. The following figures show the results.

The results are more spread among the issuers, especially in the case of the upside crash — but it may be caused by the rather too strong assumption

TABLE 12
Results of the simulation of crash on bonds

Issuer	Upside crash		Downside crash	
	Results Million FF	Share Net Worth (per cent)	Results Million FF	Share Net Worth (per cent)
BNP	−19	−0.04	68	0.14
Citibank	−1,333	−1.59	−705	−0.85
Credit Lyonnais	10	0.02	223	0.48
Paribas	−409	−1.02	405	1.01
Société Générale	−719	−1.19	1,073	1.99

— as noted before — that an upside crash behaves like a downside one. In a downside crash, Citibank may have a slight problem.

3. CONCLUDING REMARKS

The description of the warrants market in Paris shows that it is an attractive "option" market for the investors because of the very large diversity of underlying assets and maturities it offers. It helps the Paris financial market to be more "complete". But it remains to be demonstrated that it is efficient! Indeed, in this respect, it has a somewhat dubious reputation: the spreads offered by the market-makers are said to be certainly too wide, especially when the market follows a strong trend.

About the security of this market, one may conclude that the hedging process seems adequate — except the Société Générale case. But nevertheless, *there seems to subsist a systemic risk due to the real influence of the hedging operations on the underlying assets*, even when they are as liquid as the future CAC-40.

This fact warrants further research. And an immediate research should be undertaken *in order to know the true size of the OTC market* and to know if it is really **9 times** larger than the "official" one If this was proved to be true, it would be difficult to believe that this market is a "prudentially safe" market. Such research can only be made by, or under the auspices, of one of the two regulatory bodies, the Commission de Bourse (C.O.B). or the Commission Bancaire.

NOTES

1. Contrarily to the Anglo-Saxon markets, the stocks are divided in Paris into two separate markets: those traded on a "future-forward" market (called Rèlement Mensuel, RM) and those on a "cash" or "immediate delivery" market (Règlement Immédiat, R.I.).

2. Curiously, the regulatory agency, the Commission de Bourse, COB, does not seem to have any information on this OTC Market.

3. Option Finance no. 371, 25-9-1995, pp. 24-30.

4. The Treasury issues on several occasions bonds with the *same* characteristics of coupon and maturity; so the amount of a given bond becomes larger and its very size prevents any risk of manipulations.

5. Cited by COB: *Bulletin* no. 269, May 1993, p. 6.

6. One may nevertheless wonder if the members of the Commission Bancaire have the competence to really check the sophisticated models presented by teams of financial mathematicians ... .

7. We also simulated the sub-portfolios of warrants on currencies but the results obtained are not coherent; needing further research.

8. Only the amounts of warrants on CAC-40 are taken into account. No extrapolation to the whole portfolio is made since the hedging of these other underlying assets would take place on their own markets.

REFERENCES

Acard, C. and M. de Varax (1994). Les warrants financiers, un instrument "apatride" du droit financier, *Les cahiers MTF Haute Finance* no. 9, supplément au no. 66, Décembre.

Aglietta, M. and A. Brender (1990). Globalisation financière et risque de système, *Cahiers Economiques et Monétaire*, no. 37.

Commission Bancaire (1994). *Rapport.*

Commission des Opérations de Bourse, Années 1989 à 1993. *Rapport au Président de la République,* Journal Officiel, Ed. des Documents Administratifs.

Berthon, J. and G. Gallais-Hamonno (1994). *Les options négociables*, PUF, Collec. QueSais-Je?, Paris, 128 p.

Fonds Monétaire International (1994). Les produits dérivés: un nouveau risque financier, *Bulletin du FMI*, 28 Février.

Goldstein, M. and D. Folkerts-Landau (1991). International Capital markets, Part II: Systemic Issues in International Finance, *Etudes Economiques et Financières du Fonds Monétaire International.*

Gregoir, O. (1994). Les marchés des produits dérivés, *Banque* no. 548, Mai.

Hannoun, H. (1994). Les banques centrales renforcent la surveillance prudentielle, *Marchés et Techniques Financières,* Octobre-Décembre.

Marchés et Techniques Financières (1994). Produits dérivés: réglementer ou ne pas réglementer? no. 61, Juin.

Nouy, D. (1994). La surveillance prudentielle des dérivés, *Banque*, no. 548, Mai.

O'Hagan, C. (1995). *Dérivés: une méthodologie d'analyse des risques, Marchés et Techniques Financières*, no. 71, Juin.

OCDE (1991). Nouveaux instruments financiers, *Harmonisation des normes comptables*, no. 6.

Rohmer, X. (1995). Régime juridique et fiscal des warrants financiers, *Option Finance*, no. 347, Mars.

G21

224-51

UK

Asset and Liability Management in Retail Banking

Summary

This paper examines asset and liability management in retail banking. Efficient management of the interest rate risk and funding requirements arising from retail banking operations necessitates that these exposures be consolidated, along with positions arising from other operational divisions, under an integrated risk management structure. For this risk transfer process to function effectively, risks in retail banking business must be identified and measured accurately, products need to be grouped into categories according to their repricing and funding characteristics, and product margins and transfer prices determined.

Based on the experiences of a British bank, the practical difficulties which need to be overcome when modelling assets and liabilities and simulating decision-making parameters are illustrated. The paper is divided into three parts. The first considers the sources of interest rate risk in retail banking. A number of distinct product types — variable rate, fixed rate, and zeros — clearly exist in retail banking but careful analysis is needed to distinguish contractual terms from customer behaviour governing factors such as the duration of core funding, repricing terms, basis risk in matched wholesale funding, forward funds delivery, drawdown delays and early repayment. These are considered in the second part of the paper along with the mechanics of the portfolio risk transfer process. Finally, a sensitivity analysis is conducted on the bank's risk transfer book using Monte Carlo techniques.

Mervyn K. Lewis is Midland Bank Professor of Money and Banking and Course Director of the MBA in Financial Studies in the School of Management and Finance at the University of Nottingham, and Visiting Professor in Economics at the Flinders University of South Australia. He has published ten books and numerous articles on monetary economics, his most recent book being *Financial Intermediaries, The International Library of Critical Writings in Economics* (Edward Elgar, 1995).
Phillip Morton graduated from the University of Nottingham in 1994 with an MBA in Financial Studies, and was awarded the prize for the top dissertation. He is presently working in Uruguay as Manager, Product Development, Lloyds Bank (BLSA), Montevideo.

XIII. Asset and Liability Management in Retail Banking

MERVYN K. LEWIS and PHILLIP MORTON

1. INTRODUCTION

Every business is faced with a number of risks: operations risks, product risk, credit risks, commodity price (basis) risk, conglomerate risk, capital adequacy, liquidity risk, foreign exchange risk, interest rate sensitivity. These risks also confront banks and other financial institutions. This is in part because some risks are inherent to any commercial enterprise. But it is also because a 'risk transfer' process operates in financial markets whereby some risks are routinely transferred to banks, and this is the case with interest rate risk.

In their off-the-balance-sheet activities, banks provide customers with tailor-made instruments for hedging interest rate exposures. On the balance sheet, banks accept interest rate risk as part of their normal operations when as financial intermediaries they accommodate to customers' demands for assets and liabilities which have different maturities (e.g. short-term deposits and long-term loans), different interest rate reset terms, and different degrees of interest rate flexibility. Customers are given the option to withdraw deposits at short notice and repay and renegotiate loans.

These factors are especially important for banks with extensive retail operations, offering their customers a wide variety of deposits and loans with different maturities and contractual and non-contractual interest reset arrangements. These activities leave their net interest income vulnerable to changes in market interest rates. Effective management of this risk is fundamental to retail banking.

This paper examines interest rate risk management in retail banking.[1] Section 2 considers the sources of interest rate risk in retail banking operations. Section 3 examines how the risks are managed in practice by a British retail bank. Section 4 looks at the application of simulation models to provide sensitivity testing of the risk transfer process, and Section 5 considers some implications of the results.

2. Interest Rate Risk in Retail Banking

Interest rate risk is present when the interest rates earned on assets do not adjust to an equal extent or at the same time as the interest rates paid on liabilities. This may occur because:

- the maturity of assets and liabilities differ;
- contractual interest rate re-setting arrangements are different;
- competition and other factors inhibit repricing adjustment for products with non-contractual resets; or
- options to prepay loans or redeem deposits are utilised.

Mismatching of contracts by maturity is a feature of most intermediation and this forms the basis for the models of 'interest rate uncertainty' of Niehans (1978) and Niehans and Hewson (1976). Viewed in terms of forward contracts, fixed price, fixed quantity forward contracts are written on one side of the balance sheet (long-term loans for example), but not on the other (e.g. deposits at call). Where the fixed price liabilities have a longer maturity than assets, the intermediary is faced with the necessity to reinvest funds which become available when assets mature. Uncertainty exists because of the difficulty, in the absence of hedging on futures markets, of foretelling the yield which will be received on those reinvested funds relative to the costs in the form of interest and expenses of carrying the liability portfolio. Conversely, in the case of positive maturity transformation, a situation when assets have a longer maturity than liabilities, there is a need for the intermediary to refinance its asset holdings by the issue of new liabilities. Risk arises from the uncertainty surrounding the interest rate which will need to be paid to attract funds or, alternatively, from the need to sell (liquidate) assets at an uncertain market price, if refinancing is not to be pursued. The bank in this case is 'liability sensitive' and increases in interest rates which adversely affect its net interest income also reduce the market value of assets and its liquidity.

The incentive for banks to take on such risks arises from the potential profits available from maturity transformation when yields in markets of different maturity exhibit differences. Depositors may prefer short-term deposits to long-term deposits and be willing to accept less interest in return, while borrowers may want long-term funds and be prepared to pay a premium to avoid unpredictable changes in their monthly payments caused by interest rates. Positive maturity transformation by retail intermediaries serves to meet these different preferences and, at the same time, allows the institutions to earn a spread between interest income and interest expense for bearing this risk.[2]

TABLE 1

Maturity analysis of Sterling business of British Banks with UK residents[1] (percent of assets and liabilities)

	All banks		Retail banks		British non-retail banks		Overseas banks	
	A	L	A	L	A	L	A	L
0–7 days	6.48	67.32	3.09	74.89	14.78	51.43	9.93	40.07
8 days–1 month	5.51	14.06	2.92	10.60	4.44	18.50	11.74	23.58
1–3 months	7.46	9.60	6.11	7.04	8.18	14.32	11.51	23.67
3–6 months	4.39	3.26	3.52	3.46	8.17	6.87	5.38	7.64
6 months–1 year	5.77	2.59	4.63	2.80	11.10	3.48	6.87	3.09
1–3 years	11.49	1.75	8.22	0.26	21.88	2.20	18.72	0.73
3 years+	58.90	1.42	71.51	0.95	31.45	3.20	35.85	1.22
Total	100.00	100.00	100.00	100.00	100.00	100.00	100.00	100.00

[1] As at first quarter 1995 for All banks. Other classifications as at May 1993. Source: Bank of England.

Measuring the extent of maturity transformation in retail banking is hampered by the difficulty of distinguishing retail from other operations. In the UK there are wholesale banks, but no *purely* retail banks, limiting themselves to the tapping of retail deposits markets and lending only in retail loan markets. All banks in the UK are to some extent multimarket. Nevertheless, the division between retail/domestic, wholesale/foreign currency (i.e. Eurocurrency) does differ amongst the categories of banks, and the classifications in Table 1 are based on these divisions. Retail banks comprise the clearing banks and others, numbering 22 banks in all, which form the basis of the payments mechanism and have an extensive network of branches and agencies in the UK. The other banks are divided into 210 British non-retail banks, specialising in merchant banking or wholesale banking activities, and 286 branches, subsidiaries and joint ventures of banks owned and registered overseas. Like most of the British non-retail banks, these overseas banks have few branches in the UK and have little involvement in the payments system. In fact, only about 10 per cent of their business is in Sterling, the rest being in foreign currency, with US Dollar business dominant.

Table 1 sets out the maturity analysis of the banks' sterling business with UK residents where assets (A) and liabilities (L) are classified according to the remaining period to maturity. Maturity mismatching is clearly not confined to the retail banks, and the total sterling balance sheet of all banks is not 'matched'. There is an excess of liabilities over assets at the short end of the scale, and conversely at the long end. With non-bank customers, 67 per cent of liabilities mature either on demand or at 7 *days* or less notice, while 58 per cent of assets had a residual maturity of 3 or more *years*. When the various categories of banks are compared, the retail banks have an even more mismatched balance sheet (both in total and with non-bank customers) than the other banks. For non-bank business, 84 per cent of liabilities of retail banks are in the 0–7 days category and 66 per cent of assets have a maturity of three years or more.

Some features of the way maturities are classified by the banks should be noted. In general, the most 'pessimistic' view is taken, and this presents problems of interpretation in three main areas. First, the maturity of deposits is defined in terms of the earliest possible repayment date. Thus a deposit at call which may stay with a bank for six months is called a 'sight' deposit. A second difficulty comes from the existence of overdrafts. Because very often they are allowed to run on for long periods, overdrafts tend to be all lumped into the longest maturity asset category. Third, there is the treatment of rollover credits. Many of the sterling assets are loans nominally for terms in excess of one year, some of them well in excess of five years, renegotiated ('rolled over') on a three- or six-monthly basis at variable interest rates. These are classified according to the period remaining to the ultimate maturity date of the loan and not to the next rollover date.

This last feature is important in transforming the nature of the risk borne by retail intermediaries. Were maturity transformation of one short-term deposit into one longer-term asset the only activity undertaken by an intermediary, its portfolio management would involve deciding at what point the increases in expected profit from increased maturity transformation (assuming a positively sloped yield curve) cease to outweigh the extra uncertainty of outcome thereby created. The answer, not unexpectedly, depends upon the attitude to risk of the intermediary's owners, the term premium, the intermediary's expectation of future yields, and the resource cost of intermediation. In practice, most banks undertake some combination of fixed and variable rate financing. Rather than entering implicit forward contracts specifying fixed price and quantity, a price contingent upon spot market developments is specified and the interest rate is adjusted periodically in some manner in response to market developments.

The point is that the repricing term is not the same as maturity, and interest rate risk arises primarily from mismatches of repricing terms, and only partly from mismatches of maturities. Retail banks face special factors in repricing terms due to the distinction between items with contractual rate resets and those with non-contractual rate resets. A contractual rate reset occurs when the interest rate is fixed until a predetermined time. A term deposit has a contractual reset point at maturity, while a ten-year term loan linked to 3-month Libor has a contractual repricing term of 3 months. Repricing arrangements may be formal, as is often the case in wholesale markets where the interest rate charged is linked to some overall market indicator rate, or informal, as in some retail markets where variations in the yield may be at the lender's discretion or negotiated between borrower and lender. In similar vein, the timing of adjustments may be at prespecified dates, or discretionary. Those products with non-contractual rate resets (e.g. variable rate housing loans) typically respond to market rates with a lag and with a lower amplitude.

Because interest rates on loans are usually adjusted less frequently than deposit rates change, banks are not completely absolved from interest rate risk due to maturity mismatching. It is normal for loan contract rates to be revised at set intervals (called interest rate periods). Banks are thus insulated from interest rate risk (but not funding risks) across interest rate periods. Within interest rate periods, the loan rate is effectively fixed, and banks bear interest rate risk from liabilities of shorter duration than the interest rate period. The more closely the interest rate follows the market, the more the risk is shifted to the customer. Those customers who accept market-related terms are likely to be those more able to bear the risk (Green, 1995). Returns to the bank are a combination of contrast rates and default losses. While interest rate risk is transferred from the bank to the borrower, this transfer alters the ability of the borrower to meet the remaining contractual repayment obligations. Those seeking more stable rate arrangements from banks may be those less able to bear interest rate risk, and imposing variable rate loan contracts on them may transform interest rate risk to credit risk rather than remove the risk. Even where variable loan and deposit rates are market-determined, the bank still incurs risk to the extent that loan and deposit rates are imperfectly correlated (Carhill, 1994).

The interaction of interest rate and credit risk is only one of the ways in which interest rate risk management forms part of asset and liability management more generally. Custom pricing is the norm in many retail markets, and this involves banks accepting onto their balance sheets whatever changes in assets and liabilities result from the posted rates. At one extreme, a bank could fix deposit interest rates and allow the scale of the asset portfolio to vary in line with the quantity of deposits forthcoming at the posted rates (pure asset management). Alternatively, by adjusting interest rates paid on liabilities so as to induce a quantity of deposits equal to the pre-existing stock of assets, all of the liquidity disturbances could fall upon prices (pure liability management). When liabilities are at call, the interest rate needed to maintain the deposit stock constant is, in effect, varying continuously, as indicated by the variability in the deposit stock arising from withdrawals and deposits when the interest rate is held constant. Because such variations are largely self-correcting, it is often cheaper for the bank to accept the quantity variation rather than adjusting and readjusting deposit interest rates. This is especially so for chequeing deposits and the usage of credit lines where the averaging process inherent in large numbers makes the stochastic element relatively small and predictable.

Such behaviour extends to other retail operations: for example, a bank may post terms for fixed rate mortgages, leaving uncertain how many loans are made, the timing of draw downs, and the maturities selected by customers. Figure 1 shows the typical booking and draw down profile for a £50m fixed rate mortgage offer in England. Pre-arranged matched funding with wholesale funds of the same term and maturity date as the mortgage offer will not eliminate interest risk for a number of reasons. First, the offer may take many weeks to sell and in the meantime the banks must invest the excess funds. Second, customers will typically be given the option to select the length of the fixed rate term, and the mix of terms chosen may vary from that forecast when pre-arranging matched funding. Third, customers are allowed

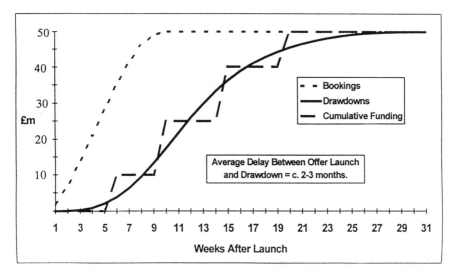

Fig. 1. Typical booking and drawdown profile for fixed rate mortgage offer in England.

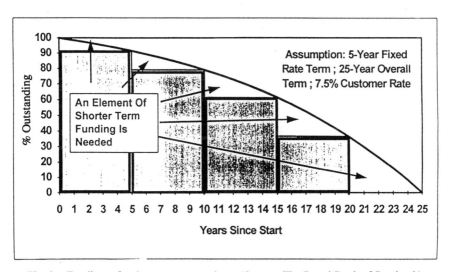

Fig. 2. Funding a fixed rate repayment loan. (Source: The Royal Bank of Scotland.)

to delay draw down of funds, and the average delay between the launch of the campaign and draw down is typically several weeks. Again, short-term deployment of funds may be at a rate below cost. Fourth, if interest rates fall before the funds are drawn down and the customer backs out, the bank will incur a re-investment loss.

Once the offer is closed, interest rate risks remain. Repayment mortgages with an amortising balance are more difficult to fund than an interest-only mortgage because of the reducing balance over the life of the loan. Figure 2 shows the funding requirements and the mixture of longer-term and shorter-term funding needed. Early prepayment of the loan adds another dimension of risk. The experience of the savings and loan associations in the United States in the early 1980s is often cited as an example of the dangers of funding long-term fixed rate mortgages with short-term deposits, with losses resulting when deposit rates had to follow market rates upwards. This story has a sequel, for the thrifts believed that they could avoid making the same mistakes if they used long-term fixed rate funds to fund the new mortgages written at the then higher interest rates. The result was that fixed rate mortgages issued at 15 per cent were financed with long-term funds borrowed at a half point lower. This strategy overlooked that borrowers held the option of refinancing and repaying the loan if interest rates fell. When interest rates did subsequently fall, borrowers repaid the 15 per cent mortgages and replaced them with 9 per cent borrowings. The institutions were then left with long term fixed rate funds at 14.5 per cent which had to be reinvested at a net interest loss (Lucas, 1994). The potential losses from prepayment of loans can be large. Consider a 10-year fixed rate term loan written with a cost of funds of 9 per cent p.a. Suppose that the loan is repaid after two years when 8-year funds have fallen to 6.5 per cent p.a. In simple terms, the funding loss [(9 per cent–6 per cent) × 8 years] represents 20 per cent of the outstanding principal.

All of these examples illustrate that the management of interest rate risk must be rooted in a clear understanding of the characteristics of the products offered, and of customer relationships and behaviour. It must also take account of the broader objectives of asset and liability management.

3. RISK MANAGEMENT IN PRACTICE

The Royal Bank of Scotland Group plc is a diversified financial services group engaged in a wide range of banking, financial and finance-related activities in the United Kingdom and abroad. Most of the Group's business is centred, however, in Britain. The Group is organised as five operating divisions supported by a central function dealing with finance, strategy, legal and regulatory matters and external affairs. The Royal Bank of Scotland plc

(RBS) is the Company's sole direct operating subsidiary and it controls and directs the business activities of the five divisional units.[3]

The Royal Bank dates back to 1727 and currently has 413 branches in Scotland and 339 in England and Wales as a result of the merger in 1985 with Williams & Glyn's Bank. At 30th September 1993, it had total assets of £36.2 billion, financed by £32.8 billion in deposits and other liabilities and £3.4 billion in equity, and employed 23,896 staff in the UK The five operating divisions of the RBS are Branch Banking Division, Corporate and Institutional Banking Division, Direct Line (Insurance), Citizens Financial Group Inc. (of the USA) and Operations Division. Our principal concern is with the Branch Banking Division (BBD), the retail arm, which provides a full range of banking and other related financial services to the personal and commercial markets up to and including the medium sized corporate customers.

3.1. The Management Structure

In broad terms, the Royal Bank's approach to interest rate risk management involves the following elements. First, the strategy has the dual objective of stabilising product margins and measuring their profitability. Second, the interest rate risk has to be identified and measured. Third, the risk is transferred from the divisions to the bank Treasury function to manage, via appropriate transfer prices. At the divisional level, these transfer prices separate asset product funding cost from liability product funds values. Fourth, risks of the operating divisions are consolidated for the Bank as a whole and managed by Treasury — on a hedging or positioning basis.

Stability of earnings and capital is important for customer and investor confidence, and for the growth of the Bank. As for any other business, retained profits are a primary source of capital generation for the RBS, capital which is needed to support balance sheet growth as well as the expansion of infrastructure.

Net interest income (NII) from retail banking represents a significant contribution to the Bank's net profits. Small changes in NII will create considerable volatility in net profits and consequently in the generation of capital.

Net interest income in turn can be seen as the sum of product balances and margins. Stability of NII thus requires the maintenance of product balances and margins through time. Product balances are relatively stable in retail banking, and so in practice the management of NII stability reduces to managing the stability of product margins. The size of the margin and also the riskiness or volatility of that margin have to be managed effectively.

The main objective, then, of the management of interest rate risk at RBS can be summarised as stabilising net interest margins (NIM) and protecting them from interest rate fluctuations. This goal is achieved by minimising interest rate exposure at the division level, by transferring the risk positions to the centre where they are managed at a consolidated level, for the Group as a whole. There is thus a two-tiered approach:

1) At the divisional level, the aim is to minimise volatility and stabilise margins. The divisions will only be making the credit margin (within a context of profit maximisation) whilst their interest rate exposure will be picked up by the centre to be managed on a consolidated basis.

2) At the Group level or centre, a management vehicle is created by which the objectives set out by the Bank's senior management, at a strategic level, are met by either running a position or hedging it in the market.

Group Treasury Services (GTS) is the organisational unit responsible for the management of Group interest rate risk on an aggregate basis, within guidelines and limits established by the Asset and Liability Committee (ALCO), the body in the organisational structure with the role of managing interest rate risk at the strategic/tactical level. The advantage of this strategy is that GTS, with the support of efficient information systems, can have a global perspective of the Bank's balance sheet and can therefore hedge or take positions against the known consolidated position of the Bank as a whole. This helps to avoid the situation in which several units of the Bank may independently be managing their own exposures, taking hedging or positioning decisions whilst inadvertently increasing the exposure of the Bank on an aggregate basis, which could lead to increased risks and/or losses for the Group as a whole.

In addition, the centralisation of overall funding and interest rate risk in the Group Treasury enables the bank to take advantage of natural hedges within its own balance sheet, to realize market opportunities by the size of the transactions it executes, and to control more effectively the net structural risk position of the Bank. Also, the consolidated management of interest rate risk is important for the effectiveness of the Asset and Liability Committee's (ALCO) decision making process and control.

Figure 3 shows a simplified organisational chart of the Group Risk Management structure. At the highest level is the Asset and Liability Committee (ALCO), the main body with the responsibility of managing the balance sheet of the Bank at a strategic and tactical level. The ALCO is an Executive Committee of the Bank which reports to the Board of Directors. It is a policy-setting and monitoring body which usually meets every month and the objectives of which are to develop the RBS's assets and liabilities, to manage

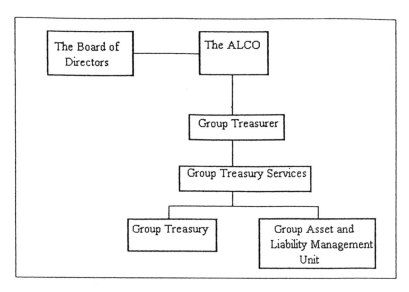

Fig. 3. Integrated risk management structure at The Royal Bank of Scotland. (Source: The Royal Bank of Scotland.)

the Bank's risk profile, and to optimise the investment of the free capital. The ALCO is chaired by the Group Chief Executive and comprises the Deputy Group Chief Executive, Group Finance Director, Director of Treasury and Capital Markets, Chief Economist, Head of Group Risk Management, and the heads of significant business areas.

This committee is supported by GTS, which is responsible for providing the ALCO with informational and technical support as well as executing the ALCO's risk management strategies. It comprises two distinct units: the Group Asset and Liability Management Unit, responsible for providing full technical support to the ALCO; and Group Treasury, which is responsible for the position management according to the strategies defined by the ALCO.

3.2. Risk Management Procedures

All divisional interest rate exposures are concentrated in GTS. The business units transfer their net risk positions to GTS at an agreed transfer price which reflects the cost of hedging those positions for GTS. In this way the units are freed from managing the mismatches in their balance sheets themselves and, theoretically, their interest rate risk exposure should be reduced to zero. GTS then manages the net interest rate exposure within the limits and guidelines set by the ALCO. It can lay-off the risk positions it receives from the divisions with the Treasury and Capital Market's Interest Rate Derivatives Desk (basically through the use of swaps, futures or any other hedging instruments deemed appropriate).

In order for the divisions to transfer their risk positions to GTS, the amount and term of the risk transfers has to be determined. The idea is to establish a basis for the risk transfer pricing between GTS and the divisions. To obtain this, what needs to be ascertained are the repricing characteristics of all products, both on the asset and the liability side of the balance sheet at division level. This process is initiated with a thorough analysis of each of the asset and liability products that the Bank offers to its customers through the different business units, examining the historic behaviour of the bank's products to determine the repricing characteristics and balance stability for each one.

In broad terms it can be said that RBS has three different types of products categorised by repricing characteristics. These are depicted in Figure 4.

- Variable Rate Products: predominantly Base Rate lending (overdrafts and term loans) and numerous deposit products. For most of these there is a no contractual repricing basis linked to defined market rates, and it is necessary to determine the behavioural pattern of these products to establish the repricing terms empirically. Once this is done, a wholesale market rate that best matches the pricing behaviour is selected to protect margin stability.
- In some cases the repricing characteristics of some products cannot be readily matched, e.g. those products which are priced at a spread off Base Rate. Most of the Bank's lending products are linked to this rate. The problem is that Base Rate is not a wholesale funding rate; banks cannot fund themselves in the market at Base Rate. Furthermore, there are few deposit products linked to this rate. What needs to be done in these cases is to determine a wholesale interest rate that most closely resembles the behaviour of Base Rate over time.

  For example, comparing the movement of Libor for 1, 3, 6 and 12 months with Base Rate (quarterly interest applications) has shown that the rolling one month Libor rate best matches the volatility of Base Rate (see Figure 5). Consequently, matching Base Rate linked assets in the one month wholesale market minimises the basis risk that exists in volatility of net interest margins.
- Zero Rate Products: for example Non Interest Bearing Deposits (personal and commercial). These deposits have no contractual maturity. Their repricing characteristics are determined by analysing their historic behaviour and their likely duration in time. The more volatile portion is

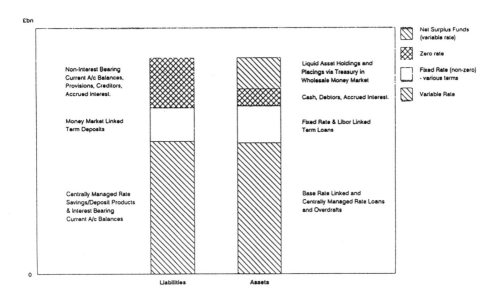

Fig. 4. Repricing characteristics of retail bank balance sheet (excl. capital and fixed assets). (Source: The Royal Bank of Scotland.)

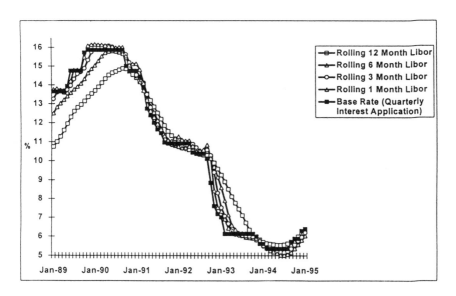

Fig. 5. Base rate vs. rolling wholesale rates. (Source: The Royal Bank of Scotland.)

distinguished from the more stable core long-term balances. A long-term market rate is selected to match the performance of the core portion whilst a short-term rate is selected for volatile/non-core balances.
- Fixed Rate Products: fixed rate mortgages and business term loans. These loan products are matched by contractual repricing term, mainly by bid deposits. However, the matching is never perfect due to the variation of mortgage loan outstanding as a consequence of early repayments and customer withdrawal behaviour.

Once the repricing terms have been determined the next step is to allocate the projected product balances to the selected repricing terms. A negative net balance on BBD's books denotes an excess of rate sensitive liabilities (RSL) over rate sensitive assets (RSA). This means that for that specific repricing term BBD has excessive rate sensitive funds over placements and will therefore be placing funds with GTS for that amount and repricing term. A positive net balance on the other hand reflects an excess of RSA over RSL's, and BBD will take funds from GTS for the selected repricing term. For example, suppose that in the 3 month exposure category, BBD shows an excess of rate sensitive assets (RSA) over rate sensitive liabilities (RSL). That means that the division would be exposed to interest rate movements in that amount. In order to eliminate that exposure it would need to match the excess assets with an equal amount of funding for that same term. This could be obtained by borrowing funds from GTS for three months in exchange for lending funds to GTS for one month. BBD would be exchanging (or swapping) one month funding for three month funding, eliminating its exposure to interest rates in the process.

By means of these transactions, BBD's net risk positions for each repricing term are cancelled out by mirror transactions with GTS. In reality, there is no effective movement of cash between GTS and the divisions. The risk positions are transferred to GTS by means of interest rate swaps by which only interest cash flows will be exchanged in the future between the parties.

In order to stabilise interest margins, the risk transfers are set up simulating a rolling term structure. This structure helps to smoothen out the effects of changes in interest rates over time. For example, a 5 year risk transfer of £300 million could be in the form of a single five year deposit from BBD for that notional amount for which it could arrange to pay, say, a fixed rate of 8.5 per cent p.a. In five years time, upon maturity, these funds would be rolled over at the rate prevailing at that time, say 5 per cent, for another 5 year period, then at the end of this period, at 10 per cent and so on. Alternatively, the risk transfer could be split into twenty equal tranches of, say, £15 million each and placed with GTS out to five years on a laddered quarterly basis. Each time a tranche matures it would be rolled over for a five year period so that at the end of the first five years, the whole balance would be placed for five years but on a rolling basis. Each time a tranche falls due, it would rollover at the prevailing rate but the rest of the balance would still be accruing interest at the initial rates. This helps to stabilise margins as the change in the average interest rate on the total balance every time a tranche rolls over will not be as abrupt as in the previous case.

The number of tranches into which each risk transfer can be divided will depend on the size of each tranche, the term of the risk transfer and the processing/administrative costs associated with managing the risk transfer book. In principle, the shorter the rolling period the more stable the margin will be. However the shorter the rolling period the greater the number of tranches and therefore the higher the administrative costs incurred in managing the book. On the other hand if the tranches are too big (or too small) the Treasury might have difficulties in handling the transactions in the market. So in practice, the risk transfer balances need to be split into tranches of manageable size both from an operational and cost effective point of view, bearing in mind the ultimate goal of minimising margin volatility within a given level.

Once the risk transfers have been determined and set up as a rolling structure, the task of GTS is to manage the exposure to interest rate risk. Depending on the strategy adopted by the ALCO, it will either run the positions or hedge them in the market.

4. ASSET AND LIABILITY MODELLING

One of the responsibilities of Group Treasury Services at The Royal Bank of Scotland is to provide a modelling and simulation risk/reward package for Group market risk exposure management. This section reports on some experiments with commercial software developed specifically for asset/liability management purposes.

Usually simulation models relate dependent variables (such as Net Interest Income or Net Profit) to independent variables over which the bank has some sort of control, for example volume and mix, as well as to variables beyond the control of the bank such as exchange and market interest rates. Simulation can help overcome some of the limitations of traditional gap (and duration) analysis, which are important in showing what is the current exposure, but only in a static sense and cannot deal with the effects of future courses of action or reaction to interest rate exposure (French, 1988). Many of the first attempts of modelling within the asset/liability management context were

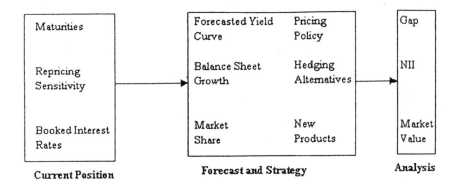

Fig. 6. Typical interest rate model structure. (Source: Elliot (1992).)

performed precisely with the intention of animating or articulating the basic static gap report (Hempel and Simonsen, 1992), resulting in the so-called dynamic or forward gap, which estimated the static gap that would occur in the future. But the emphasis was on the gap itself rather than the variation of earnings and the total balance sheet, whereas simulation better allows asset and liability management to be integrated into the overall planning process, including budgeting, strategic planning and marketing (Glomski, 1993).

Most simulation models for balance sheet management have the same basic structure. Figure 6 depicts a simplified model for managing interest rate risk exposure. The starting point of any model will be the current or initial position. Usually information on current balances, rates and maturities and repricing characteristics will be requested by the system. The future business to be generated plus the forecasted forward yield curve are then entered into the model. A single simulation or run will produce a base case which can later be tested for sensitivity by running different interest rate scenarios or changing some of the other variables that define the model.

Simulation packages developed during the 1980s allowed for simulation under three different interest rates scenarios: most likely, rising and declining rate scenarios (Bennett, 1992). Additionally a probability of occurrence could be attached to each scenario. Simulations were run for each of the scenarios and the results compared, allowing management to select an appropriate risk reward trade-off. The main drawback to these models was that interest rate scenarios were subjectively, rather than randomly, determined. Models now developed create many rate scenarios by randomly generating interest rate paths. Monte Carlo simulation techniques are used to generate these paths (Rubenstein, 1981; Brooking and Magee, 1991).

Short-term net income is usually the control variable in interest rate risk management, with models showing the sensitivity of net interest income (NII) or net income (NI) to changes in interest rates. Some models also incorporate the calculation of market values, duration and convexity providing a complete framework for the analysis of total return (that is, sensitivity of NII plus the change in market value of portfolio equity).

4.1. The Model

The modelling reported here was based on Group Treasury Services' risk transfers book using the Possibilities software package. The risk transfers book is a simple balance sheet in which the net positions received from the divisions are recorded. The objective was to create a model that could be used for simulation purposes, as a tool for managing the interest rate exposure of the risk transfers portfolio using a total return approach, but initially evaluating the effects of interest rate movements on net interest income (NII).

Possibilities[4] is an accrual based modelling package which allows for the simulation of a bank's balance sheet under different interest rate scenarios. The software package consists of a series files held in two dimensional matrices which appear to the user as multiple spreadsheets with the time periods across the top and the account lines on the left hand side of the matrices. By establishing relationships between the independent and dependent variables, a model which simulates a bank's balance sheet can be developed using the features contained in the package. Variables can be further related by writing equations which link them in many different ways. Perhaps the most salient feature of the package is that it contains a Monte Carlo Income Simulation option which allows for the generation of up to 300 different interest rate scenarios chosen at random by a Monte Carlo process.

An interest risk model has two parts:

– an historical (current) position model; and
– a forecast of future operations.

Standard maturity gap and duration gap are based on historical positions. Simulation of net interest income uses both the historical position and forecasts of future operations.

As in any asset/liability modelling package, the starting point to the modelling process is to define the account lines that will constitute the model

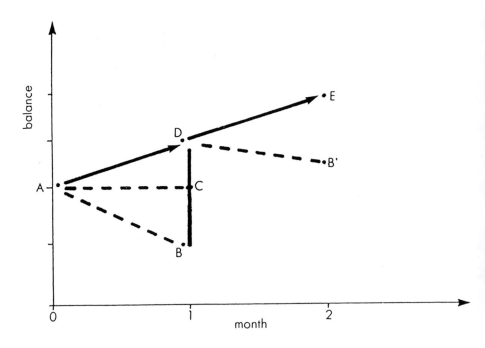

Fig. 7. Modelling behaviour of term deposits. (Source: Smith (1991).)

Forward Market Yield Curve - Semi Annual Basis

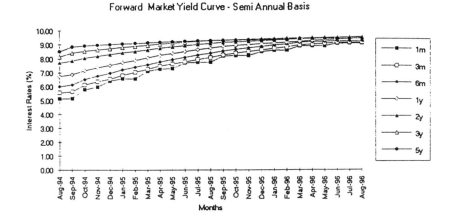

Fig. 8. Forecasted mid-market yield curve. (Source: The Royal Bank of Scotland.)

and to set up the account specifications. The definition of account lines includes the account names, account types (asset or liability and equity), accrual methodology (for calculating interest), interest rate calculation basis (fixed, floating etc.), tax status, the day in which trading will take place, on average, every period and the forecast methodology that will be used for each account line.

Once the structure of the balance sheet and income statement have been defined and the account specifications established, data is loaded into the model. The first set of data to be loaded into the model is the current position, that is, the initial situation of the bank's balance sheet. Although a product's beginning balance is a stock, and therefore relates to a point in time, it can be de-composed into amounts with different contractual maturity dates and interest reset points. Information is required on a product (or account line) basis showing current balances, booked rates, maturities and repricing frequencies. This will build the current position showing the actual outstanding balances, the rates at which they are booked and in what manner these balances will mature in the future.

Next, the future business is forecast. The marginal volumes and rates have to be provided as well as the maturity profile of this new business. To illustrate, suppose that we are modelling a term deposit with a fixed maturity and rate of interest. In Figure 7 the current position is a starting balance of A, and the forecast or target balances for term deposits are D for the end of month one and E for the end of the second month. If all deposits maturing in month one are not renewed and no new term deposits are lodged, balances would fall to B. The amount CB represents the runoffs in month one. New volumes are DB constituting both the volumes rolled over on maturity and marginal (new) business. New volumes less the runoffs equals the net movement in balances over the month. However, the weighted average interest rate of the runoff CB may not be the same as the weighted average rate at A, as different parts of the portfolio will have different interest rates depending on when each deposit was booked. Interest rates on new volumes are likely to differ again, as they would be set according to the interest rate regime prevailing at that time.

For products with contractual rate resets before maturity (for example, a term loan with quarterly rate resets), information is also required on reset amounts and existing rates on these volumes. In the case of products with non-contractual rate resets (e.g. floating rate loans with discretionary repricing), information on runoffs is not required because the whole balance reprices.

The following conditions were set for the simulation exercise.

1.   Volumes were assumed to remain flat throughout the planning period. Subsequently, the TARGET method was chosen to forecast future average

balances. This method implies that the average balances for each of the forecasted periods must be given and Possibilities then calculates the necessary new business to arrive at the supplied averages for the period.

2.   All new business was priced off a forward yield curve. A yield curve with seven points (1,3 and 6 months and 1,2,3 and 5 years) was forecast, off which all marginal business is priced in the future. This yield curve was constructed using the spot rates for the short end of the curve (1 to 6 months) and the swap equivalent rates for the rest of the points and was provided by Group Market Risk Unit. Figure 8 shows the shape of the forward yield curve used in the model.

3.   The interest rate for each account line was tied to the forward yield curve plus/minus a spread. The spread applied to each account line depends on the term of each transaction and the deal size of the individual transactions that are aggregated into the account line totals. This spread is added or subtracted (for assets and liabilities respectively) to the forward yield curve picked up by the equation which calculates the interest rate applicable to each account line.

4.   Two set of swaps were entered, effectively simulating the transactions closed by GTS to manage interest rate risk of the portfolio. The first swap, the 'short' swap starting in November 1994 and ending in February 1996, is a quarterly amortising swap, with decreasing notional amounts. The second forward starting swap, the 'long' swap, is initially an accreting swap, as it starts increasing in notional amount from February 1996 until it reaches a maximum in August 1997, and then turns into an amortising swap, decreasing in notional value every quarter until May 1999.

4.2. Sensitivity Analysis

Sensitivity analysis of any model involves testing for the effects of different balance sheet structures and interest rate scenarios. The balance sheet structure governs an institution's interest rate exposures, and the interest rate scenario which unfolds determines the outcome which transpires. Within limits, an institution's balance sheet structure can be altered by varying target balances and shortening or lengthening the maturity profile of new business. However, the institution has no control over the interest rate scenario. For this reason, an examination of different paths for interest rates is central to sensitivity testing.

The model was used to run both rate shocks and Monte Carlo simulations For the rate shocks, the model was tested using the standard parallel movements of the yield curve (incremental/decremental movements up to

TABLE 2
Impact of interest rate shock on net interest income

Change in Interest Rates (bp)	Effect on NII			Effect on NILAS		
	Key Income (£000s)	Change from Base (£000s)	% Change from Base	Key Income (£000s)	Change from Base (£000s)	% Change from Base
+200	-679	-2,181	-145	856	-508	-37
+100	412	-1,091	-73	1,110	-254	-19
+50	957	-545	-36	1,237	-127	-9
+10	1,393	-109	-7	1,338	-25	-2
0	1,502	0	0	1,364	0	0
-10	1,611	109	7	1,389	25	2
-50	2,048	545	36	1,491	127	9
-100	2,593	1,091	73	1,618	254	19
-200	3,684	2,181	145	1,872	508	37

+/-200 bp respectively). Table 2 gives the results of the interest rate shock exercise. The table shows that if there is an upward parallel movement in the yield curve, NII will fall; if the yield curve moves down in parallel, then net interest income will rise. This result is a consequence of the particular gap structure. The gap is negative for the first month (RSL>RSA) but then turns positive for the rest of the planning horizon (RSA>RSL); consequently, the gap ratio is less than one for the month of August 1994 (0.64) and is greater than one from then on. Thus the book is strongly 'liability sensitive' in the first month and then turns 'asset sensitive' in the rest of the months. Consequently, as interest rates rise the liabilities in the short end of the structure will reprice before the assets. To a certain extent, yield curve risk is also having an impact. The forward market yield curve structure shown in Figure 8 has a steeper increase (i.e., larger percentage increase) in the low end of the curve than in the higher end. Therefore, RSL in the first month will not only be repricing faster than assets but also at rates that are increasing at higher relative terms than rates on assets.

Table 2 is also useful to evaluate the effects of the swap hedge on NII. It can be seen that the result of the hedge has been to limit the downside risk of a fall in NII by a substantial amount. For the maximum upward shift in the curve (+200bp) the fall in NIIAS from the base case is 37 per cent as compared to 145 per cent in the unhedged situation. Nevertheless, the swap also has the effect of decreasing the upside potential of making a profit. Indeed, both the base case scenario (zero shift in the curve) and the maximum downward shift (–200bp) show a lower net income figure than the unhedged situation. This is obviously the trade off to hedging a position: the potential for making a loss is diminished but so is the potential for making a higher profit, which can be interpreted as the 'cost' associated with the insurance being purchased.

The Monte Carlo technique is a simulation controller that generates numerous random interest rate paths/scenarios (as many as 300 different random paths can be generated) and then runs a calculation of the complete model for each path to ascertain the effects on Net Interest Income. In addition to the forecasts of rates, the degree of variation of the rates in the future have to be supplied to generate the rate paths. The interest rate paths resulting from the Monte Carlo method will therefore be constrained by the distribution of rates, one year out, supplied by the user. Thus, the process is not totally random. Figure 9a illustrates the generation of random interest rate paths by Possibilities.

Possibilities provides two methods of establishing the user-supplied distributions: volatility or standard distribution.[5] Both measure the rate and range of the up and down movements of interest rates one year out. Numerically, for

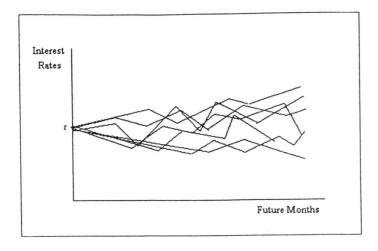

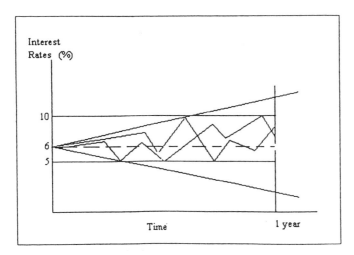

Fig. 9. (a, *Top*) Random paths of interest rates. (b, *Bottom*) Limiting the random rate generator. (Source: Brooking/Magee (1992).)

example, a 10 per cent volatility per annum means that with approximately 68 per cent probability the interest rate levels at the end of one year will be within 10 per cent of the starting level on either side. With 95 per cent probability, the rates will be within a range twice as large, i.e. within 20 per cent of the starting level.

In addition to specifying the possible distribution of interest rates one year out, Possibilities contemplates the alternative of limiting the random rate generator to keep the rates produced by the random process within 'realistic' levels. The Monte Carlo simulation will generate interest paths within a band specified by the user defined by the maximum and the minimum level that interest rates for each term may reach any time within the next year. This is illustrated graphically in Figure 9b where the interest rate paths are maintained within a specified band, with a ceiling of 10 per cent and a floor of 5 per cent from a starting rate of 6 per cent.

For all simulations, the volatility of interest rates one year out was estimated as being 15 per cent for all rates, although the 3 month rate was chosen as the target rate. Figure 10 shows, for illustrative purposes, the distribution of net interest income to changes in interest rates under these assumptions. What this graph is showing is that there is a 100 per cent chance that NII for the period under analysis will be above £–0.4 million; 80 per cent chance that it will be above 1 million; 50 per cent chance that it will be above £1.5 million and no chance that it will be above £2.6 million.

Figure 11 shows, again for illustrative purposes, the dispersion of Net Interest Income with respect to the different levels of the 3 month rate which was targeted. Each point on the graph is the result of an individual simulation (or sample). It can be seen that there is a very strong linear relationship between NII and the level of interest rates. The higher the rate, the lower the level of income and vice versa. The linear relationship identified is in part a consequence of the simple assumptions which were taken when defining the model. The balance sheet is deterministic in the sense that balances are not affected by movements in interest rates. The assumption made was that balances would remain flat over the planning period. Movements in interest rates usually bring about substantial modifications to the structure of the balance sheet as a consequence of, for example, changes in customer behaviour. This typically results in a non-linear relationship between changes in interest rates and net interest income.

5. CONCLUSION

Following on from the last observation, the conclusion must be that however valuable computer simulations are for testing the sensitivities of net interest income to movements in interest rates, they should be used in conjunction with other methods and techniques that a bank has at its disposal for risk exposure management. It should be clear by now that measuring interest rate risk in retail banking is very difficult, despite its importance for earnings growth and stability. Further, the maturities and repricing characteristics of

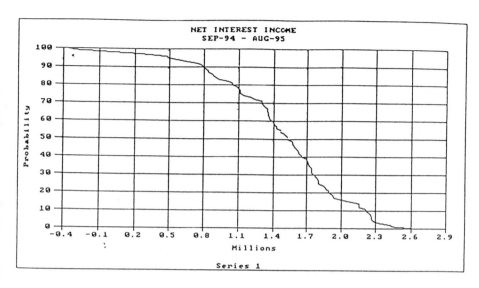

Fig. 10. Cumulative probability distribution of net interest income (NII). (Source: see text.)

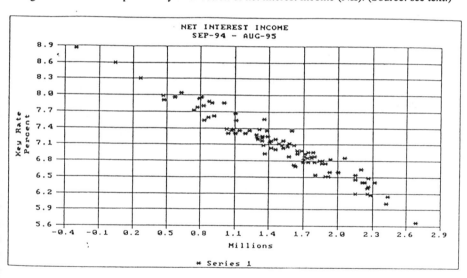

Fig. 11. Dispersion of earnings-NII vs. 3 month rate. (Source: see text.)

an institution's assets and liabilities are apt to change significantly over time as it reinvests cash flows and refinances liabilities. These volumes depend in a complicated way on the inherited balance sheet, the shape and movements of the yield curve, and the impact of these upon product balance growth

Mervyn K. Lewis, Phillip Morton

and customer behaviour. For such reasons, asset and liability management is demonstrably more of an art than a science.

NOTES

1. This paper is based on a seven week internship spent by Phillip Morton at the Royal Bank of Scotland while completing his dissertation for the MBA in Financial Studies at the University of Nottingham under the supervision of Mervyn Lewis. The paper also draws on presentations at the University given by Mr Phil Leverick, Head of the Asset and Liability Management of the Bank. The authors thank the Royal Bank of Scotland for sponsoring this project.

2. In the absence of liquidity preferences in the term structure, the risk arises not from interest rate increases *per se*, but from increases that are unexpectedly large relative to the market consensus at the time when the bank took its position. By 'riding the yield curve', the bank believes that interest rates are going to rise by less then was reflected in the term structure (see Lewis and Davis, 1987).

3. The following information is based on data contained in the Prospectus of the £11.5 billion Euro Medium Term Note Programme dated 22nd February 1994 issued by The Royal Bank of Scotland plc.

4. Possibilities and Monte Carlo Income Simulation are trademarks of the Bennet Management Services, Inc. Possibilities is a DOS based simulation package that can be run on a standard PC with an Intel 80386 or higher processor, 640k of memory and a hard disk drive of 5MB of free memory.

5. The difference in using volatility or the standard deviation as the measures of variance is based on the difference between the normal and the log-normal process of generating the rates at random. The normal process is an additive process. The random rate changes, which tend to be of the same relative size regardless of the level of interest rates, are simply added to the previous period's interest rate to generate the rate for any given period. A normal distribution, therefore, implies equal probability of equal absolute change. The log-normal process, on the other hand, is a multiplicative process. The amount of change is directly related to the level of interest rates of the previous period. The normal process implies, then, equal probability of equal percentage change.

Either rate generation process may be selected for a Monte Carlo simulation. The use of one method or the other will depend on which process is selected to generate the interest rate paths and, in turn, these will be dependent on the assumptions being made on the shape of the future distribution of interest rates.

REFERENCES

Bennett, D. (1992). 'Into the Next Generation', *Balance Sheet* 1, No.2, Summer. pp. 28-32.

Brooking, C. and D. Magee, D. (1991). 'Using Monte Carlo Simulation to Manage Interest Rate Risk', *Bank Accounting and Finance*, Boston, Fall, Vol. 5:1. pp. 48-54.

Carhill, M. (1994). 'Information and Accuracy in Interest-Risk Simulation', Comptroller of the Currency, Economics and Policy Analysis Working Paper, 94-7.

Elliott, A. (1992). 'Asset and Liability Management – a case study' in Whitley, J. (editor), *The Alco: Strategic Issues in Asset and Liability Management.*

French, G.I. (1988). 'Measuring the Interest-Rate Exposure of Financial Intermediaries', *FDIC Banking Review*, Vol. 1, Fall, pp. 14-27.

Glomski, T. (1993). *Bankmaster. Banking Decision Systems,* Duration Primer.

Green, C.J. (1995). *Banks as Interest Rate Managers*, Cardiff Business School, January, mimeo.

Hempel, G. and D. Simonsen (1991). *Bank Financial Management, Strategies and Techniques for a Changing Industry*, John Wiley and Sons, New York.

Lewis, M.K. and K.T. Davis (1987). *Domestic and International Banking*, Oxford: Philip Allan.

Lucas, C. (1994). 'Financial Innovation' in *Current Legal Issues Affecting Central Banks,* Vol. 2, ed. R. C. Effros, Washington: International Monetary Fund.

Niehans, J. (1978). *The Theory of Money*, The John Hopkins University Press.

Niehans, J. and J.R. Henson (1976). 'The Euro Dollar Market and Monetary Theory', *Journal of Money, Credit and Banking* 5(1) Pt.2: pp.465-504.

Rubinstein, R. (1981). *Simulation and the Monte Carlo Method*, John Wiley and Sons, New York.

Smith, P. and M. Benci (1991). 'Measuring and Managing Interest Rate Risk' in *Risk Management* in: *Financial Institutions* ed. K. Davis and I. Harper, Sydney: Allen & Unwin.

Part D
Policy Implications

Is Central Bank Intervention Effective in Stabilizing Exchange Rates?

Summary

The key issue discussed in the paper is how the G-3 and EMS countries have conducted central bank intervention, and whether such intervention was coordinated, sterilized and effective. It is found that G-3 as well as EMS intervention was apparently sterilized, both in its immediate impact and in its long-run consequences. Second, intervention by the G-3 and EMS countries was ineffective in the sense that it did not significantly stabilize bilateral exchange rates in the long-run. It is argued that the predominant use of sterilized intervention, which represents the most ineffective means for stabilizing exchange rates, must be seen as the prime cause for the collapse of the narrow exchange rate bands of the EMS.

** **Axel A. Weber** studied economics at the University of Konstanz, and obtained both his Ph.D. and his *Habilitation* at the University of Siegen. In 1994 he was appointed as Professor for Economic Theory at the University of Bonn. Professor Weber is a research fellow of the Centre for Economic Policy Research in London, an associate editor of the *European Economic Review* and a member on the panel of *Economic Policy*. In his research he has visited the Queen Mary College at the University of London, the Brookings Institution and the Research Department of the International Monetary Fund in Washington D.C. He has been an adviser to the Commission of the European Communities and to the European Parliament. He has published mainly on exchange rates, monetary policy, international finance, and trade.

** Prix Marjolin.

This paper was awarded the Prix Marjolin of ECU 2000 for the best contribution to the 1995 SUERF Colloquium by an author of less than forty years of age. (See also Editors' Introduction).

XIV. Is Central Bank Intervention Effective in Stabilizing Exchange Rates?

AXEL A. WEBER*

1. INTRODUCTION

The present paper deals with the issue of whether or not central bank's foreign exchange intervention is effective in stabilizing exchange rates. The aim of the paper is to question the validity of commonly held views about intervention within the framework of the G-3 consultations (between the United States, Japan and Germany) and the European Monetary System (EMS), and to provide new empirical evidence on how intervention within these systems was conducted and why it may have failed in maintaining stable exchange rates in the long run.

The paper first regards G-3, in particular transatlantic exchange rate management and foreign exchange intervention. After a period of benign neglect for the exchange rate prior to 1985, the United States reportedly changed its attitude towards exchange rate policies with the Plaza-Louvre agreement in 1985. Following an initial period aimed at driving down the value of the dollar, the G-3 countries switched towards a policy of targeting their dollar exchange rates within wide unofficial bands of ±12 per cent (see Funabashi, 1988, or McKinnon, 1993). The collapse of the narrow exchange rate target zones of the EMS in August 1993 has also resulted in a system of wide exchange rate bands of ± 15 per cent around the unchanged old parities. Both systems may therefore currently operate in a quite similar fashion, and it is thus interesting to analyse whether the past experience of G-3 countries with exchange rate management and central bank intervention in the framework

*This work is also part of a CEPR research programme on *Macroeconomics, Politics and Growth in Europe*, supported by the Commission of the European Communities under its Human Capital and Mobility Programme (No. ERBCHRXCT930234). Financial support by the Commission of the European Communities and by the Deutsche Forschungsgemeinschaft, Sonderforschungsbereich 303, is gratefully acknowledged. The author thanks Joseph Gagnon, Christian Bordes and Mathiew Canzoneri for detailed comments on earlier drafts of the paper. The usual disclaimer applies. All programmes and data (except the confidential daily intervention data) used in this paper are available on request.

of wide exchange rate bands holds any lessons for the future of the EMS. In order to pass such judgement, a quantitative evaluation and comparison of both the G-3 and the EMS experience is in order.

The key issue to be discussed in the present paper is how the G-3 and EMS countries have conducted central bank intervention, and whether such intervention was coordinated, sterilized and effective. It is found that G-3 intervention during the Plaza-Louvre period appears to have displayed three main characteristics: first, as postulated by McKinnon (1993), intervention was coordinated between the Bundesbank and the Federal Reserve, but there is much less evidence of coordination between these two central banks and the Bank of Japan. Second, G-3 intervention was apparently sterilized, both in its immediate impact and in its long-run consequences. Third, intervention by G-3 countries was ineffective in the long-run in the sense that it did not significantly reverse the trend of bilateral exchange rates. The present study thus confirms results reported previously by Obstfeld (1988), Bordo and Schwartz (1991), Klein and Rosengren (1991), Ghosh (1992), Kaminsky and Lewis (1992), and Lewis (1992) that sterilized intervention has had no lasting exchange rate effects.

Similar evidence is obtained for the EMS. It is shown that intervention by all EMS countries was sterilized in its effect on the monetary base. Furthermore, such sterilized intervention is found to have been ineffective in stabilizing EMS exchange rates. It is argued that ultimately the predominant use of sterilized intervention, which represents the most ineffective means for stabilizing exchange rates, must be seen as the prime cause for the collapse of the narrow exchange rate bands of the EMS.

The paper is organized as follows: Section 2 presents a summary of commonly held views about G-3 intervention and exchange rate management, and confronts these views with the data. Section 3 provides similar evidence for the EMS. Section 4 concludes the paper with a summary of the main findings and an outlook on to the future of European monetary and economic integration.

2. G-3 INTERVENTION AND EXCHANGE RATE MANAGEMENT

In a recent paper McKinnon (1993) summarizes a number of distinctive characteristics of the international monetary order. McKinnon's (1993) view of the "rules of the game" is derived from economists' interpretation of G-3, G-5 or G-7 declarations and Funabashi's (1988) transcripts of interviews with policy-makers involved in these events.[1] McKinnon (1993) thereby differentiates between the pre-1985 *floating rate dollar standard* and the post-1985 *Plaza-Louvre intervention accords for the dollar exchange rate* primarily on the basis of issues related to exchange rate management and foreign exchange intervention. For example, McKinnon (1993) postulates that the United States remained passive in the foreign exchanges prior to 1985, but became more active thereafter. Germany and Japan, on the other hand, are supposed to have used the dollar as an intervention currency in order to smooth near-term fluctuations in dollar exchange rates without committing to a par value or to long-term exchange rate stability prior to 1985. In the Plaza-Louvre accord of 1985 the G-3 central banks then agreed to set broad target zones for the mark/dollar and yen/dollar exchange rate (of approximately ± 12 per cent), but they did not announce the agreed-on central rates, and left the zonal boundaries flexible. In case of substantial disparities in economic fundamentals among the G-3 an adjustment of the implicit central rates occurred, but otherwise infrequent concerted intervention was supposed to reverse short-run trends in the dollar exchange rate. The G-3 central banks thereby signalled their collective intentions by not disguising these concerted interventions. McKinnon (1993) further states that G-3 central banks agreed to sterilize the immediate monetary impact of intervention by not adjusting short-term interest rates, whilst in the long-run each country aimed its monetary policy towards stabilizing the national price level of traded goods — thus indirectly anchoring the world price level and limiting the drift of the (unannounced) exchange rate target zones.

An obvious question is whether or not the above propositions are consistent with the stylized facts reported about intervention in the literature. This issue is discussed in the following section, whereby special attention will be paid to the objectives governing foreign exchange intervention, their degree of domestic sterilization and international coordination as well as their effectiveness in influencing the exchange rate. In addition to reviewing the literature, the present paper also reports some new empirical evidence.

2.1. Stylized Facts About G-3 Interventions

Catte, Galli and Rebecchini (1992) report that G-3 intervention was rare and concentrated in time, and that during 1985–92 each of the G-3 central banks was on the market for less than one out of six trading days. Figure 1, which displays the US Dollar/DM market interventions by the Bundesbank (BBK) and the Federal Reserve (FED), shows that this fact only holds for the post-1985 intervention. Unilateral intervention by the Bundesbank in the pre-1985 period occurred regularly and not sporadically: the Bundesbank was on the market for the majority of trading days, and frequently with substantial amounts. Also, the Federal Reserve intervened frequently prior to 1981, but completely abstained from intervention during the early Reagan years (1981–1985).

Catte, Galli and Rebecchini (1992) also report that the G-3 countries never pursued conflicting intervention. Panel (a) of Figure 2 clearly supports this statement for the US Dollar/DM market. When the Federal Reserve was on the market to support the dollar, the Bundesbank was either absent from the market or was doing the same thing, and *vice versa*. Panel (b) of Figure 2 further shows that the Fed never pursued inconsistent intervention. When the Federal Reserve was on the US Dollar/Yen market to support the dollar, it was either absent from the US Dollar/DM market or was also intervening in support of the dollar there, and *vice versa*. Catte, Galli and Rebecchini (1992) further report that the timing of G-3 intervention clusters almost always coincides for at least two of the three countries, which strongly suggests that the bulk of the post-1985 intervention was coordinated amongst pairs of G-3 central banks.[2]

The effectiveness of foreign exchange intervention is also discussed by Catte, Galli and Rebecchini (1992). The authors identify 19 non-sporadic, prolonged and concerted intervention episodes between 1985 and 1991, 18 of which they classify as aimed at countering the trend of the dollar ('leaning-against-the-wind'). The authors report the following stylized facts about the effectiveness of coordinated central bank intervention: (i) all episodes were successful in temporarily inverting the trend of the dollar, and in 9 out of 19 cases intervention was definitely successful in the sense that the next concerted intervention took place in the opposite direction; (ii) all major turning points of the dollar coincided with concerted intervention; (iii) in the majority of the intervention episodes the very short-term interest rate differentials moved according to the exchange rate objective pursued by the authorities, that is, helped the intervention.

The problem with this evidence is that it is purely descriptive and not based on any formal testing. Also, as Truman (1992) points out, adopting a slightly different criterion for the evaluation of the effectiveness of intervention leads to the conclusion that at the best 5 out of 19 episodes were partially successful. Figure 3 reproduces the graphical evidence from Catte, Galli and Rebecchini (1992) for the US Dollar/DM exchange rate. Whilst it is true that intervention occurred at many turning points of the exchange rate, there also exist many turning points at which no intervention at all occurred. This strongly supports Truman's (1992) scepticism with respect to the claim of Catte, Galli and

(a) Bundesbank intervention, sales (-) and purchases (+) of dollars for DM, 1977-1992

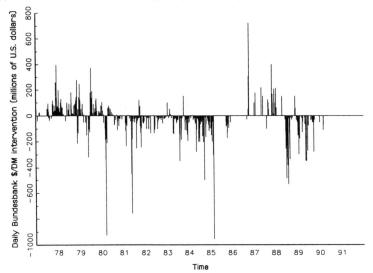

(b) Fed intervention, sales (-) and purchases (+) of dollars for DM, 1985-1992

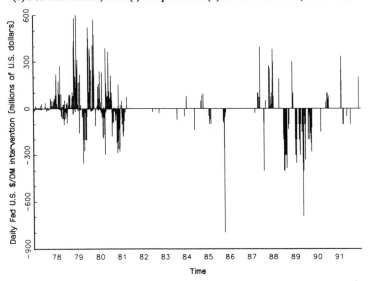

Fig. 1. Bundesbank and Fed interventions (billions of US Dollars).

(a) Coordination between the Bundesbank's and the Fed's $/DM interventions

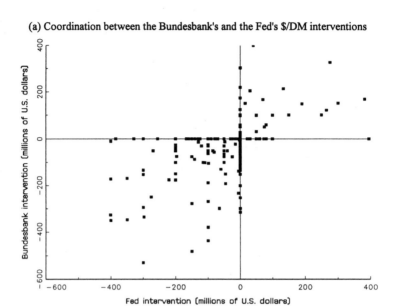

(b) Coordination between the Fed's $/DM and $/Yen interventions

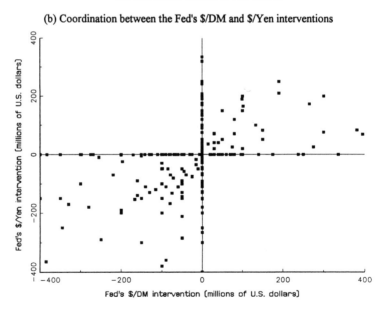

Fig. 2.   Bundesbank and Fed intervention coordination, 1985–1992.

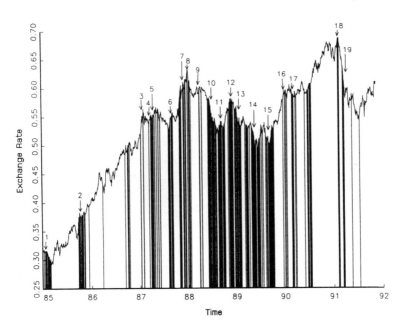

Fig. 3. Coordinated daily central bank intervention and the US$/DM exchange rate, second sub-sample (1-1-1985 – 31-12-1991).

Rebecchini (1992) that coordinated intervention was definitely effective in influencing the exchange rate in the short run.

A more differentiated view with respect to the effectiveness of central bank intervention is suggested by Figure 4, which displays the US Dollar/DM exchange rate jointly with a coding of foreign exchange trading days with sales (panels a and b) and purchases (panels c and d) of foreign exchange by the Bundesbank and the Federal Reserve. The most obvious fact from Figure 4 is the difference in the Bundesbank's intervention behaviour prior to 1985 and thereafter. Prior to 1985 the Bundesbank pursued frequent unilateral leaning-against-the-wind intervention by selling dollars when the $/DM rate rose (1977–81) and buying dollars when it declined (1981–85). After 1985 the Bundesbank appears to have intervened much less frequently by buying dollars when the level of the exchange rate was relatively high and selling dollars when it was relatively low. This suggests that the Bundesbank may have switched from a first difference to a level target for the exchange rate. Figure 4 also points out that the link between intervention policy and exchange rate movements must be studied carefully, since it may simultaneously reflect

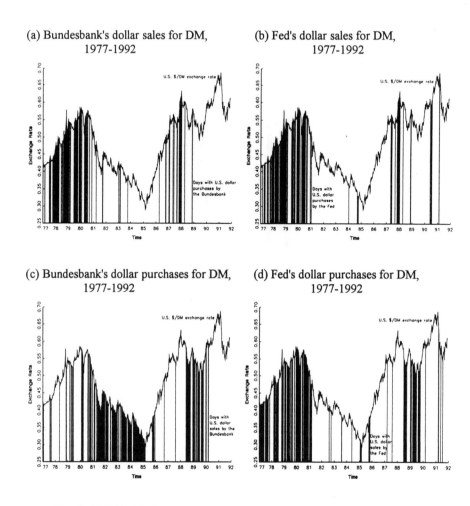

Fig. 4.   US$/DM exchange rate and Bundesbank's and Fed's interventions.

both the central bank's reaction function as well as measuring the effectiveness of intervention.

This brings me to the question of what objectives govern central bank intervention. Figure 5 looks at a number of potential arguments which are frequently referred to in studies of central bank reaction functions. Panel (a) of Figure 5 reveals that for the post 1977 period the Bundesbank on average bought dollars when the exchange rate was below a value of 0.45 $/DM and sold dollars when it was above. Furthermore, massive intervention occurred

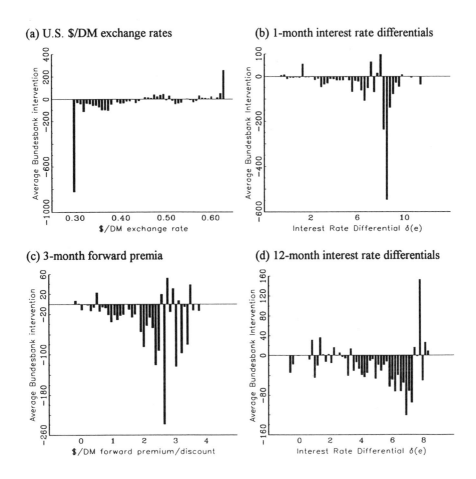

Fig. 5. The relationship between Bundesbank interventions and exchange rates, interest rate differentials and forward premia/discounts, 1977–1992.

when the exchange rate took extreme values. In terms of a level target this would suggest that during the post-1977 sample period the Bundesbank aimed at a target zone with a 0.45 $/DM (=2.22 DM/$) parity and fluctuation bands of ±33 per cent on either side of the parity. Such a level target is, however, only a poor description of the Bundesbank's intervention pattern in the $/DM market. Similar poor representations of a Bundesbank intervention objective are obtained when average intervention is displayed against short-term and

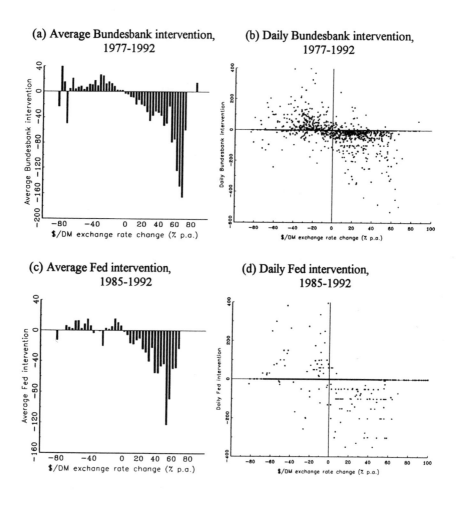

Fig. 6. The relationship between Bundesbank and Fed interventions and US$/DM exchange rates (over 8 week interval, in % p.a.).

medium-term interest rate differentials (panels b and d) or expected exchange rate movements, as reflected by the forward premium (panel c).

The best explanation of Bundesbank and Federal Reserve intervention in the $/DM market is obtained when short-term leaning-against-the-wind behaviour is postulated, as is shown in Figure 6. Panel (a) displays the Bundesbank's average intervention against the change of the $/DM exchange rate over an eight week period. The Bundesbank purchased dollars when the $/DM rate was falling and sold dollars when the DM/$ rate was rising. The average intervention amounts increased as the short-term drift in the exchange rate accelerated, suggesting that leaning-against-the-wind intervention was stronger the more exchange rates changed. The same intervention pattern is revealed in panel (c) for the Federal Reserve in the post-1985 period. Both results strongly suggest that intervention by G-3 central banks was governed by attempts to smooth near-term fluctuations in the dollar exchange rate without committing to a par value or long-term level target for the exchange rate.

So far it was established that G-3 intervention was largely coordinated and likely to have been aimed at stabilizing near-term exchange rate movements by leaning-against-the-wind. In order to judge the effectiveness of intervention it is further important to establish whether or not intervention was sterilized, since theoretical arguments in favour of the effectiveness of sterilized intervention are weak, as will be discussed in more detail below. Sterilization is typically judged by comparing intervention or the corresponding changes in central bank's net foreign assets with corresponding movements in the domestic credit component of the monetary base. Complete sterilization implies that the intervention leaves the monetary base unaltered and is off-set by a corresponding contraction in domestic credit. Two issues have to be discussed here. First, balance sheet data on changes in the net foreign asset component of the monetary base are typically used as a proxy measure for central bank intervention. The validity of this approximation has to be questioned. Second, the degree of sterilization has to be assessed.

Figure 7 shows that for the United States and Germany, the two countries where daily intervention data are publicly available, the approximation of central bank intervention by changes in the balance sheet data on net foreign assets works quite well: between 1977 and 1992 the correlation between intervention and changes in net foreign assets is 58.9 per cent for the United States, and 42.1 per cent for Germany. Thus, in order to obtain comparative international evidence, the remainder of the study is based on the monthly proxy of intervention.

Figure 8 shows that for the United States and Germany some weak evidence of sterilization exists, as measured by a negative correlation between changes in the domestic credit and net foreign asset components of the monetary base. This link is, however, far from being contemporaneously complete.

2.2. Empirical Evidence About G-3 Intervention

Before reporting any empirical results about the effectiveness of intervention, it is important to highlight some problems faced by any empirical study of this

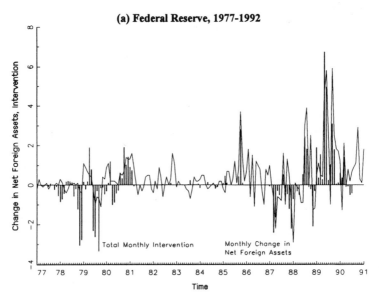

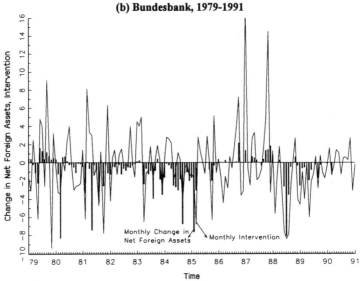

Fig. 7. Monthly sums of daily interventions and monthly changes in the net foreign assets of the Federal Reserve and the Bundesbank.

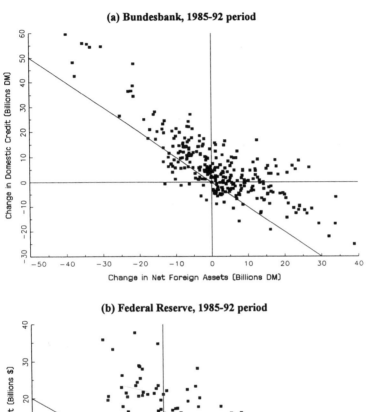

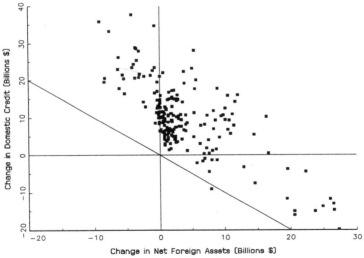

Fig. 8. Domestic credit growth, intervention and the sterilization hypothesis.

issue. In my view the key problem is that the effectiveness of intervention, the degree of sterilization and the degree of coordination of intervention must not be viewed as separate issues, as will be discussed in more detail below.

One potential link exists between the coordination and the effectiveness of intervention. For example, Catte, Galli and Rebecchini (1992) argue that coordinated intervention is likely to have more substantial effects than non-coordinated intervention. A second and more important link exists between the sterilization of intervention and its effectiveness. For example, the Jurgensen (1983) report did not view sterilized intervention as an effective policy instrument. According to the Jurgensen (1983) report, the effect of unsterilized intervention, which directly affects a country's monetary base, has to be considered to be much larger than that of sterilized intervention. Funabashi (1988) also reports that the Bank of Japan at times conducted unsterilized intervention in order to maximize its effectiveness. In general, whilst the effectiveness of unsterilized central bank intervention is unquestioned in the theoretical literature, there exists considerable controversy over the effectiveness of sterilized intervention. To date only two channels have been identified through which sterilized intervention may affect the exchange rate: the expectations or signalling channel and the portfolio channel.

The signalling channel has first been formulated by Mussa (1981), who points out that if uncovered interest rate parity holds, then sterilized intervention which leaves interest rates unaltered can have an indirect effect on the spot exchange rate by changing the expected future exchange rate. This may be the case if current intervention is perceived by market participants as a signal of future changes in monetary policy and hence future exchange rate changes. However, the empirical evidence in support of this expectations or signalling channel is weak, and most empirical studies, such as Klein and Rosengren (1991), Ghosh (1992), Kaminsky and Lewis (1992), and Lewis (1992) provide rather unfavourable results.

The portfolio channel literature postulates that due to foreign exchange risks domestic and foreign assets are imperfect substitutes. Risk averse agents then have to be compensated for the higher risk of holding foreign bonds by being paid a risk premium. Sterilized intervention, that is a change in the supply of domestic relative to foreign assets then requires a change in the risk premium for portfolio investors to maintain asset market equilibrium. This risk premium is typically measured as the deviation from uncovered interest rate parity. Thus, for given exchange rate expectations and a given interest rate differential the change in the risk premium requires a corresponding change in the spot exchange rate. The exchange rate effects of sterilized intervention thus depend critically on the imperfect substitutability of domestic and foreign assets. Whilst Dominguez and Frankel (1992, 1993) report some empirical evidence in favour of the portfolio channel by using survey data on exchange rate expectations, most of the empirical literature finds little or no evidence in its support, as Rogoff (1984), Obstfeld (1988) and Bordo and Schwartz (1991) point out.

To summarize, the existing literature strongly questions the effectiveness of sterilized central bank intervention, both on theoretical and empirical grounds. The following section reconsiders this evidence by first evaluating the effectiveness of intervention and then testing whether or not intervention was sterilized.

The Effectiveness of G-3 Intervention

The problem with the proposed empirical study is that in order to judge the effectiveness of intervention it is necessary to relate central bank intervention to its ultimate objective. To be more precise, the discussion of the daily intervention data above has revealed that intervention by the Bundesbank and the Federal Reserve may best be explained in terms of a leaning-against-the-wind objective: in the event that the Bundesbank buys US dollars through sales of German marks ($\Delta f > 0$) in order to support the dollar, such stabilizing intervention should be negatively correlated with present or past changes in the \$/DM exchange rate ($\Delta e < 0$). If such intervention ($\Delta f > 0$) were effective, it should further cause current and/or future exchange rate changes in the opposite direction ($\Delta e > 0$). Thus, in order to capture both aspects of intervention, the present paper reports empirical results obtained by estimating the simultaneous two equation system:

$$\Delta e_t = \lambda_{ef}\Delta f_t + \sum_{j=1}^{p} \alpha_{ee}^j \Delta e_{t-j} + \sum_{j=1}^{p} \alpha_{ef}^j \Delta f_{t-j} + \varepsilon_t^\nu, \tag{1}$$

$$\Delta f_t = \lambda_{fe}\Delta e_t + \sum_{j=1}^{p} \alpha_{ff}^j \Delta f_{t-j} + \sum_{j=1}^{p} \alpha_{fe}^j \Delta e_{t-j} + \varepsilon_t^\eta, \tag{2}$$

whereby Δf and Δe represent the changes in the net foreign assets component of the monetary base and changes of the exchange rate (measured as the ratio of foreign to domestic currency units) respectively. The above two equation system clearly points out the simultaneity problem between the causes and the effects of intervention. This problem has been completely disregarded in the previous literature, but will be the prime focus of the analysis below.

In order to estimate the coefficients in this vector autoregressive system the 2SLS instrumental variable techniques developed in King and Watson (1992) and discussed in more detail in Weber (1994a,b, 1995) is used. This simultaneous equation approach has two major advantages over the previous empirical literature: first, the estimates explicitly allow intervention to be both predetermined ($\lambda_{fe}=0$) and/or exogenous in the long-run [$\gamma_{fe}=\alpha_{fe}(1)/\alpha_{ff}(1)=0$ with $\alpha_{fe}(L)=\lambda_{fe}+\sum_{j=1}^{p}\alpha_{fe}^{j}L^{j}$ and $\alpha_{ff}(L)=1-\sum_{j=1}^{p}\alpha_{ff}^{j}L^{j}$] without necessarily imposing these restrictions onto the data. Second, equations (1) and (2) provide a natural framework within which the concept of immediate effectiveness ($\lambda_{ef}=0$) versus long-run effectiveness [$\gamma_{ef}=\alpha_{ef}(1)/\alpha_{ee}(1)=0$ with $\alpha_{ef}(L)=\lambda_{ef}+\sum_{j=1}^{p}\alpha_{ef}^{j}L^{j}$ and $\alpha_{ee}(L)=1-\sum_{j=1}^{p}\alpha_{ee}^{j}L^{j}$] can be formalized and tested empirically. In the discussion below the long-run effectiveness of intervention will be of prime interest.

The simultaneous equation system (1) and (2) is econometrically unidentified. In the present context this implies that the effectiveness of intervention is no longer testable when intervention is endogenous. Thus, even if the hypothesis that the shocks εt^{ν} and $\varepsilon_t \eta$ are uncorrelated is maintained, one additional restriction is required in order to identify the linear simultaneous equation model. In the literature only one identifying restriction is to be found: it is common practice to assume that intervention is exogenous, so that $\gamma_{fe}=(\lambda_{fe}+\sum_{j=1}^{p}\alpha)/(1-\sum_{j=1}^{p}\alpha)=0$, which holds, for instance, if one imposes $\lambda_{fe}=\alpha_{fe}^{1}=\alpha_{fe}^{2}=...=\alpha_{fe}^{p}=0$. Another, less restrictive approach is to assume that the model is recursive, so that either $\lambda_{ef}=0$ or $\lambda_{fe}=0$ applies. Finally, long-run ineffectiveness of intervention with $\gamma_{ef}=(\lambda_{ef}+\sum_{j=1}^{p}\alpha_{ef}^{j})/(1-\sum_{j=1}^{p}\alpha_{ee}^{j})=0$ may be assumed in order to identify the system and estimate the remaining parameters. In principle it is possible to identify the above simultaneous equation model by specifying a value of any one of the four parameters λ_{ef}, λ_{fe}, γ_{ef}, or γ_{fe} and then finding the implied estimates for the other three parameters. This is in fact the approach taken by King and Watson (1992) and Weber (1994a,b), but rather than focusing on a single identifying restriction, the authors report results for a wide range of identifying restrictions by iterating each of the four reaction coefficients (λ_{ef}, λ_{fe}, γ_{ef}, and γ_{fe}) within a reasonable range, obtaining each time estimates of the remaining three parameters and their standard errors.

The empirical evidence about the effectiveness of G-3 intervention uncovered by this approach may best be discussed by referring to Figure 9, which displays the estimates for the effectiveness of Bundesbank interventions in the pre-1985 period (panel a) and the post-1985 period (panel b). Long-run ineffectiveness of Bundesbank intervention is consistent with the pre-1985

(a) pre-1985 period

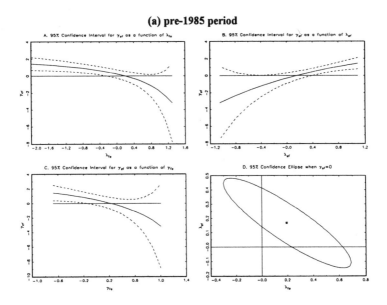

A: 95% confidence interval for γ_{ef} as a function of λ_{fe}; B: 95% confidence interval for γ_{ef} as a function of λ_{ef}; C: 95% confidence interval for γ_{ef} as a function of γ_{fe}; D: 95% confidence Ellipse, when $\gamma_{ef} = 0$.

(b) post-1985 period

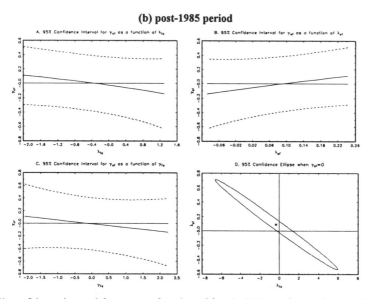

A: 95% confidence interval for γ_{ef} as a function of λ_{fe}; B: 95% confidence interval for γ_{ef} as a function of λ_{ef}; C: 95% confidence interval for γ_{ef} as a function of γ_{fe}; D: 95% confidence Ellipse, when $\gamma_{ef} = 0$.

Fig. 9.   Long-run ineffectiveness of the Bundesbank's $/DM interventions.

data only within a narrow range of identifying parameter restrictions, whilst it cannot be rejected over the entire range of possible identifications in the post-1985 sample. Figure 9 thus clearly suggests that Bundesbank intervention in the post-1985 period has been ineffective in altering the dollar exchange rate in the long-run, irrespective of the possible identifying restrictions on the coefficients λ_{fe}, γ_{fe} and λ_{ef}. Imposing long-run ineffectiveness ($\gamma_{ef}=0$) reveals no significant short-run effects ($\lambda_{ef}\neq0$) of predetermined intervention ($\lambda_{fe}=0$), as is indicated by the fact that the origin lies within the 95 per cent confidence ellipse for the long-run ineffectiveness hypothesis. In contrast, a rather different result is obtained for the pre-1985 period. Although both predetermined and long-run exogenous inter-vention ($\lambda_{fe}=0$, $\gamma_{fe}=0$) are again found to be ineffective in the long-run, modestly leaning-against-the-wind intervention ($\lambda_{fe}<-0.1$ and $\gamma_{fe}<0.09$) is found to have significant long-run exchange rate effects. Moreover, imposing long-run ineffectiveness ($\gamma_{ef}=0$) reveals significant short-run effects ($\lambda_{ef}>0$) of predetermined intervention ($\lambda_{fe}=0$) since the origin lies outside the 95 per cent confidence ellipse for parameters satisfying the long-run ineffectiveness restriction.

Weber (1994b, 1995) also reports similar evidence for all combinations of G-3 exchange rates and intervention policies. The long-run effectiveness of intervention is rejected by all the data for the post-1985 period, and imposing long-run exchange rate neutrality of intervention reveals no significant short-run effects. For the pre-1985 period the long-run effectiveness of intervention is not rejected over such a wide range of identifying restrictions. Predeter-mined ($\lambda_{fe}=0$) or leaning-against-the-wind intervention ($\lambda_{fe}<0$) typically has significant positive long-run effects ($\gamma_{ef}>0$). Furthermore, intervention by the Bank of Japan in the DM/Japanese Yen market and by the Federal Re-serve in the DM/$ market has significant short-run effects even if long-run ineffectiveness is imposed upon the data.

The Degree of Sterilization of G-3 Intervention

The degree of sterilization of intervention is analyzed in Weber (1994b, 1995) by using the methodology outlined above. More specifically, these papers report estimates for the *simultaneous* two equation system:

$$\Delta m_t = \lambda_{mf}\Delta f_t + \sum_{j=1}^{p} \alpha_{mm}^j \Delta m_{t-j} + \sum_{j=1}^{p} \alpha_{mf}^j \Delta f_{t-j} + \varepsilon_t^m, \qquad (3)$$

$$\Delta f_t = \lambda_{fm}\Delta m_t + \sum_{j=1}^{p} \alpha_{ff}^j \Delta f_{t-j} + \sum_{j=1}^{p} \alpha_{fm}^j \Delta m_{t-j} + \varepsilon_t^\eta, \qquad (4)$$

with Δf and Δm as changes in net foreign assets and changes in the monetary base respectively. As above, intervention or changes in net foreign assets are allowed to be both predetermined ($\lambda_{fm}=0$) and/or exogenous in the long-run [$\gamma_{fm} = \alpha_{fm}(1)/\; \alpha_{ff}(1)=0$ with $\alpha_{fm}(L)=\lambda_{fm}+ \sum_{j=1}^{p} \alpha_{mf}^{j}L^{j}$ and $\alpha_{ff}(L)=1-\sum_{j=1}^{p} \alpha_{mf}^{j}L^{j}$] without necessarily imposing these restrictions onto the data. Equations (3) and (4) may then be used to test degree of immediate sterilization ($\lambda_{mf}=0$) versus long-run sterilization [$\gamma_{mf}=\alpha_{mf}(1)/\alpha_{mm}(1)=0$ with $\alpha_{mf}(L)=\lambda_{mf}+ \sum_{j=1}^{p} \alpha_{mf}^{j}L^{j}$ and $\alpha_{mm}(L)=1- \sum_{j=1}^{p} \alpha_{mm}^{j}L^{j}$].

The sterilization issue has been estimated in a large number of studies before. The evidence from these studies is somewhat mixed. Some early studies find that the Bundesbank completely sterilized its interventions (Herring and Marston, 1977a, 1977b, Obstfeld, 1983, Mastropasqua, Micossi and Rinaldi, 1988), whilst others find that sterilization was less than complete (Neumann, 1984, Gaiotti, Giucca and Micossi, 1989), in particular in its long-run effects on base money growth (von Hagen, 1989, Neumann and von Hagen, 1991). Empirical studies for Japanese data, on the other hand, largely reveal complete contemporary sterilization (Gaiotti, Giucca and Micossi, 1989, Takagi, 1991).

The empirical evidence on the degree of sterilization derived in Weber (1994b, 1995) is reported in Figure 10, which displays the estimates for the Bundesbank's sterilization attempts for the pre-1985 period (panel a) and the post-1985 period (panel b). Long-term sterilization of Bundesbank intervention is consistent with the pre-1985 data only within a narrow range of identifying parameter restrictions, whilst it cannot be rejected over the entire range of possible identifications in the post-1985 sample. For the case of predetermined ($\lambda_{fm}=0$) or long-run exogenous ($\gamma_{fm}=0$) intervention, which is typically analysed in the literature, the data reject long-run sterilization in the pre-1985 period, but not in the post-1985 sample. Furthermore, in the first sub-sample short-run sterilization ($\lambda_{mf}=0$) does not guarantee long-run sterilization ($\gamma_{fm}=0$), and *vice versa*. Rather, the estimates suggest that in order to achieve long-term sterilization the Bundesbank would have had to overcompensate the effects of intervention by a more than proportional reduction of the domestic credit component. I view this as evidence against the long-run sterilization hypothesis for Bundesbank intervention prior to 1985. Given its very frequent and in part substantial daily intervention activities in the first sub-sample, it is scarcely surprising that the Bundesbank was unable to safeguard the domestic money supply completely from the long-run consequences of its foreign exchange operations, even if sterilization of any immediate impact was possible at times.

(a) pre-1985 period

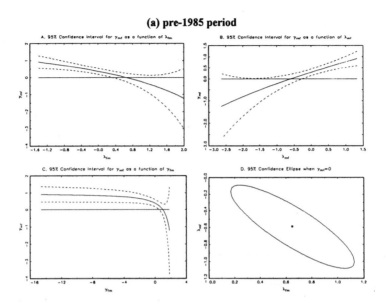

A: 95% confidence interval for γ_{mf} as a function of λ_{fm}; B: 95% confidence interval for γ_{mf} as a function of λ_{mf}; C: 95% confidence interval for γ_{mf} as a function of γ_{fm}; D: 95% confidence Ellipse, when $\gamma_{mf} = 0$.

(b) post-1985 period

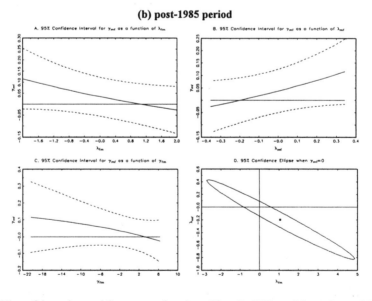

A: 95% confidence interval for γ_{mf} as a function of λ_{fm}; B: 95% confidence interval for γ_{mf} as a function of λ_{mf}; C: 95% confidence interval for γ_{mf} as a function of γ_{fm}; D: 95% confidence Ellipse, when $\gamma_{mf} = 0$.

Fig. 10.   Long-run sterilization of Bundesbank interventions.

Weber (1994b, 1995) also reports empirical results on the degree of sterilization for the post-1973 period and the two sub-periods postulated in McKinnon (1993). This evidence reveals that for the United States and Japan both predetermined and long-run exogenous intervention are compatible with long-run sterilization in both sub-samples. The point estimates under long-run sterilization of intervention suggest that the Federal Reserve in both sub-samples has tended to reduce the foreign component when the monetary base increased ($\lambda_{fm}<0$), whilst for Japan and Germany positive but insignificant coefficients ($\lambda_{fm}>0$) are found for the post-1985 period.

The above findings of long-term non-sterilized intervention by Germany in the pre-1985 period and sterilized intervention otherwise is broadly consistent with the results reported in the previous literature. As in the papers by Gaiotti, Giucca and Micossi (1989) and Takagi (1991), the data suggest complete sterilization for Japan. The pre-1985 result for Germany further explains why long-run sterilization ($\gamma_{mf}=0$) is frequently rejected in single equation studies, such as von Hagen (1989) and Neumann and von Hagen (1991), which imply $\gamma_{fm}=0$. Finally the present study also shows that failure to sterilize the long-run impact of intervention does not rule out that the immediate impact of intervention may have been sterilized, as has been suggested by Herring and Marston (1977a,b) and Obstfeld (1983).

To summarize, G-3 intervention during the Plaza-Louvre period appears to have displayed the following two main characteristics: first, as postulated by McKinnon (1993), G-3 intervention was apparently sterilized, both in its immediate impact and in its long-run consequences. Second, intervention by G-3 countries was ineffective in the long-run in the sense that it did not significantly reverse the trend of bilateral exchange rates. A major finding of the present paper therefore is that sterilized G-3 intervention has had no lasting exchange rate effects. The evidence on the effectiveness of central bank intervention obtained by the simultaneous equation approach of the present paper is therefore also consistent with previous results reported in Obstfeld (1988), Bordo and Schwartz (1991), Klein and Rosengren (1991), Ghosh (1992), Kaminsky and Lewis (1992), and Lewis (1992) for the post-1985 period. Furthermore, the present paper reveals a striking parallel between the degree of sterilization of intervention and their ineffectiveness in influencing the exchange rate. This strongly supports the results pointed out by the Jurgensen (1983) report, which views sterilized intervention as an ineffective policy instrument for influencing the exchange rate.

3. EMS Intervention and Exchange Rate Management

In order to compare the EMS and the G-3 experience with foreign exchange intervention, Weber (1994b, 1995) also conducted the tests reported in the previous section for the original EMS member countries, Germany, France, Italy, the Netherlands, Belgium, Denmark and Ireland, and in addition for the United Kingdom.

3.1. The Effectiveness of EMS Intervention

EMS intervention during the post-1985 period is found in Weber (1994b, 1995) to have been ineffective in stabilizing DM exchange rates in the long-run, regardless of the possible identifying restrictions on the coefficients λ_{fe}, γ_{fe} and λ_{ef}. The only major exception is the Bundesbank's intervention with respect to the Italian Lira exchange rate, where significant positive long-run effects are obtained no matter what identifying restrictions were placed on λ_{fe}, γ_{fe} and λ_{ef}. The positive sign thereby suggests that Bundesbank intervention has without doubt been unsuccessful, as it appears to have destabilized ($\lambda_{ef} > 0$) rather than stabilized ($\lambda_{ef} < 0$) the Lira exchange rate.

3.2. The Degree of Sterilization of EMS Intervention

Weber (1994b, 1995) also reports estimation results for the sterilization issue within the EMS. As for the G-3 countries above, there is little evidence about long-run non-sterilized intervention in the post-1985 period. Except for Germany and France in the pre-1985 period and the Netherlands and Ireland in the post-1985 period, pre-determined intervention ($\lambda_{fm}=0$) and long-run exogenous intervention ($\gamma_{fm}=0$) are found to have been sterilized in the long-run ($\gamma_{mf} \neq 0$). Also, short-run sterilization ($\lambda_{mf}=0$) does not guarantee long-run sterilization ($\gamma_{mf}=0$) for France in either sub-sample. Finally, the point estimates under long-run sterilization of intervention suggest that most European central banks in the post-1985 period have tended to increase the foreign component when the monetary base increased ($\lambda_{fm} > 0$), although the coefficient λ_{fm} is only statistically significant for Ireland.

To summarize, central bank intervention in the EMS exhibited the following two characteristics: first, intervention by all EMS countries, and not only German intervention as postulated by McKinnon (1993), has been sterilized in both its immediate impact and in its long-run consequences for national money supplies. Second, intervention by EMS central banks was ineffective in the long-run in the sense that it did not significantly stabilize bilateral exchange rates. This finding is consistent with the non-formal evidence reported in Weber (1994b) that the Bundesbank only participated in mandatory intervention at the margins of the bands. The fact that such marginal intervention typically occurred prior to EMS realignments in itself suggests that it was unsuccessful in defending the pre-realignment exchange rate target zone. The key point is that the predominant use of sterilized intervention by all EMS member countries may have strongly undermined any potential disciplinary effects arising from quasi-fixed exchange rates. This long-run ineffectiveness result for the EMS is furthermore consistent with the evidence reported for intervention in the G-3 context: sterilized intervention is unlikely to be an effective means for stabilizing exchange rates.

4. SUMMARY AND POLICY CONCLUSIONS WITH RESPECT TO THE FUTURE OF EMU

In this paper I have reviewed the evidence on the degree to which intervention policies differ between G-3 countries and the EMS. Foreign exchange intervention activities are found to have been very similar within the G-3 and the EMS context. Two sets of issues have been discussed: first, intervention was shown to have typically been sterilized. Second, such sterilized intervention was not found to have had significant long-run exchange rate stabilization effects. This is not surprising, given that sterilization aims at delaying or avoiding precisely those domestic monetary policy adjustments which would be necessary for guaranteeing long-run exchange rate stability.

In my view the sterilization of intervention by all EMS countries and not just by Germany is in part responsible for the collapse of the exchange rate mechanism of the EMS. Sterilized intervention signals a non-credible commitment to long-run exchange rate stability. Foreign exchange markets understood this signal perfectly well and hence have launched a speculative attack. These speculative attacks were successful for two reasons: first, it was commonly known that the German Bundesbank preferred to sterilize the effects of its foreign exchange intervention. Under sterilized intervention any accumulation of foreign assets in support of the Italian Lira and British Pound would have had to be offset by a corresponding decline in German domestic credit. Such a tightening of German domestic credit in the face of the huge private and public investment demand in the aftermath of German unification would have been very unpopular, and may have further driven up German domestic interest rates. The other option was not to sterilize the intervention in support of the Italian Lira and British Pound. However, this would have driven German domestic interest rates down and may ultimately have added to German inflation, which for the Bundesbank at the time was an even less appealing option. Against this background the reluctance of the Bundesbank to intervene at all in support of the Italian Lira and the British Pound was well understandable. The second reason for the success of the speculative attacks is that the evidence reported in the present paper suggests that EMS intervention was not able to stabilize exchange rates in the long-run or even in the short-run. This empirical finding holds for both the rare German obligatory marginal intervention and the intramarginal intervention by the remaining EMS central banks. The evidence of the present paper further reveals an apparent correlation between the ineffectiveness of inframarginal intervention and the fact that the bulk of EMS intervention was sterilized. For the Bundesbank the sterilization of intervention was a necessary prerequisite for the pursuit of an independent monetary policy aimed at anchoring the price level. For the remaining EMS countries sterilization clearly violates the *implicit* rules of the EMS as a "DM-zone", as portrayed by McKinnon (1993). The use of sterilized intramarginal intervention is motivated by the desire of the non-German EMS central banks to maintain some degree of monetary independence from Germany. Ultimately this signals a non-credible commitment to long-term exchange rate stability, and markets fully understood this signal.

The failure of the EMS may best be understood in terms of violations of *implicit* "rules of the game" on both sides. The Bundesbank is to blame in part for not having intervened sufficiently at the margins of the bands in support of the weak EMS currencies, but such intervention was undesirable at the time. The central banks of the weak EMS currency countries are to blame in part because they did not aim at stabilizing exchange rates intramarginally by their most effective means, the use of non-sterilized intervention. Ultimately the collapse of the EMS was caused by the fact that neither the Bundesbank nor the central banks in the remaining EMS countries were prepared to give up some monetary autonomy for the sake of exchange rate stability. This clearly points out the failure to co-ordinate monetary policy within the EMS.

In my view the key to future successful exchange rate targeting lies alone in international policy coordination, which needs to be re-enforced in the EMS. Economic and Monetary Union differs from the old EMS primarily in the degree to which monetary policy is coordinated and subject to joint decision making. Stage 2 of the transition to EMU should therefore strengthen the policy coordination and consultation process within the EMS. The new Community institutions, such as the European Monetary Institute, will greatly enhance this process. In my view the old EMS has placed too much emphasis on exchange rate stability as a means for enforcing policy coordination and convergence. But exchange rate stability must be viewed as the outcome of a process of policy coordination and convergence in Europe, and not *vice versa*. The current wide-band EMS therefore exemplifies the need for increased policy coordination much more clearly than the old EMS system ever did.

TIME SERIES AND DATA SOURCES

The paper uses both daily and monthly data. The econometric evidence is based on monthly data. Whenever original data were not seasonally adjusted, seasonal adjustment was carried out using the multiplicative adjustment procedure in MicroTSP 7.0. The time series and data sources used were:

Monthly data

Base money: IMF, *International Financial Statistics*, various issues, line 14.

Net foreign assets: IMF, *International Financial Statistics*, various issues, calculated as the difference between foreign assets (line 11) and foreign liabilities (line 16c)

Daily Data

Intervention: Bundesbank intervention in the DM/US Dollar market and in the EMS, Deutsche Bundesbank, *unpublished data*.

Federal Reserve intervention in the DM/US Dollar and Yen/US Dollar market, Federal Reserve Board of Governors, *unpublished data*.

Interest rates: Bank for International Settlements, *unpublished data*.

Exchange rates: Bank for International Settlements, *unpublished data*.

Forward premia: Bank for International Settlements, *unpublished data*.

NOTES

1. The G-3 countries are the United States, Japan and Germany, the G-5 countries consist of the G-3 plus the United Kingdom and France, and the G-7 additionally include Canada and Italy.

2. Due to the lack of Japanese intervention data this proposition cannot be re-confirmed here and is merely reported as it stands.

REFERENCES

Bordo, Michael D. and Anna J. Schwartz (1991). 'What has Foreign Exchange Market Intervention Since Plaza Agreement Accomplished?' *Open Economies Review 2*, pp. 39-64.

Catte, Pietro, Giampaolo Galli and Salvatore Rebecchini (1992). 'Concerted Intervention and the Dollar: An Analysis of Daily Data', Mimeo.

Dominguez, Kathryn M. (1990). 'Market Response to Coordinated Central Bank Intervention', in: Meltzer, Allan. H. and Charles Plosser, eds. *Carnegie Rochester Conference Series on Public Policy, 32*, pp. 121-163.

Dominguez, Kathryn M. (1992). 'Does Central Bank Intervention Increase the Volatility of Foreign Exchange Rates?' Harvard University, Mimeo.

Dominguez, Kathryn M. and Jeffrey Frankel (1992). 'Does Foreign Exchange Intervention Matter? Disentangling the Portfolio and Expectations Effect for the Mark', University of California at Berkeley, Mimeo.

Dominguez, Kathryn M. and Jeffrey Frankel (1993). 'Does Foreign Exchange Intervention Matter? The Portfolio Effect', *American Economic Review 83*, S. 1356-1369.

Edison, Hali (1993). 'The Effectiveness of Central Bank Intervention: A Survey of the post-1982. Literature', Division of International Finance, Board of Governors of the Federal Reserve System, Mimeo.

Funabashi, Yoichi (1988). *Managing the Dollar: From Plaza to the Louvre*, Institute for International Economics, Washington D.C.

Gaiotti, E., P. Giucca and S. Micossi (1989). 'Cooperation in Managing the Dollar 1985-1987: Interventions in Foreign Exchange Markets and Interest Rates', Banca d'Italia Discussion Paper No. 119.

Ghosh, Atish R. (1992). 'Is it Signaling? Exchange Intervention and the Dollar-Deutschemark Rate', *Journal of International Economics 32*, pp. 201-220.

Hagen, Jürgen von (1989). 'Monetary Targeting with Exchange Rate Constraints: The Bundesbank in the 1980s', *Federal Reserve Bank of St. Louis Review*, September/October.

Herring, R. J. and R. Marston (1977a). *National Monetary Policies and International Financial Markets*, North-Holland Publishers, Amsterdam.

Herring, R. J. and R. Marston (1977b). 'Sterilization Policy: the Trade-off Between Monetary Autonomy and Control Over Foreign Exchange Reserves', *European Economic Review*.

Humpage, Owen F. (1991). 'Central Bank Intervention: Recent Literature, Continuing Controversy', *Federal Reserve Bank of Cleveland Economic Review 27*, pp. 12-26.

Jurgensen, Philippe (Chairman) (1983). 'Report of the Working Group on Exchange Market Intervention', Mimeo.

Kaminsky, Graciela L. and Karen K. Lewis (1992). 'Does Foreign Exchange Intervention Signal Future Monetary Policy', Division of International Finance, Board of Governors of the Federal Reserve System, Mimeo.

King, Robert G. and Mark W. Watson (1992). 'Testing long run neutrality', *National Bureau of Economic Research Working Paper No 4156.*

Klein, Michael and Eric Rosengren (1991). 'Foreign Exchange Intervention as a Signal of Monetary Policy', *New England Economic Review*, (May/June), pp. 39-50.

Lewis, Karen K. (1992). 'Are Foreign Exchange Intervention and Monetary Policy Related and Does It Really Matter', *National Bureau of Economic Research Discussion Paper No. 4377.*

Mastropasqua, Christina, Stefano Micossi and Roberto Rinaldi, (1988). 'Interventions, Sterilization and Monetary Policy in the European Monetary System Countries 1979-87', in Giavazzi, F.S. Micossi and M. Miller, eds. *The European Monetary System*, Cambridge University Press, pp. 252-287.

McKinnon, Ronald I. (1993). 'The Rules of the Game: International Money from a Historical Perspective', *Journal of Economic Literature 31*, pp. 1-44.

Micossi, Stefano (1985). 'The Intervention and Financing Mechanisms of the EMS and the Role of the ECU', *Banca Nazionale del Lavoro Quarterly Review 155*, pp. 327-345.

Mussa, Michael (1981). 'The Role of Official Intervention', Group of Thirty Occasional Paper No. 6, New York, Group of Thirty.

Neumann, Manfred J.M. 'Intervention in the Mark/Dollar Market: the Authorities' Reaction Function', *Journal of International Money and Finance 3*, pp. 223-239.

Neumann, Manfred J.M. and Jürgen von Hagen (1991). 'Monetary Policy in Germany', in: Fratianni, Michelle and Dominik Salvatore, eds. *Monetary Policy in Developed Economies*, Handbook of Comparative Economic Policies, Vol. 3, pp. 299-334, Greenwood Press, Westport, Connecticut, and London.

Obstfeld, Maurice (1983). 'Exchange Rates, Inflation and the Sterilization Problem: Germany 1975-1981' *European Economic Review, 21*, pp. 161-189.

Obstfeld, Maurice (1988). 'The Effectiveness of Foreign Exchange Intervention: Recent Experience', *National Bureau of Economic Research Discussion Paper No. 2796.*

Obstfeld, Maurice (1990). 'The Effectiveness of Foreign Exchange Intervention: Recent Experience: 1985-1988' in: William Branson, Jacob Frenkel, and Morris Goldstein, eds. *International Policy Coordination and Exchange Rate Fluctuations*, NBER Conference Volume, Chicago University Press, Chicago.

Rogoff, Kenneth (1984). 'On the Effects of Sterilized Intervention: An Analysis of Weekly Data', *Journal of Monetary Economics 14*, S. 133-150.

Takagi, Shinji (1991). 'Foreign Exchange Market Intervention and Domestic Monetary Control in Japan 1973-89', *Japan and the World Economy*, 90, pp. 147-180.

Truman, Edwin M. (1992). Comments on paper entitled: 'Concerted Intervention and the Dollar: An Analysis of Daily Data', Mimeo.

Weber, Axel A. (1991). 'Credibility, Reputation and the European Monetary System', *Economic Policy 12*, pp. 57-102.

Weber, Axel A. (1994a). 'Testing Long-run Neutrality: Empirical Evidence From the G7-Countries with Special Emphasis on Germany', in: Meltzer, Allan. H. and Charles Plosser, eds. *Carnegie Rochester Conference Series on Public Policy 41*, pp. 67-117.

Weber, Axel A. (1994b). 'Foreign Exchange Intervention and International Policy Coordination: Comparing the G-3 and EMS Experience', *Centre for Economic Policy Research Discussion Paper No. 1038*, forthcoming in: Matthew Canzoneri, William Ethier and Vittorio Grilli, ed. *The New Transatlantic Economy*, Cambridge University Press, Cambridge.

Weber, Axel A. (1995). 'Exchange Rates and the Effectiveness of Central Bank Intervention: New Evidence from the G-3 and the EMS', in: Girardin, Eric, ed. *European Currency Crisis and After*, Manchester University Press, Manchester, England, pp. 202-235.

The Emerging Framework of Bank Regulation and Capital Control

Summary

This paper has three objectives: it sets out to provide a theoretical rationale for banking regulation in terms of a brief survey of recent academic research in the area; it attempts to provide a critical appraisal of the evolution of bank regulation in recent years, with a discussion of the pros and cons of existing rules and a (sometimes subjective) assessment of the principal problems which the bank regulatory framework faces today; and it assesses the viability of alternative solutions such as a narrow bank, a limitation of deposit insurance or a shift towards universal banking.

Julian Alworth obtained his D.Phil. from Oxford University in 1984, and his Laurea in Economia Commerciale from the University of Rome in 1975. He worked at the Bank for International Settlements from 1981 to 1993, before joining Mediolanum Consulenza. He is also a Visiting Professor at Universita Luigi Bocconi. His research includes work on tax policy, international finance, and financial regulation.

Sudipto Bhattacharya obtained his Ph.D. in 1978 from the Massachusetts Institute of Technology, and his B.Sc. in Physics from the University of Delhi in 1971. He has taught at the Universities of Chicago, Stanford, California (Berkeley), Michigan, Delhi and Louvain, before joining the London School of Economics in 1995 as Professor of Finance. His publications include *Frontiers of Financial Theory* (Volumes 1 and 2, Rowman and Littlefield, 1989) edited with George M. Constantinides. His research interests include topics in corporate finance, banking, economics of R&D and intellectual property, and the theory of contracts under asymmetric information.

XV. The Emerging Framework of Bank Regulation and Capital Control

Julian S. Alworth and Sudipto Bhattacharya*

INTRODUCTION

Bank regulation and capital requirements are presently at the centre stage of practical and theoretical discussions: trade journals such as $Risk^{TM}$ carry in nearly every issue articles on capital ratios and organise conferences for practitioners on sophisticated models for managing complex interest rate exposures; a host of specialised central bank committees have been set up in recent years under the auspices of the Basle Supervisors to monitor the application of the Basle Capital Accord and to provide the conceptual framework for the implementation of capital requirements on market risks; and a number of books and a spate of articles in academic journals have appeared since the early 1980s attempting to address the theoretical underpinnings of banking regulation as well as the more general role of financial intermediaries in the economy.[1]

Several parallel developments have spurred this widespread interest in the role of capital requirements and explain the different types of discussion to which they have given rise. One broad set of reasons relates to the changes in the institutional context of financial markets which has occurred in recent decades. In the first place, the elaborate framework of banking regulation which had been enacted in many countries during the 1930s — involving controls on interest rates and capital movements, restrictions on the composition of portfolios (such as types of asset held) and the segmentation of financial institutions (geographically, by maturity of borrowing and lending activity, by nature of involvement in the securities markets etc.) — was eased considerably in the 1980s on the grounds that this would lead to a more efficient financial system.[2] At the same time in most countries it was generally recognised that the greater degree of freedom allowed to financial institutions as a result of deregulation should be accompanied by wider and stronger

*The authors are grateful to Riccardo Rovelli for comments on a previous draft of this paper.

powers for the supervisory authorities, though it is interesting to note that the nature of the regulatory mandate (higher capital ratios, greater reliance on external accountants, or more frequent audits by the supervisors) differed from country to country and that no explicit conceptual framework for this form of "re-regulation" seems to have been discussed openly by the authorities.

A related development behind the renewed interest in bank capital requirements, especially the manner in which regulatory changes have been enacted, is the internationalisation of banking activity. It is no mystery that the creation of a "level playing field" among competing financial institutions of differing nations was one of the main aims of the Basle Capital Accord of 1988. The existence of a shared interest among supervisory authorities also provided part of the impetus to greater international cooperation in this area (for example, the creation of a formal Secretariat for the Basle Committee). Finally, it is also apparent that existing capital requirements in the 1980s (as well as banks' own internal risk management systems) were ill-suited to confront the changes in banking exposures and practices arising from the growing complexity of transactions and the expansion of off-balance sheet business, particularly in the form of derivatives.[3]

A somewhat different set of reasons which have stimulated interest in banking regulation arise from the number and magnitude of bank failures in the 1980s and early 1990s and the severity of some the resulting conseqences: S&Ls in the United States, banking problems in the Nordic countries, BCCI etc.[4] These crises have called into question the basic premises on which banking regulation is based and induced many observers to conclude that the moral hazard problems and the perverse incentive schemes in existing regulations were at the origin of the failures and subsequent bail-outs of the troubled financial institutions. Such systemic concerns — possibly deriving from a potential malfunctioning of payments mechanisms — also appear to have been implicitly at the origin of some of the peculiarities of the Basle Capital Accord. In particular the relatively high risk asset ratio attaching to interbank deposits — especially if considered in relation to the average maturity of such transactions — may be interpreteed as having been motivated by a desire to reduce the volume of business among banks and the possibility of costly bank runs via domino and "contagion" effects.[5]

Finally, one broad strand of the academic literature on issues relating to banking regulation can be attributed to a revived interest in understanding the fundamental characteristics of financial intermediation. Since the early 1980s much effort has been spent in explaining the nature of contractual relations, the functioning of markets in which economic agents operate under conditions of imperfect or asymmetric information and the type of "market failures" to which such circumstances can give rise. The aim of many of these studies has been to provide explanations for the existence of deposit insurance, equity constraints on banks and the role of the lender of last resort. Another and more practical strand of academic research has been aimed at the application of advanced mathematical and statistical techniques to the pricing of complex cash flows and the management of risk. Indeed many of the changes in banking which have taken place in recent years originate in the Black-Scholes (1973) options pricing formula and arbitrage free pricing. It is interesting to note that, somewhat belatedly, bank regulators appear to have paid greater attention to understanding how these approaches might be useful in assisting their supervisory mandate by allowing more precise measurement of the riskiness of banks' asset portfolios and the resulting bankruptcy risk.

This paper has three objectives.

Firstly, it sets out to provide a theoretical rationale for banking regulation in terms of a brief survey of recent academic research in the area looking at questions such as:

(a) What is special about banks and why might equity based capital requirements be desirable?

(b) Is market discipline sufficient to impose the socially desirable level of bank capital, if the latter can be indeed defined? How should the role of the regulator be interpreted, and what is a desirable scheme of incentives among the regulator, the regulated bank and society at large?

(c) How extensive should the safety net be?

(d) How and in what interests should the behaviour of financial intermediaries with insured liabilities be regulated? What role should capital requirements have in this context?

Secondly, this paper attempts to provide a critical appraisal of the evolution of bank regulation in recent years, a discussion of the pros and cons of existing rules and a (sometimes subjective) assessment of the direction which bank supervision might take in the future. Some of the specific issues which are addressed concern questions such as:

(a) How far has deposit insurance or the "too big to fail rule" induced undesired behaviour by financial intermediaries?

(b) What are the limits of equity based capital incentives on counterparty credit risks?

(c) Can market risks of complex investment portfolios be meaningfully quantified and at what cost?

While interesting in and of themselves these questions take for granted the existing supervisory framework and the overarching system of implicit incentives on which it is based. It also assumes that the "incremental approach" of gradually adjusting existing regulations to their defects as they emerge can be sustainable in the long run.

The *final* objective of this paper is more speculative. It attempts to sketch an outline of some of the *desiderata* of a regulatory framework, and to outline the design of a supervisory system if it were possible to start again from scratch. The starting points of the discussion are the narrow bank proposal and a recent proposal issued by the Federal Reserve Board (1995) which for the first time appears to address directly the potential incentives arising from different forms of regulation.

The remainder of this paper is accordingly divided into four sections. The first examines the rationale for banking regulation drawing in particular on recent research in the area of imperfect information and contract design. The second section examines briefly some issues arising from the changes in financial markets in the 1980s, and provides a partial assessment of the Basle Supervisory Accord of 1988 and the more recent attempts at extending the accord to covering market risks. The third section considers some possible modifications to the regulatory framework of many countries: (i) the implementation of an optimal incentive scheme for deposit insurance; (ii) limitations to deposit insurance; (iii) narrow banking and (iv) universal banking. Some concluding comments close the paper.

1. THE UNIQUENESS OF BANKING AND THE NEED FOR REGULATION

1.1. The Specificities of Banks

Many disparate reasons have been given for the purported uniqueness of banks and the need for heavy regulation. Some of these consider the prevalence of banking relative to market-based financing (and the difference between banks and other companies more generally) as attributable to the historical evolution of the interrelationships between the oligopolistic structure of the banking industry and the rigid regulatory framework constructed around it (Miller, 1995). Another view prevalent among central bankers is that banks play a unique role in the payment system: the rationale for bank regulation derives from the need to safeguard the payment system from possible systemic shocks. The necessity for the public provision of the "safety net" is that private provision would give rise to unsurmountable "moral hazard" problems if the restrictions on risk taking and portfolio choice were unenforceable.[6]

Finally, others identify the specificity of banks in the fundamental role of financial intermediaries in operating a qualitative transformation of assets by altering the risk and maturity (liquidity) attributes of financial claims. Two types of comparative advantages in risk transformation appear to be crucial.

(i) Diversification of credit risk in the presence of informational problems

In the presence of asymmetric information between borrowers and potential lenders, financial institutions can have a comparative advantage in providing intermediation services by reducing overall monitoring cum bonding or signalling costs. This comparative advantage can take various forms: a borrower might be prepared to reveal information to a bank, but not be willing to disseminate information to financial markets; or a bank may invest in information acquisition over time owing to an enduring relationship with the borrowers. Intermediation, moreover, reduces duplication in the acquisition of information.[7] Portfolio diversification by intermediaries (across imperfectly correlated projects) permits the benefits of this process to be passed on to the ultimate/primary investor (Diamond, 1984).[8]

A related approach to financial intermediaries is to view the role of these institutions as that of reducing or eliminating problems of moral hazard in relations between firms, their managers and ultimate investors (Hart, 1991; Hellwig, 1992). These problems arise because there are costs of monitoring managerial effort, the riskiness of firm strategies and the ex-post realisations of returns. Intermediaries are viewed as reducing these difficulties by engaging in monitoring and controlling activities in which presumably there are natural scale economies: it is less costly for a single intermediary to monitor a firm than a multiplicity of investors. In addition if the intermediary holds a well-diversified portfolio of firms, then the relation between the intermediary and final investors need not be equally affected by moral hazard and asymmetric information. It is possible for such a financial institution to issue a riskless security — if there are no scale economies associated with diversification Diamond (1984) — or to reduce the signalling costs (of undiversified private shareholding) borne by its insiders (Leland and Pyle, 1977), even if there are diseconomies of scale such as *internal* incentive problems with intermediaries (of duplicated monitoring).

(ii) Providing insurance against unexpected changes in the timing of consumption

By providing liquidity on demand, simple deposit contracts can insure against random shocks to investors' preferences affecting the desired timing of consumption. Bank debt contracts play a unique role in completing markets: in comparison to other financial instruments representing a direct (non-traded) claim on capital, and hence they permit the hedging (or risk sharing) of uninsurable risks to individuals' endowments such as employment, health etc. (Bryant, 1980; Jacklin, 1987). Owing to private information about such shocks (i.e. whether withdrawals are due to consumer impatience or to the fear of insolvency) deposit contracts may lead to coordination failures: if a sufficiently large proportion of depositors attempts early withdrawal, others attempt to join them. Runs on banks can be prevented by the suspension of convertibility, the introduction of deposit insurance or the existence of lender of last resort facilities[9] (Diamond and Dybvig, 1983); Jacklin and Bhattacharya, 1988)).

As already mentioned the uniqueness of banks from the standpoint of the authorities stems from their role as intermediaries in creating liquid liabilities in the face of relatively illiquid individual assets through at least partial diversification (aggregation) of both investment and liquidity risks on the two sides of their balance sheet. Hence, for example, it is usually the case that: (a) the debt to asset ratio of banks is higher than that of other non-financial firms; and (b) a far larger proportion of bank debt is short-term and directly demandable (from the issuer), than is the case for non-financial firms.

Some authors, such as Calomiris and Kahn (1991) have argued that the issuance of short-term (demandable) debt is also important for non-intermediary firms, in order to enable their lenders to exercise greater discipline on their managers, who are subject to the problems of moral hazard arising from shirking, the consumption of perquisites, the "private benefits" of excessive expansion (Hart, 1991; Hart and Moore, 1995), or excessive risk-taking in the interest of highly-leveraged equity holders (Jensen and Meckling, 1976). Recently Peters (1994/5) has shown that, given the deadweight costs associated with early liquidition of long-term (illiquid) asset investments, the optimal deposit contract allows for runs by informed depositors with sufficiently bad news about their banks' asset returns (in order to discipline bank management ex-ante) but that it also involves partial insurance of such deposit contracts, so that only some of the depositors choose to become informed. Broaddus (1994) provides a practitioner's recommendations for a regulatory framework along similar lines. A full analysis of both (i) the comparative statics of optimal deposit cum insurance contracts vis-à-vis asset risk (and managerial discretion) attributes of firms as well as (ii) general equilibrium modelliing of the contagion effects of runs and the endogenous determination of the interim liquidation (secondary market) values of firms' long-term investments is still lacking.

1.2. The Rationale for Banking Regulation

There are two separate elements to understanding the role of capital requirements in the context which has just been described. One important rationale
for the regulation of banks can be traced to their role as creators of liquidity,
and the mechanisms used to reduce the likelihood of "bank runs". Deposit
insurance and lender of last resort mechanisms suffer from moral hazard problems — on the one hand, shareholders of insured banks have the incentive
to invest in high-risk assets leaving the insurance fund to bear the downside
risks; on the other hand, insured depositors have no incentive to choose banks
according to the risks of their portfolio. Monitoring, capital requirements and
rights to close insured banks are natural ways for resolving or reducing the
moral hazard problem. At the same time the existence of bank examinations,
minimum equity standards and closure rules affect the incentives resulting
from deposit insurance, the scale of bank operations and risktaking behaviour
possibly in a perverse fashion. In other words "optimum" deposit insurance
must be decided jointly with the regulatory framework.

The second leg of this argument derives from the observation that one of the
major, if not foremost, mandates of central banks is to preserve the purchasing
power of the currency. An important instrument in maintaining the integrity
of this public good is to ensure that the payments system operates efficiently
and to minimise the probability of undesired contractions of the monetary
base arising from liquidity shocks, possibly amplified by investors' reactions
such as bank runs and panics. A role for the supervision and regulation
of commercial banks arises from the fact that bank deposits are the most
common means of payment in an economy, and that the facilitation of trade
(and investment) via money is a public good in modern economies.

A related approach to the role of bank regulators has been suggested by
Dewatripont and Tirole (1994) drawing on the corporate governance literature. They suggest that prudential regulation bears strong similarities to loan
agreement covenants whereby lenders (or insurers) attempt to restrict the
activities of borrowers by imposing constraints, by setting minimum levels
for a number of financial indicators, and by forcing default if covenants are
violated.

Some criticism has been addressed recently to these rationale for banking
regulation and specificaly to high levels of deposit insurance. Dowd (1993)
contends on the basis of his reading of the period of free banking in the
United States that in relatively unregulated systems banks with strong capital
positions retained depositor confidence. Safety net provisions, on the other
hand, had the effect of weakening the banking system. A somewhat different

set of considerations has been put forth recently by Broaddus (1994) who has advocated a partially insured deposit contract, with much lower limits (than the present $100,000 per deposit account in the United States). He contends that regulators can distinguish the difference between purely liquidity-based high withdrawals, or panics, and rational runs based on sufficiently low asset returns prospects of the issuing banks. An important issue in the design of the regulations is to analyse the additional bargaining power with respect to bank management, that the regulator obtains when he is "aided" (from an ex-ante perspective) by the illiquidity created by a run by partially insured, and informed, depositors. Such "aiding" may be important because uninsured depositors may react to information (signals) that are *not* externally verifiable and, hence, allowing *regulators* to react to such signals independently (forcing out bank management, for example) could lead to problems of potential corruption.

Another critical view of government intervention per se is that much of the role for a regulator, in the form of a central bank as advocated by Peters (1994) and Broaddus (1994) and implicit in most discussion, could be potentially performed by interbank clearing houses or clubs. Some, such as Kaufman (1994) have argued that this is essentially what these associations did in the free-banking era.

However, an argument can be made that such a role should be undertaken by a disinterested party (not competing with a bank), in these circumstances a public regulator (*qua* honest broker) could be the best agent to perform such a function (Marquardt, 1987). This argument is valid even in the *absence* of realistic differences such as the greater potential resource base, via taxation powers, of the state as a deposit insurer and also without any doubts about the ability of rival banks in the club to commit to view the underlying asset quality of a distressed bank subject to a run and/or illiquidity in an objective manner. The argument essentially is that judging asset quality objectively would necessarily often involve acquiring proprietary knowledge about the quality of a bank's specific borrowers and investments, and it would be extraordinarily difficult for rival banks to precommit not to use such knowledge to further their own interests.

1.3. The Role of Capital Ratios and Equity

As with all credit risks, holding all other things equal (such as underlying asset portfolio choice, debt repayment levels and maturity structure, managerial effort/efficiency levels etc.), higher equity capital reduces any firm's probability of default on its debt. In this respect, a bank is no different from a

non-financial firm (Miller, 1995). However, several circumstances are somewhat more specific to banking than other industries in respect of their "market
determined" (privately optimal) choices of equity capital ratios, and also of
the desirability of regulatory intervention (over and above market-oriented
creditor actions) in the mandated choices of (a) equity capital standards, and
(b) closure rules for declaring the debtor in default.[10] Prime among these
differences are:

(i)   The far greater and increasing over time (for example in the United
States between 1850 and 1945) geographical and inter-industry diversification
of bank asset (loan) portfolios, leading to sharply lower variability of asset
portfolio returns and market determined equity capital ratios.[11]

(ii)   The heightened importance of a large, regulatory "effective creditor"
in the form of a deposit insurance fund and its reluctance or inability to fully
adjust deposit insurance premia to reflect lower capital ratios and/or higher
risk estimates of individual banks based, for example, on examinations.[12]
This is in contrast with the presumed greater flexibility of private creditors
in adjusting credit terms (such as interest rates, maturity, early withdrawal
rights) to reflect the specificity of debt covenants and capital and dividend
standards, line of business restrictions etc.

(iii)   An incremental rationale for any divergence between market-determined and "socially optimal" regulated standards on equity capital in
banking may arise from the greater externalities associated with bank failures
compared to the bankruptcy of a non-financial firm, for reasons such as:

- the possibility of "contagion" (panic) runs spreading to the depositors of
  other fundamentally sound banks;
- "gridlocks" in the payment systems and the need for quick, and costly
  (monitoring and) intervention by regulatory authorities. In the case of
  gridlock of the payment system it is difficult even on the part of the central
  bank to observe whether a bank is illiquid or insolvent;[13]
- the non-substitutable loss (at least in the short-term) of "informational capital" on individual borrowers accumulated by particular banks (as compared to the "market niche" of a normal firm, in, say, an industry with
  monopolistic competition and product diversity).[14]

It has to be kept in mind that, leaving aside the deadweight costs (for example,
of taxation) involved in raising resources to pay off insured depositors of
failed banks ex-post, some recent research, by Samartin, suggests that with
significant deadweight costs of taxation suspension of convertibility may be
superior to deposit insurance for agents with moderate risk-aversion. The goal
in devising a socially optimal scheme of regulation, as well as the associated

insurance premia and closure rules, should *not* be the minimisation of the market or discounted expected value of anticipated losses to the creditor and/or deposit insurance agency arising from the potential bankruptcy of the debtor bank in the future. Instead, the appropriate objective should be that of encouraging socially optimal asset portfolio choices given an underlying space of risk/return tradeoffs by the debtor bank (Kane, 1995).

In the corporate finance literature on optimal capital structure, the distinction between default-risk-minimising and optimal-choice-encouraging debt equity ratios cum debt covenants is well recognised. In essence, in the absence of externalities arising from creditor losses or debtor bankruptcy per se, ex-post, the optimal choice of debt terms such as its level, interest rates and mandated covenants including capital standards leads to overall portfolio value maximising choices of asset investments by the debtor or a manager acting (in part) in the stakeholder's interest. Tradeoffs involved in such overall value maximisation include (a) tax shields on debt interest (possibly unimportant for a socially optimal choice), (b) any efficiency benefits, vis-à-vis managerial slack, arising from higher debt payment obligations,[15] (c) the anticipated value of (discounted expected) direct and indirect bankruptcy costs (such as business disruption etc.), (d) the impact of higher debt levels on the induced risk-taking incentives of debtors acting solely in the interest of the levered equity holders, who do not lose ex-post (after the debt contract) from any downside losses to the creditors.[16] As a methodological matter, an appropriate and convincing model of such optimal capital structure tradeoffs should also be of a dynamic nature, to reflect the ongoing nature of the debtor firm, both literally and to stress the importance of (risk control and managerial effort) incentives arising from anticipated rents to equity holders and managers, from the continuation (as opposed to earlier bankruptcy) of the debtor-firm in the future,[17] and also to allow the possibility of refinancing (equity issue) and renegotiation by the (bank) debtor with its creditors and regulators.

2. WHAT HAVE WE LEARNED IN THE 1980S AND 1990S?

The process of financial and banking deregulation that swept through many OECD countries in the 1980s was accompanied by three developments: (1) a much greater incidence of banking failures than in the preceding decades (in some instances on the verge of financial collapse); (2) a wave of financial innovation, most notably in the area of derivatives, and a greater emphasis on securities markets; and (3) a much more pronounced internationalisation of financial flows and a greater integration of financial markets. These developments were accompanied and in part stimulated by the introduction of new supervisory rules and international co-ordination among regulatory authorities. In the first part of this section we begin by examining some of the weaknesses of the regulatory framework in existence in the 1980s and early 1990s in the light of the experiences with banking failures and crises. We then turn to a discussion of some of the issues for bank risk management resulting from the wave of financial deregulations and innovations. The second part of this section examines various aspects of the Basle Committee framework. We review the nature of and effects of the 1988 Accord, the proposals concerning interest rate risk, the arrangements concerning netting and some aspects of the decision process, in particular the benefits and drawbacks from the peculiar "international" status of the committee. The third part discusses briefly FDICIA and a recent proposal by some members of the staff of the Federal Reserve Board. Some very tentative assessments close the section.

2.1. The Changing Financial Environment

2.1.1. The failures of the 1980s and the problems of the 1990s: deposit insurance, too big to fail and the operation of the safety net

The second half of the 1980s and early 1990s witnessed a sharp deterioration in asset quality among many banks in numerous countries with very different institutional frameworks. Not surprisingly actual experiences have been varied. At one extreme one can speak of widespread financial distress in the case of the United States, Norway, Sweden, Finland, and Japan.[18] In other instances deterioration in asset quality led governments to provide open assistance to specific institutions (the United Kingdom, France and Spain). Yet in other examples, public ownership of financial intermediaries prevented latent problems in institutions' portfolios from surfacing (Italy).

The problems were most acute and widespread in the Nordic countries, where institutions which failed or received assistance from governments accounted in some instances for about one half of total industry assets. By comparison in the United States the number of institutions (largely Savings & Loans) was much larger but affected a smaller per centage of total assets. The cost of coping with such financial crises has been very large and imposed heavy burdens on deteriorating government finances. Again this was especially true in the case of the Nordic countries where governments support to shore up the banking system is estimated to have ranged from 2.8 to 4 per cent of GDP, but also in the United States where the total cost of the resolution of distress since 1980 can be estimated to be some 3 per cent of 1992 GDP (BIS, 1993), or about $150 billion.

A number of common features characterised the emergence of these problems. In the first place, problem loans were the result of major expansions in lending and greater competition amongst financial institutions which followed deregulation measures, such as the lifting of (asset portfolio?) constraints. In many instances perverse tax incentives encouraged excessive leverage in the housing sector thus fueling the build-up in real estate prices and the over-appreciation of collateral values. As a result many institutions were exposed to interest rate risks to a much greater extent than they had anticipated either directly through the mismatching of maturities or indirectly because borrowers were unable to service their debt and collateral values vanished when housing price "bubbles" collapsed.

Secondly, the mounting crises were characterised in many instances by a weakening or relaxation of regulatory standards. In the United States, technically insolvent institutions were allowed to continue operating in the hope that the problems would be temporary. This policy of forbearance — or "buying time" — in fact often produced greater losses and financial distress than if earlier closure had taken place.[19]

Thirdly, the regulation was rife with "moral hazard" problems. Many authors (Bhattacharya, 1982 and Kane, 1985) already in the early 1980s had drawn attention to the problems with deposit insurance mechanisms based on fixed premiums unrelated to the underlying risk of individual financial institutions and to the perverse incentives this created for risk-taking.[20] Another element exacerbating moral hazard was the wide disparity of treatment among different financial institutions which took place after the problems actually materialised. In the United States, for example, smaller institutions were typically liquidated whereas larger institutions were taken over or received assistance without being closed down ("too big to fail"). These approaches also had the consequence of distorting competition and raising questions of fairness: in the Nordic countries but also France, notably in the recent case of Credit Lyonnais, weakly capitalised institutions were granted assistance whereas the healthy ones were not.

These developments highlight several weaknesses of the application of capital standards and the approaches taken to cope with distressed banks, and as we shall see below in some respects led to changes in regulatory procedures. Firstly, existing regulations failed to recognise the importance of systematic undiversifiable risks such as those arising from a generalised increase in interest rates. This in turn raised a conflict of interest for central banks: between the monetary and the safety net responsibilities. Secondly, the regulatory frameworks appeared ill-equipped to cope with mounting problems in the financial sector. For example, no explicit system of penalties applied to banks for failing to comply with the capital standards. Thirdly, the process of assistance to problem banks in and of itself created distortions to the regulatory framework by increasing the risks of moral hazard. Finally, recent experience has highlighted that the impact of specific regulations cannot be assessed in isolation without a knowledge of the wider economic context. For example, in the case of the US, S&L's strict regulation of balance sheets in the 1960s and 1970s coupled with a relatively stable interest rate environment and high rents from the charter meant that there were virtually no cases of distress and deposit insurance funds were not at risk.[21] By contrast in the early 1980s following deregulation — and in a volatile financial environment — the S&L's proved extremely vulnerable. Recent moves by regulators appear to be an attempt to redress some of these problems.

2.1.2. *Financial Innovation and Risk Management*

The wave of financial innovation and changing character of banking activity, which has swept through financial markets since the 1980s, raised several doubts about the adequacy of financial institutions' risk management procedures and contibuted to several changes in the existing regulatory framework. The new instruments have also drawn attention to areas where financial risks were previously thought to be relatively unimportant.

The foremost challenge of derivatives concerns the assessment of the typical risks involving financial transactions: market risk, credit risk, legal risks, settlement risks, operating risks and systemic risk. Derivatives require that both banks and regulators acquire more technically complex systems and skills for managing the risks as well as a greater degree of understanding of the nature of exposures.[22] To monitor the many dimensions of risk it has become necessary to keep multiple sets of electronic books to which information is provided almost continuously for trading purposes and at the end of the day for the overall risk evaluations. It is important that risk management committees meet often and include senior managers.

As far as *market risks* are concerned, the introduction of derivatives has rendered obsolete "objective" quantifiable ex-ante measurements of the riskiness of financial institutions according to traditional accounting measures, including marking to market. Given the highly nonlinear payoffs only model-based estimations assessments or simulations can permit an assessment at a particular moment in time of the actual value of the capital base of a bank.[23] These evaluations, however, are model dependent, to some extent judgemental (alternative hypotheses or historical episodes result in different outcomes) and inevitably destined to change over time as a result of the development of new market instruments and pricing formulae.[24]

The expansion of derivatives has contributed to underscore the close nexus between market and credit risk: recent problems with derivatives (for example, the default by Orange County) have shown vividly how changes in macroeconomic variables can result in a rapid deterioration in the credit quality of counterparties. The interaction between market and credit risk and how these two factors should be blended together with an assessment of portfolios of exposures appears only to have been considered by the regulators in relation to netting arrangements.

Legal risks have been in the forefront of the preoccupations of participants in the derivatives markets in large measure because existing laws are often difficult to interpret in the light of the new instruments. One area which has created many problems is the enforceability of contracts. The notorious case in which the House of Lords in the United Kingdom considered the derivative transactions by some London local council authorities as being "ultra vires" had profound implications for the assessment of counterparty risks.[25] Another area of private contracting, which also has implications for regulators, has been the manner in which derivatives are handled in the case of the early termination of contracts as a result of bankruptcy, insolvency or liquidiation of counterparties. For example, there is the risk that netting provisions might not be recognised in a particular bankruptcy proceeding and that this could lead to higher exposures than anticipated. Furthermore, automatic stay on terminating contracts typical of bankruptcy proceedings could contribute to uncertainties about exposures and the eventual recovery of funds from a bankrupt counterparty.

Finally, the changing character of *operating risks* resulting from exposure to loss resulting from inadequate risk management and internal control has certainly been an important aspect of concerns for regulators. The emphasis here has tended to be centred on seeing that senior management of individual institutions has developed and understands sophisticated internal control systems of credit and market risks. However, operating risks also apply to the regulators themselves who in several instances (particularly in the beginning of the 1980s) failed to appreciate the changes in the character and nature of risks arising from the activities of banks which they were mandated to supervise.

Another general consequence of the growth of derivatives is that it complicates the operation of the lender of last resort function by central banks, implies a very different time framework for assessing risk exposures and may accelerate the build-up of systemic risks. Moreover, the complexity of exposures can lead to difficulties in the ex-post verifiability of the actual positions of single institutions and even complicate liquidation proceedings.[26]

Finally the growth of derivatives and concommitant changes in banking technology have accelerated the breakdown of barriers between institutions subject to different regulatory frameworks. This has produced potential competitive distortions between institutions subject to differing regulatory authorities and access to the "safety net". It also raises the more fundamental issue addressed in Section 3 concerning the boundaries of banking i.e. which institutions should have access to the lender of last resort.

2.2. The Evolution of Banking Supervision

The changing character of banking activity which we have just described has been brought about, and in part been stimulated by, developments in the regulatory framework. The most important development was no doubt the Basle Capital Accord of 1988 but also a number of other changes have had or in the near future are likely to have a major impact on the conduct of banking activity: the Report on Interbank Netting Schemes, and the Proposals on the application of capital ratios to market risk. In what follows we shall provide a short critical assessment of the main features of the changes brought about by the new regulations, drawing attention to some of their potential impact on bank behaviour particularly in respect of attitudes towards risktaking.

2.2.1. The Basle Capital Accord 1988

The Basle Capital Accord was meant to represent a major break from previous definitions of minimum capital ratios. The following appear to be the principal novelties:

(a)   it represented an international agreement (not an international treaty) between all the major bank regulators and given the membership of the committee concerned nearly all (internationally active) major banks in the world.[27]

(b)   The regulations applied to the worldwide consolidated balance sheets of banks.

(c)   The Accord established that capital requirements should not be merely based on a simple measure of leverage. Rather minimum capital adequacy ratios should be based on *risk-weighted* assets, with different types of counterparty receiving different weights (for example OECD area governments 0 per cent, banks 20 per cent others 100 per cent).

(d)   Various categories of off-balance sheet activities with a clear on balance sheet equivalent exposure (such as letters of credit, loan committments etc.) were taken into account in constructing the capital ratios and weighted according to the perceived riskiness of the operations.

(e)   Conversion factors were developed to provide so-called credit equivalent measures of risk necessary for converting the notional off-balance amounts of transactions into values comparable to on-balance sheet exposures.[28]

(f)   Two different qualities of capital were defined: tier 1 or "core" capital representing paid-up stock and disclosed reserves; and tier 2 or "supplementary" capital including elements such as undisclosed reserves, longer term subordinated debt and shares redeemable at the option of the issuer.[29]

It is fair to say that after nearly seven years these requirements have achieved their primary objective: namely that of forcing the recapitalisation of the banking systems of many countries and particularly that of the United States. Nevertheless, in the light of subsequent changes in the regulation it is also difficult to dispute that the original measures which were devised represented a somewhat distorted assessment of the actual weighted risk credit exposures of single financial institutions. Indeed virtually all of these different novel features has in some way come under criticism, been the object of sometimes long negotiations with representatives of particular sectors of the banking industry or induced unexpected behaviour including avoidance schemes.[30] Among the latter some changes in behaviour by market participants — such as the adoption of netting arrangements (to be discussed below) — have resulted in reduction of systemic risks. However, others such as the much greater reliance on trading in government securities as a source of profits have had somewhat more dubious effects.

Somewhat different issues in respect of the new capital requirements concern whether they will actually succeed in staving off banking crises or assist in helping to identify problem banks. As far as the first concern, the Basle Accord does not take account of systemic risks: changes in the overall level of interest rates may have an impact on creditworthiness in ways which would not be identifiable from the riskweightings. Using the levels of capital to identify problem banks may also be difficult. A recent study by Jones and King (1995) applies the definitions of the Basle Accord to a confidential data set of US banks in the 1980s and finds that a number of institutions which would have exceeded the 8 per cent hurdle would in fact with a very high probability have been insolvent within two years.

2.2.2. Netting Agreements and Credit Risk Exposures of Derivatives

In order to a avoid the possibility that if a default occurs on a derivative contract with negative market value, the non-defaulting counterparty is free to reap a windfall gain, netting agreements specifiy that the net exposure of a portfolio of contracts with a single counterparty is equal to either the current market value of the portfolio or zero, whichever is lower.

There are various forms of bilateral and multilateral netting agreements. Recent amendments to the Basle Capital Accord recognise close-out netting agreements which provide for the exchange of a single net close-out amount for all covered transactions when one counterparty defaults on its derivatives contract. Close-out netting is now a standard provision of master agreements that serve as legal documentation of OTC derivative transactions including the ISDA Master Agreement.

Allowing for netting has two implications for the measurement of credit exposures. First, the *current* gross credit exposures — the mark-to-market value of outstanding positions — between counterparties tend to be much larger than net positions. Second, *potential* gross exposures arising from un-predictable price movements in underlying assets (exchange rates, interest rates, commodity prices etc.) are in all likelihood larger and more variable than net exposures. Under the original framework of the Basle Accord potential exposures were subject to so-called add-on provisions which differed according to the remaining maturity (more or less than one year) and nature of contracts (interest rate or foreign exchange). A netting agreement with a single counterparty covering diversified portfolios lowers volatility (if the positions are not perfectly correlated) because of offsetting movements in the value of individual contracts: this reduces the value of add-on needed to cover potential exposures (Hendricks, 1994). This reduction in potential exposures has now been recognised by the Basle Committee.

2.2.3. The Debate over the Measurement of Interest Rate Risk

The long debate over the application of capital ratios to market risks both within the supervisory community and between the regulators and private financial institutions highlights many other problems at the heart of the current approach to the supervision of risk exposures.

Although no public information is available concerning the varying ap-proaches considered by the Basle Committee in regard to market risks, it appears that work on developing such measurements was well under way soon after the approval of the Basle Capital Accord in 1988. Initially the supervisors believed that it would be possible to segment market risks into various baskets (interest rates, exchange rates, etc.) in a manner somewhat reminiscent of that taken for credit exposures. It was soon realised that the character of market risk exposures and their complex interrelationships did not easily lend themselves to traditional methods although a modified version of this approach is still found in current proposals.

It was also felt that introducing capital charges on portfolios of traded debt and equity had important implications for banks' competitive positions in the securities markets and that it would be preferable to develop a joint framework with the regulators of these markets. After long negotiations disagreement openly broke out between then heads of the SEC Breeden and the Chairman of the Basle Supervisory Committee, Corrigan, illustrating the pronounced differences in approach between the different regulatory bodies.[31] More recently, however, limited agreement was finally reached in respect of the subject of management controls and on the information that regulators should have in respect of the derivative activities of securities companies and banks (Basle Committee and IOSCO, 1995).

The Basle committee finally issued in April 1993 a consultative document with a proposal for extending the 1988 Capital Accord to incorporate foreign exchange risks in the bank as a whole (subject to some discretion over structural foreign exchange positions) and the price risks in traded debt and equity instruments. After a first round of discussions with market participants a second consultative document was issued in April, 1995. It envisages two possible approaches. The first known as the "standardised" or "building blocks" approach envisages separate rules for various asset classes and general market risks, a method already adopted in the European Union Capital Adequacy Directive (CAD) which should come into effect on 31 December 1995.[32] The various weightings and charges on individual items have been constructed on the basis of simulation studies carried out by the central banks for market shocks roughly equivalent to 95 per cent confidence intervals for historic twoweek changes in various market factors. The overall capital charge under the standardised measurement will be the arithmetic sum of the risk measures over the various categories (debt securities, equities, foreign exchange, commodities, and a special basket for options). A number of other special adjustments are made to take account of non-parallel interest rate shifts, options, etc.

Several criticisms have been levelled at this approach: the "haircuts" are based on historical volatilities, and no procedure is envisaged for attempting to update the weights ("the system is cast in stone"); no account is taken of covariances — indeed adding up individual measures for independent risks is incorrect since in these circumstances cumulative risks are equal to the square root of the sum of squares of exposures;[33] and the so-called "vertical disallowance" is too onerous (Gumerlock, 1993).

The present Basle proposal states that banks' capital adequacy charge can also be computed on the basis of "internal risk management models".[34] Banks must meet a number of qualitative criteria to be permitted to use a models-based approach and the qualitative criteria may influence the severity of capital charges. Banks will have flexibility in devising the precise nature of their models (variance-covariance matrices, historical simulations or Monte Carlo simulations) but minimum standards apply for the purpose of calculating the capital charge. Correlations are recognised within but not across broad risk categories. The measurement of risk exposure will be the higher of the previous day's value at risk (VAR) and the average daily VAR over the past sixty days.[35] The resulting figure is then multiplied by a scaling factor of at least three to be determined by the relevant central bank.[36]

In a discussion very much reminiscent of the debate concerning credit equivalent risk measures the banking community has responded to this proposal by noting that many institutions that have developed sophisticated risk management systems would opt to use the standardised method for supervisory purposes because it generated lower capital requirements than the internal model because of the risk weighting and time horizon.[37] This would create the rather perverse incentive that banks which attempt to introduce more sophisticated monitoring systems would not be rewarded by having lower capital adequacy requirements. Moreover it could lead to the paradoxical outcome that any in-built conservative elements in the models might be clawed back to reduce the impact of the multipliers.

More recently the debate concerning risk management systems has given rise to a yet more fundamental criticism of the approach taken by the regulators and by many financial institutions which aim at deriving a single indicator of risk (i.e. the price risk of a portfolio in terms of the frequency with which a loss is likely to occur). Namely what is the ultimate goal served by the risk ratios and internal management systems such as VARs? Is the purpose of internal risk management systems to guard against events which fall within the range of reasonably forecastable events (or more typically historical data) or should the aim be to test existing exposures under situations of stress? Should bank management be concerned with the number of times a loss will occur or with the size of the loss? Are internal risk management procedures appropriate for the objectives pursued by regulators?

Kupiec and O'Brian (1995) have recently argued that, indeed model based internal risk assessments suffer from various problems: they do not provide suitable estimations of true risk exposures over a relatively lengthy horizon;

their ability to incorporate option value sensitivities over wide ranges of price movements is limited; they ignore the endogeneity of trading risk and the effects of risk management on returns. They conclude that capital charges assessed according to internal models could be very misleading.

2.2.4.   The Regulatory Framework: The International Nature of the Accord

Since the Herstatt failure of 1974 and the subsequent Basle Concordat the international character of modern day banking activity has been at the forefront of the preoccupations of regulators. The experiences of the 1980s and 1990s suggest that these issues, far from having been solved, remain a point of weakness of the existing regulatory framework and that the issue has only been addressed seriously in the wake of acute problems (BCCI, Barings and the like).

More fundamentally the present regulatory framework relies in different measure on co-ordination and harmonisation to function effectively. Co-ordination (in the form of exchange of information, assignment of responsibility for supervision etc.) is necessary to ensure the working of supervision on a consolidated basis. In its absence bank supervisors would fail to achieve the objective of reducing systemic risk: the implications of the fragmentation and lack of communication between supervisory authorities was apparent in the build up to the Barings crisis. Harmonisation is also an essential ingredient in order to avoid the possibility of regulatory arbitrage by banks setting up their head offices in centres with lax supervisory authorities. It is not surprising, therefore, that supervisory authorities from the dominant players in the international financial markets — the United States, Japan and the United Kingdom (as a financial centre with a reputation at stake) — took the leading role in initiating the Basle Accord and applied significant pressure on other countries — including the offshore centres — to accept the agreement.

It is difficult to say to what extent multilateral negotiations such as those of the Basle Supervisory Committee can be expected in the future to be as successful in obtaining a consensus over co-ordination and harmonisation as they have been in recent years. To be sure, in comparison with other multilateral fora concerned with economic negotiations (GATT, OECD, EC, etc.) the Basle Committee has several advantages. First, the growing internationalisation of banks implies that narrow national self-interests are less important and that it is more difficult to form blocking coalitions among countries.[38] Second, it is easier for supervisors to define and agree upon a common goal which extends beyond national boundaries — such as the reduction of systemic risk. It is interesting to note in this respect that the extension of capital requirements to other types of financial institutions where regulators do not share the same preoccupations has met with great difficulties. Third, the highly technical nature of many agreements has tended to keep discussions outside of national legislative bodies. Finally, the uncertain legal status of the agreements from the standpoint of international law has permitted the negotiators a greater room for maneouvre than if the agreements were subject to the formalities of international treaties.

At the same time, several factors may render the consensus approach difficult to uphold in the long run. The existence of differing national legal systems may impair desirable changes to regulations — the difficulty of agreeing to netting and the uncertainties surrounding derivatives are telling examples of these problems. More significantly in situations of financial distress regulatory authorities and governments have taken different approaches to coping with problem banks. In the long run it is difficult to see how the competitive distortions which arise from these divergences can be compatible with harmonised supervisory standards. Another important issue for the maintenance of consensus is that even within a group with common goals participants may not necessarily agree on the most adequate method for achieving the common good. Consensus requires that "doves" and "hawks" must ultimately reach a compromise; in technical matters such outcomes may be far from second best solutions. The process of "ad hoc" adjustment to existing regulations of the Basle Accord may in part be due to this type of phenomenon.

2.3. Regulatory Developments in the United States

FDICIA Act of 1991

The Federal Deposit Insurance Corporation Improvement Act of 1991 (FDICIA) was in large measure a reaction of the US Congress to the perception that regulatory restrictions on bank risk-taking were inadequate to protect the federal safety net. Its main aim was to preclude supervisory forbearance by reinforcing existing capital requirements and by mandating a system of discipline. Under the framework, each bank is placed in one of five zones based on its regulatory capital position: (i) well capitalised; (ii) adequately capitalised; (iii) undercapitalised; (iv) significantly undercapitalised; (v) critically undercapitalised. Penalties escalate the more an institution violates the capital standards. This escalation ("prompt corrective action") is meant to mimic indirectly risk-based insurance premia (i.e. to circumvent the moral hazard problem in flat insurance premia such as those mandated by FDIC) and ensure that private stakeholders in an undercapitalised institution bear part of the costs of insolvency. In addition, the formalisation of the process of penalisation is meant to limit supervisory discretion which had characterised regulation in the past and thereby reduce forbearance.[39,40]

Pre-Commitment Approach to Capital Requirements for Market Risk

Mention should be made of a novel proposal for improving the capital requirements for market risks put forth by members of the Federal Reserve Board Staff (Kupiec et al., 1995). The proposal would require a bank to specify the amount of capital it chose to allocate to support market risks and to commit itself to manage its trading portfolio so as to limit any cumulative trading losses over some subsequent interval (e.g. a month, a quarter) to an amount less than the capital allocation. Failing to limit losses to the capital commitment would trigger economic costs or "penalties" for the management and shareholders of the bank.

One of the major motivations for this proposal is to provide greater flexibility in the measurement of market risks which as we have just seen has been constantly evolving and where cast iron regulations might risk giving rise to perverse incentive mechanisms. In this respect it represents a clear break from the existing VAR framework and a welcome step in the right direction.

A closer examination of the proposal reveals, however, that the approach is much less novel than the authors suggest as far as the purported incentive mechanisms are concerned. A system of penalties is already present in the FDICIA Act of 1991.[41] It is also not clear from the theoretical literature whether imposing penalties entailing higher levels of capital would necessarily lead to a reduction in risk-taking. Finally, if — as the proposal suggests — regulators were allowed to waive the right to penalties under certain circumstances forbearance could potentially reappear through the back door.

2.4. Existing Banking Regulation: A Tentative Evaluation

Many strides have been made in recent years in respect of the assessment of various types of risks by both regulators and market participants. There is much greater understanding of the nature of risks and of how they should not be measured, and much more care in weighting different types of exposure. In addition there have been many attempts to reduce risks at both the macro and micro level. Among the former the most important is the ongoing work on the nature and management of payment systems while among the latter probably the most significant is the recognition of close out netting agreements for the purposes of evaluating counterparty risks.

At the same time our discussion has identified several drawbacks of the existing regulatory framework.

(1) The notion of risk

It is not clear to what extent the existing differential capital requirements capture actual differences in risk:

- Risk-adjusted weightings, for example, do not deal adequately with the divergence of risk within asset classes. For example, AAA non-banks are subject to higher risk weightings than AA-sovereign entities.
- With the exception of netting (and only implicitly) the benefits from diversification across risky instruments is not recognised. There is also no attempt to differentiate among macro-concentrations of counterparty risk. A geographically well diversified portfolio should attract lower ratios than one which is concentrated on a narrow group of borrowers.
- The risk ratios do not protect against aggregate or systematic risk which is undiversifiable (Hellwig, 1993). In practice this means that a portfolio of government bonds with a default premium that is correlated with the level of international interest rates is potentially as risky as one of non-bank loans of a shorter maturity.

(2) Timing

The recent Barings experience suggests once again that purportedly adequate capital can be eroded very quickly when financial markets are volatile and portfolios are complex. In these circumstances it is difficult for supervisory authorities to devise measures which can be at all times up to date on potential exposures without relying heavily on the risk management systems of individual financial institutions.

(3) Traditional product categories have become obsolete

"Financial engineering" has increasingly blurred the boundaries between various types of financial instrument (most importantly the differentiations between debt and equity) and nature of exposure (such as the character of exposures to counterparties which can be markedly different in the risk asset weightings if on or off the balance sheet). The most dramatic examples of these reconstructions of exposure are offered by the swap market and options which can be recombined in a variety of ways each with potentially a different capital weighting.

(4) Traditional institutional categories have become obsolete

It is possible for instruments traditionally offered by one type of financial institution to be offered by other institutions. This is most clearly exemplified by structured notes bearing all the characteristics of an insurance policy.

(5) Existing accounting valuations — even those based on marking to market —fail to take account of risk allocations where contracts have zero net present values but alter the future stream of cash flows

One of the most common positions which has been upheld by both private observers and regulators is that public disclosure of banks' activities would be a way of indirectly achieving regulatory objectives particularly in respect of the monitoring of risk exposures. The recent highly technical and hotly debated discussions held by the Basle Supervisory Committee with the banking community in respect of market risks suggest that there is presently no generally agreed synthetic measurement of overall exposures. Arguing at this stage for greater disclosure — particularly in the highly imperfect fashion suggested by FASB Statement no. 119 — should be considered very carefully and could actually be counterproductive.

This has implications for the benefits of disclosure, which is required for a variety of financial activities albeit to a widely varying extent across countries. It is commonly argued that disclosure increases efficiency as a result of a reduction in the costs of obtaining information by a depositor in respect of the riskiness of a bank's portfolio or from the sharing of information between financial intermediaries about the exposures and creditworthiness of individual counterparties. However, disclosure requirements may not always be beneficial. For example, in some situations excessive information may result in non-price and wasteful competition, or in other cases firms may respond to a requirement by simply increasing the amount of information they disclose thereby giving rise to an "overload" (high ratio of noise to signal; Shaffer, 1995). More significantly, the release of misleading information which receives an implicit seal of approval — say by the auditors — could in the end lead to inappropriate incentives for firm managers.

3. An Appropriate Framework for Banking Regulation: Issues in the Reform of Regulatory Mechanisms

In this section, we consider three somewhat interrelated, but also conceptually rather distinct issues that are important vis-à-vis any attempt to understand the desiderata of a comprehensive and coherent, regulatory framework for banking activities. First, we revisit the issue of optimal capital regulation, coupled with deposit insurance and closure rules in a dynamic framework, with a focus on generating efficient risk-taking incentives by banks. Second, we consider the issue of a "fairly" priced deposit insurance scheme (including possibly the socially optimal subsidies to liquidity-enhancing deposit creation) and the generation of adequate capital standards in the face of market risks connected with interest rate movements in the presence of complex instruments used by banks to control some of these risks (hedging) or given the inappropriate incentives to speculate based on its assumptions about such risky dynamics.

The third point addressed in this section is the set of issues pertaining to fundamental reforms of the regulatory framework of banking, in the forms of (i) elimination or drastic curtailment of the extent of bank deposit insurance limits per account; (ii) the *alternative* (due to Irving Fisher in the 1930s, revived by Friedman (1960) and recommended in Miller (1995)) of basing the payment mechanism (and demand deposits) only on 100 per cent reserves, or alternatively of restricting banks' investments to short-term (Treasury) bills; (iii) easing non-banking portfolio restrictions, such as underwriting or even direct stock ownership — a policy prescription diametrically opposite to (ii) — by creating "universal banks" that may (as some suppose) enhance the monitoring cum corporate control functions of such financial intermediaries as delegated monitors.

3.1. Reforming Capital Regulation and Retaining Deposit Insurance: Mechanisms for Controls, Closure Rules and Risk Choices in a Dynamic Model of Banking

Theories of liability insurance (Scott and Mayer, 1971) and put option pricing (Merton, 1977 and 1978) have been applied to determining the optimal deposit insurance premium, but many authors have recently found this approach to be inadequate.[42] Ronn and Verma (1986), for example, estimated "fairly priced" insurance premia for US banks that were *smaller* than existing ones, which seems to be counterintuitive in the light of the commonly held view that subsidies to deposit insurance encouraged excessive risk taking by intermediaries, such as the S&Ls, in the 1980s. Later estimates by Pennacchi (1987) and others, using perpetual rather than finite maturity variants of the put option pricing models, showed that the current levels of the insurance premia could indeed be lower than the actuarially fair levels for the risks involved, but these results confirm that as a practical matter it may be extremely difficult to implement premia based strictly on put pricing formulae.

A more substantial criticism is that the analytical framework does not adequately endogenise the choice of risk-taken by banks in an integrated fashion:[43,44] where insurance premia are set before portfolio choices, banks will undertake riskier projects if monitoring is imperfect. A model of bank capital regulation and closure rules should take account explicitly of the endogenous choices (and asset values) by banks in the interests of their levered equity holders. To be realistic the model ought to allow for the banks to be an ongoing concern with *perpetual debt* and the possibility of *new equity financing* (to preserve the value of the bank charter) by the bank owners subject to the regulatory pressure or denial. Such a model with a flexible ex-ante chosen safety barrier, a firm value floor below which equity financing is *not* allowed, can be found in the recent work of Leland (1994).[45] The model has the advantage of allowing for simple power function solutions for equity and risky debt values as functions of (i) the underlying asset value of the bank V; (ii) its continuous-time (diffusion process) rate of return variance per unit of time, σ^2; (iii) the precommitted rate of coupon payments, C; (iv) the riskless interest rate, r ; and (v) the tax rate (shield) on deductible interest payments, t which can also be interpreted as the benefits arising from the bank charter;. (vi) the safety barrier level F such that the firm is liquidated with loss of future tax shield on debt if the condition $V \geq F$ is not satisfied at any point in time.

In Leland's model, the equity value is given by

$$E(V, \sigma^2, r, t, F) = V - (1 - t)\frac{C}{r} + \frac{[(1 - t)C/r] - F}{(V/F)^x},$$ (1a)

where

$$x = 2r/\sigma^2$$ (1b)

and the last term in (1a) represents the balance between (i) the option value of defaulting on debt, but (ii) also the potential loss of future tax shields on debt interest. Leland assumes unrealistically, that all debt interest (coupon) payments have to be financed by equity holders from new equity issues, rather than operating earnings on assets, but this can be easily rectified to allow a total proportional payment from retained earnings at a rate ρV per unit of time, where $0 \leq \rho \leq r$, as in Black and Cox (1976). The important point to note is the following: if there exists an $F = F^* = (1-t)C/r$ such that, unlike in finite maturity standard call option pricing models

$$\frac{\partial E(V, \sigma^2, r, t, F)}{\partial \sigma^2} = 0, \tag{2a}$$

so that maximising equity value would be coincident with the efficiency criterion of maximising V, i.e. moral hazard with respect to excessive risk-taking is eliminated.

Two aspects of the above "optimal control investment" of a safety barrier or firm value floor, should be noted. First it is the case that

$$\frac{(1-t)C}{r + 0.5\sigma^2} = F^o < F^* < \frac{C}{r}, \tag{2b}$$

where F^o is the voluntarily chosen point at which, when $V = F^o$, equity holders would have elected to stop financing coupon payments with new equity issues (in the prospect of the ongoing option value of new earnings). But at the same time $F^* < C/r$, the floor on V which would have made the debt riskless, given the assumed continuous observability of the underlying firm value V on the part of creditors as well as the equity holders and managers. Second F^* (given that V can be accurately measured) is independent of σ^2, i.e. risk-assessment per se by the creditor is "only" required for fair pricing of default risk but not for optimal control of risk choice by the debtor. In summary the optimal regulation, therefore, entails a closure rule that neither makes the debt entirely safe (which would generate risk aversion on the part of equity holders) nor takes it to the point of *laissez faire* with respect to voluntary capitalisation by bank shareholders (which would make them risk-loving).

The assumption that the firm's value V follows a diffusion process and is continuously verifiable by the creditor/regulator, makes the Leland model inadequate for a theory of bank capital standards, unless one is to interpret $(C/r - F^*)$ as the optimal (maximal) negative capital (forbearance or closure) standards. Hence for an adequate theory of capital regulation the model needs to be augmented by either or both (i) the possibility of discontinuous (downward) jumps in the asset value V (Merton, 1976) or (ii) random discrete audits (because of costs) so that $V < F$ within an audit interval becomes possible as in Merton (1977,1978).[46] Then if V can discontinuously (in time) drop to (at least) μV, $0 < \mu < 1$ one may (for illustration purposes) wish to recommend a regulatory policy having (something like) the two components of, say, $\{[(F^*/\mu) - C/r]/V\}$ as the optimal capital standard and $V \geq F^*$ as the closure point with $F^*/\mu > C/r > F^*$. Further analysis along these lines, using the techniques of the Black-Scholes (1973) option pricing paradigm, augmented by realistic assumptions such as asset value discontinuities and infrequent or imperfect observability of bank portfolio values, would make for an important addition to the conceptual framework of bank capital regulation. The endogeneity (to policy) of the debt tax-shield, t, or the rent coefficient on deposits, generated through controls on bank charters etc., should also form parts of a satisfactory model.

3.2. *Limiting Deposit Insurance and Private Market Discipline*

Some criticism has been addressed recently to the rationale for having banking regulation in the public sector, and specifically to high levels of deposit insurance. Dowd (1993) contends on the basis of his reading of the period of free banking in the United States that in relatively unregulated systems banks with strong capital positions retained depositor confidence. Safety net provisions, on the other hand, had the effect of weakening the banking system. An analogous set of arguments — cast in the present institutional framework and somewhat less radical — is that lower deposit insurance can help to discipline bank behaviour: the threat of withdrawal by uninsured (or partially insured) depositors would induce bank management to behave in a more conservative fashion.

Another set of considerations has been put forth recently by Broaddus (1994) who has advocated a partially insured deposit contract, with much lower limits (than the present $100,000 per deposit account in the United States). He contends that regulators can distinguish the difference between purely liquidity-based high withdrawals, or panics, and rational runs based on sufficiently low asset returns prospects of the issuing banks.[47]

Another critical view of government intervention implicit in most discussion is that much of the role for a regulator could be potentially performed by interbank clearing houses or clubs. Some, such as Kaufamn (1992) have argued that this is essentially what these associations did in the free-banking era. Even Dowd (1993) concludes that there is a rationale for banking clubs, owing to purposes ranging from (i) serving as a clearinghouse for settling notes and checks; (ii) lowering transactions and monitoring costs for interbank borrowing and lending to cope with liquidity shocks (iii) regulating liquid asset reserves, to manage the "externality" of reserves for banks as a whole; (iv) manage bank runs, before they lead to contagion, through emergency lending or through the club providing a signal that the bank subject to a run is indeed unsound, leading to resolution of depositors' claims within a short period of time. All of these functions require that the club monitor the quality of bank assets, both to ensure their liquidity and to decide whether or not to support the bank during a run.

However, an argument can be made that such a role should be undertaken by a disinterested party (not competing with a bank); in these circumstances a public regulator (*qua* honest broker) could be the best agent to the perform such a function (Marquardt, 1987). This argument is valid even in the *absence* of realistic differences such as the greater potential resource base, via taxation powers, of the state as a deposit insurer and also without any doubts on the powers of rival banks in the club to commit to view the underlying asset quality of a distressed bank subject to a run and/or illiquidity in an objective manner. The argument essentially is that judging asset quality objectively would necessarily (often) involve acquiring proprietary knowledge about the quality of the banks' specific borrowers and investments, and it would be extraordinarily difficult for rival banks to precommit not to use such knowledge to further their own interests.

3.3. Narrow Banking

One drastic solution to the vulnerability to liquidity crises ("runs") which would result from the elimination of government deposit insurance is the extension of the role of money market mutual funds or the creation of "narrow" banks. Money market mutual funds whose assets consist of short-term marketable securities (Treasury bills commercial paper, etc.) already provide checking account services. The novelty would lie in having the fund back directly checkable deposits. According to McCulloch (1993) because of the liquidity of the assets, deposit insurance would not be required and recent historical experiences suggest that runs on the funds would not give rise to liquidity crises.[48]

The various forms of the "narrow bank" proposal have encountered several criticisms. First the volume of short-term securities necessary to cover the present size of demand deposits may be too small. The extent to which this criticism is valid depends on whether the economy has surplus liquidity and liquidity creation by banks is no longer necessary for the functioning of the economy. If the bank were extended only to (short-term) demand deposits it is probable that this would not pose a serious problem. However, with a wider spectrum of deposit maturities (that are still demandable with some penalties), narrow banking would not be feasible. A second criticism goes to the heart of the nature of deposits. If bank deposits are meant to provide a shield or insurance against shifts in preferences then a narrow bank with a marking to market of positions would not be able to insulate depositors from exogenous shocks. This would be true if the assets held against the deposits were not perfectly liquid. Term deposits in particular would not be compatible with narrow banking: even matched maturities would be subject to problems if deposits could be withdrawn before maturity (at a penalty). However, the extent to which deposits actually protect against preference shocks is an empirical issue which the rise of money market funds tends to question. Hellwig (1994) attempts to model the optimal (multi-period) deposit contract in the presence of shocks to future (interim) interest rates. However, he makes the strong assumption of ex post corner preferences of depositors, over consumption in two different periods, thus ruling out interesting substitution and income effect reactions to interest rates.

Another criticism concerns the scope of the narrow bank proposal. While accepting that the narrow bank scheme is a viable solution for retail customers and would be a substitute for deposit insurance, it is not clear to what extent it would reduce overall systemic risks. Payment systems risks — particularly those associated with large funds transfers and settlements of transactions in securities — are affected only to a very minimal extent by the proposals. It is not difficult to think of situations of financial distress and possibilities of contagion occurring among uninsured financial institutions with a wide network of creditor relationships and an active membership in clearing houses (as, for example, if there were a run on a major securities company). Indeed, if the narrow bank participates in the clearing and settlement mechanisms it is not clear whether it might not also incur counterparty risks under certain types of arrangements.

Finally, it is also not clear whether financial intermediaries might not continue to offer uninsured deposits which would compete with the money market funds but be subject to "runs".

3.4. Universal Banking

Recent studies have begun to pay more attention to issues relating to banking scope, i.e. the degree to which banks can engage in different activities. There are three separate but interrelated aspects that are often confused. The first concerns the distinction between universal banking (in a rather narrow sense) and functionally separated banking, i.e. the extent to which banks are allowed to perform both investment and commercial banking functions, and the insurance business. The second relates to the extent to which banks are allowed to hold equity stakes in non-financial companies of which they are often creditors. This is the wider and more common usage made of universal banks. The third concerns the relationship between banking and commerce, i.e. the extent to which non-banks are allowed to hold stakes in a banking institution.

It is not surprising that these issues should be receiving attention at this stage in view of the weakening of banks' competitiveness vis-à-vis non-bank financial intermediaries and companies. The question of universal banks is also related to the surge in consolidations taking place in various countries.

The principal argument in favour of abolishing the separation of commercial and investment banking is that artificial limitations constrain the laissez-faire configuration of banking. In other words that separation impairs the cross-sectional reusability of information between commercial and investment banking: the information gathered by banks about their borrowers may lead to less adverse selection and hence lower underwriting spreads in issuing securities. In a wider sense universal banks which have equity stakes in non-financial entities are said to be able to internalise situations of financial distress better than commercial banks and securities markets (Mayer, 1988). On the other hand there are several arguments against universal banks: there could be serious conflicts of interest; the development of capital markets could be impaired; non-competitive market conditions would become more prevalent and as a consequence the "too big to fail" syndrome would be likely to escalate.

These arguments have been recently formalised by a number of authors but the questions appear ultimately to be an empirical matter.[49] Some tentative albeit at times surprising conclusions appear to be emerging with regard to the question of conflict of interest affecting universal banks. Kroszner and Rajan (1994), for example, find that contrary to widely held views, prior to the Glass-Steagall Act, US banks did not misrepresent the financial condition of a borrower in order to use the proceeds of capital market issue for the purpose of repaying a bank loan. Market discipline according to these authors appears to have been effective in preventing abuses. There also appears to have been a recent reassessment of the behaviour of German banks in the light of an initial superficial reading of the operations of institutions. In practice, German banks do not have much equity in well-functioning firms (most of their voting power comes through proxy rights). Moreover, the role of banks in corporate control is also more dubious than originally believed. Finally, it is worth noting that flexibility in US banking law is such that banks can in fact assume equity stakes in borrowers in bankruptcy proceedings, so that their liquidation versus continuation incentives are aligned with those of universal banks.

The scope of banking also raises questions which are of direct concern to the framework of banking regulation. The internationalisation of banking has focused attention on very pronounced differences in banking structures across countries: one important element, here, is how banking regulations which are meant to be uniform across countries can be constructed so as to limit potentially competitive distortions. Universal banks also raise risk management issues which have not attracted much attention to date but may have signifcant implications for the structure of capital requirements. One reason for advocating universal banks is the existence of synergies between various parts of financial market activity. For example, lending activity or providing guarantees may be a complement to fee income generating acitivities such as underwriting or payments services. The complex nexus of bank/client relationship arising in these circumstances raises several issues for bank regulation, particularly in respect of how to assess the riskiness of portfolios and the risk/return profile of specific assets. A universal bank is likely to have a loan portfolio vis-à-vis a particular client which is difficult to 'mark-to-market' and at the same time a series of complicated transactions vis-à-vis the same client which are adjusted at every moment to reflect market prices sometimes induced by changes in the credit risk of the counterparty. It is not clear how the Basle Accord would take account of this factor. More significantly the existence of differences in banking structure creates competitive distortions between banks both in terms of their ability to weather shocks to their balance sheets as well as in respect to capital.

4. CONCLUDING REMARKS

As we approach the end of the millenium it is important to ask oneself what shape do we desire our financial system to take in the years to come. The 1980s and early 1990s heralded a wave of financial changes which potentially can improve the efficiency of the financial system by enhancing the opportunities for risk sharing, lowering transactions costs and reducing asymmetric information and agency costs. It is along these lines that one must be forward looking in thinking of regulatory frameworks which can meet the challenges posed by the changing technological and institutional environments. As noted by Merton (1995) the dynamics of institutional and technological change should be an explicit element in the analysis of regulatory policies towards financial institutions (and more generally other areas of interest to central banks). Unfortunately current developments indicate that such an approach is not being currently contemplated.

In most respects we believe that many of the institutional features of bank regulation should remain in their present form. In particular, bank regulation and the "safety net" should remain in the hands of the central bank or of an institution closely associated to it. At the same time the debate over the nature of banking contracts and the incentives faced by bank managers, shareholders, depositors (of various types) and regulators have shown that the actual traditional forms of regulation are fraught with perverse incentives.

With respect to the new supervisory frameworks developed in recent years — the Basle Capital Accord, FDICIA and recent proposals to cope with market risk — it is possible to draw several tentative conclusions from the discussion in this paper. First, it is necessary to subject the present system of capital ratios to a period of stress in order to appreciate whether the capital requirements have indeed been able to safeguard the financial system. The little evidence available regarding US banks in the 1980s suggests that the current capital ratios would have been of little use in protecting banks from insolvency. Second, risk-sensitive capital requirements are potentially useful tools in the arsenal of bank regulators. However, practical measurement appears fraught with problems. In particular, present market and credit risk measurements appear to be poorly integrated with one another, and it does not appear that this can be easily accomplished if the present structure of capital requirements is maintained. Third, the incremental complication which accompanies each revision of the guidelines in order to take account of distortions is likely to be a never ending process. Indeed, the current overflow of proposals and guidelines being issued by the Supervisory Authorities appear increasingly inconsistent with one another.

More fundamentally looking into the future it is not clear what type of structure of the banking system is implicit in the capital requirements and how adaptable the current framework is to technological and economic changes. Narrow bank and "free banking" proposals whatever may be their many defects attempt to address these questions directly. The studies by central banks on the mechanics of payment systems and netting arrangements also reflect a considerable degree of foresight.

NOTES

1. See, for example, Bhattacharya and Thakor (1993), Dewatripont and Tirole (1994) and the Symposium on Bank Regulation in the July 1995 issue of the *Journal of Banking and Finance*.

2. In many countries the barriers arising from the elaborate regulatory framework had been gradually eroded through complex avoidance schemes or loopholes in the legislation. A cross-country comparison of the interrelationships between the process of deregulation and financial innovation in the early 1980s is described in Akhtar (1983). A later study which

provides a blow by blow account of the Japanese experience is Takeda and Turner (1993). See also the evaluation in BIS (1992).

3. See for example BIS (1986) chapter 12 and Miller (1994).

4. Many of the bank failures were partly attributable to the changes in financial markets taking place in the early 1980s and the slow — and in some instances perverse — changes in regulations which took place in those years.

5. See for example Jacklin and Bhattacharya (1988), Chari and Jagannthan (1988), and Kaufman (1992), for discussions of bank runs and contagion effects, and Bhattacharya and Gale (1987) for a theory of interbank relationships. The central bank concerns with interbank activity are set out in BIS (1982 and 1992).

6. Broaddus (1994) draws interesting analogies between elements of the safety net and the structure of typical private contracts. Deposit insurance is similar to a third-party guarantee; discount window lending is like a collateralised line of credit and the central bank's participation in the payments system is analogous to a clearinghouse overdraft facility.

7. In many respects these functions do not need to be carried out on the balance sheet of a bank. See Boot (1995) for a survey of the importance of securitisation and of the relationships between borrowers, investors and intermediaries.

8. Two drawbacks of these models is that they do not explain the existence of equity and do not account for the impossibility of diversifying systemic risk.

9. Jacklin and Bhattacharya (1988) as well as Chari and Jagannthan (1988) construct models in which investors' private information about their (idiosyncratic) "preference shocks" is coupled with (some) depositors having private, interim, knowlege of their banks' antic-ipated investment returns. the resulting bank runs that may arise, when depositors have significantly adverse information, are unique equilibria unlike the panic (sunspot) runs in Diamond and Dybvig (1983). Nevertheless, the resulting outcomes are not necessarily socially efficient as there is undesirable interim randomisation in withdrawals (and con-sumption) among investors who genuinely wish to withdraw early for consumption versus those who do so because they have bad news about their banks' investments (with suspen-sion of convertibility); alternatively, there are deadweight tax costs of providing deposit insurance to eliminate such runs. Furthermore, if depositors are uncertain about the mag-nitude of the interim liquidity-based demand for withdrawals by others, even uninformed depositors may aggravate the liquidity problem, by trying to withdraw because they fear others may have bad news about their bank's invests. Such "rational panics" may also provide a basis for contagion phenomena, across banks whose investment returns on their asset portfolios are highly correlated, but not more generally; see Kaufmann (1992) for empirical evidence on these topics and de Bondt (1994) for further modelling.

10. Much of the literature on bank regulation, including very recent articles by Berger et al. (1995), treat (a) in isolation from (b). In our discussion below we shall argue that such a separation of concerns is highly undesirable.

11. Berger et al. (1995) provide evidence that average US bank equity capital ratios declined sharply between 1840 and 1945 from around 55 per cent of assets to around 6–8 per cent of assets, stayed within that range from 1945–90, and then have been rising to the mandated (8 per cent on average) ratios of the FDICIA Act of 1991 and Basle Accord.

12. Several authors have examined these issues. With regulatory standards on capital respond-ing inflexibly to interbank heterogeneity on asset (monitoring) quality (ability), it is even possible for higher capital standards to lower average asset quality through incentive or entry effects.

13. Failures to effectuate payment can have important knock on effects (Borio and van den Bergh, 1993, for example) the difficulty on the part of the central bank to distinguish a liquidity from a solvency crisis at a bank is one of the central concerns of central banks with the growth of derivatives.

14. The evidence in Kaufman (1992) suggests (but does not fully convince) that contagion effects may not be important outside the group of banks with very closely correlated (and different from others) asset portfolios, compared to the insolvent or illiquid banks. Broaddus (1994) opines, from a regulatory standpoint, that allowing for the possibility of bank failure from runs by uninsured depositors is likely to be socially desirable for regulators such as the Federal Reserve Board and its regional affiliates, who have the ability to distinguish liquidity crunches (or panic runs) on sound banks from rational withdrawals from fundamentally unsound banks. Presumably, the non-verifiability of the information on which such rational runs are based leads regulators such as Broaddus to desire the "aid" of uninsured depositor runs triggering regulators' intervention, since allowing regulators *per se* to respond to such unverifiable information (with insured depositors) may lead to possibilities of corruption, etc.

15. In a banking context, rents to having deposits may also include (a) privately beneficial rents (to bank equity) from entry barriers and interest rate controls which are sustainable owing to the greater liquidity of demandable debt, and (b) the social importance of providing such liquidity to otherwise incompletely insured investors.

16. A significant emerging literature, exemplified by Hart (1991), emphasises the importance of modelling managerial incentives per se for the optimal capital structure tradeoff, and questions the appropriateness of ascribing solely shareholder oriented criteria to debtor management. These debt-related "controls" may be less important in the banking context with small and unsophisticated creditors, who would be unable to coordinate on disciplining management.

17. Keeley (1992) provides compelling evidence that banks with higher market to book value asset ratios undertook less risky portfolio strategies in the 1980s, Bhattacharya (1982) and Flannery (1991) analyse some of the tradeoffs involved.

18. An excellent description of the genesis and development of these banking crises is provided in Bank for International Settlements (1993), Chapter 7.

19. The present position taken by the Japanese authorities vis-à-vis several financial institutions is very reminiscent of the US experience in the 1980s, see Boot, Greenbaum, and Thakor (1993) for a model of *ex post* regulatory forbearance based on regulators' incentives to protect their reputation for correct *ex ante* monitoring of banks' assets and liabilities.

20. In general market forces prevent shareholders from taking advantage of the put options implicit in limited liability whereby the net worth of corporation cannot fall below zero. The cost of debt tends to increase with the riskiness of a corporation; bond covenants and the need to refinance short-term debt also restrict portfolio choice. In the banking sector with insured deposits or implcit guarantees of bail-out debtholders are indifferent about the riskiness of banks and do not demand higher interest rates from risker banks. Therefore, banks enjoy risk-insensitive funding contracts and have greater incentives to take risks than if deposits were not insured.

21. See Keeley (1990) for a study of the change in value of the banking charter in the United States during this period, and for tests of the incentive effects of charter values on risk-taking by banks.

22. Barone-Adesi (1995) presents an assessment of conventional and new methods of assessing asset and liability management risk.

23. In actual fact many traditional instruments can have non-linear pay-offs. The specific issue with derivatives is one of volume as well as degree of complexity.

24. As we shall see below, bank regulators have been quick to recognise the implications of complex payoff structures for the measurement of credit risk by accepting (a) the distinction between notional values and actual exposures in the Basle Capital Accord of 1988 (b) the reduction of risk resulting from netting arrangements in situations where two counterparties have a number of creditor/debtor relationships with one another.

25. A recent Group of Thirty (1993) survey reported that, besides municipalities, derivatives market participants were wary about entering into contracts with sovereign entities, pension funds and to lesser extent unit investment trusts and insurance companies.

26. The debate (see Edwards and Canter (1995), for example) over the Metalgesellschaft's derivatives losses, the interpretation over whether the company was in fact following a hedging strategy or riding the yield curve, and the behaviour of the liquidators is a noteworthy example of this point.

27. It is interesting to note that many supervisory authorities from countries not represented in the Basle Supervisory Committee have since the signing of the Accord agreed to its enactment for banks under their purview operating internationally.

28. Two choices of treatment were permitted, subject to approval by the national supervisors. In the approach more commonly used, the so-called "current exposure" method, the credit risk in derivatives is assessed by calculating the current replacement cost (which equals the "mark-to market" value if positive and zero otherwise) and by adding a factor designed to reflect potential exposure during the remaining life of the contract (the so-called "add-on"). The add-ons are based on the notional principal of each contract and vary depending on two factors: first, foreign exchange contracts have higher weights than interest rate contracts because of higher volatility and because foreign currency swaps typically involve an exchange of principal at maturity; second, contracts with a residual maturity of one year bear higher weight than those under one year. The alternative method of measuring the credit risk in derivatives, the "original exposure" method does not take the current value of the contract into account, but is expressed solely as a fraction of notional principal.

29. Tier 2 capital cannot exceed 100 per cent of Tier 1 capital as a contribution to total capital. Shares redeemable at the option of the issuer and subordinated debt cannot exceed 50 per cent of Tier 1 capital. There are other provisions concerning "general reserves".

30. In addition to some of the problems discussed in the text it is worth mentioning: (a) the international agreement was between hardline and market-oriented supervisors. Subsequent amendments suggest that compromise solutions have not been sustainable. (b) consolidation has proved far more difficult to implement than originally envisaged particularly in respect of financial conglomerates (c) risk weightings for different assets appear to have resulted in significant shifts in portfolio composition away from commercial bank lending towards investments in government securities (Haubrich and Wachtel, 1993), and from traditional interbank activity to collateralised repo transactions; (f) banks issued a number of exotic debt instruments in an attempt to have these recognised as capital. The ambiguities over the character of these instruments led to some unfortunate incidents in the markets (the collapse of floating rate note market).

31. One fundamental reason for the breakdown in the negotiations was that liquidity risks play a much more important role than market or credit risk for securities companies than banks. It also appears that there were strong personality conflicts involved in the discussions.

32. The Basle proposals and CAD differ in some points of detail.

33. It appears that when this observation was put to the authorities responsible for CAD the response was "square roots are inappropriate to international regulators" (quoted in Gumerlock, 1993)

34. Internal risk management systems can be used subject to six conditions: (i) general adequacy of the risk management system; (ii) qualitative standards of internal oversight, notably by management; (iii) guidelines for specifying an appropriate set of market risk factors; (iv) quantitative standards setting minimum statistical parameters for measuring risk; (v) validation procedures for external oversight of the models; (vi) rules for banks which use a mixture of models and the standardised approach.

35. JP Morgan (1994) describes a very popular proprietary model used for calculating VAR.

36. The proposal also sets requirements on confidence intervals, a 10-day holding period and limitations on the values of correlations necessary to determine the aggregate value at risk.

37. In a submission to the Basle Committee by the London Investment Banking Committee it was reported that in the case of one financial institution utilising both the "standardised" and the Basle VAR models resulted in 40 per cent higher capital charges in the latter case (Elderfield, 1995).

38. One attempt at creating a differential treatment of banking institutions arose at the time of the Discussion of the Second Banking Directive of the EC concerned with national treatment and reciprocity. This issue, however, did not concern directly the activities of the Basle Supervisory Committee.

39. FDICIA also attempts to reduce the regulatory burden for banks. It requires the FDIC to select the least cost method of resolving failed depository institutions and to document its decision. It also contains provisions designed to discourage discount window lending to critically undercapitalised institutions and in some circumstances imposes losses on the FED in the event a borrower fails.

40. Not all obervers believe that FDICIA will be successful in eliminating the adverse incentive structure of existing regulations. For a critical assessment, see Kane (1995).

41. We do, however, share the proposal's criticism of the present VAR approach to bank capital regulation.

42. See Kane (1995) who provides a detailed summary and critical review of these approaches.

43. Flannery (1991), for example, considered capital controls and deposit insurance premia as imperfect subsitutes when risk is measured with error and there are costs associated with both errors in insurance pricing (from "unfair" competition among banks) and in "excessive" equity levels (of inadequate liquidity enhancing deposit creation) in a static model.

44. Kane (1995) lists other problems, such as the fat lower tails of bank returns not allowed for by the Black-Scholes formula, and particularly regulatory forbearance of seemingly insolvent banks upon inspection thereof.

45. The model is an extension — with a value augmenting tax shield of corporate debt — of the pioneering work of Black and Cox (1975).

46. Neither Merton model has perpetual debt or (flexible) safety barrier covenants on firm value.

47. An important issue in the design of the regulations is to analyse the additional bargaining power with respect to bank management, that the regulator obtains when he is "aided" (from an ex ante perspective) by the illiquidity created by a run by partially insured, and informed, depositors.

48. Between November 1982 and May 1983 money market mutual funds in the United States suffered a 24 per cent loss in their deposits as a result of a shift to newly created money market deposit accounts at banks. This shift had no notable impact on the funds (McCulloch, 1993).
49. See Bhattacharya, Boot and Thakor (1995).

REFERENCES

Akhtar, A. (1983). "Financial Innovations and their implications for monetary policy: an international perspective", *BIS Economic Papers*, No. 9.

Bank for International Settlements (1982). *The International Interbank Market ("Holland Report")*, *BIS Economic Paper*, No. 8.

Bank for International Settlements (1992). *Recent Developments in International Interbank Relations*.

Bank for International Settlements (1986). *Recent Innovations in International Banking*, Basle.

Bank for International Settlements (1992). *Annual Report*, Basle.

Bank for International Settlement (1993). *Annual Report*, Basle.

Bank for International Settlements (1994). *Public Disclosure of Market and Credit Risks by Financial Intermediaries*, Basle, (September).

Bank for International Settlements (1994). *Public Disclosure of Market and Credit Risks by Financial Intermediaries*, Basle, (July).

Barone-Adesi, G. (1995). "ALM in Banks", mimeo.

Basle Committee on Banking Supervision (1993a). *The Supervisory Treatment of Market Risks*. Consultative Proposal, Basle.

Basle Committee on Banking Supervision (1993b). *Measurement of Banks' Exposure to Interest Rate Risk*, Basle.

Basle Committee on Banking Supervision (1994a), *Basle Capital Accord: The Treatment of the Credit Risk Associated with Certain Off-Balance Sheet Items: Netting-Amendments and Add-ons-Proposals*, Basle, (July).

Basle Committee on Banking Supervision (1994b). *Risk Management Guidelines for Derivatives*, Basle, (July).

Basle Committee on Banking Supervision (1995). *Basle Capital Accord: Treatment of Potential Exposure for Off-balance Sheet Items*, Basle, (April).

Basle Committee on Banking Supervision (1995). *Planned Supplement to the Capital Accord to Incorporate Market Risks: Consultative Proposal*, Basle, (April).

Basle Committee on Banking Supervision and Technical Committee of the International Organisation of Securities Commissions (1995). *Framework for supervisory information about derivatives activities of banks and securities firms*, Basle, (May).

Berger, A.N., R.J. Herring and G.P. Szego (1995). "The role of capital in financial institutions", *Journal of Banking and Finance*, 19, pp. 393-430.

Bhattacharya, S. (1982). "Aspects of monetary and banking theory and moral hazard", *Journal of Finance*, 37, pp. 374-84.

Bhattacharya, S., and D. Gale (1987). "Preference Shocks, Liquidity, and Central Bank Policy", in W. A. Barnett and K. J. Singleton (eds.), *New Approaches to Monetary Economics*, Cambridge University Press.

Bhattacharya, S., and A. Thakor (1993). "Contemporary banking theory", *Journal of Financial Intermediation*, 3, pp. 2-50.

Bhattacharya, S., A. Boot, and A. Thakor (1995). "The economics of bank regulation", *TRACE Discussion Paper*, 95-163.

Black, F., and J.C. Cox (1976). "Valuing corporate securities: some effects of bond indenture provisions", *Journal of Finance*, 31, pp. 351-68.

Boot, A. (1995). "Challenges to competitive banking", paper presented at the Universita Bocconi Conference.

Boot, A., S. Greenbaum, and A. Thakor (1993). "Reputation and Discretion in Financial Contracting", *American Economic Review*, 83, 1993, pp. 1165-1181.

Broaddus, A. (1994). "Choices in banking policy", *Economic Quarterly*, Federal Reserve Bank of Richmond, 80(2), pp. 1-11.

Calomaris, C., and C. Kahn (1991). "The role of demandable debt in structuring optimal banking arrangements", *American Economic Review*, 81, pp. 497-513.

Chari, V.V., and R. Jagannathan (1988) "Bank panics, information and rational expectations equilibrium", *Journal of Finance*, 43, pp. 749-61.

Corrigan, E.G. (1992). "Challenges facing the international community of bank supervisors", *Federal Reserve Bank of New York Quarterly Review*, 17(3), pp. 1-9.

Dewatripont, M., and J. Tirole (1994). *The Prudential Regulation of Banks*, Cambridge, Massachusetts: The MIT Press.

Diamond, D. (1984). "Financial intermediation and delegated monitoring", *Review of Economic Studies*, 51, pp. 393-414.

Dowd, K. (1993). "Deposit insurance: a sceptical view", Federal Reserve Bank of St. Louis Review, 75(1), pp. 14-17.

Edwards, F., and M. Canter (1995). "The collapse of Metallgesellschaft: unhedgeable risks, poor hedging strategy or just bad luck?", *The Journal of Futures Markets*, May.

Elderfield, M. (1995). "Capital incentives", *Risk*, 9(8), pp. 20-21.

Flannery, M. (1991). "Pricing deposit insurance when the insurer measures bank risk with error", *Journal of Banking and Finance*, 15, pp. 975-998.

Friedman, M. (1960). *A Program for Monetary Stability*, New York, Fordham University Press.

Group of Thirty (1993). *Derivatives: Practices and Principles*, New York.

Gumerlock, R. (1993). "Double trouble", *Risk*, 9(6), pp. 80-91.

Hart, O. (1991). "Theories of optimal capital structure: managerial discretion perspective", National Bureau of Economic Research, Reprint Series.

Haubrich, J.G., and P. Wachtel (1993). "Capital requirements and shifts in commercial bank portfolios", *Economic Review*, Federal Reserve Bank of Cleveland, pp. 2-15.

Hellwig, M. (1991). "Banking, financial intermediation and corporate finance", in A. Giovannini and C. Mayer (eds.), *European Financial Integration*, Cambridge: Cambridge University Press.

Hellwig, M. (1994). "Liquidity provision, banking and the allocation of interest rate risk", *European Economic Review*, 38, pp. 1363-89.

Hendricks, D. (1994). "Netting agreements and the credit exposures of OTC Derivative Portfolios", *Quarterly Review*, Federal Reserve Bank of New York, 19(1), pp. 7-17.

Jacklin, C., and S. Bhattacharya (1988). "Distinguishing panics and information based bank runs: welfare and policy implications", *Journal of Political Economy*, 96, pp. 568-92.

James, C. (1991). "The losses realised in bank failures", *Journal of Finance*, 46, pp. 1223-1242.

Jensen, M., and H. Meckling (1976). "The theory of the firm, managerial behaviour, agency costs and ownership structure", *Journal of Financial Economics*, 3, pp. 305-60.

Jones, D. S., and K. K. King (1995). "The implementation of prompt corrective action", *Journal of Banking and Finance*, 19, pp. 491-510.

JP Morgan (1994). RiskMetrics™ Technical Document: Second Edition, New York.

Kane, E. (1985). *The Gathering Crisis in Federal Deposit Insurance*, Cambridge, Massachusetts, M.I.T. Press.

Kane, E. (1995). "Three paradigms for the role of capitalisation in insured financial institutions", *Journal of Banking and Finance*, 19.

Kaufman, G.G. (1991). "Capital in banking: past, present and future", *Journal of Financial Services Research*, 5, pp. 383-402.

Kaufman, G.G. (1992). "Bank contagion: theory and evidence", Federal Reserve Bank of Chicago.

Keeley, M. (1990). "Deposit insurance, risk and market power in banking", *American Economic Review*, 80, pp. 1183-1200.

Kroszner, R., and R.G. Rajan (1994). "Is the Glass-Steagall Act justified? A study of the US experience with universal banking before 1933", *American Economic Review*, 84, 810-32.

Kupiec, P., and J. N. O'Brian (1995). "Internal Affairs", *Risk*, 8(5), pp. 43-47.

Kupiec, P. (1995). "Techniques for verifying the accuracy of risk measurement models", Federal Reserve Board, mimeo.

Kupiec, P., J.N. O'Brian and P. Parkinson (1995). *Precommitment Approach to Capital Requirements for Market Risk*, Federal Reserve Board, mimeo.

Leland, H. (1994). "Corporate debt value, bond covenants and optimal capital structure", Working Paper, University of California, Berkeley.

Leland, H., and D. Pyle (1977). "Informational asymmetries, financial structure and financial intermediation", *Journal of Finance*, 32, pp. 371-87.

Marquardt, J. (1987). "Financial market supervision: some conceptual issues", *BIS Economic Paper*, 19.

Mayer, C. (1988). "New issues in corporate finance", *European Economic Review*, 32 pp. 1167-1188.

McCulloch, J.H. (1993). "Banking without tax-backed deposit insurance", *The Federal Reserve Bank of St. Louis Review*, 75(1), pp. 18-21.

Merton, R.C. (1976). "Option pricing when underlying stock prices are discontinuous", *Journal of Financial Economics*, 3, pp. 125-44.

Merton, R.C. (1977). "An analytical derivation of the cost of deposit insurance and loan guarantees; An application of modern option pricing", *Journal of Banking and Finance*, 1, pp. 3-11.

Merton, R.C. (1978). "On the cost of deposit insurance when there are surveillance costs", *Journal of Business*, 51, pp. 439-52.

Merton, R.C. (1995). "Financial innovation and the management and regulation of financial institutions", *Journal of Banking and Finance*, 19, pp. 461-81.

Miller, M. (1995). "Do the M&M propositions apply to banks?", *Journal of Banking and Finance*, 19, pp. 483-89.

Pennacchi, G. (1987). "Alternative forms of deposit insurance", *Journal of Banking and Finance*, 11, pp. 291-312.

Peters, S. (1994). "Why are Deposits Sequentially Service Constrained and Insured?", Working Paper, University of Connecticut.

Ronn, E.I., and A.K. Verma (1986). "Pricing risk-adjusted deposit insurance", *Journal of Finance*, 41(4), pp. 871-95.

Scott, K.E., and T. Mayer (1971). "Risk and regulation in banking: some proposals for deposit insurance reform", *Stanford Law Review*, 23, pp. 857-902.

Shaffer, S. (1995). "Rethinking disclosure requirements", *Business Review: Federal Reserve Bank of Philadelphia*, (May, June), pp. 15-29.

Takeda, M., and P. Turner (1993). "The liberalisation of Japan's financial markets: some major themes", *BIS Economic Papers*, No. 34.

Tripartite Group (1995). The Supervision of Financial Conglomerates: A Report by the Tripartite Group of Bank, Securities and Insurance Regulators, Basle.

Monetary Policy and Liberalisation in Poland, Russia and the United Kingdom

Summary

In this paper we present new empirical work to examine whether monetary aggregates can serve a useful role as intermediate targets for reducing inflation in two transitional countries — Poland and Russia. Partly because few data are yet available for such economies, we compare this with the UK's experience over the past quarter-century which — in admittedly different circumstances — has witnessed marked financial liberalisation and where a succession of intermediate targets, including the exchange rate, has been used.

In successful transitional economies, including Poland, fixed exchange rate regimes have come under strain from capital inflows. A possible alternative for central banks is to allow greater exchange rate flexibility and to pursue their domestic policy objectives using monetary targets. In Russia and Poland, there is evidence that monetary aggregates have been a useful guide to future inflation. The lags appear to be shorter than in western economies where inflation rates are lower. But we find evidence that money velocities became less predictable as inflation fell in 1993–94.

Such relationships are in any case subject to change as a result of competition and innovation in the financial system, so it is impossible to be confident that a particular target range for any monetary aggregate will deliver desired monetary objectives and it would be unwise for either Russia or Poland to base monetary policy on monetary targets to be adhered to rigidly and unthinkingly. Better would be to identify monitoring ranges for monetary aggregates.

William A. Allen, Deputy Director, Monetary Analysis, at the Bank of England is a graduate from Balliol College, Oxford, and holds a Masters degree from the London School of Economics. He joined the Bank in 1972, where he worked in economics, was seconded to the Bank for International Settlements 1978–80 and later headed, in turn, the Gilt-Edged and Money Markets and Foreign Exchange Divisions.

Glenn Hoggarth, graduated in economics at Warwick and gained a Masters degree at Cambridge University. He joined the Economics Division of the Bank of England in 1989 advising mainly on UK monetary policy, after seven years as a private sector economist. In 1994 he was appointed Advisor on Monetary Policy at the Bank's Centre for Central Banking Studies and is also an IMF external adviser on monetary operations and policy in eastern and central Europe and Asia.

Lionel Price, Director of the Bank of England's Centre for Central Banking Studies, joined the Bank in 1967 from Cambridge University. He was UK Alternate Executive Director at the IMF 1979-81 and on return to the Bank headed, in turn, the Information, International, European and Economics Divisions. He is currently responsible for training provided to foreign central banks.

XVI. Monetary Policy and Liberalisation in Poland, Russia and the United Kingdom

BILL ALLEN, GLENN HOGGARTH and LIONEL PRICE*

1. INTRODUCTION

The main task of most central banks is to use monetary policy to keep inflation low. But many have found it difficult to do this because the effect of changes in monetary policy on inflation has not always proved easy to predict. This problem has been only too familiar over the last twenty years in western countries where the financial system has been increasingly liberalised. A similar and more acute problem is now confronting the formerly planned economies as economic and financial markets rapidly develop there.

In a liberalised or liberalising economy, policymakers often adopt a two-step approach to controlling inflation. First, they change their policy instruments to influence some measure of monetary conditions, such as broad or narrow money, credit, or the exchange rate. Secondly, they predict how this intermediate target will affect price inflation — the final goal of monetary policy. Each of these two stages is complicated by the *process* of liberalisation. The instruments used to control money and credit change during the transition period as market interest rates play a progressively more important role and financial flows become more sensitive to changes in interest rates. The relationship of money and credit with inflation may also be unstable. In particular, moving from a high to a low inflation environment — something which has happened in the successful transitional economies — is likely to reduce the velocity of money — but not necessarily in a predictable way.

A fixed nominal exchange rate, even against a country with low inflation, ensures low inflation in the home country only in the long run and only for internationally tradeable goods and services. If the exchange rate is fixed at an undervalued level — as appears to be the case in many transitional countries — net inflows of foreign exchange are to be expected, and inflation is likely to

---

*The views are those of the authors and not necessarily those of the Bank of England. They thank Andrew Haldane and Jagjit Chadha for their comments on an earlier draft and Andrew Brigden for research assistance.

be the means by which the real exchange rate adjusts to equilibrium. Convergence of prices (and inflation rates) should occur only in the *tradeable* sector. If domestic demand is growing fast, non-tradeable inflation, and therefore inflation in the economy as a whole, is likely to remain higher than tradeable inflation. For example, the Hong Kong dollar has been fixed against the US dollar since 1983. Although Hong Kong has witnessed a convergence of price inflation in the tradeable sector to the low rates witnessed in the United States, consumer price inflation remains quite high — around 10 per cent per annum — because of relatively high inflation in the non-tradeable sector.

In this paper we present new empirical work to examine whether monetary aggregates can serve a useful role as intermediate targets for reducing inflation in two transitional countries facing financial liberalisation — Poland and Russia. Partly because few reliable data are yet available for the transition economies, we compare this with the UK's experience over the past quarter-century which — in admittedly different circumstances — has witnessed marked financial liberalisation and where a succession of intermediate targets have been used.

2.

2.1. Intermediate Targets in Poland, Russia and the United Kingdom

Since the beginning of its reform programme *Poland* has pursued a policy of targeting the exchange rate. The zloty exchange rate has been kept within a band; since October 1991, the band has depreciated (a "crawling peg") broadly to offset the difference between Poland's inflation and inflation in the major industrialised countries.

Until the middle of May 1995, Poland's exchange rate band was fairly narrow. Although this allowed the National Bank of Poland (NBP) some degree of discretion in interest rate policy, the extent of that discretion decreased as Poland became more integrated into world financial markets. Because of the exchange rate commitment, however, the NBP had only limited power to control monetary growth, which has since late 1994 been greatly stimulated by very large inflows of foreign exchange, leading to growing inflationary pressures.

This has posed a major dilemma for monetary policy in Poland (similar to that faced by several other countries). Smaller inflows of foreign exchange would help to reduce the dilemma. For example, they could be encouraged by (i) a further liberalisation of outward trade policy to stimulate imports (which would also help to reduce the price level) and/or (ii) liberalisation of outward capital movements — for example withdrawal of the requirement that exporters must sell 100 per cent of foreign currency export proceeds for zloty. Another possible way of making the dilemma less acute would be to reduce the budget deficit. This would in theory lower the equilibrium real exchange rate and make it possible to lower interest rates without making the outlook for inflation worse; lower interest rates would reduce the incentive for capital inflows. In principle, greater restrictions on capital inflows would also make the dilemma less acute, but they would also set back the growing integration of Poland into international financial markets. These measures might help ameliorate the dilemma but it is not certain that they would be sufficient to resolve it.

The underlying problem *may* be that the Polish authorities are trying to hold the real exchange rate below its equilibrium path. Real exchange rates in transition economies have usually fallen sharply at the beginning of the transition process but have then tended gradually to appreciate as productivity improves. In Poland this appreciation has been stemmed since 1992 by the exchange rate policy adopted. Halpern and Wyplosz (1995) compare real wages in various countries to try to judge whether actual exchange rates are above or below equilibrium levels. In the Polish case, they say that the real exchange rate is no longer *clearly* undervalued, but they do show that the zloty is some way below their central estimate of its equilibrium level.

If the real value of the zloty is undervalued, then the undervaluation can be corrected in either of two ways: the inflation rate can remain high with no nominal exchange rate appreciation, or the nominal exchange rate can appreciate. There may be no option but to take risks with one or both of the policy objectives of low inflation and strong exports and domestic activity, and to decide which of the policy options — accepting continued inflows of foreign exchange, adjusting interest rates, adjusting the rate of crawl of the exchange rate band, and a step exchange rate appreciation — involves the most acceptable risks. If inflation control is paramount, one possible way of resolving the dilemma would be to accept more flexibility in the exchange rate, thereby stopping, or at least greatly reducing, the scale of external flows and reasserting domestic control over some measure of Polish monetary growth.

In contrast to Poland, monetary policy in *Russia* during the transition period has been eclectic but, until recently, generally independent of exchange rate objectives. Until early 1993 real interest rates were very negative and short-run maintenance of output appeared to take precedence over control of inflation as the main final goal of policy. But since early 1993, central bank lending rates have been set at positive real rates to help reduce inflation.

Monetary aggregates, particularly M2, have been used as a guide to short-run inflationary pressures while central bank credit has been a performance criterion under the IMF standby arrangement. Until recently, there has been no explicit exchange rate objective. At times the Central Bank of Russia (CBR) has intervened to steady the value of the rouble, as in October 1994 when the rouble fell sharply, and since May this year in response to upward pressure on the rouble caused by capital inflows. In July, policy was formalised and made more explicit. The aim in the second half of this year is to keep the nominal exchange rate within 6.5 per cent of $/rouble 4,600 (i.e. a range of 4,300–4,900). Although the target range for the exchange rate seems quite wide, there could arise a policy conflict between the exchange rate on the one hand and the targets for inflation and the growth in the monetary base on the other. In fact, this has happened already in recent months. Facing large capital inflows the CBR has allowed reserve monetary growth and inflation to rise above target rather than allowing the rouble to appreciate further.

Over the last 20 years the *UK* has guided monetary policy by means of a succession of intermediate targets. The breakdown of the Bretton Woods fixed exchange rate system in 1971, and a rapid exit from the EC snake in 1972, had left the UK without an anchor for its monetary policy and — as inflation accelerated — increasing attention was paid to monetary aggregates. But their behaviour was already being affected by moves to increase competition in the banking system announced in 1970 and it proved difficult to judge how far an unexpected fall in the velocity of broad money should be attributed to structural shifts and how far it represented an easing of monetary policy. Despite these uncertainties, a broad money target was announced in 1976 (followed a few months later by the adoption of domestic credit ceilings under an IMF programme). But velocity then rose again, in part because new restraints on banks' behaviour prompted disintermediation, permitting a new, though less severe, surge in inflation at the end of the decade.

The ending of exchange controls and a series of moves to liberalise the financial system through the early 1980s prompted a new and continuing fall in the velocity of broad money but, even though various definitions of broad money were tried, it proved very difficult to find satisfactory econometric explanations of these changes. As in the early 1970s, it was impossible to know how much of the fall in velocity to attribute to liberalisation; in the second half of the 1980s, rapid broad money growth was insufficiently heeded and inflation once more accelerated towards the end of the decade. Although broad money was targeted until 1988, attention increasingly shifted to a very narrow monetary aggregate, M0, which is little more than the note circulation. M0 was adopted as a target in 1984, at first alongside broad money and then alone. Although the velocity of M0 was itself steadily rising, it proved much easier to explain this in terms of interest rates which not only represented the opportunity cost of holding cash, but on which the rate of innovation in finding ways of economising on cash holdings (such as increased use of credit cards and automatic cash dispensers) also seemed to depend.

But continuing concern about the predictability of M0 left many looking for a more robust anchor for monetary policy and there was much debate about sterling joining the European exchange rate mechanism. An informal attempt in 1987–88 to hold the exchange rate against the Deutsche Mark in a narrow range was abandoned after sizable foreign exchange inflows. It appeared that the exchange rate ceiling had been set too low and, as may be the case in some central and eastern European economies today, it represented too easy a monetary policy and faster inflation ensued. The period from 1990 to 1992 of sterling's formal participation in the ERM was for a time very successful in enhancing the credibility of UK monetary policy — inflation came down to rates similar to France and Germany's — but eventually the opposite problem — of massive foreign exchange outflows — forced sterling out of the ERM. ERM membership in effect required sterling interest rates to be held above German rates and this no longer seemed sensible in view of the very different conjunctural positions of the two economies in 1992.

Withdrawal from the ERM left the UK again without a monetary policy anchor. After the earlier problems with monetary targets, the authorities decided to operate without an intermediate target. Instead UK monetary policy now focuses on a final target of keeping inflation at $2\frac{1}{2}$ per cent or less per annum. Interest rates are adjusted in the light of projections of inflation over the following two years. Developments in narrow and broad money are taken into account when projecting inflation but so are many other economic variables. Although "monitoring ranges" have been set for M0 and M4, they do not have the status of intermediate targets. Movements of M0 and M4 outside their monitoring range may be discounted if other information suggests the inflation target will be achieved.

2.2. *Velocity of Money and Financial Liberalisation*

As can be seen from the UK's experience, it is difficult to use an intermediate monetary target unless it has a stable, or at least predictable, relationship with the final target of policy — usually price inflation. In transitional economies, after a big initial rise following price liberalisation, the velocity of broad measures of money has tended to fall but — as in the UK — not necessarily in an easily predictable way. There are two main, but interrelated, reasons for this: (a) macroeconomic stabilisation, which can be expected to reduce the growth in the velocity of circulation temporarily during the period in which inflation is squeezed; and (b) liberalisation of the banking system, the effect of which on monetary growth is likely to be spread out over a longer period.

Following very rapid inflation rates, many of the transitional countries have tightened monetary (and fiscal) policies to reduce and then stabilise inflation. For those countries which have been successful, this has created and gradually developed confidence in domestic currency assets, and increased the financial attractiveness of savings (see Figure 1). In an environment of lower inflationary expectations, a larger share of the stock of broad money will likely be willingly held for savings purposes rather than held temporarily ready to spend. This may mean less of the money supply is likely to affect future prices.

The stage of transition may also affect the length of the *time lag* between a change in money growth and its effect on inflation. Opposing forces are at work. On the one hand, the time lag would be expected to be shorter in more developed market economies, assuming that supply, demand and relative prices are more flexible there. On the other hand, transitional countries have higher rates of inflation. In periods of fast monetary growth and high inflation, the costs of not adjusting prices, including the exchange rate, are larger and more visible. Changes in money growth should quickly result in changes in inflation. Therefore not only may a falling inflation rate reduce the *extent* to which money growth affects future inflation but the time lag of monetary policy may be permanently lengthened once a lower inflation rate has been secured.[1] (It may be the low *variability* of inflation associated with low inflation, rather than low inflation itself, which lengthens the time lag; but there is insufficient information in the data to distinguish between these two possibilities.)

Over time, it is also likely that liberalisation will increase financial sector activity. An increase in competition between banks should result in narrower spreads between bank deposit and lending rates and a greater array of saving and borrowing products. This would result in an increase in M2 and bank credit in the economy, relative to incomes.[2]

These influences have resulted in a decline in broad money and credit velocity in many countries in both the developing and developed world, including the UK, which have liberalised their financial markets (see Figure 2). In contrast, the development of other means of payment has led to economies in the use of cash and sight deposits and continuing rises in the velocity of narrower monetary aggregates. In view of the previous lack of non-cash

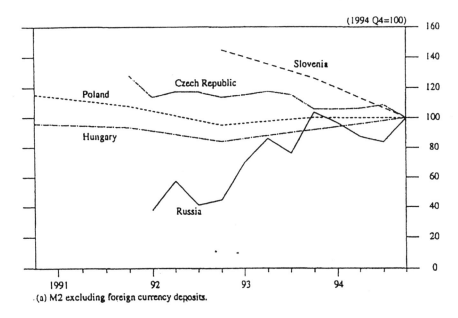

(a) M2 excluding foreign currency deposits.

Fig. 1.   Income velocity of broad money in Central Europe and Russia. M2 excluding foreign currency deposits. (Source: Poland, Hungary, Czech Republic and Slovenia, IMF staff estimates; Russia, Russian Economic Trends).

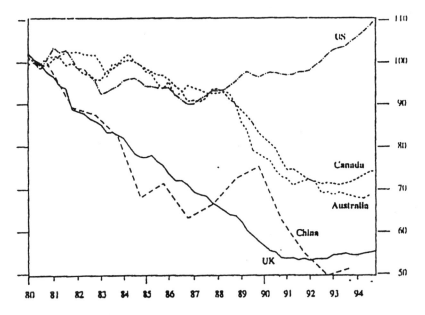

Fig. 2.   Income velocity of broad money (1980=100) in selected countries facing financial liberalisation. M2 for United States, Canada and China; M3 for Australia; M4 for United Kingdom.

means of payment, rapid rises in narrow money velocity were to be expected, and are being seen, in the transition countries.

2.3. Controllability

Central banks normally provide banknotes on demand, and have little opportunity therefore to control the supply of notes directly. In countries where commercial banks hold substantial voluntary deposits with the central bank, however, the monetary base (including these deposits) may be controllable through open market operations. For example, open market sales of securities will squeeze the banking system's deposits with the central bank, and push up interest rates other things being equal; counterwise, open market purchases will cause interbank rates to fall.[3]

That possibility apart, both narrow and broad money are normally influenced indirectly by interest rate management. The general level of short-term interest rates is an indicator of the opportunity cost of holding non-interest bearing money, so that a rise in interest rates can be expected to compress the demand for it. The opportunity cost of holding broad money depends on the return on broad money relative to other assets; these relative returns are not easily predictable. Nevertheless a rise in interest rates is likely to influence the demand for broad money, if only by reducing income growth.

3. EMPIRICAL WORK

Using data for Poland and Russia, we analysed (i) the *leading indicator* properties of a variety of monetary variables for inflation and (ii) the impact of various interest rates on money growth, the potential intermediate target (and on inflation, the final target).

(i) is a measure of the stability of the relationship between money growth and inflation; (ii) is a measure of the controllability of money. Both conditions are necessary if money is to serve as a useful intermediate policy target.

In particular we wanted to test:

(a) whether money growth has had a weaker effect on future inflation in more recent years as the inflation rate fell and real bank deposit rates increased;

(b) whether the lags from money growth to future inflation differ between countries and over time, owing to, for example, different rates of inflation or different stages of financial liberalisation; and

(c) whether across all countries money growth and inflation are more sensitive to changes in interest rates in floating exchange rate regimes than in fixed rate ones, and in the period since market-based monetary policy has become more established.

3.1. Method

The monthly data sets start after the recent bouts of near-hyperinflation in each country — early 1990 and 1992 in Poland and Russia respectively. A theoretical approach was adopted. To test (a) and (b) above, monthly price inflation was regressed by means of OLS techniques on numerous lags of money, using a variety of measures, and a one-month lag of the dependent variable (to capture inertia).[4] In both Poland and Russia, cash and M2 excluding foreign currency deposits were used as measures of narrow and broad money respectively. In addition, reserve money (excluding obligatory deposits) and M2 including foreign currency deposits were used in Poland. For Poland, where unlike Russia there are sufficient available data, a structural equation for the demand for zloty M2 was also estimated. The purpose was to identify the demand for money, so as to test the hypothesis that only actual money supply in excess of its long-run demand (MEXCESS) adds to future inflation as agents adjust their money holdings to desired levels (equation 1b). To test (c) above, equations (2) and (3) were estimated regressing, in turn, money growth and inflation on past central bank interest rates (R). Parsimonious forms were derived by sequentially dropping statistically insignificant lags. So for example:

$$\text{Inflation}_t = \text{constant} + a_i M_{t-i} + \lambda_1 \text{ inflation}_{t-1}, \tag{1a}$$

$$\text{Inflation}_t = \text{constant} + b_i \text{ MEXCESS}_{t-i}, \tag{1b}$$

$$M_t = \text{constant} + c_i R_{t-i} + \lambda_2 M_{t-1}, \tag{2}$$

$$\text{Inflation}_t = \text{constant} + d_i R_{t-i} + \lambda_3 \text{ inflation}_{t-1}. \tag{3}$$

Because of the limited available data set, particularly for Russia, the lags were restricted to six months and a rolling window approach was adopted to search for the most significant lag lengths. The detailed results are shown in Tables 3–10 while a summary of the relationships between monetary growth and inflation is shown in Table 1 below.

3.2. Monetary Growth to Inflation

Table 3 shows the results using the whole sample period — 1990M3–1994M12 for Poland and 1992M5–1994M12 for Russia. The results suggest:

TABLE 1
Summary of estimated impact of past M2 and cash growth on inflation[1]

Sample Period	Average monthly inflation rate (per cent)	Average monthly real interest rate (per cent)*	Per cent point impact on inflation rate of a 1 per cent increase in past monetary growth		Significant lag length (months)		Equation's fit (R-Bar Squared)	
			M2	Cash	M2	Cash	M2	Cash
(i) Russia								
1992M5–94M12	$17\frac{1}{2}$	−3	0.94	1.00	3.4	3.6	0.71	0.72
1992M5–93M10	20	−9	0.84	1.09	3.4	3.6	0.61	0.55
1993M11–94M12	$10\frac{1}{2}$	4	0.54	0.23**	6	6	0.69	0.48
(ii) Poland								
90M3–94M12	$3\frac{1}{2}$	−2	0.18	0.24	12	10.11	0.38	0.45
90M3–92M12	4	$-2\frac{1}{2}$	0.18	0.26	12	10.11	0.38	0.51
93M1–94M12	$2\frac{1}{2}$	−1	**	0.15*	**	14	**	0.06

* monthly central bank lending rate deflated by monthly consumer price inflation (a proxy for monthly inflation expectations).

** statistically insignificantly different from zero.

[1] M2 excluding foreign currency deposits.

- in both Poland and Russia past movements in the growth of money alone, on all definitions, can explain between 1/5 and 1/2 of the movement of current inflation (as reflected in the $\bar{R}_s^2$). In Russia, inclusion of the lagged value of inflation increases the explanatory power for both narrow (cash) and broad money (rouble M2) from 43 per cent and 36 per cent respectively to 72 per cent and 71 per cent, perhaps reflecting a partial adjustment of inflation to past changes in monetary growth.
- to the extent that the estimated relationships are causal over this sample period, changes in monetary growth had a *larger* and *quicker* impact on inflation in Russia than in Poland.[5] A 1 per cent point increase in rouble M2 growth added 0.17 per cent points to Russian inflation after 3 months, 0.44 per cent[6] points after 4 months and eventually 1 per cent point. The effects in Poland took longer and were more muted. The most powerful effect was for M2. Here a 1 per cent point increase in money growth added 0.32 per cent points to Polish inflation after 7 months and eventually (after 12 months) 0.54 per cent points. The statistically significant individual lags of money all appear in 3–6 month range in Russia and 6–12 months in Poland.

Tables 4 and 5 show the results after splitting the sample periods in the middle. In both countries inflation was significantly lower and real interest rates higher in the latter period (see Table 1). Because of the small data sets, particularly for Russia, these sub-period results need to be treated with caution. With this caveat borne in mind, over the early sample period the results are similar to the whole sample period estimates described above. The one clear exception is that in Poland, zloty M2 growth had a noticeably more powerful effect on future inflation over the 1990–92 period than is suggested by the whole period results.

In the second sub-period, however, most of the money growth-future inflation relationships broke down with the exception of those involving rouble M2 in Russia and reserve money in Poland. For narrow money in Russia and particularly for broad measures of money in Poland there is no evident relationship between past money growth and present inflation. In the lower inflation environment in Russia in 1994, the impact of rouble M2 growth appears to have become both weaker and more protracted. Here the most significant lag lengths occur at 6 months rather than 3–4 months and the long-run impact on inflation of a 1 per cent point increase in money growth is about 1/2 per cent point rather than 1 per cent point.[7]

The impact of narrow measures of money in Poland (both cash and reserve money) also became weaker and more protracted in the more recent lower inflationary period. Polish reserve money had its largest impact after about 1 year compared with an estimated 6 months in the earlier period.

Therefore, there is some evidence, comparing both across countries and over time, that lower inflation both *weakens* and *protracts* the impact of money growth on future inflation. In western economies, where inflation is generally much lower, the lags between monetary *policy* changes and inflation are longer still.[8] For example, Astley and Haldane (1994) find that in the United Kingdom inflation shows a systematic response to an increase in currency in circulation from the third quarter to around $2\frac{1}{2}$ years out. Similar responses are harder to determine for broader monetary aggregates in the UK, which do not seem to offer very much by way of leading indicator information. Amongst the various aggregates, a Divisia index seems to perform best, especially when split into corporate and personal holdings. These exhibit even longer lags, persisting for more than three years.

If the monetary authorities do not allow for such changes in the money growth-inflation relationship, there is a danger that their policy actions based on intermediate monetary targets may destabilise rather than stabilise the macroeconomy.[9] In periods of rising inflation, monetary growth may understate the immediate inflationary pressure and policy actions based on money targets may be too loose. In contrast, as inflation falls, money growth may overstate the near-term inflationary threat. If no allowance is made for this shift in the demand for money, policy may be excessively tight.

This latter effect can be illustrated by using the results for rouble M2. Tables 4 and 5 and Figure 3 show the closest relationships between past rouble M2 and current inflation in the two periods 1992M5–93M10 and 1993M11–94M12. The equation estimated over the earlier sample period (fitted1) tracks actual inflation well over this period. But as shown in the chart, its (dynamic) forecast — the line 'predicted' — overstates inflation, and thus understates real monetary growth, during the disinflationary period in the first three quarters of 1994. Monetary policy based on such a relationship would have been too tight for a given inflation objective.

This smaller quantifiable effect of money growth on inflation in 1994 reflects an increase in real money holdings. This was probably due to an increased willingness to hold bank deposits in Russia as inflation was reduced, at least for a while, to single digit monthly rates.[10] Moreover, the relationship fitted 2 accurately predicts the return of monthly inflation to single digit rates during the first half of 1995.

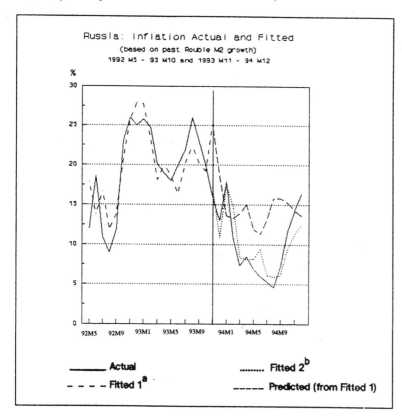

Fig. 3.   [a] Fitted 1 = 2.7 + 0.16 M2 growth t–3 + 0.31 M2 growth t–4 + 0.44 Inflation t–1 (estimated over 1992M5–1993M10); [b] Fitted 2 = 1.5 + 0.23 M2 growth t–6 + 0.57 Inflation t–1 (estimated over 1993M11–1994M12).

3.3. The Demand for Money in Poland

In principle, the changing relationship between money growth and inflation in Poland and Russia could have reflected a change in either velocity growth or GDP growth. To try to discover more, we estimated for Poland, where sufficient reliable data are available, a demand-for-money relationship for zloty M2.

The explanatory variables used were prices (with an expected unit coefficient), real GDP (proxied by monthly retail sales)[11] and the real bank deposit interest rate (a measure of the "own interest rate" on zloty M2 relative to inflation protected assets). As shown in Table 2 (i) the variables have similar time-series properties. The log of money, prices and retail sales volume are on the border line of being trend-stationary variables while real interest rates are clearly trend-stationary. When estimating the relationship using Johansen techniques, four cointegrating vectors are found between these variables. However, only one can be interpreted as a money-demand equation — vector (2) — where the price level has a unit coefficient and real interest rates and retail sales volume are correctly signed (positive). The coefficients also seem to be of a plausible magnitude (similar results were found when estimating by OLS instead). The residual from this vector was interpreted as the difference between *actual money and its long-run desired level*. As this residual increases, and actual money stock rises further away from its long-run equilibrium position, inflation should be higher in the future as agents offload their excess money balances. When testing for lagged values of the residuals affecting monthly inflation there was a *strong effect after 12 months* (see Table 2(iii)). Almost 60 per cent of the change in inflation can be explained by changes in the 12th lag of this disequilibrium variable alone. The explanatory power over the earlier sample period was *70 per cent* — twice as large as reported in Table 4 where the *actual* value of money growth 12 months ago is used as the explanatory variable.

This suggests that by stripping out the component of money which is held willingly, *more of future inflation can be explained*. However, as in the earlier results, the disequilibrium term fails to explain the movement of inflation over the second half of the period, suggesting the money demand relationship does not capture all the factors affecting Polish (zloty M2) money demand.

What then explains this poor relationship in Poland between broad money growth and inflation since the beginning of 1993? One possibility is that because the variability of inflation and monetary growth has been much smaller since 1993 than before it is difficult to establish a robust statistical relationship in the more recent period. An alternative economic explanation lies in the factors behind the increase in the supply of foreign exchange. For example, there may have been an increase in demand for money in Poland — not captured in our demand equation for broad money — reflecting a greater expected relative return on zloty deposits than on foreign currency assets, but we are not able to demonstrate this from the present data.

3.4. Controllability: Interest Rates and Future Monetary Growth

Table 6 shows the whole sample period results in Russia and Poland of regressing measures of the growth in the money supply on lagged values of the central bank's refinance rate to test whether the policy instrument systematically affected the growth in the money supply.

TABLE 2
Demand for Zloty M2

(i) Data Properties

Variable	ADF Statistic (with trend)
(log of) nominal Zloty M2 (LZM2)	–2.3
(log of) prices (LP)	–2.7
(log of) retail sales volume (LRS)	–4.2
real monthly deposit interest rate (RR)	–5.3
critical value	–3.5

(ii) Long Run Demand for Money Equation, LZM2 (1990M3–94M12)
4 Co-integrating vectors (var=3)

	(1)	(2)	(3)	(4)
LP	0.9	1.1	1.0	6.9
LRS	1.5	0.9	–0.1	7.1
RR	–4.0	0.12	–0.4	–0.9

(iii) Excess Monetary Growth to Future Inflation
Dependent Variable: Monthly Inflation

	90M12–94M12	90M12–92M12	93M1–94M12
Explanatory variable: $Res(2)^*_{t-12}$			
Coefficient (s.e.)	2.4(0.29)	2.4 (0.32)	–1.0(1.31)
Standard error of regression	1.4	1.4	1.2
R-bar squared	0.57	0.69	–0.05
DW-Statistic	1.8	2.2	1.4
LM(12)	13.3	9.5	13.6
Number of observations	49	25	24

* Res(2) are the residuals – the difference between actual and fitted – from vector
(2) in Table 2 (ii) above.

Over the whole sample period there appears evidence that changes in the monthly lending rate affected monetary growth in Russia after 3 months, particularly on the cash measure of money (R-bar squared 0.33). But when the sample is split in two parts there is no evidence of an effect in either sub-period. These results are however inconclusive since the split sample periods are very short and the estimates may not be very reliable.

TABLE 3
Leading Indicator Properties of Monetary Growth for Inflation — *Whole period*; Dependant variable: Monthly Inflation (%)

	Russia		Poland			
	92M5–94M12	92M5–94M12	90M12–94M12	90M9–94M12	91M1–94M12	91M1–94M12
Explanatory variable	Cash	Rouble M2	Cash	Reserve Money*	Zloty M2	M2
M_{t-3}	0.20 (0.08)	0.17 (0.08)				
M_{t-4}		0.16 (0.08)				
M_{t-5}						
M_{t-6}	0.19 (0.09)			0.15 (0.06)		
M_{t-7}				0.18 (0.06)		0.32 (0.13)
M_{t-8}						
M_{t-9}						
M_{t-10}			0.11 (0.04)			
M_{t-11}			0.13 (0.04)			
M_{t-12}					0.18 (0.03)	0.24 (0.05)
Inflation $_{t-1}$	0.61 (0.11)	0.65 (0.11)				
SEE	3.63	3.69	1.56	1.89	1.64	1.55
R-bar-squared	0.72	0.71	0.45	0.20	0.38	0.45
DW-Statistic	1.70	1.85	1.88	1.55	1.57	1.86
Durbin H-statistic	1.01	0.55				
LM(12)	9.3	7.6	9.9	12.0	18.2	15.6
Number of observations	32	32	49	52	48	48

M is the monthly growth of the specified monetary aggregate (%); Standard errors in parentheses;
* Cash plus free bank reserves at the National Bank of Poland.

TABLE 4

Leading Indicator Properties of Monetary Growth for Inflation - *Earlier period*; Dependant variable: Monthly Inflation (%)

Explanatory variable	Russia		Poland			
	92M5–93M10 Cash	92M5–94M10 Rouble M2	90M12–92M12 Cash	90M9–92M12 Reserve Money*	91M1–92M12 Zloty M2	91M1–92M12 M2
M_{t-3}	0.27 (0.13)	0.16 (0.09)				
M_{t-4}		0.31 (0.10)				
M_{t-5}						
M_{t-6}	0.24 (0.11)			0.16 (0.09)		
M_{t-7}				0.23 (0.09)		0.59 (0.18)
M_{t-8}						
M_{t-9}						
M_{t-10}			0.12 (0.57)			
M_{t-11}			0.14 (0.56)			
M_{t-12}					0.18 (0.05)	0.22 (0.06)
$Inflation_{q-1}$	0.53 (0.17)	0.44 (0.16)				
SEE	3.68	3.43	1.83	2.23	2.06	1.68
R-bar-squared	0.55	0.61	0.51	0.21	0.38	0.59
DW-Statistic	2.03	1.92	2.02	1.68	1.58	2.20
Durbin H-statistic	–0.09	0.2				
LM(12)	10.9	15.3	4.3	9.1	10.5	10.3
Number of observations	18	18	25	28	24	24

M is the monthly growth of the specified monetary aggregate (%); Standard errors in parentheses;

* Cash plus free bank reserves at the National Bank of Poland.

TABLE 5

Leading Indicator Properties of Monetary Growth for Inflation — *Later period*; Dependant variable: Monthly Inflation (%)

	Russia		Poland			
	93M11–94M12	93M11–94M12	93M1–94M12	93M1–94M12	93M1–94M12	93M1–94M12
Explanatory variable	Cash	Rouble M2	Cash	Reserve Money*	Zloty M2	M2
M_{t-3}						
M_{t-4}						
M_{t-5}						
M_{t-6}	0.09 (0.13)	0.23 (0.08)				
M_{t-7}						
M_{t-8}						
M_{t-9}						
M_{t-10}					No Relationship	No Relationship
M_{t-11}						
M_{t-12}				0.15 (0.06)		
M_{t-13}				0.11 (0.05)		
M_{t-14}			0.15 (0.09)	0.10 (0.06)		
Inflation $_{t-1}$	0.61 (0.21)	0.57 (0.15)				
SEE	3.23		2.51		1.11	1.03
R-bar-squared	0.48		0.69		0.06	0.20
DW-Statistic	1.55		1.0		1.40	1.31
Durbin H-statistic	1.3		2.3			
LM(12)	0.6[1]		4.7[1]	17.7	15.4	
Number of observations	14	14	24	24		

[1] LM(1); M is the monthly growth of the specified monetary aggregate (%); Standard errors in parentheses;

* Cash plus free bank reserves at the National Bank of Poland.

For Poland, over the 1990–92 period there is evidence that the changes in central bank credit rate in the past affected current *broad* money growth with a short lag (one month) but there is no evidence that the NBP's lending rate affected any measure of money growth in 1993–94. However, replacing the NBP's refinance rate with the Treasury bill rate provides some evidence that (the change in) the past TB rate affected current *narrow* money growth (see Table 9).[12]

Following the introduction of open market operations in Treasury bills in Poland, the TB rate has become increasingly important as an indicator of the stance of monetary policy. There is some evidence of a systematic effect of changes in the TB rate on the growth in the size of the NBP's own balance sheet. However, the controllability of broad money disappeared in the more recent period.

These results are broadly consistent with the monetary approach to the balance of payments (MABP).[13] For a country pursuing a fixed exchange rate policy, changes in interest rates will not affect monetary growth *if the economy is open and the foreign exchange market efficient.* By 1993–94 Poland had many of these features. Imports had risen to 22 per cent of GDP and the money market was growing rapidly. In contrast, in 1990–92 the economy had been less open and the foreign exchange market less liquid and efficient. This meant that over this earlier period, and despite the fixed exchange rate policy, an increase in interest rates could, at least for a time, reduce the growth in money *as well as* domestic credit since it would not be fully offset by higher capital inflows. In contrast, the more open capital markets witnessed since 1993 may have reduced the ability of the NBP to affect money growth given its exchange rate objective.

In Part 2 of this empirical section, we found that although in the earlier period money had played a useful leading indicator role in both Russia and Poland, this was less evident in the later period, particularly in Poland. Now we find also that the controllability of money through policy instruments — which are focusing increasingly on market interest rates as the financial markets become more liberalised — is not very strong or robust.

3.5. Interest Rates and Future Inflation

But is there any evidence that changes in interest rates are having more powerful effects on inflation as financial markets are liberalised and deepen? This question was addressed for the UK by Easton in Easton and Stephenson (1990). He found clear econometric evidence that the effects of interest rates on demand, and thereby on inflation, had become more powerful during the

TABLE 6

Controllability: Leading Indicator Properties of Interest Rates for Monetary Growth — *Whole period* Dependent Variable: Monthly Growth of the Specified Monetary Aggregate (%)

	Russia		Poland			
	92M5–94M12	92M5–94M12	90M7–94M11	90M8–94M9	90M7–94M12	90M7–94M12
	Cash	Rouble M2	Cash	Reserve Money*	Zloty M2	M2
r_{t-1}			−0.03 (0.08)			
Δr_{t-1}					−0.18 (0.05)	−0.11 (0.03)
r_{t-2}			0.08 (0.06)			
Δr_{t-2}				−0.20 (0.08)		
r_{t-3}	−1.0 (0.25)	−0.82 (0.29)				
SEE	7.33	8.31	3.11	4.03	2.57	1.69
R-bar squared	0.33	0.19	0.03	0.09	0.16	0.15
DW-Statistic	1.74	1.93	1.8	2.5	0.98	1.6
LM(12)	10.5	6.5	8.1	12.9	18.0	7.1
Number of observations	32	32	53	50	54	54

Explanatory variable r is the monthly central bank lending rate (%); Standard errors in parentheses;

* Cash plus free bank reserves at the National Bank of Poland.

TABLE 7

Controllability: Leading Indicator Properties of Interest Rates for Monetary Growth — *Earlier period* Dependent Variable: Monthly Growth of the Specified Monetary Aggregate (%)

	Russia		Poland			
	92M5–93M10	92M5–93M10	90M7–92M12	90M8–92M12	90M7–92M12	90M7–92M12
	Cash	Rouble M2	Cash	Reserve Money*	Zloty M2	M2
r_{t-1}			-0.06 (0.04)			
Δr_{t-1}		-1.10 (0.76)			-0.16 (0.05)	-0.11 (0.03)
r_{t-2}			0.07 (0.07)			
Δr_{t-2}				-0.18 (0.08)		
r_{t-3}	-0.79 (0.57)					
SEE	6.94	10.00	3.51	4.71	2.64	1.6
R-bar squared	0.05	0.06	-0.04	0.12	0.20	0.23
DW-Statistic	1.64	2.07	1.8	2.7	0.82	1.4
LM(12)	5.74	13.07	6.8	13.5	12.9	8.8
Number of observations	18	18	30	29	30	30

Explanatory variable r is the monthly central bank lending rate (%); Standard errors in parentheses;
* Cash plus free bank reserves at the National Bank of Poland.

TABLE 8
Controllability: Leading Indicator Properties of Interest Rates for Monetary Growth — *Later period* Dependent Variable: Monthly Growth of the Specified Monetary Aggregate (%)

	Russia		Poland			
	93M11–94M12	93M11–94M12	93M1–94M11	93M1–94M9	93M1–94M12	93M1–94M12
	Cash	Rouble M2	Cash	Reserve Money*	Zloty M2	M2
r_{t-1}			−0.5 (0.77)	−0.7 (0.70)	−0.4 (0.28)	−0.3 (0.24)
Δr_{t-1}						
r_{t-2}				0.8 (0.72)		
Δr_{t-2}						
r_{t-3}	0.34 (0.78)	0.69 (0.44)				
SEE	7.26	4.14	2.46	3.87	1.81	1.58
R-bar squared	−0.07	0.10	−0.02	0.01	0.06	0.04
DW-Statistic	2.61	2.01	2.17	1.80	2.0	2.1
LM(12)	1.95[1]	0.02[1]	13.8	15.0	15.1	16.9
Number of observations	14	14	23	21	24	24

Explanatory variable r is the monthly central bank lending rate (%); Standard errors in parentheses;
* Cash plus free bank reserves at the National Bank of Poland.

TABLE 9

Controllability: Leading Indicator Properties of Interest Rates for Monetary Growth — *Later period* Dependent Variable: Monthly Growth of the Specified Monetary Aggregate (%)

	Russia		Poland			
	93M11–94M12 Cash	93M11–94M12 Rouble M2	93M11–94M11 Cash	93M1–94M9 Reserve Money*	93M1–94M12 Zloty M2	93M1–94M12 M2
rTB_{t-1}	−0.55 (1.56)	−1.13 (0.91)	−0.64 (0.22)	−0.5 (0.23)	−0.13 (0.10)	−0.07 (0.19)
ΔrTB_{t-1}						−0.02 (0.18)
rTB_{t-2}						
ΔrTB_{t-2}						
rTB_{t-3}						
SEE	7.28	4.27	2.12	3.56	1.85	
R-bar squared	−0.07	0.04	0.24	0.15	0.02	−0.05
DW-Statistic	2.44	1.70	1.9	2.0	1.9	2.0
LM(12)	0.94[1]	0.31[1]	14.7	10.6	15.6	20.2
Number of observations	14	14	23	21	24	24

[1] LM(1); Explanatory variable rTB is the monthly rate on 3M Treasury Bills (%) for Poland and the interbank rate for Russia (%); Standard errors in parentheses.

* Cash plus free bank reserves at the National Bank of Poland.

TABLE 10

Leading Indicator Properties of Interest Rates for Inflation Dependent Variable: Monthly Inflation (%)

	Russia		Poland			
	92M6–94M12	92M6–93M10	93M11–94M12	90M12–94M12	90M12–92M12	93M1–94M12
r_{t-5}	−0.3 (0.15)	1.0 (0.67)	−1.88 (0.27)			
r_{t-6}				−0.17 (0.04)	−0.20 (0.05)	
r_{t-7}				0.17 (0.04)	0.16 (0.04)	
r_{t-8}						
r_{t-9}						−0.30 (0.11)
r_{t-10}						0.28 (0.11)
Inflation$_{t-1}$	0.70 (0.12)	0.34 (0.26)				
SEE	3.65	3.86	1.74	2.07	1.05	0.17
R-bar-squared	0.72	0.47	0.78	0.32	0.37	0.17
DW-Statistic	1.50	1.41	2.11	1.59	1.77	1.45
LM(12)	8.8	12.6	0.15[1]	15.9	13.9	14.2
Number of observations	31	17	14	49	25	24

[1] LM(1); Explanatory variable r is the monthly central bank lending rate (%); Standard errors in parentheses.

1980s. This increased responsiveness to interest rates was largely ascribed to the deregulation and structural changes in financial markets. In the UK, the greater scope for substitution effects of interest rate changes to play a role in freer markets was reinforced by shifts in the exposure of different economic agents to the income effects of interest rate changes. Following liberalisation of access to credit, personal sector borrowing increased rapidly and the sector's liabilities bearing floating interest rates came to exceed its floating-rate assets, so that rises in interest rates rapidly cut net personal sector income. As the most exposed borrowers tend to be credit-constrained and have higher than average marginal propensities to consume from income, the income effects of interest rate changes became stronger, augmenting the usual substitution effects.

A survey by Stephenson in the same paper found that distributional effects in household sectors were important in some other major economies, but less so than in the UK. Generally, these other economies did not show the clear increase in responsiveness to interest rates seen in the UK, but the results did indicate that changes in the size and type (floating or fixed rate) of different sectors' assets and liabilities were important in determining the effects of changes in interest rates on the real economy and inflation.

For Russia in 1993–94, there is stronger evidence of a direct link from interest rates to inflation than from either interest rates to money supply growth or from money growth to inflation (see Table 10). This does not however apply to Poland. Again the lag lengths are shorter in Russia than in Poland: almost 80 per cent of the change of the fluctuations in inflation between 1993M11–94M12 can be explained by movements in the refinance rate five months earlier (similar results are found when using the inter-bank rate instead). Higher interest rates also seem to have reduced real output, at least on the official monthly measures.[14] In Poland the relationship is weaker but nonetheless almost 20 per cent of fluctuations in inflation can be explained over the 1993–94 period by changes in interest rates nine and ten months earlier.

In Russia, although not in Poland, interest rates seem to have had more effect on future inflation in 1993-94 than before. This may reflect the growing importance of changes in financial prices — interest rates and exchange rates — in the transmission of Russian monetary policy as market forces came to play a larger role. Since 1993 there has been a marked reduction in directed credits at subsidised interest rates. Primary auctions of Treasury bills were introduced in May 1993, credit auctions were introduced in February 1994 and since April 1994 the CBR refinance rate has been kept above the interbank reference rate.

The apparently weaker effect on inflation of interest rates in Poland than Russia may reflect the differing monetary policy regimes. Poland has pursued a fixed exchange rate policy implying that the effects of changes in interest rates on domestic inflation and demand would be offset by changes in capital flows. The offsets are likely to have become quicker-acting as the economy has become more open. This is supported by the empirical results which show a smaller interest rate effect on inflation in 1993–94 than in 1990–92. Gerlach and Smets (1994), who found weaker effects on inflation of changes in interest rates in France and Italy than in the other G7 economies over the 1979Q1–93Q4 period, attribute this to the absence of an exchange rate response since Italy and France were pursuing an exchange rate target within the ERM for most of this period.

4. CONCLUSIONS

Governments and central banks around the world have given a higher priority to reducing inflation in recent years. Some central banks have used an intermediate exchange rate target fixed against a low inflation country to help achieve this. Although fixed exchange rate regimes may ensure currency stability for small economies with relatively large tradeable sectors, they ensure low inflation only in the tradeable sector, rather than in the economy as a whole. In addition, in successful transitional (and developing) economies, including Poland, fixed exchange rate regimes have come under strain from capital inflows.

A possible alternative for central banks is to allow greater exchange rate flexibility and to pursue their domestic policy objectives through independent monetary policies. Over the past twenty years, many central banks have used broad money targets, at one time or another, to guide their monetary policy. In Russia and Poland, there is evidence too in recent years that monetary aggregates have been a useful guide to future inflation. The lags appear to be shorter than in western economies where inflation rates are lower: in Poland they seem to be around 12 months and in Russia, where inflation has been higher still, no more than 6 months.

In several western countries, financial liberalisation and innovations have, however, weakened the relationship between the monetary aggregates and inflation, making the monetary aggregates less useful for target purposes. The recent results for the UK point to some measures of money, particularly cash, serving a useful indicator role but there is insufficient confidence in the stability of the relationships to give monetary aggregates an intermediate target status (see Astley and Haldane (1995)). Similarly, there is some evidence, albeit based on a limited number of observations, that money velocities became less predictable in Russia and Poland as inflation fell in 1993–94, with the effect of changes in broad money growth on future inflation appearing to have become both weaker and more protracted.[15]

A number of countries, including the UK, have reacted to the difficulty in predicting the velocity of money, particularly when faced by liberalisation, by abandoning intermediate monetary targets in favour of final target (ranges) for price inflation.[16] Nevertheless the UK has retained monitoring ranges for both narrow and broad monetary aggregates. In face of high capital inflows Poland has widened its exchange rate band. Russia, in contrast, where the currency has been appreciating, has recently introduced a short-term exchange rate target range to operate alongside a central bank credit ceiling under the IMF programme.

The results do not give a clear indication as to which definition of money would be best adapted for target or guideline purposes in Poland: there is no great difference between narrow and broad definitions in their power to predict future inflation. An additional criterion is controllability: there is not much point in setting a target for an uncontrollable variable. On this criterion, reserve money (which can be controlled to some degree through open market operations) scores more highly than cash. As to broader definitions, the econometric results suggest that there is no significant difference in the responsiveness of zloty M2 and total M2 to interest rate fluctuations. If there were to be more exchange rate flexibility, zloty and foreign currency deposits would become less close substitutes, and it seems likely that zloty M2 would become more easily controllable than total M2 than with a fixed exchange rate. As seems to have been the case in Russia, if Poland switched to a floating rate regime interest rates too would have a more powerful effect on inflation.

The econometric relationships between money and inflation described in this paper are based on the experience of only a few turbulent years and where the data are unlikely to be fully reliable. Such relationships are in any case subject to change as a result of competition and innovation in the financial system. For these reasons it is impossible to be confident that a particular target range for any monetary aggregate will deliver desired monetary objectives, so it would be unwise for either Russia or Poland to base monetary policy on monetary targets to be adhered to rigidly and unthinkingly. Better would be to identify monitoring ranges, perhaps for both broad and narrow monetary aggregates: a shift of either broad or narrow money growth outside the monitoring range should be regarded as *prima facie* evidence that domestic monetary objectives were unlikely to be met and that corrective action would be needed unless other evidence indicated clearly that the monetary aggregates were giving a misleading signal.

DATA APPENDIX

Russia. All data are taken from Russian Economic Trends, various issues.

Poland. Obligatory deposits and foreign currency deposits in M2 from the National Bank of Poland. All other data are taken from IMF International Financial Statistics.

The Polish monthly monetary data are available from December 1989. There was a break in the monetary series when the new monetary sector was established in December 1991. As an estimate of this break, currency, the monetary base (excluding obligatory deposits), zloty M2 and M2 have been revised downwards prior to December 1991 by 8 per cent, $5\frac{1}{2}$ per cent, $9\frac{1}{2}$ per cent and $7\frac{1}{2}$ per cent respectively. (This break appears only to have affected the currency component of reserve money). This is a rough estimate based on a mixture of the usual growth in December and the monthly growth rates in the months around end 1991. These adjustments only affect one observation in each of these monetary *growth* series.

The NBP refinance rate is available over a long historical period but the (1-month) money market rate and (3-month) TB rate at auctions are only available from 1990M12 and 1992M1 respectively. Data on obligatory deposits were used until 1994M9 after which a new method of measurement was introduced.

Order of Integration
Poland (sample 90M3-94M12) - 12 lags

Variable (Y)	ADF(Y)	ADF(ΔY)
%ΔP	–6.3*	
%ΔC	–3.3*	
%ΔRM	–1.8	–1.6
%ΔZM2	–2.8	–2.3
%ΔM2	–2.9*	
RR	–5.8*	

Critical value –2.9

Russia

Variable (Y)	ADF(Y)	ADF(ΔY)
%ΔP	–1.8	–3.4*
%ΔC	–1.5	–3.0*
%ΔRM2	–1.9	–3.1*

Critical value –3.0

* significant at 95% critical value
Δ first difference
%Δ monthly growth (per cent)
P price level
C notes and coin
RM reserve money (excluding obligatory reserves)
ZM2 Zloty M2
RM2 Rouble M2
RR nominal central bank lending rate (per cent)

In Poland, inflation and the NBP's lending rate are clearly stationary variables. The growth in currency, broad measures of money and, to a lesser extent, reserve money are on the border line of being stationary variables. In Russia, inflation, narrow and broad growth are only stationary in first difference terms (i.e. I(1) variables).

NOTES

1. In technical jargon, the short-run Phillips curve may be flatter at low rates of inflation than at high rates.

2. For developed countries most research suggests that the removal of constraints on lending is the dominant effect. Thus after liberalisation, credit has increased more rapidly than deposits resulting in a decline in saving rates. (See Bayoumi (1993), Japelli and Pagano (1989), Lehmussaari (1990), Levy and Ostry (1994) and Miles (1992)). For a sample of mainly developing countries, however, Edwards (1995) finds that financial deepening *increases* the saving rate of the private sector.

3. During the transition process, open market operations typically increasingly replace less market-oriented methods of monetary control such as direct credit limits and changes in obligatory reserve requirements.

4. The lagged dependent variable was insignificant in the Polish equation. This is to be expected as Polish monthly inflation is a stationary variable.

5. A causal relationship in Russia may reflect, as suggested by Fischer (1994), the effect of higher money growth on rouble depreciation and the effect of higher bank credit growth on state sector wages.

6. $0.17+0.16+0.17*(0.65)$.

7. In the long run, once the inflation rate and velocity growth stabilise, a 1% increase in monetary growth should be associated with a 1% increase in inflation.

8. Gerlach and Smets (1994) find in recent VAR simulations that monetary policy effects are *broadly* similar across G7 economies.

9. See Dornbusch and Simonsen (1988).

10. In principle, an increase in real money holdings (M/P) could be due to a rise in real output (Y) rather than resulting from a decline in velocity (V). But, on the basis of the official data at least, the reverse happened in the first half of 1994, with real GDP dropping further.

11. GDP is available only on an annual basis in Poland.

12. The TB rate in Poland is only available from 1992M1.

13. See, for example, Frenkel and Johnson (1976).

14. The simple correlations between interest rates lagged 3 months and the growth in real GDP and industrial production in Russia over 1993M11-94M12 are −0.64 and −0.90 respectively. Output growth is measured on a 12-month basis to avoid the problem caused by monthly seasonal movements. It probably does not capture accurately the growth in private sector output. So tighter monetary policy may have only resulted in a switch in production from the old state sector to the private sector rather than to a reduction in *total* output.

15. These results from transitional countries may have wider implications. For example, the present very low inflation rates seen in a number of major economies could, in principle, increase the time lag of monetary policy.

16. Inflation targets are now set in Canada, Finland, Israel, New Zealand, Spain, Sweden and the United Kingdom.

REFERENCES

Astley, S.A. and A.G. Haldane (1995). *Money as an Indicator*, Bank of England Working Paper, No. 35, May.

Bayoumi, T. (1993). 'Financial Deregulation and Household Saving', *The Economic Journal* 103, No. 421 pp. 1432-43.

Dornbusch, R. and M. Simonsen (1988). 'Inflation Stabilization: The Role of Incomes Policy and Monetization' in: Dornbusch, R. (ed.) *Exchange Rates and Inflation*.

Easton, W.W. and M.J. Stephenson (1990). 'The Interest Rate Transmission Mechanism in the United Kingdom and Overseas', *Bank of England Quarterly Bulletin*, May 1990.

Edwards, S. (1995). 'Why Are Saving Rates So Different Across Countries?: An International Comparative Analysis', National Bureau of Economic Research Working Paper, No. 5097.

Fischer, S. (1994). 'Prospects for Russian Stabilization in the Summer of 1993' in: Aslund, A. (ed.) *Economic Transformation in Russia*.

Frenkel, J.A. and H.G. Johnson (eds.) (1976). *The Monetary Approach to the Balance of Payments*.

Gerlach, S. and F. Smets (1994). 'The Monetary Transmission: Evidence from the G7 Countries', Bank for International Settlements.

Government of the Russian Federation, *Russian Economic Trends*, various issues.

Haldane, A. (1995). 'Inflation Targets', *Bank of England Quarterly Bulletin*, August.

Halpern, L. and C. Wyplosz (1995). 'Equilibrium Real Exchange Rates in Transition', CEPR Discussion Paper No. 1145, April.

Hoggarth, G. (1995). 'Monetary Policy in Russia', Chapter 3 of *Russia's Financial Markets and Banking Sector in Transition*, Series A, Bank of Finland.

Jappelli, T. and M. Pagano (1989). 'Consumption and Capital Market Imperfections: An International Comparison', *The American Economic Review*, 79 No. 5.

Koen, V. and M. Marrese (1995). 'Stabilization and Structural Change in Russia, 1992-94', *IMF Working Paper* 95/13.

Lehmussaari, O.P. (1990). 'Deregulation and Consumption: Saving Dynamics in the Nordic Countries', *IMF Staff Papers* 37, pp. 71-93.

Levy, J. and J.D. Ostry (1994). 'Household Saving in France: Stochastic Income and Financial Deregulation', *IMF Working Paper* No. 94/136.

Miles, D. (1992). 'Housing Market, Consumption and Financial Liberalisation in the Major Economies', *European Economic Review* 36, pp. 1093-1136.

Nijsse, E. (1994) 'Household Money Demand and Savings in Poland: An Explanatory Approach' *National Bank of Poland Research Department Paper* No. 10, March.

Part E
The Marjolin Lecture

Central Banking and Market Volatility
The Marjolin Lecture

Summary

As a consequence of the globalisation of capital markets of all kinds, monetary policy has had to become more market-oriented. Market expectations play an important rôle and entail increasing volatility on interest rates and exchange rates. The latter may remain misaligned for a while compared to current fundamental indicators; although they are influenced by the latter, expectations reflect changing medium-term views of market operators. This is why central banks have to build up credibility, take a forward-looking approach and apply a careful communications policy, while they cannot rely as much as before on intermediate targets.

At the same time, spillover effects of decisions made at a national level or of shocks have brought international co-operation to the fore. Such co-operation should not apply exclusively to monetary policy, but should also include fiscal policy, a sensitive issue for market expectations. At a regional level, there is more than a good case for establishing tight cooperation. In particular, the adoption of a single currency is a normal feature of a single multinational market. This was the vision of Robert Marjolin in as early as 1962. It was elaborated in subsequent reports, leading to the Maastricht Treaty.

Robert Raymond has spent most of his career with the Bank of France. After several years in the Foreign Department, he became Head of the Research Department (dealing with economic, statistical and monetary matters) before his transfer to become Director General in charge of money market and credit operations. In February 1994, Mr Raymond left the Bank of France following his appointment as Director General of the newly created European Monetary Institute.

XVII. Central Banking and Market Volatility

The Marjolin Lecture

ROBERT RAYMOND

I knew Robert Marjolin quite well during the last twelve years of his life. In autumn 1973, as the Head of the Balance of Payments Division in the Bank of France, I was appointed as the rapporteur of the Commission of the Plan organisation in charge of international affairs. This Commission had to work under challenging circumstances. Robert Marjolin was the Chairman.

Robert Marjolin came from a modest family. With the assistance of a grant, he studied in the United States at the beginning of the 1930s. He became Jean Monnet's assistant in the United States during the war; they were the representatives of the Free French in that country, in charge of procurement for the Free French army. They conceived the Plan to be applied after the war to help rebuild the French economy. Very soon after the war, Robert Marjolin was one of the French negotiators for the Marshall Plan. He was selected as Secretary General of the new OEEC and he set up the organisation from scratch. He installed it where the OECD still stands today, in the Chateau de la Muette in Paris. Much later, he became one of the French negotiators of the Rome Treaty, and the first member of the Commission (as Vice President) in charge of economic affairs. When I met him, he had left public duties behind and served instead on many panels and major company boards.

He had a particular interest in monetary policy. He was the co-author of the Marjolin-Sadrin-Wormser report which recommended in 1969 a simplification of the instruments of monetary policy in France. This led soon after to the abandonment of rediscount operations and the use of private paper as collateral for repos on equal footing with Treasury Bills, a reform which could still be recommended to several European central banks. As early as 24 October 1962, a Marjolin Report underlined the necessity for the Common Market to enjoy stable exchange rates, thus leading to the adoption of a European currency.

Robert Marjolin died suddenly at home, in his sleep, after lunch one day. He died as he lived, with more than a touch of class, making short and simple what is usually long and painful.

I accepted the task of delivering this memorial speech, in order to pay my own tribute to this noble man and great European. In doing so, I am aware that I am compelled to follow four guidelines:

- first, referring to Robert Marjolin, as a monetary analyst and a founding-father of the European Union;
- second, dealing with issues related to the topic of our colloquium;
- third, drawing on my current experience;
- and fourth, applying the basic rule for lectures: being boring.

I assure you that in what follows, I will do my best to do so.

* * *

No central banker could deny that the job has changed dramatically during the last ten to twenty years, and even more if I remember how my professional life was at the beginning. In the good old days, the concept of money was a by-product of accounting. Money creation was curbed by administrative ceilings on credit expansion and credit policy was only part of a global governmental economic policy. Since then central banks have been eager to conquer their autonomy, whilst in most cases they unfortunately lost track of money. Life is never as it should be!

More recently, confidence in market ability to improve growth has led to deregulation in many sectors, especially in financial activities. The abolition of capital controls, widespread financial innovation, the growth of public debts and the increasing role of institutional investors led to globalisation, what our colleague Richard O'Brien called: "the end of geography". These factors increased price volatility on financial markets, notably for exchange rates and long-term interest rates. Exchange rates, in particular, are shaped by capital movements more than by international trade. Therefore trade and activity are influenced, at least in the short-run, by exchange rate volatility. Volatility is triggered by spontaneous changes in expectation, while globalisation facilitates transmission of external shocks. Such volatility has entailed not only day-to-day or intraday fluctuations, but also medium-term deviations from levels consistent with fundamentals.

Instead of a photograph of money as a portion of banks' accounts, we are now watching a movie in which Lucky Luke shoots so fast that you do not always see who has been hit. The intrusion of time and space in monetary policy has had a strong impact on policymaking and on techniques of intervention.

1. TIME

As far as time is concerned, the market place has become a battlefield on which speculators' and central banks' views and wishes come into conflict. While in the past central banks had the power to rule, the game today is better balanced. Therefore central banks must be convincing in order to influence operators' behaviour and to make the fight less bloody. Let us consider both antagonists one after the other.

Price volatility on financial and exchange markets is steered by capital movements and portfolio arbitrage, based on *market expectations*. Central banks always run the risk of being taken by surprise. They should be forgiven if volatility reflects unforeseeable events. At least they should try to understand the genesis of expectations. When they complain about the non-rational character of market behaviour, this mirrors either their ignorance of the motivation of market participants or more likely a difference of opinion with markets about future developments.

I will not refer here to the attempts which were made to modelise the so-called overshooting phenomena, by which a price deviates from the long-term equilibrium level in an increasing manner. I would prefer to comment briefly on more trivial observations.

Firstly, the usual criticism is that markets pay less attention than before to fundamentals. We should first try to agree on what is fundamental. Common sense would focus on prices of goods — mainly the CPI — and real growth, adding to this a few complementary indicators such as the fiscal stance, the trade balance or the current account, and some monetary aggregates.

It would be wrong to think that markets do not pay attention to such fundamentals. New data on prices, foreign trade or current accounts may trigger moves on interest rates at given maturities before central banks act or speak, to the extent that market operators will feel that current policies are not sustainable any more and may anticipate a policy change. Therefore these data do not matter so much by themselves, as the market knows that they are used by central banks as an input for the elaboration of their strategy. Market expectations are based on the reaction functions of central banks as they are perceived. They also include an assessment of the lag with which the expected policy move will prove to be effective. The combination of both the reaction function and the transmission mechanism explains why markets are deeply influenced by past records. Several institutions, including mine, noted that exchange rate depreciation and long-term interest rate differentials in 1994–95 are correlated with average inflation over the previous ten years.

The fiscal stance also has a bearing on expectations. It is not clear if it is considered as a fundamental, or as a potential threat to monetary and financial stability. Such concerns underpin the Maastricht fiscal criteria.

Secondly, markets may very well keep quiet when some fundamentals are moving and then suddenly change their minds. Central bankers and academics are usually surprised by such reassessments. Part of the explanation can be found, in my judgement, in the concept of sustainability and how it is interpreted. Let me take two examples.

The dominant view is that when a new situation is created, it will continue, until it is considered to be unsustainable. When this happens, all participants revise their own positions simultaneously. Market psychology and dynamics clearly play a role. The last of many liquidity crises in Latin America, namely the Mexican crisis a year ago, is a good illustration. There was no hyperinflation and the fiscal stance was satisfactory. At some stage, however, the trade deficit appeared to be on the wrong track and not sustainable at the existing exchange rate. Then operators focused on the fact that large capital inflows in early 1990 had accompanied and hidden a decline in savings.

Symmetrically, the market may not be satisfied by what is usually called fundamental, if some other factors inspire doubts about the sustainability of such a good combination of indexes. Public acceptance of current policies and political instability are factors that decision-makers tend to minimise, while they may be perceived as a source of uncertainty by market operators. Market suspicion about the acceptability of the rate of unemployment or repeated political turmoil belong to this category. Therefore, the assessment of sustainability may be a cause of conflict between authorities, including central banks, and the main players. This lack of mutual understanding can be associated with many shocks observed recently, including ERM crises in the 1990s.

Thirdly, the predictability of decision-makers' reactions and therefore the confidence in the sustainability of a policy are enhanced by credibility. This is an important but emotional concept. Should I go as far as to say that volatility and credibility are two pedantic words which are very useful since they allow analysts to conceal their ignorance: volatility when they cannot explain why it is moving when it shouldn't, credibility when they cannot explain why it is not moving when it should?

Credibility is a medal that you can only win after years of effort without any break, being fully independent from external influences including political or market pressures, and acting according to your own rules, provided this does not prompt any disaster. Only survivors can be credible.

It is easier for individuals and independent central banks to be credible, that is to say, reliable, than for Governments, as they cannot abstract from political pressure, by definition. Government policies can only be credible to the extent they express a strong social consensus.

Central banks had to adapt their strategy to new market conditions, and pay greater attention to time, its cost and its power, than to the straightforward interpretation of data.

During the last half-century there has been a long-lasting training process by which the ability to forecast has increased. This has been based on standardised national accounts, the use of complex models for forecasting future developments and analysing variants with different policy contents. These activities have been developed by national agencies and international organisations. As sophisticated as they can be, these tools proved persistently unable to foresee the big events which occurred in the economic field or on markets: oil shocks, the big inflationary wave, stock and bond market crises. A recent example on which I shall comment later occurred at the end of 1993, when the majority of experts felt that the dollar was starting to appreciate. The difficulty of foreseeing the date of future economic changes is partly related to the volatile nature of financial market expectations.

In spite of such weaknesses, central banks have become much more forward-looking.

First, in general, most of them can no longer rely on a strict correlation between some intermediate target of money stock and inflation. This link either was broken or became weaker. When it was possible to stick to such a target in the spirit of a monetarist approach, it was very helpful and made monetary policy both effective and predictable. Where it is still possible to use some M as a benchmark, it is appropriate to continue and it has obviously a very good pedagogical impact. But in several countries, authorities consider that - unfortunately - they cannot make use of it any more.

Second, however, central banks have a better perception of the time lag with which prices are influenced by policy action. They move earlier than before. This is why we experienced early rises in money rates in the United States, Italy and the United Kingdom in 1994-95, despite low levels of current inflation. Central banks are aware now that a wide range of factors or indicators may reveal inflationary trends, including financial market yields and derivative contracts.

Third, at the same time, they feel less strictly bound to the cyclical pattern and nearly exclusively committed to price stability. Maintaining low inflation and being independent for that purpose now is normally enshrined in their Statutes.

As a result of these three characteristics, central banks have developed a medium-term vision of the optimal path between counterinflationary action and sustainable growth.

The communication policy of central banks vis-à-vis market and public opinion has been adapted to the new environment. When I was a young central bank officer, Governors were silent Gods. Today they have to be media experts. This does not mean that they apply a uniform communication policy. I would distinguish between two main streams, or principles, which may seem incompatible at the first glance, but which might not be so in reality.

There are good arguments in favour of transparency. Explaining the objectives and what is expected from any new decision may contribute to narrowing down differences of interpretation and avoid conflicts with market forces. Ex post hearings are one of the normal counterparts of central banks' autonomy, a tribute to be paid to public accountability. Communiqués and public statements concomitant with decisions have become more usual. After a while, or if rules of the game are well known, changes in official rates or semi-official rates (such as rates for periodical repos) are understood as being messages as well as having a direct impact on the yield curve. It is well known that limited intervention on the foreign exchange market, when a great fuss is made about it, may give food for thought to speculators. It may have a strong impact when market psychology is well judged, as with the dollar in mid-August. However, it has to be significant enough, and repeated if need be, to be made credible and express a clear commitment. If not, it is much ado about nothing, and it will be interpreted as a substitute for action and finally be detrimental.

Another view, which might be considered as opposite, is market aversion: never do what the market is expecting. This is based on the trade-off between a market-led approach and the search for credibility. It is a disaster for portfolio managers, as they are taken by surprise and have to overreact. It is a godsend for financial intermediaries on derivative markets as it increases volatility.

As usual, there should be a way of reconciling both parties. No pre-announcement can be envisaged by central banks. In normal conditions, transparency is useful as a pedagogical approach. This is why targeting is welcome where it still works. As for market aversion, it cannot be a system, but it does entail the sensible view that market pressure should never per se be an excuse to act. In his memoirs, Leo Melamed, one of the fathers of derivative activities in Chicago, recommended that markets should be loved, not hated. Being more cautious, I would recommend that they be understood, not ignored.

Some years ago, I would have said that the development of financial markets would make it appropriate for central banks to act as if they were regular market operators, therefore abandoning official rates of intervention. However, such rates are still in use in most countries. This expresses the wish to send signals to the markets, as part of a communication policy. This is especially clear when the size and frequency of interventions at official rates is limited compared to interventions at or near market rates.

Whatever progress is made by markets and officials on the road towards co-operation, volatility will still be there for a long time. Academics would see it as the flexibility needed to absorb the effects of asymmetric information, the lack of consensus on analysis and the imperfections of economic systems. In the monetary and financial sectors, short-term volatility illustrates market aversion to uncertainty, while bubbles imply ill-founded certitude or a taste for risky exposure. Given the much more rapid adjustment of financial markets than goods markets, the Corporate sector is often a victim. In addition, volatility entails uncertainty, an obstacle to planning and investment. Firms can suffer from a loss of competitiveness as a result of exchange rate overvaluation, or be misguided by accidental and transitory competitiveness gains. They bear the cost of hedging operations. Adherence to the purchasing power parity is their out-of-reach dream. This is why they like the idea of a monetary union.

2. SPACE

When considering the intrusion of space into central bank strategy, one has to keep in mind that space is not homogeneous. Portfolio diversification may give the wrong impression that financial globalisation is the ultima ratio. However, portfolio arbitrage is based on the existence of differentiated currencies belonging to very different countries, with their individual exchange rate and yield curve behaviour. The main effect of financial globalisation was to accelerate the transmission of shocks from one currency area to another. However, room is left for decoupling. A shock may and should have differentiated impact on the various currencies. Consequences for prices and growth are more uneven, as the transmission mechanism differs from country to country, depending for instance on the degree of openness or the proportion of short-term versus long-term debt outstanding.

No country is sheltered from such external shocks, all are exposed to the resulting volatility. Those who, like Robert Marjolin and the Commission in the Plan organisation I mentioned, had to cope with the effects of the first oil shock in the mid 1970s, remember the high degree of uncertainty which prevailed at that time. The same is true of the impact of a sudden change in the market value of a major currency such as the dollar, or of a shock on the bond market. Although it is not possible to prevent such shocks, a cooperative solution may be preferred to disorderly conditions, at least to minimise their impact. Such co-operation may be expressed in different ways. It may be a loose cooperation when nothing better can be done, such as the G7 concertation. It may be a more automatic system based on the philosophy of Bretton Woods, to which the EMS referred to some extent. Finally, as heterogeneity in space leads to currency differentiation, it may lead to a reduction in global volatility by merging currencies, as in the European Monetary Union.

Preventing shocks or reacting properly to them within the framework of a loose cooperation mainly based on national goodwill can only be a global strategy. I remember the doctrine according to which monetary policy co-ordination would be sufficient to stabilise exchange rates. In theory, this could be achieved by pegging the exchange rate to a basket of currencies. In practice, it has led to pegging exchange rates to an anchor currency. The dollar played this role in the Bretton Woods system, and the Deutsche Mark as well in the more recent experience of the EMS.

Therefore, $n-1$ countries would lose autonomy in the monetary field. It was argued that national initiative could sufficiently be based on the fiscal stance. We know that in general this strategy did not work. This is for several reasons.

Firstly, interest rate policy can only be exclusively geared by external constraints in small, open economies. Elsewhere the final objective of price stability in medium and large economies requires a more complex approach, dealing with other factors.

Secondly, as I already mentioned, markets pay a great deal of attention to the fiscal stance, including the central government deficit and social transfers. Any significant fiscal imbalance contributes to a depreciation of the exchange rate and to the triggering of interest rate differentials, both as a policy reaction at the short end of the market — as a tool to avoid imported inflation — and spontaneous at the long end of the market, because of risk premiums. Therefore, no change in the fiscal stance can be made, assuming that everything else will remain unchanged.

Thirdly, in such circumstances, relying exclusively on interest rates cannot be credible for long as the problem is not a question of how to administer drugs, but of eradicating the cause of the disease.

Some co-ordination, sometimes active, but more often passively endured as a consequence of external constraints, explains why the world economy has experienced long periods of relatively similar evolution across countries, such as the great inflation of the 1970s or the great depression in the 1930s. It can be argued that this similarity makes policy mistakes very dangerous if they are to be generalised. This gives dominant economies a special responsibility. This is not enough to discard cooperation, as a cooperative approach should not necessarily lead to imitation, but to the best possible combination of action.

The recent depreciation of the dollar is one among many events which are a test for cooperation. In fact, this depreciation derives from a non-cooperative attitude of the United States and Japan, the former country being reluctant to cut imports and budget deficits, the latter to open its domestic market. Traders were therefore right in requiring a huge undervaluation of the dollar to correct these imbalances.

Co-operation could, in theory, be more justified and more easily applied at a regional level, when the mutual openness of the economies involved would make any deviation of exchange rates vis-à-vis some measure — which can only be approximate — of the purchasing power parity very harmful. Such deviation in one country directly impacts on the economic situation both internally and in partner countries.

In Europe, the memorandum that Robert Marjolin issued as a member of the Commission, rests on this principle. So do the many more recent statements according to which a monetary union is part of a single domestic market in Europe.

If the target can easily be determined, difficulties lie in the transition. This is what it is all about today, on the basis of the Maastricht Treaty.

A first difficulty comes from the nationalistic negative reaction to the loss of the domestic currency, especially where public opinion has good reason to be proud of it. Globalisation would *a priori* please financial intermediaries (except those specialising in foreign exchange transactions) and businesses which favour free competition on active markets - not those which are sheltered from competition. Explaining to the public at large that this will support job creation and increase the average standard of living is more complex, as this requires sophisticated economic analysis. A second difficulty is the need for economic convergence among those countries whose currencies should be merged. If not addressed, monetary unification would create a shock in those countries where some fundamental factors are still diverging. For instance, if nominal costs tend to rise more than average in part of the currency area, firms would soon lose competitiveness and be ousted by others. Therefore it is better to adjust beforehand.

Similarly, the global outstanding amount of savings in a single currency area is a kind of common public good. Any major borrower, especially if it is the government of a major member country, could create crowding-out effects which would be detrimental to other players, public or private. Therefore fiscal adjustment and co-ordination are necessary. This is especially important in Europe, as no big federal budget could be used to regulate the fiscal stance.

A third difficulty is to change current practices. It should be considered first from the point of view of ordinary people, households and individual or small businesses, as they will have to change the unit of account they currently use to measure the value of goods. They have to be convinced that this effort is worthwhile.

For banks, big financial institutions, and big firms, monetary unification will bring about adaptation costs. It can also be argued, however, that it will provide an ideal opportunity for the modernisation of operating systems. An important concern, on which experts are working today within the framework of European Union, is to minimise such costs and avoid technical failure or any other kind of systemic risk. The challenge is to find the optimal path between some flexibility which would be compatible with the variety of individual situations and a smoothly organised transition.

Finally, central banks will also have to adapt their techniques. By boosting the globalisation of financial markets in Europe — a process already launched by several Community directives — monetary unification will make it even more necessary than today to rely on market mechanisms. However, a lot of progress has already been made during the last ten years. Any observer can see that, step by step and on a voluntary basis, European central banks have harmonised their operations to a great extent, making use of regular repos, containing the flexibility of very short term monetary market rates within a channel with a policy function, eliminating some — if not yet all — of the major differences in the way they assess the usefulness of reserve requirements.

The very functioning of markets itself is involved in such a monetary reform. However, this is not a new story, as huge international markets have expanded already long ago, such as the foreign exchange market worldwide, or Euromarkets of the main currencies, or derivative markets. Guidelines for various ratios, in particular capital adequacy, have been elaborated in the wake of the Lamfalussy report and subsequent documents, and in the framework of the G-10 countries. They have already been translated into the Community legislation. By forcing banks to restructure those assets whose quality has been downgraded as a result of the recession, such regulations may reinforce the cyclical downward adjustment of the economy. However, this — to the extent it can be seen as a short-term threat by some economic agents — has two merits. One is to reduce the systemic risk and create conditions for an orderly cyclical pattern. The other is to avoid a lasting inflationary wave which might delay the necessary adjustment but would make it more painful when it comes. Maintaining sound medium-term anti-inflationary policies should contribute to the provision of a more stable and comfortable environment for markets and industrialists.

Most of my remarks have been to do with the trade-off between price volatility on markets and policy-making.

Shifting from a strictly regulated and segmented world to a globalised and market-oriented one may recall to mind the historical evolution of maturing economies from authoritarian monarchy to democracy. Granting private actors more freedom to express their views and to make decisions, either by voting or by pricing assets, can lead to a harmonious society provided some rules of the game avoid chaos and secure free competition.

Therefore, as uncertain as it seems to be, the present world should not impede progress towards a better global or regional organisation, leaving enough room for flexibility.

It may be that this liberal and elusive environment creates by itself the need for a better understanding of what is good for all. It would then make it necessary to reach a consensus on an ethic in many fields, including the economy, especially where people's lives are closely interdependent. May we assume that this was the ideal of Robert Marjolin and others who promoted with him a global alliance within Europe as well as with other parts of the world.